W9-DFN-902

GROWTH THROUGH COMPETITION, COMPETITION THROUGH GROWTH

GROWTH THROUGH COMPETITION, COMPETITION THROUGH GROWTH

Strategic Management and the Economy in Japan

HIROYUKI ODAGIRI

CLARENDON PRESS · OXFORD
1992

Oxford University Press, Walton Street, Oxford OX2 6DP
Oxford New York Toronto
Delhi Bombay Calcutta Madras Karachi
Petaling Jaya Singapore Hong Kong Tokyo
Nairobi Dar es Salaam Cape Town
Melbourne Auckland
and associated companies in
Berlin Ibadan

Oxford is a trade mark of Oxford University Press

Published in the United States
by Oxford University Press, New York

British Library Cataloguing in Publication Data
Data available

Library of Congress Cataloging in Publication Data
Odagiri, Hiroyuki, 1946–
Growth through competition, competition through growth: a study of Japanese management/Hiroyuki Odagiri.
p. cm.
Includes bibliographical references and index.
1. Industrial management—Japan. 2. Competition—Japan.
I. Title.
HD70.J30295 1992 338.6'048'0952—dc20 91-20437
ISBN 0–19–828655–4

Typeset by Best-set Typesetter Ltd.

Printed and bound in
Great Britain by Bookcraft (Bath) Ltd.
Midsomer Norton. Avon

PREFACE

Books on Japanese management abound. So why another? My first answer is that so many works ignore the presence of universally applicable principles behind the ostensible peculiarities, cultural or otherwise, of Japanese management. I am tired of hearing simple-minded arguments that what the Japanese have been doing is totally different from the *laissez-faire* economy of the West. In my opinion, the Japanese economy and Japanese management are based just as firmly on competition as those in the West, possibly more so. The Japanese internal labour system does not indicate corporate paternalism. It is an economically rational system, and it is a competitive system. This competition is enhanced by the preference of Japanese management for growth, and competition, in turn, makes growth feasible. Hence the title, *Growth through Competition, Competition through Growth.*

Secondly, in my opinion, the existing literature has never really studied the consequences of the Japanese management system on its industrial organization and macroeconomy. Of course, many academic and non-academic authors have discussed the behaviour and performance of Japanese industries and the Japanese economy with reference to management style. However, no effort has been made to integrate these microeconomic and macroeconomic aspects in a comprehensive manner. It was to redress this failing that the author was prompted to write the present book. It starts with a discussion of the motivation, behaviour, and organization of Japanese management, and then proceeds to examine the industrial and macroeconomic consequences. A plan of the book and a summary of the contents of each chapter appear in Section 1.5.

Although this book may be regarded generally speaking as an economic study, it is not sophisticated theoretically. Very few mathematical equations have been used and the discussion is descriptive, with occasional tables and regression results. A knowledge of basic microeconomic theory concerning production and discounting, for example, would be helpful, but there is no need for any familiarity with more elaborate theory, and even a reader without such knowledge should be able to follow the argument without difficulty. The only difficulty may arise in Section

9.2 where, although the basic idea is simple, some readers may find the theoretical manipulation hard to follow; but this section may be omitted. Thus, although the book is primarily aimed at researchers in the fields of the theory of the firm, industrial organization, and Japanese studies, I firmly believe that it will be useful and comprehensible to a wide body of readers, including business people and students in business schools and undergraduate economics and management courses.

It would not have been possible for me to write this book without the two-year research period I spent at the Centre for Business Strategy at the London Business School. Not only did the CBS allow me to concentrate on my writing, it also provided many opportunities to learn about differences between management in Japan and the UK and to get reactions to my arguments. I would like to thank everybody at the CBS and particularly John Kay, the director, and Paul Geroski. I am also grateful to the Institute of Socio-Economic Planning, University of Tsukuba, for generously allowing me to take two years' leave in order to pursue my research at the CBS. The list of people both in England and in Japan who offered helpful comments is unfortunately too long to be included here. However, special thanks must go to Robin Marris, who has not only commented on my work but also offered constant encouragement since I initially conceived it.

I have utilized the results of my earlier studies in many parts of the book, and would like to thank my collaborators on those studies for allowing me to do so. These include Hideki Yamawaki in Louvain (previously in Berlin), and Naotake Fujishiro, Tatsuo Hase, Kyoichi Suzuki, and Takashi Yamashita all four of whom, at one time or another, wrote a master's thesis at the University of Tsukuba. Chapter 5 appeared in a slightly different version (jointly with Tatsuo Hase) in the *International Journal of Industrial Organization*, and I thank them for allowing me to reproduce it here.

Last but not least, I cannot thank my family, Mari, Kosuke, and Shinsuke, enough for their tolerance and encouragement. Without their support and affection I would not have been able to maintain the spirit and energy to complete my work. This book is theirs as much as mine.

H.O.

London, Summer 1990

CONTENTS

LIST OF FIGURES AND TABLES

Figures

Tables

PART I

HOW IT WORKS

1

Introduction

1.1. THE FIRM AS A COLLECTION OF HUMAN RESOURCES

This book takes the view that the firm should be viewed primarily as a collection of human resources. That the firm is a collection of productive resources was first emphasized by Penrose: 'a firm is more than an administrative unit; it is also a collection of productive resources the disposal of which between uses and over time is determined by administrative decision' (Penrose 1959, 24). To her the firm is an organism and hence the 'growth' of the firm, like the growth of an organism, is an appropriate subject of study.

We take a similar view in this book. The resources of the firm can be separated into two categories—physical and financial on the one hand, and human on the other—as Penrose also did. We suggest that a particular emphasis should be placed on human resources. Although Penrose nowhere compared the relative importance of the two categories, the following sentence suggests that she too regarded human resources as essential: 'there is one type of productive services which, by its very nature, is available to a firm in only limited amounts. This is the service of personnel, in particular, of management, with experience within the firm' (Penrose 1955, 534). As suggested here, the importance of human resources stems from the fact that knowledge and experience are increasingly important in our lives. Knowledge has three salient features. First, it is largely embodied in individual workers (from blue-collar workers to management staff), so that the loss of a worker immediately causes a loss of knowledge to the firm. Second, to a significant extent knowledge is specific to each worker and to each firm, for one person cannot have exactly the same background, the same training, or the same experience as others inside or outside the company. Third, knowledge is a capital stock that can be accumulated only through investment in education and training, and through gaining experience.

Thus 'individuals with experience within a given group cannot be hired from outside the group, and it takes time for them to achieve the requisite experience' (Penrose 1959, 47). Consequently, human resources constitute a more fundamental constraint on the growth of a firm than financial and physical resources. The neoclassical view of capitalism, in which capital hires labour, may well be obsolete: in a modern corporation, it may be that labour hires capital, in the sense that the level of human resources determines the speed and direction of the firm's growth and the capital required is then financed accordingly. Therefore, any study of the firm is meaningless unless its human aspects are fully investigated. Only by this means is it possible to arrive at a new way of looking at a firm, a way hitherto overlooked in neoclassical theory.

Take lifetime employment, for instance. Given that every worker is different from any other and is to a considerable degree indispensable to the firm, the knowledge he has accumulated is fully valuable only when he[1] keeps working with the same firm. It is thus to the firm's advantage to retain the worker for his lifetime, and to the worker's advantage that he stays with the firm. That is, 'a man whose past productive activity has been spent within a particular firm can, because of his intimate knowledge of the resources, structure, history, operations, and personnel of the firm render services to that firm which he could give to no other firm without acquiring additional experience' (ibid. 54). Only by continuously working in the same firm can a worker fully utilize his knowledge and be motivated to accumulate it. Only by continuously employing the worker can a firm derive full productivity from him, and maintain an efficient production/management team. Lifetime employment can be a perfectly rational arrangement to make the best use of human resources: it can never be regarded as a norm solely on the basis of historical convention or corporate paternalism. The same can be said of internal promotion, because the efficient operation of the firm is best maintained by promoting an employee who has the highest chance of having such 'intimate knowledge and experience'. Internal promotion also fosters competition, and thereby increases effort.

We intend to argue in this book that many of the labour practices that have been taken as peculiarly Japanese are in fact

[1] Throughout the book he will be used to indicate he/she.

economic and rational, and that these have important consequences for corporate behaviour and organization, which in turn influence the national economic performance.

1.2. GROWTH PREFERENCE AND COMPETITION: TWO KEY CONCEPTS

It is now easy to understand why a strong preference for growth results. When a man expects to work with a single firm for his lifetime, the future of the firm—its size and prosperity—is naturally of the greatest concern to him. Moreover, where there is internal promotion, expansion will bring increased opportunities for the worker to achieve the higher income, the enhanced social status and the greater psychological satisfaction that promotion brings.

Growth creates opportunities to utilize the firm's human resources fully and to enrich and expand them, because only a growing firm can create challenging jobs that force the workers to expand their knowledge and experience. The human resources thus accumulated in a successfully growing firm then become the basis for the firm's further growth, creating further opportunities for the employees to gain economic, social, and psychological attainments.

Such desire for growth on the part of employees cannot but influence corporate decision-making. When the workers are endowed with specific knowledge and cannot be replaced by outside workers without a loss in productivity, they tend to possess a degree of power that cannot be ignored by the legal owners of the firm. The owners, on the other hand, are now dispersed and lack controlling power. Take-overs and proxy fights, considered by some authors to be an effective control device, are nowhere entirely successful in this respect; and this is particularly true of countries other than the USA and the UK, most notably Japan. Managers—from chairman or president to middle management—are now mostly internally bred, having worked with the same firm for many years and gradually climbed up the promotion ladder. They do not own a significant share of the firm; even if they do, they do not regard themselves primarily as the shareholders. Instead, they feel they belong to the employees. All these factors point to management behaviour which will seek to maximize growth. This tendency must be stronger where the mechanism of shareholder control is less effective, where human resources are more widely recognized as a vital part of corporate organization, or where all workers, from shop floor to senior executives, are more homogeneous and more cohesive. These conditions, we intend to show, are most apparent within Japanese firms.

The pursuit of maximum growth has serious industrial and macroeconomic consequences. For one thing, it affects inter-firm and intra-firm competition. When a firm intends to grow, it must expand its business, either horizontally, vertically, or by diversifying, and whichever way is chosen will lead to confrontation with firms already in business or those with plans to enter into business, thus intensifying competition. Competition develops not only in markets but also within firms because, under the system of lifetime employment and internal promotion, the welfare of any worker is directly related to his prospect for promotion, and striving to be selected for promotion will result in internal competition. This competition can be more intense than the competition in external labour markets, which is presumed to play a central role in neoclassical theory, because in the internal labour market workers are acutely aware of the presence of the rivals, whereas in the external markets they respond passively to given wage offers. Internal competition is further intensified as continuous evaluation is made and opportunities are repeatedly provided for promotion or relocation—a process of long-term competition. Again we intend to show that the practices in Japanese firms are working very much in this direction.

In a very simplified way, therefore, the scheme of this book may be illustrated as in Fig. 1.1. As regards the firm, it is necessary to investigate motivation, organization, and behaviour. These are of course influenced by the human and physical (and financial) resources; yet, we will put greater emphasis on how the human resources are managed. The outcome of this investigation will be summarized together with the two key concepts of growth preference and competition. Their consequences will then be investigated for many aspects of our economy, such as industrial organization, the macroeconomy, the dynamics of technological progress and economic growth, and international activities. Finally, these in turn provide an environment in which the firms operate. A circle of causes and effects is thus apparent.

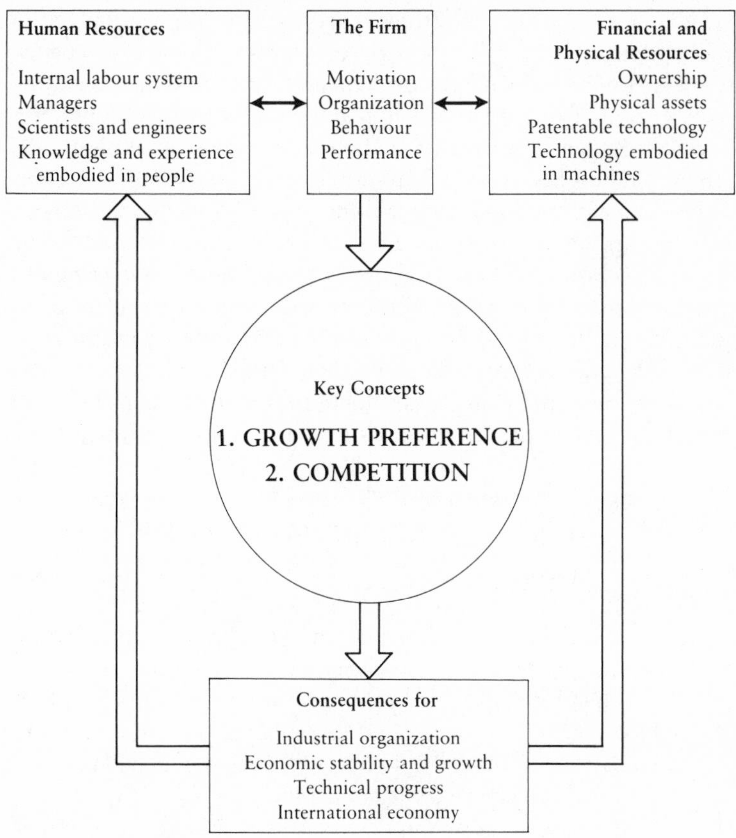

FIG. 1.1 Analytical framework

The diagram is excessively simplified. Many problems that need to be discussed are not in the diagram, nor are many factors that affect corporate behaviour or economic performance. None the less, the simplified picture given here will help the reader to gain a quick image of the way Japanese management is to be discussed in this book.

1.3. COMPETITION: ALTERNATIVE CONCEPTS

In view of the important part that the concept of competition plays in this book, and in view of the fact that the concept is often used in a confused way (from a specific definition adopted by mathematical economists to a loose definition implicitly used by non-academics), it will be useful to discuss competition in some detail here. Let us classify it under four headings: (1) competition in terms of quantity as opposed to non-quantity variables; (2) competition in the short as opposed to the long term; (3) competition by exit as opposed to by voice; and (4) competition with incentives given according to the absolute level as opposed to the relative level of merit. The traditional discussion of competition in economic theory has been biased toward competition in terms of quantity, in the short term, by exit, and with incentives given according to the absolute level of merit. Other modes of competition are increasingly important and may be particularly so in internal organizations (as opposed to markets) and in Japan.

1.3.1. Competition in Terms of Quantity as Opposed to Non-Quantity Variables

In textbook microeconomics, a perfectly competitive firm determines the quantity of output given prices. In the Cournot–Nash model of oligopoly, a firm determines the quantity of output given the quantities produced by rival firms. In either model, the policy variable is quantity. Provided that the marginal cost schedule is upward-sloping for a relevant range of output, a more efficient firm (that is, one with a lower marginal cost schedule) will produce more, thereby causing a positive efficiency–quantity correlation. For this reason people tend to identify a larger quantity of output with competitiveness on the part of the firm. However, there are also models which treat non-quantity variables as policy variables.

Example 1, price: the Bertrand model. Suppose that in an oligopolistic market the firm determines its price given its rivals' prices. The result will depend on whether the products are homogeneous or differentiated between the firms. If differentiated, the consequence may be similar to the Cournot solution because the demand is still positive, though smaller, with a price higher than the rivals'. By contrast, if the products are homogeneous no customer will be attracted by a price higher than the rivals'. There is a strong incentive to undercut the rivals' prices and capture the entire market: that is, the demand is either all of the market demand or none as the price is lower or higher than the rivals'. Because of this discontinuity, there is a strong motivation to undercut the rival prices; consequently, the equilibrium price is forced down to the level of the minimum unit cost, provided this cost is identical among the firms. Both in terms of behaviour and of consequence (but not structure), the market is undoubtedly competitive. The result of this so-called Bertrand equilibrium is noteworthy because social optimality is attained irrespective of the number of firms, as long as there are two or more.

Example 2, entry: the contestable market model. If the incumbent firms want to prevent entry, they cannot price their products at a level higher than the potential entrant's minimum unit cost. Particularly, if no sunk cost is needed in entry and the cost conditions of entrants are the same as those of the incumbents, the incumbents can only charge a price equal to the minimum unit cost. Such a market is called perfectly contestable and the equilibrium has the same property as in the Bertrand model (Baumol *et al.* 1982).

Example 3, innovation: Schumpeterian competition. Competition also takes place in terms of innovation and marketing. Competition in innovation means that the firm strives to develop a new product or to attain a higher quality either in the sense of a physically better product (for instance, a higher capacity of computer) or of characteristics closer to the target consumers' taste (for instance, compatibility with a widely accepted standard). Competition in marketing takes place in the areas of establishing and maintaining a brand, packaging, delivery, and after-sales services. The most influential writer to stress this aspect of competition is Schumpeter, for whom the essence of competition was never in terms of quantity or price but 'the competition from the new commodity, the new technology, the new source of supply, the new type of organization—competition which commands a decisive cost or quality advantage and which strikes not at the margins of the profits and the outputs of the existing firms but at their foundations and their very lives' (Schumpeter 1942, 84). As in the Bertrand model, a large number of sellers and buyers is not a prerequisite for market competition. It is well known that Schumpeter further asserted that competition in innovation is the indispensable engine for economic development or 'the process of creative destruction'.

In forms of competition with non-quantity variables, relative superiority is more important than absolute superiority, and the cost of losing is large. If you invent a better product or invent a new product earlier, you succeed in capturing the market. If you fail in innovation, that is, if you only come up with a product inferior to the rival's or at a later time, you may lose the whole market and risk your costs. In the Bertrand model, it is more a relative position that matters, that is, whether your price is higher or lower than your rivals', than the absolute price level. If your price is higher, you lose your whole market, and this forms a contrast to the Cournot model, in which a smaller output means only a proportionally smaller profit. Losing in non-quantity competition can be really painful and the only thing you can do to avoid this misery is to strive hard: competition is bound to be intense as a result.

A lesson to be learnt from this discussion is the danger of inferring the strength of market competition from structural variables such as concentration ratios. A positive link between concentration and profits (or social welfare) has been proved to exist when firms compete in a Cournot manner (Cowling and Waterson 1976; Dansby and Willig 1979). It no longer exists if they compete in terms of non-quantity variables. Even if the concentration ratio is high and stable, a small number of firms may be vigorously competing with each other *à la* Bertrand or Schumpeter, or with potential entrants, thereby gaining no excess profits and approximating a socially desirable level of market production. This fact suggests that the extent of competition may be better inferred from performance measures, such as profits, than from structural measures. If we find no evidence of the industry earning excess profits, it is likely to be sufficiently competitive. In Chapter 8 we shall compare the average profit rate and its inter-firm dispersion internationally, to suggest that Japanese industries are generally more competitive than those in the USA or the UK.

1.3.2. Competition in the Short as Opposed to the Long Term

The form of market competition discussed in textbook economics applies best to spot markets (of crude oil, most typically) or stock-markets where one is supposed to sell and buy instantaneously whenever there is an opportunity for profit. Transactions are intertemporally independent; that is, the terms you offer today and the terms you are offered today are not affected by your decisions in the past or your past relation with other market participants. It is competition in the short term, and, whether you win or lose today, competition starts afresh tomorrow. There is also a form of competition which operates in the long term and in an evolutionary manner.[2] Even if A's offer is less favourable than B's, you may decide to buy from A because your past relationship with A makes it attractive to maintain the relationship. Yet, as the evolutionary process of natural selection is a long-term process of gradual but incessant change, A's rank among your suppliers will be gradually lowered under A's lack of improved performance and eventually you will decide to terminate the relationship.

Example 1, labour. Competition prevails in the short-term sense for some types of labour, such as temporary labour and unskilled or unspecialized manual work. In these cases, hiring worker A today does not preclude you from hiring B tomorrow; and working for company X today does not preclude you from working for Y tomorrow. Whether you hired A or B yesterday, today you will hire the worker who demands the lowest wage: whether you worked for X or Y yesterday, today you will apply for the highest-paid job. By contrast, in the labour market for workers with firm-specific skills, both the firm and the worker have a strong incentive to maintain a long-term employment relationship as discussed earlier. If you have worked for company X, you must have acquired skills that increase your productivity while you work in X but not in any other firm. If you have hired A yesterday, A must have gained specific skills that B does not have, and you will employ A again today even if A's pay demand exceeds B's to a certain extent. The resulting long-term attachment between workers and employers does not imply a lack of competition. Although the firm will not immediately fire a worker with poor performance, it can punish him by awarding a below-average pay rise or delaying promotion. Similarly, a company offering poor pay today will not face immediate defection by its workers; yet, in the long run, a bad reputation will spread, causing the firm to receive fewer applications from desirable workers. Competition is at work in the long term.

[2] For an 'evolutionary' economic process, see Nelson and Winter (1982).

Example 2, materials and intermediate goods. In spot markets for materials and intermediate goods, competition in the short term prevails. You buy from whoever offers the cheapest price, irrespective of your source of supply yesterday. In contrast, a long-term relationship between suppliers and buyers is observed in some markets; for instance, purchases of components for automobile assembly, and dealership. Even if supplier B offers a cheaper price than the current supplier A, the assembler may not stop buying from A immediately; yet, the threat will be felt by A and, if A cannot match B's offer for some time, then there will be a change in the source of supply.

Example 3, financial markets. A relationship between a bank and its customers is another example. A bank with a long-term view will not immediately withdraw its loan even if the borrower's business is thought to be risky now.

Competition in the long term is more commonly observed when asset specificity or switching costs are higher. A higher asset specificity means that you have made an investment which is valuable only when you maintain your relationship with your current trading partner. A higher switching cost means that you will incur substantial costs if you change partner. The two are, of course, related since a higher asset specificity results in a higher switching cost. Under these circumstances, it is unwise for the players to change partners even if outside offers are attractive today. More wisely, they will retain current relations and persuade the partner to match the outside offer. It is likely, therefore, that the use of the voice mechanism to persuade the partner must be more common where competition in the long term is prominent.

Reputation plays an important disciplinary role when competition is operating in the long term. Once you acquire a bad reputation, you will lose a long-term relation, and this is more costly than losing just for today. Consequently, opportunism is less likely: even if you can make money by behaving in an opportunistic manner, you are likely to suffer from a bad reputation in the long run. The longer the relationship, the larger the cost of any bad reputation will be.

Competition in the long term must be more effective if the economy, industry, or firm is expected to grow and if the discount rate is lower, because under these conditions securing future returns is more important than making a short-term opportunistic gain: you will be tempted to maintain a long-term relationship even if that entails sacrificing short-term gains. In this light, the coexistence of growth maximization and long-term competition shown in Fig. 1.1 is easy to understand.

1.3.3. Competition by Exit as Opposed to by Voice

In any society, misbehaviour and malfunction are facts of life. An important question is what mechanisms there are to remedy deviation and force miscreants to revert to proper behaviour. Hirschman argued that there are two options for such mechanisms. One is called 'exit', which is 'withdrawal from a relationship that one has built up as a buyer of merchandise or as a member of an organization such as a firm, a family, a political party or a state'; and the other is called 'voice', which is 'the attempt at repairing and perhaps improving the relationship through an effort at communicating one's complaints, grievances and proposals for improvement' (Hirschman 1987, 219). In textbook economics, a customer who is dissatisfied with a seller stops buying from that company or individual and switches to a rival. This is the use of the exit option. Instead, he may express his dissatisfaction directly to the seller and suggest an improvement. This is the use of the voice option. When the exit mechanism occurs, demand on the firm decreases, thereby giving a signal that consumer dissatisfaction is getting serious. When the voice mechanism is used, management will learn of the problem as long as intra-firm communication is smooth. Either of the two options, therefore, sends a message to the management that something is wrong. Despite traditional disregard of the voice option, it may be more effective than the exit mechanism in many situations. For one thing, an awareness of customer exit alone may not tell the management what is wrong; hence, there is a possibility that the management will fail to understand the real problem or that it has to spend resources to discover it. Such costs will not be necessary under the voice option. For another thing, the exit option may entail switching costs for the participants. A customer who has been using a particular computer may have to rewrite programs when switching to another firm's computer. A producer supplying a component to an assembler may have to change moulds and tools to produce a component that fits another assembler's requirements. The more different the operating systems of the two computers or the less standardized the two different components are the higher must be the switching cost. In other words, the presence of asset specificity makes the exit option more costly and the use of voice increasingly attractive.

On the other hand, a free-rider problem may make the voice option less effective because any service improvement attained as a result of one customer's voice may benefit all the customers. They can free-ride on someone else's voice, and the private benefit of voice is less than the social benefit. As a result, the voice option will be employed less often than is socially optimal. Obviously, this free-rider problem is more serious when each participant's share in the market is smaller. This fact probably explains why the voice mechanism has been disregarded in the neoclassical economic theory that takes atomistic markets as ideal. If, on the contrary, either a buyer or a seller holds a significant share of the market, his private gain from exercising the voice option is commensurate with the social gain; hence, he may prefer the voice to the exit mechanism. In the market for intermediate goods, such as automobile components, the buyers, namely, the assemblers, tend to use the voice option more frequently because they have a large share in the supplier's sales. By contrast, the consumer of beer will opt to switch brand.

Another reason why the use of voice is more common in intermediate goods markets than in consumer goods markets is the difference in the amount of knowledge. Because an assembler in the case of the component market has a great deal of information on what is wrong and what should be done to improve the situation, he can make suggestions as to how such improvement could be effected. The more information that the buyer (or seller) has, the more informative the voice option will be to the seller (or buyer).

The assembler–supplier relation is not the only example where the use of the voice option is frequently observed. Other examples follow.

Example 1, trade unions. If wages are low and working conditions poor, the worker has to rely on either exit (leaving) or voice to improve the situation. The use of voice on an individual basis is costly because, as a single person in a pool of possibly thousands, the worker may find that the employer chooses the exit option, which in this case is dismissal or, less drastically, damage to future career prospects. The trade union is a device to avoid such costs to individual workers. By expressing dissatisfaction collectively, each worker can remain anonymous, thereby avoiding personal loss. The union can force the employer to listen to the voice because it makes it difficult for the employer to use the exit option (dismissal). If the management responds to the voice positively and improves working conditions so that there is a productivity increase, and/or if the union uses the voice option also to improve efficiency in the workplace, the union contributes to the advancement not only of its members but of society at large. If, on the contrary, the union uses its monopoly power only to pursue higher wages, the consequences may be socially undesirable. Freeman and Medoff (1984) called these two opposing effects the 'two faces' of unionism—'the collective voice/institutional response face' as opposed to 'the monopoly face'. They emphasized the efficiency-enhancing effect of the first: 'the voice/response face directs attention to the possibility that, because of incomplete information, lack of coordination in an enterprise, and organizational slack, management can respond to unionism in more creative ways, which may be socially beneficial' (ibid. 11). It is important that management has a constructive attitude in its reaction to the voice: 'If management uses the collective bargaining process to learn about and improve the operation of the workplace and the production process, unionism can be a significant plus to enterprise efficiency. On the other hand, if management responds negatively to collective bargaining (or is prevented by unions from reacting positively), unionism can significantly harm the performance of the firm' (ibid. 12). With the use of quantitative results, they found that 'productivity is generally higher in unionized establishments than in otherwise comparable establishments that are nonunion' (ibid. 180). We will argue later in this book that the enterprise unionism prevalent in Japan encourages the constructive use of the voice mechanism.

Asset specificity again plays an important role here. The relevant asset here is the skills possessed by workers. If these skills are more firm-specific, the exit mechanism is costly for both the worker and the employer. The workers are more inclined to use the voice option, giving them a strong incentive to make a better use of the union. The management has more incentive to listen to the voice because the use of the exit option (dismissals) is costly due to the lack of required skills among outside workers. If the union–management relationship can maintain a constructive atmosphere, voice can become a far more effective option than exit to remedy disorders and dissatisfaction and to increase efficiency.

Example 2, shareholders. When the shareholder is dissatisfied with the management, he can either express his voice to the management or exit by selling his shares. When shareholding is widely dispersed, each shareholder's stake in the firm becomes very small and, as the argument above has suggested, his gain from expressing voice is also small. Thus, the voice option is increasingly less likely to be exercised. This fact explains the tendency in the USA and the UK to rely on take-overs, which are used to take advantage of the shareholders' exit option, as a mechanism for corporate control (Jensen 1988). By contrast, the large shareholdings by banks common in Germany and, to a lesser extent, in Japan may make the use of the voice option by these banks more viable.

Example 3, banks. Banks may also exert influence through loans because, if they are dissatisfied with the decisions or performance of the client company, they can either withdraw their loans (the exit option) or give advice on improving performance (the voice option). The close bank–firm relationship in Japan is well known. It was established during the 1950s when excess demand for funds was a permanent phenomenon. The use of the exit option, namely, switching of banks, was difficult for firms, who therefore had a strong incentive to listen to the banks' voice. Although, with the disappearance of excess demand, firms now have more freedom to use the exit option, long-term relationships with banks are still widespread. The voice option is also used by the firm against the bank, when other banks offer better terms. Instead of switching banks immediately, the firm can ask for similar or better terms from that bank with which it has a continuing relationship. Insofar as the bank responds positively to this voice, the relationship remains stable and long-term.

As these examples imply, the threat of exit plays a powerful role in forcing individuals or firms to listen to the voice seriously and react to it in a positive manner: 'the availability and threat of exit on the part of an important customer or group of members may powerfully reinforce their voice' (Hirschman 1987, 220). Under the threat of loan withdrawal (and given a lack of alternative banks to borrow from), the firm has a strong incentive to take the bank's voice seriously. The trade union's voice is taken seriously because it has an option to strike, that is, to exit from the workplace. The supplier listens to the assembler's voice because there are other firms who wish to supply the same products to the assembler. The producers are concerned with the voice of important customers, because the loss of sales to these customers can have a damaging effect.

Thus, continuous use of voice by no means implies a lack of competition. A continuous relationship with a single trading partner may be maintained, with a continuous threat of switching to rivals, and it is in this situation that the voice mechanism achieves its full effect of curing disorders and increasing efficiency. Just as the concept of competition has been extended by the contestability theory to include rivalry between incumbents and potential entrants, it can usefully be extended to include the use of voice accompanied by the threat of exit, namely, the threat from potential rivals. 'Competition by voice' is an appropriate expression for this mechanism. It forms a contrast to 'competition by exit', in which, as assumed in traditional economic theory, market participants express their dissatisfaction only through the use of the exit option.

1.3.4. Competition with Incentives According to Absolute as Opposed to Relative Merits

It is not difficult to find examples in which relative ranking is decisive. A school entrance examination is most typical. Because the number of total students to be admitted is fixed, what matters is not your grade itself but the ranking. Even if you work hard and succeed in doubling your grades, your chances of admission remain unchanged if all the others do the same. More appropriate examples in our context follow.

Example 1, Promotion. Promotion is awarded to the best among the candidates and not to all the workers satisfying a specified performance level. If others are working harder, you have to work equally hard just to maintain the same chance of promotion. Hence the term 'rat race' is commonly used to describe the race for promotion which, precisely for this reason, is a strong device for maintaining work incentives. This fact was the subject of a theoretical inquiry by Lazear and Rosen (1981), who gave the name 'rank-order tournaments' to the competition for promotion. Under a simplified situation of identical risk-neutral workers, they proved that the effort level of workers is identical between two compensation schemes, a rank-order tournament and a piece-rate payment. In the latter scheme the worker is paid the wage equal to the value of his marginal product, as presumed in standard economic theory, that is, incentives are given according to the absolute level of merit in contrast to rank-order tournaments in which incentives are given according to relative merits.

Example 2, the Cournot as opposed to the Bertrand model. As discussed earlier, in the Cournot oligopoly model, firms with different cost efficiency survive in the equilibrium provided the cost difference is within a certain boundary. By contrast, only the least cost firms survive in the long run in the Bertrand model or in the contestable market model. The relative efficiency is decisive in these models.

Example 3, the patent race. The salient feature of the patent is that only the first one to invent gets the patent-right. However much you have spent, you get no patent as long as you are later than your rival in coming up with the invention. You have to be first to win. Such a first-mover advantage can also be found in a broader area of innovation and marketing. If you are the first to enter the market with a new product, you may have a decisive advantage over those that follow, either because you can attain a larger cost reduction through experience on the job, or because the pecuniary and psychological cost to the consumer of switching to other brands is substantial (Schmalensee 1982; Lieberman and Montgomery 1988). Theoretical studies suggest that the patent race can become so intense as to result in socially excessive innovation efforts (Kamien and Schwartz 1982).

Needless to say, a pure rank-order tournament cannot have an incentive effect if it is possible for rivals to collude because, even if all the candidates for promotion agree to work less hard (that is, to shirk), each of them still has the same promotion chances, unless, of course, the employer can opt for outside recruitment to fill the post. Under the piece-rate scheme, by contrast, your pay will decrease if you work less hard, whether or not you collude with your colleagues, because your marginal product decreases. Rivalry is a prerequisite to efficiency under any scheme, but especially when incentives are given according to ranking.

The incentive effect of rivalry in a rank-order tournament is particularly strong when the rivals are homogeneous. In the promotion race, for instance, if the two candidates are widely different in their intrinsic ability, the lesser able will assume that his promotion chances are low anyway and may decide that the expected increase in promotion probability from working harder is not worth the disutility of the effort. Consequently he may opt to drop out of the race in pursuit of an easy life, which in turn decreases the incentive for the more able, who is now sure of his promotion even without additional effort. It is when both estimate the marginal return from doing so to be large that they will make a great effort, and this occurs when the chances are high that by working a little harder one person can exceed his rival's performance. The promotion race, therefore, is expected to be more intense and more effective in soliciting effort when workers are alike. Big Japanese companies satisfy this condition, as Japan is a more homogeneous nation than the USA or the UK and the companies undertake a careful screening process when hiring new graduates. Similarly, the innovation efforts of Japanese firms may be intense because several companies of roughly comparable size are competing in many of the markets, particularly in the high-technology industries.

We would also expect the rank-order tournament to be more effective when the difference in reward for winners and for losers is larger, because a larger difference means a larger gain from working harder. Such a large difference will exist, for instance, when outside opportunities for the losers are limited. If the pay you can get by changing your employer is reasonably high (and you expect to be able to find a new job), then the suffering incurred by losing the promotion race is small. If you lose, you just leave and look for another job. If, on the contrary, it is hard to find a job in another firm, or if the best pay you can get there is low, as in Japan, then you will not be able to leave even if you lose. The suffering incurred by losing is large, and this encourages you to strive hard to win the promotion race. The intensity of internal competition among the workers in a Japanese firm will be stressed in Chapter 4.

1.3.5. *Summary*

While the neoclassical school has mostly confined its analyses to competition in terms of quantity, in the short term, by exit, and with incentives given according to absolute levels of merit, competition in the real world has increasingly operated in terms of non-quantity variables (such as Schumpeterian competition in innovation), in the long term (that is, through an evolutionary process of competition), by the use of the voice option (reinforced by the threat to exit), and with incentives given according to relative merits (namely, rank-order tournaments). All these are forms of competition because they involve one person or firm striving against existing or potential rivals. They all provide mechanisms for encouraging effort on the part of the participants and for correcting bad behaviour. The increasing prevalence of these forms of competition coincides with an increasing specificity of assets, both physical and human. In particular, the increasing importance of specific knowledge and experience embodied in human resources, noted in Section 1.1, favours the kind of continuous relationship in employment, procurement, finance, and so on, which makes long-term competition and the use of the voice mechanism more effective. We have shown in a few instances that these considerations are more pertinent in Japan. More details will be given in other parts of this book.

1.4. JAPANESE MANAGEMENT AS VIEWED IN PAST STUDIES

The rapidity with which post-war Japan has caught up with Euro-American economic standards and even surpassed them in several sectors, has aroused considerable interest, as well as suspicion, among Westerners concerning Japan's economy and management. This tendency has been reinforced by the fact that the Japanese do not share the Protestant ethic that has been believed to be imperative to Western capitalist development (Weber 1904). The result has been the denial of a thesis that Japan followed the same ground rules of capitalist development as the West. Viewed in this way, it is no wonder that the popular explanations have stressed either cultural differences or a deliberate conspiracy undertaken by the government and industries.

According to the culture theory, Japanese culture differs from Western culture in ways which are favourable to economic development. The most frequently cited of such differences are the emphasis placed on harmony rather than rivalry in interpersonal relationships (often quoted in this connection is the first Japanese constitution established by Prince Shotoku in the year 604, which, in its first article, stated that harmony, *wa*, should be most highly respected), and the loyalty and paternalism which operate in essentially vertical social relations (Nakane 1970). These, it is alleged, have led the Japanese to create efficient teamwork, a commitment to company or social goals, and a close collaboration between labour, business, and government.

According to the conspiracy theory, the Japanese have united to achieve a shared national goal of economic growth. The government, it is argued, indicated which industries should be promoted, and guided the target industries in this direction with subsidies, unfair trade practices, or persuasion. The businesses followed this guidance and, in return, the government listened to their views and co-ordinated them to avoid damaging competition. In short, the whole economy has behaved like a single entity, a 'Japan Inc.', pursuing the common goals of attaining economic growth and succeeding in international markets, with the government acting as the supreme decision-maker.

Although these may be oversimplifications of the two theories, the point is that they accept neither the usual postulate concerning human motivation that an individual will strive to pursue self-interests that are chiefly of an economic nature, nor the role of the market in adjusting independent decisions. They negate, that is, the principle of the Invisible Hand that has been the backbone of economics since Adam Smith (and even since some authors before Smith, for instance, Cantillon).

As previous sections have indicated, this book takes the opposing view that the principle of the Invisible Hand is just as applicable to the Japanese economy (and possibly more so) as it is to the Western economies. It will argue that people in Japan are also motivated to pursue self-interests and that, if there is any difference, it is the incentive system that leads Japanese workers and management to behave differently: specifically in Japan, as in any other country, competition has been the key to performance.

We agree that there is some truth in both the culture theory and the conspiracy theory. For instance, it may well be true that cultural differences have been conducive to making long-term relationships more important in Japan than in the USA or the UK in many aspects of management. Geographical factors (for instance, dense population surrounded by sea) and demographic factors (for instance, racial homogeneity) are perhaps also relevant. Yet, can we really say that the difference between, say, Japan and Germany is significantly larger than the difference between, say, Germany and the UK? Making a list of differences leads us nowhere. More fruitfully, we can ask how the different business practices have resulted in different economic performance, and whether the consequences can be consistently explained by the logic of economic theory. Only by so doing can we discuss the applicability of Japanese management to other economies, and evaluate the universality of such economic logic as the principle of the Invisible Hand.

The same can be said of the conspiracy theory. It may well be true that the government–business relationship has been more intense in Japan than in other countries. But again the difference is not absolute but one of degree, as witnessed by the contrast between, say, France and the Anglo-American countries. We can also observe many cases where industries have developed without any government support or even despite government objections, as we shall discuss in Chapter 11. It is our contention, therefore, that, even though government involvement may have made some impact, it is overwhelmingly the entrepreneurship present in the private sector and the resulting competitive market situations that have played the major role in the course of economic development in Japan.

1.5. THE PLAN OF THE BOOK

This book is divided into three parts following the basic structure given in Fig. 1.1. Part I contains a core discussion of the motivation and behaviour of Japanese management. Part II examines organizational issues, such as mergers, divisional forms, manufacturer–supplier relations, and business groups. Part III discusses the implications for industrial organization, the national economy, government policies, and international aspects.

Part I begins with an investigation of the financial and human resources of Japanese firms, starting in Chapter 2 with an inquiry into the pattern of share-ownership. One conclusion to be drawn from an international comparison is the lack of dominant individual shareholders in Japan, the USA or the UK. Another is the greater incidence of shareholding by non-financial companies and banks in Japan as compared to the USA and the UK, though the difference is probably exaggerated in the available statistics. The influence of banks on industrial companies in Japan has been widely discussed in the West. While their role is actually important in rescue operations for failing companies, their influence otherwise seems rather restricted and has been declining. Chapter 2 also discusses the power and background of managers. The salient characteristics of Japanese management are the lack of external directors and the prevalence of internal promotion. We suggest that these factors give considerable power to the managers, who tend to be sympathetic to employees' needs. We also refer to the different background Japanese managers tend to have in comparison to American and British managers: that is, more of the Japanese managers have experienced production or technology-related positions, a fact which contrasts with the prevalence of managers with a finance background in the USA and the UK. This difference is consistent with a stronger emphasis on manufacturing and technology development and a weaker emphasis on acquisitions in Japan.

Following our inquiry into ownership and top management, the discussion inevitably turns to ordinary employees. Chapter 3 therefore examines the internal labour system, beginning with a critical appraisal of the so-called three pillars of the Japanese system: lifetime employment, the seniority rule, and enterprise unionism. Although it is true that the Japanese system has more of these elements than the American system, it is not true that they have been strictly applied in Japan or that no such practices exist in other countries. Lifetime employment, for instance, does not guarantee that an employee will never be dismissed. Yet it is also true that lifetime employment is regarded as a norm to which management is expected to conform. The discussion then moves on to examine three issues in turn: employment adjustment, skill formation, and internal competition on promotion. We note that the employment level is frequently adjusted but in such a way as to minimize redundancies (lay-offs), that training and rotation are organized to ensure that workers acquire both more advanced and more wide-ranging skills, and that internal competition to seek promotion is intense in Japanese firms. Such competition operates in the long term and in the form of a rank-order tournament. The voice mechanism also plays an important role in improving worker performance.

In Chapter 4, we hypothesize that Japanese management maximizes the rate of growth of the firm subject to a minimum valuation constraint, and present a model by which to analyse the choice of optimal growth rate under this hypothesis and compare it to the growth rate under the traditional value maximization hypothesis. We then apply the analysis in a discussion of the higher propensity of Japanese firms to invest. Growth, we argue, has to be internal and not through acquisitions, in order to fulfil the wishes of management and employees. This preference for internal over external growth prevents the firm from investing in totally unrelated businesses for which the necessary human resources are lacking within the firm; consequently, the extent of diversification is lower in Japan than in other countries. The research and development activities of Japanese firms are also discussed to suggest that the Japanese management system makes larger and more efficient R & D feasible.

Part II examines the organizational aspects of Japanese management. It starts with Chapter 5, which provides an empirical inquiry into mergers and acquisitions during 1980–7. The preference for internal growth suggests that M & As will be fewer and more of them will be used as a means of diversification because human resources with knowledge of the target industries are internally insufficient and can be reinforced by human resources acquired by M & As, though there may be also horizontal M & As to save failing firms. It can also be hypothesized that looser forms of combination are preferred to complete integration because keeping internal labour systems separate is less costly and more acceptable to the employees. Our empirical study of 243 M & As supports these hypotheses. It also finds no evidence that M & As improve the acquirers' performance.

Chapter 6 discusses several organizational issues. First, the lower popularity of the (multi)divisional business form in Japan is noted and is argued to be consistent with the internal labour system, because the divisional business form hinders the cross-divisional mobility of employees needed to attain employment adjustment with minimum lay-offs and to foster the inter-divisional transfer of knowledge. The reduced use of the divisional form also appears to contribute to a long-term managerial view. Second, hive-off is commonly used in place of the divisional form. Hive-off is particularly useful for businesses unrelated to the parent firm, where complementarity in knowledge and experience is hardly expected, and for businesses requiring only low-skilled workers for whom a lower wage scale is applied. Third, we examine the supplier–assembler relationship, taking the automobile industry as an example. Despite the ostensible stability in relationships, we emphasize that competition is very much at work. This competition operates in the long term, and the use of the voice option with the threat of exit is frequent and effective. The role of the human factor in long-term supplier–assembler relations is also noted. Fourth and finally, there is a discussion of the *keiretsu*. This is defined as a group of businesses with one dominant firm, but its form may vary, from a group composed of a parent firm and its hived-off subsidiaries, in which case the parent firm's control may be strong and the group should be effectively regarded as one company, to a group composed of an assembler and its main suppliers, in which case control is weak and does not function in terms of share ownership.

Chapter 7 discusses another form of group, called a *kigyo-shudan*, which is a loose association of essentially independent firms of equal power. The three ex-*zaibatsu* groups, Mitsubishi, Mitsui, and Sumitomo, are well known. Because they are descendants of pre-war *zaibatsu* which had a holding company at the top that controlled all the group companies, like conglomerates in the present USA and the UK, the *kigyo-shudan* is often considered to be a coherent group that has a central decision-making function. We deny such a view. To support our argument, we first describe the pre-war *zaibatsu* and then the drastic post-war policy measures taken to dissolve them. The consequence of this reform was an elimination of the central decision-making unit and of control through inter-firm share ownership. The activities of business groups today are discussed and the main motivation for individual firms to join the groups (if any) is hypothesized to be those growth opportunities created by information exchange and joint ventures, and mutual insurance. Our empirical findings do not support the view that such advantages actually exist. Furthermore, we predict a declining significance of the factors that have been raised as supporting these advantages.

Finally, Part III examines the consequences of Japanese management. The effect on industrial organization is studied in Chapter 8. Although a comparison of concentration ratios in Japan and the USA suggests that aggregate concentration is lower in Japan, it does not offer any clear conclusions about individual market concentration. Besides, as discussed earlier, concentration may not be a good measure of the intensity of market competition. Therefore, we turn to a comparison of company profit rates. Despite the difficulty in comparison owing to international differences in accounting rules, it seems reasonable to conclude that profit rates are lower on average and that inter-firm dispersion is less wide-ranging in Japan than the USA or the UK. This tendency appears to exist even in regard to predicted long-run profit rates. These results support the hypothesis that inter-firm competition is stronger in Japan, which is consistent with the growth maximization hypothesis because internal growth should either expand capacity in existing markets and intensify competition there, or foster entry to other markets and intensify contestability. Finally, we look at the change in the relationship between profitability and share (or concentration) from the 1960s to the 1980s with cross-section regression analyses. Results here are similar to the findings in the USA and are suggestive of a change in the behavioral modes of oligopolists from collusion to rivalry.

In Chapter 9, we inquire into the macroeconomic consequences of the labour-hoarding that is carried out to minimize lay-offs during recessions. A simple Keynesian–Kaldorian macro-model suggests that such hoarding stabilizes macro-fluctuation and this is reinforced by a multiplier effect. Using macro-data we find that the countercyclical movement of labour share in the GDP is most prominent in Japan, which, according to the model, must have contributed to the economy being among the most stable. This chapter also provides an empirical study of price mark-up behaviour in oligopolistic industries during the course of business fluctuation. The result does not indicate a systematic difference between highly concentrated industries and unconcentrated industries, unlike Wachtel and Adelsheim (1977) who argued that firms in US concentrated industries relatively increase mark-ups during recession and cause stagflation.

Macroeconomic growth is discussed in Chapter 10. Under certain conditions, an equilibrium model of economic growth predicts that a stronger managerial growth preference causes faster macroeconomic growth, provided that an increase in labour productivity is internally generated through conscious R & D efforts on the part of firms. Therefore, the growth maximization behaviour of Japanese management must have contributed to the rapid post-war economic growth of the country. A higher saving rate may have also contributed, and we examine the extent to which it really was higher than in other countries. In addition, there is a discussion of the relation between the rate of return on shareholding and the rate of company profit.

As argued in the previous section, the conspiracy theory attributes Japan's post-war economic growth to government policies. In Chapter 11, we offer a critical review of post-war policies—antimonopoly policy, industrial policy, and technology policy—and argue that though government measures may have helped in certain cases (for instance, the application of the infant industry theory in the automobile and electronics industries in the 1950s), the driving force was not government policies but the growth-pursuing behaviour of firms. Government policies were effective only to the extent that firms were eager to utilize the opportunities they provided; hence, if the policies of the Japanese government were more effective than in other countries, it was because firms were more keen to use the opportunities to their advantages. It should be noted that the political and bureaucratic costs of industrial policies, like those of regulation, can be substantial, and we find many such cases in the policies of the Japanese government, possibly more so than in other countries. These cases, we also note, are found mainly in those markets where competition is not at work, for instance, where competition is precluded by regulation.

Finally, in Chapter 12, we begin by re-examining growth maximization and competition, as well as the question of accountability, and then go on to discuss three issues related to international activities: overseas production, trade, and acquisitions. First, many studies show that Japanese management, or in some cases a modified form of it, is applied, with resulting high productivity, in the overseas plants of Japanese manufacturing firms, suggesting that, in contradiction to the culture theory, Japanese management is separable from Japanese culture and that such concepts as a flexible labour-force with internal competition and an emphasis on quality control and innovation are universally applicable. Second, Japanese exporters have been successful not because of governmental policies or unfair trade practices but because of the growth maximization behaviour which made long-term distribution and marketing investment in foreign markets possible. Third, Japanese acquisitions of foreign firms will increase because acquiring foreign human resources does not conflict with but rather complements the growth of domestic human resources. Foreign acquisitions of Japanese firms, on the other hand, will remain difficult because of the large share owned by financial institutions and other firms friendly to the target firm, and because the employees of target firms will regard it as an intrusion. In both trade and acquisition, therefore, international friction between Japan and other countries appears unlikely to subside. The book concludes with some thoughts on the future of the Japanese management system.

2

Ownership and Management

2.1. INTRODUCTION

Since a firm is essentially a collection of two types of resource, financial (and physical) and human, it is appropriate to start our discussion with two chapters discussing these in turn and then proceed to discuss the behaviour of Japanese management as a synthesis of the two. We shall follow traditional Western attitudes by putting the financial side of the firm first and the human side second, although this order is not intended to imply that we consider one more important than the other.

In Section 2.2, the pattern of share ownership is discussed, as well as the effectiveness of take-overs as a control device, to suggest that the control of management by the capital market is weaker in Japan than in the USA or the UK. Inter-company shareholdings and shareholdings by financial institutions are a prevalent feature in Japan and their implications on management are discussed in Section 2.3, which again suggests that management has considerable discretion in the Japanese firm. These facts suggest that to understand managerial behaviour, we need to look into the power and the origin of managers, which are the subjects of Sections 2.4 and 2.5, respectively. Section 2.6 concludes the chapter by discussing the implications for managerial motivation.

2.2. THE PATTERN OF SHARE OWNERSHIP

In Japan, as in most other industrialized countries, a major part of economic activity is carried out by joint-stock companies or *kabushiki kaisha* (KK). Actually, in terms of the number of firms or establishments, the proportion of joint-stock companies (even when *yugen kaisha*, companies with limited liability but without stock issues, are included) is less than a half, at about 40 per cent, the rest being proprietorships (*kojin kigyo*) or partnerships (*gomei kaisha, goshi kaisha*). Furthermore, the proportion of the latter is higher than in the USA. Nevertheless, in terms of economic activities, it is clearly joint-stock companies that are predominant in Japan, the USA, or elsewhere; for instance, they account for more than 90 per cent of sales in the manufacturing sector.

In a stock company, the shareholders are supposed to possess the ultimate controlling power. They elect the board of directors and, if they wish, may fire the incumbent executives at their annual or other meetings. There are several well-known limitations to this control mechanism, however. As numerous studies have shown,[1] most big companies have widely diffused share ownership, without any individual holding a sufficiently large share to control management decisions. Furthermore, as information has become more and more specific to the firm, those outside incumbent management have become less and less able to evaluate the adequacy of management decisions. This tendency is probably more evident in Japan, where management staff are less mobile across firms than in the USA or the UK.

Table 2.1 shows the pattern of share-ownership of companies in seven developed economies, classified by type of investor. Households, considered to be typical share owners in classical theories, comprise slightly less than a quarter in Japan and in European countries. It should be noted that international comparison of this kind may be affected by differences in accounting procedures and institutional factors. This raises particular difficulties when examining pension funds and retirement allowances. In Japan, it is established labour practice to make a sizeable lump-sum payment at a worker's retirement. Allowances are therefore made within the company to prepare for this payment, and these are regarded as a deferred payment to employees and treated as a company debt. This practice provides one explanation for the higher proportion of shares held by other non-financial enterprises in Japan, in comparison to the USA and the UK. Another explanation is that US data are on a consolidated basis while Japanese data are not. Therefore, although, as will be discussed in the next section, the prevalence of mutual shareholding between companies in alliance and among companies in business groups is a salient characteristic of Japanese business organization, how much of the difference in share-ownership pattern between Japan and the USA

[1] The pioneering work is Berle and Means (1932). For a more recent study, comparing the UK, the USA, and Japan, see Scott (1986).

TABLE 2.1. Share ownership by type of owner, 1985 (%)[a]

	USA	UK	Canada	Japan	FRG	France	Italy
Non-financial enterprises[b]	—	10	1	30	43	41	66
Banks[c]	0	0	4	17	8	4	3
Other financial institutions	28	52	21	22	9	8	3
Households	67	24	69	23	18	24	13
Government	0	5	2	0	9	10	9
Other[d]	4	10	4	7	13	13	5

[a] Including financial as well as non-financial companies.
[b] Not applicable for the USA because the data are on a consolidated basis.
[c] In Italy, only shares of financial companies.
[d] Mainly non-residents.

Source: Bank for International Settlements, *59th Annual Report*, June 1989.

is explained by this fact is unclear. There are also pension funds accumulated by firms, governments, and other employers which, as in the USA and the UK, are transferred to separate accounts. The increasing weight of these funds particularly in the USA has been discussed by several researchers (for instance, Mintz and Schwartz 1985). Since they are included in the table in the households category for the USA and Canada, but in the category of other financial institutions (trust banks and insurance companies) for Japan, the proportion of households is overstated for the USA and Canada.

Another possibly misleading international comparison concerns the extent of shareholding by banks. Even though the table suggests that American and British banks own no shares at all, the reality appears less clear-cut. They often hold shares of other companies temporarily, for instance, when they intervene in the management of firms in financial trouble, and many of them own shares through their trust and investment departments or subsidiaries. Thus the table exaggerates international differences and, in my view, the difference is not as obvious as is usually believed; and what disparities there are, are probably more qualitative than quantitative. In terms of bank shareholding, for instance, the important question may be whether banks hold the share to maintain a long-term relationship with the firm, or whether there is any co-ordination and exchange of information within a bank between the investment department and the lending department.

The lack of dominant individual shareholders has been evidenced by many studies since the pioneering work of Berle and Means (1932), suggesting the separation of control from ownership. Similar results have been found for Japan by several researchers, such as Nishiyama (1975).[2] Scott compared financial power in Japan, the UK, and the USA, and concluded that 'in all three economies the largest single category of control comprised those enterprises in which there was no dominant interest, the enterprises which were tied through interweaving share participa-

[2] For English readers, Nishiyama (1982) gives an excerpt from this book. For criticisms of these studies of management control, see Demsetz and Lehn (1985) and Pitelis and Sugden (1986), who argue that the lack of majority shareholding does not imply a lack of control, but merely the fact that minority shareholding has become sufficient to exert influence.

tions into a system of impersonal possession' (Scott 1986, 200). This similarity between the three economies is far more important and evident than any difference, but if there is a distinction it is that 'family control was lowest in Japan and highest in Britain; family influence within the system of impersonal possession was similarly at its lowest in Japan, but was highest in the United States' (ibid. 199).

Such lack of dominant individual shareholding makes it practically impossible for the shareholders to form a coalition or to establish a majority with proxies to influence management decisions. The cost of disseminating relevant information to other shareholders, persuading them, and reaching agreement with them is larger, the more the share-ownership is dispersed among small investors. The benefit from doing so is on the contrary smaller the smaller is the share owned by each investor, for he will receive only the fraction equal to his share in the firm of the benefit of the higher profits expected from such a move. This is a classical example of a free-rider problem, and insofar as every investor intends to free-ride on the effort of others, no one will initiate it.

Another mechanism may be present in the capital market to punish those managers not working in the shareholder's interests. Since a company with such managers will suffer poor long-run profitability and the share price is bound to be low, one consequence is the high cost of financing through new share issues. Hence, in order to keep the cost of new capital low, the management may be motivated to pursue shareholders' interests. This mechanism works when and only when the firm wishes to raise finance through new share issues, which is in fact the least preferred method, the most popular being retention of earnings, and the second choice being loans from financial institutions, because of the larger transaction costs—brokerage fees, informational requirements, and so on—required with share issues. The proportion of equity issues in industrial financing has been around a mere 3 per cent.[3] Unless the company has urgent financial problems, the mechanism is unlikely to exert a significant constraint on managerial behaviour.

[3] According to Hoddar (1988), the proportion was 3.5% in Japan and 2.6% in the USA on average in 1971–83, and in 1983 alone, 2.7% in Japan and 7.8% in the USA. The proportion is therefore small and hardly differs between the two countries. What is different is the proportion of loans from private financial

Take-overs arguably represent another device for corporate control in capital markets, since a low share price is expected to attract take-over bids by promising a high return from purchasing the firm, reorganizing it, and adopting better strategies or simply managing more efficiently. According to this view, the intensity of take-over activity observed in the USA and the UK is justified as an indication of the smoothness of capital markets, since take-overs are supposed to transfer control from an inefficient management to a more efficient one, where the word 'efficiency' is used to mean conformity to shareholder interests. The threat of take-over, therefore, provides an incentive for current management to be efficient in this sense.[4] Empirical examinations of take-overs as enhancers of efficiency have been inconclusive, as will be discussed in Chapter 5: some support the hypothesis, but others do not, arguing instead that take-overs have been made to satisfy the empire-building ambitions of the raiders without contributing to economic efficiency. The effectiveness as well as the social cost of this mechanism remains open to question, therefore.[5] This cost is not confined to pecuniary expenditure, such as legal and the brokerage fees. A possibly negative influence of frequent take-overs and sell-offs on the motivation of staff and employees appears to me a very important question which has not been investigated so far.

Obviously, the threat of take-overs as a control device is weaker the higher the costs to potential raiders. These costs may be substantial. One obvious example is the premiums to be paid to the target shareholders and the brokerage and legal fees. Less apparent, but potentially more significant, is the cost of reorganizing the acquired firm and ensuring that it pursues those strategies the raider wishes to enforce. Such costs can be very high, especially in Japan, owing to the costs related to the human aspect

institutions, which is 37% in Japan and 13.4% in the USA, though, according to Kuroda and Oritani (1980), this difference is partly due to different accounting rules and is exaggerated. Some of these differences are discussed in the Appendix to Chap. 8. A discussion of financial structure can be found in Sec. 10.6.

[4] Marris (1964) and Manne (1965) were the first to view take-overs as a disciplinary mechanism, though they differ in emphasis: Manne stressed their efficiency-enhancing effects, whereas Marris stressed the imperfectness of this mechanism. The most outspoken supporter of take-overs as an efficiency device is Jensen (1988).

[5] We will return to this topic in Sec. 12.1.

of Japanese firms as will be discussed in Chapter 5 and, as a consequence, hostile take-overs there are quite rare. Shareholder control of management through take-overs, if it exists at all, is limited in Japan.

In summary, the dispersion of share-ownership and the resulting separation of ownership from control have been as widespread in Japan as in other industrial nations, if not more so. Active take-over activities, observed in the USA and the UK and regarded by some authors as an effective reminder to the management of capital market discipline, have been and will continue to be rare in Japan. The consequence is that Japanese management possesses considerable controlling power. In other words, the motivation and interests of the managers themselves are the important factors in understanding Japanese management, suggesting a need to inquire into the origins and backgrounds of directors and presidents.

Finally, it should be noted that a disregard for shareholder interest *ex ante* does not necessarily imply that it is low *ex post*. This is particularly important when making international comparisons because the rate of return on holding a share has been higher in Japan than in the USA or the UK. What is suggested here is that the rate of return might have been even higher in Japan had management maximized it! Moreover, it is necessary to investigate macroeconomic interaction to examine the rate of return *ex post*. These questions will be raised in Chapter 10.

2.3. THE INFLUENCE OF FINANCIAL INSTITUTIONS AND INTER-COMPANY SHAREHOLDINGS

A salient feature of corporate ownership in Japan, as we have observed, is the larger proportion of shares owned by financial and non-financial companies. One explanation, the inclusion of retirement allowances in company debt, has been suggested. Another explanation that may be equally appropriate is the prevalence of inter-company shareholding.

There are basically three types of inter-company shareholding. The first includes holdings by banks and other financial institutions of their clients' shares; the second includes holdings by industrial or commercial companies of the shares of their affiliates, such as subsidiaries, subcontractors, and suppliers who are usually dependent on the parent firms for trading and technological reasons; and the third includes reciprocal holdings between basically independent companies. In Japanese the terms *kinyu-keiretsu*, (*sangyo*) *keiretsu*, and *kigyo-shudan* are used to describe these three, respectively, though the distinction is not always clear, and the terms have often been used in an obscure or misleading manner. A precise definition will be given in Chapters 6 and 7.

There are several reasons why banks might wish to own shares in client companies. First, while examining the application for loans and during the course of making these loans, they will be able to collect more accurate and detailed information on the company than that available to other investors, and will thus be in a better position to assess the risk. Second, they may wish to acquire shares in order to ensure that management co-operates in offering detailed information and, if the company gets in trouble, in order to bring pressure on management to secure the repayment of loans. Third, they may acquire shares to entice the management to make deposits, loans, and other financial transactions with them. This third factor appears to be gaining more importance now because industrial companies have recently accumulated more and more internal funds so that they now depend less and less on loans. Fourth, in view of the high rate of return from shareholding attained in the past, banks may have simply chosen to purchase shares as profitable investment opportunities.

The influence of banks on management should not be exaggerated. It is true that the bank, particularly the so-called *main* bank, which is usually the bank holding the largest debts of the firm, tends to influence the management when it is in trouble by, for instance, persuading the firm to take on a bank representative in some senior position, such as vice-president, to accept a less ambitious strategy, to sell some of the assets to reduce the debt, or even to agree to acquisition by a healthier company. A list of such cases between 1975 and 1984 can be found in Sheard (1989). Probably two of the best-known cases are Toyo Kogyo (now Mazda Motor), which was successfully revived with the support of the Sumitomo Bank (Pascale and Rohlen 1983), and Ataka & Co., a trading company. Ataka was forced to cut its work-force by more than two-thirds and was then acquired by C. Ito, but it was said that C. Ito would not have agreed to acquire the ailing company without the urging of the Sumitomo Bank, one of C. Ito's main banks.

Sheard argues that the main-bank system in Japan provides a quasi-internal capital market and that 'the main bank substitutes for the missing *external* markets for corporate control and monitoring services' (ibid. 413, his emphasis). A similar argument has been made by Cable (1985) with regard to the role of West German banks. Although these authors imply that the Japanese and German system offers a contrast to an Anglo-American system, in which banks play a more passive role and management control is effected externally through take-overs, the difference should not be exaggerated. Even in the USA and the UK, banks sometimes intervene in their borrowers' management. They may send personnel to the companies and dictate managerial changes in return for extended loans and short-term shareholdings. Such cases in the USA are listed in Mintz and Schwartz (1985). They counted forty-two cases in the five-year period 1977–81 mostly from a reading of *Business Week*. These were only the major cases, however, and the total number must be much larger. Compare this to the twenty-seven cases of major bank assistance or bank intervention that Sheard found for Japan in the ten-year period 1975–84, mainly from *Nihon Keizai Shimbun*. Needless to say, the comparison is not entirely meaningful because the numbers are not exhaustive and the extent of intervention varies widely between countries and cases. Yet, it appears very difficult indeed to conclude that bank intervention is rare in the USA but common in Japan.

Whether in the USA, the UK or Japan, the fact is that, however conspicuous such cases as that of Mazda may be, main banks rarely attempt to influence the management of client companies unless the latter are in deep financial trouble. For one thing, management, quite understandably, does not welcome what it sees as intervention in its authority. Unless the company desperately needs to secure loans, it has an incentive to avoid banks with an interventionist reputation and to diversify the source of loans so that none of the lenders have a decisive influence. A dilemma facing the management is that, on the one hand, it will wish to avoid becoming too dependent on a particular bank, but that, on the other hand, the more dependent it is on a particular bank, the more likely this bank will be to come to the rescue when the firm's financial situation deteriorates. Diversifying the source of funds and depending less on a particular bank must become more attractive as the company's internal funds grow larger or the management becomes more confident in its future. This tendency, in fact, seems to be under way now.

The firm usually obtains loans from a number of banks. Some firms even switch their main bank. Yet, a stable bank–client relationship has been quite common without this apparently resulting in either side influencing the decision-making of the other. For instance, the Mitsui Bank has always been the main bank for Sony, and the Mitsubishi Bank for Honda. It is of course inconceivable that Sony's management has been influenced by Mitsui or Honda's by Mitsubishi: otherwise, why should Mitsubishi Motor and Honda be competing so fiercely with each other? Equally, Sony has never been regarded as belonging to the Mitsui Group or Honda to the Mitsubishi Group. Stability in bank–company relationships does not necessarily imply either influence in management or any special connection apart from ordinary financial transactions. Stability has its own advantages which, as discussed in Chapter 1, are larger as asset specificity is higher. A good bank–customer relationship, based on accumulated knowledge of each other's management and accumulated confidence, is an asset and, insofar as the terms offered by banks are similar, the firm has little incentive to switch to another lender. The advantage of long-term transactional stability is well known, as in the case of the supplier–assembler relationship to be discussed in Section 6.4, and in this respect financial transactions are the same as any other.

The absence of bank control, except in cases of failing companies, need not be affected by the share-ownership of financial institutions. This is partly because the Japanese Antimonopoly Law restricts shareholding by a bank (or any other non-insurance financial institution) to a maximum of 5 per cent of the company share.[6] The effect of this restriction, made to prevent the re-emergence of a *zaibatsu*-type giant trust with financial institutions at its centre, is apparent in the fact that the largest shareholders of many companies are financial institutions, each holding the maximum 5 per cent. Hence, the average 17 per cent owned by banks (see Table 2.1) must be in the hands of at least four different banks. This pattern of share-ownership by several banks

[6] For insurance companies, the maximum is 10%. (See also Chap. 7 n. 6.)

must imply that the controlling power of each bank is limited and that probably none of them has any real control. It is true that, if the major banks collude, they will be able to acquire decisive controlling power. However, such collusion is prohibited under the Antimonopoly Law and is, furthermore, extremely unlikely in view of the keen competition between banks. There have been reports of conflicting opinions among shareholding banks about how to rescue firms on the brink of bankruptcy. If agreement is difficult even when repayment of debts is at stake, what incentive is there to seek agreement in normal circumstances?

Shareholding by non-financial companies, as explained earlier, may be separated into two categories: holding shares of subsidiaries or affiliates, and holding shares of intra-group companies on a bilateral basis. The first, needless to say, aims at real control. For instance, Toyota owns shares of many of the firms that it buys components from or that it subcontracts with, in order to facilitate smooth overall production plans and to create harmonized investment and other strategies. In addition, many firms hive off parts of businesses as subsidiaries. Such shareholding is common in other countries as well. To the extent that hive-off is more popular than divisional forms within a company, and that a long-term subcontracting or purchasing relation is more common and more advantageous in Japan, shareholding associated with it may be also more common (see Chapter 6 for further discussion).

The other type of inter-company shareholding is found between companies in some forms of alliance and within business groups such as Mitsui, Mitsubishi, and Sumitomo. Since there is a detailed discussion on corporate groups in Chapter 7, we shall confine ourselves here to emphasizing that within groups firms are basically independent and equal in power. The proportion of mutual shareholding, that is the proportion in total shares of the shares held by all other members, amounts on average to one-quarter or one-third. Yet each company possesses only a small share in any other, which, together with the bilateral nature of the shareholding, makes it very unlikely that this is used as a means of control. This represents a crucial difference between modern groups and their predecessors, the pre-war *zaibatsu*, in which the majority share of every member firm was owned by a holding company that acted as central decision-making unit.

Shareholding may also occur, often on a bilateral basis,

between two independent companies without any relation to these groups. In many cases, mutual shareholding is designed to foster co-operation in product development, marketing, joint ventures, and so forth, without damaging the independence of either company. Increasingly the formation of such alliances is a common strategy adopted by firms in any country, for instance, to create global networks for marketing or research. They often involve some form of capital participation, which is increasingly used as a substitute for mergers and acquisitions because of the costs and difficulties involved in acquiring and integrating another organization (see Chapter 5 for details). To conclude, shareholding by financial institutions is more common in Japan than in the USA and the UK, and so is inter-company shareholding. Both forms are generally used to reinforce other forms of inter-company relations, such as lending, supplies of components, strategic alliance, and corporate grouping, and are rarely used (or usable) as a means of corporate control. An exception to this observation may be made when the company is in financial difficulty, because banks then tend to interfere with management so as to revive the company or to liquidate it with as little hardship as possible to creditors and shareholders as well as to employees. Otherwise, management decisions in Japan are less likely to be influenced by concern for shareholders than in other countries.

2.4. THE POWER OF MANAGERS

In Japan, as in any other country, every stock company must hold an annual shareholders' meeting, at which the board of directors is elected, and the report of accounts is approved. The process will be little more than a formality in normal circumstances: candidates for the board are proposed by the current chairman and approved without much debate. Even for more substantial matters, such as changes in the articles of association (the certificate of incorporation) due to the addition of new business fields, for instance, antagonistic arguments against management proposals are rare. The average length of the annual shareholders' meetings held in June 1987 by 1,082 listed companies (70 per cent of all listed companies), was only twenty-nine minutes, suggesting that little more than the straightforward approval of management proposals took place.[7]

There are, of course, exceptions. The longest on record is the thirteen and a half hours that Sony had to endure in 1984 to answer questions and complaints from the shareholders on the unpopularity of the Beta VTR system that the company had developed. Thus, when firms are in trouble, shareholders may use the meetings to give the incumbent management a hard time. Yet despite this, the Sony management succeeded at that meeting in winning approval for all its proposals, as is customary at virtually all shareholders' meetings.

In typical Japanese companies, most of the directors are internally promoted, and have been working with the firm for many years, often since joining the business immediately after graduation from university. There are exceptions. If the company has a dominant shareholder, as in the case of a subsidiary company, it is usual to have a representative from the parent or shareholding company on the board. Companies in business groups (*kigyo shudan*) often have directors who sit on more than one board. Companies with financial, technological, marketing or historical links may receive a director from their partners, probably on a reciprocal basis. Table 2.2 shows that more than 90 per cent of the major firms have at least one director from outside. In about a half of the firms one or more of the directors have come from the largest shareholder and a similar number from the largest lender (which may be the largest shareholder as well). An unknown proportion of these directors had once been, but were no longer outside the firm. Some of them, therefore, may have been recruited as directors not because of their links with former employers but simply because of their ability.

Yet a majority of the directors in large Japanese companies are insiders, and this stands in considerable contrast to American and British firms, where outside non-executive directors tend to be in a majority on the board. According to Kagono *et al.* (1985), the percentage of companies in which outside directors form a majority

[7] *Nihon Keizai Shimbun*, 12 June 1988. As shown in the text, more than two-thirds of the listed companies hold their meetings in June, because an accounting year ending in March, which is the same as the government fiscal year and the school year, is most popular, and three months are needed to prepare financial statements.

TABLE 2.2. Outside directors of listed Japanese firms, 1980

Number of directors	Breakdown of firms (%) according to number of directors formerly or concurrently from			
	Outside the firm	Largest shareholder	Largest source of borrowings	Civil service or government
1	11.9	19.3	33.1	17.9
2	12.6	11.1	11.7	5.3
3	11.0	6.4	3.4	3.6
4	11.7	3.3	0.7	2.5
5	10.1	2.3	0.4	1.7
6 or more	33.2	10.4	0.0	2.0
None	9.5	47.1	50.7	66.4

Note: The total number of firms, all listed in Tokyo Stock Exchange, First Section, is 809. For 'largest source of borrowings' the total number is 761 because 43 firms had no borrowings, and for 5 firms the largest source of borrowings could not be identified.

Source: Sheard (1989).

is zero in Japan but 83 (industrials) and 88 (non-industrials) in the USA. Therefore, the role of outside directors in Japanese companies cannot be more than advisory. They do not actively participate in the daily management decisions, unless, again, the company is in difficulty and an outside director, such as somebody from the main bank, is forced to take action to protect the interests of the bank or whichever company he represents.

The company usually has a chairman and a president, who are of course on the board. The division of power and responsibility between the two varies from one company to another, but typically the president takes care of most managerial matters, being equivalent to an American chief executive officer (CEO) or a British managing director (MD). Basically his power comes from his control of managerial appointments. He nominates both candidates for the board and, under normal circumstances, the person who is to succeed him after his retirement. By so doing, he may eliminate, if he wishes to, anyone he regards as unsuitable or hostile to his leadership. Such oppressive management is unusual, because it will evoke resentment and sabotage among the rank and file, and damage social reputation, and because his predecessor is unlikely to have nominated such a person to the post. Even so there have been cases. One example is Mitsukoshi, a prestigious and long-established department store—the Harrods of Japan—under the presidency of Okada in 1972–82. Okada was initially respected as an energetic manager with fresh ideas but he became dictatorial and made decisions that worried several of the directors. Nevertheless, he was able to maintain his power by demoting directors with opposing views or waiting until they became discouraged and resigned. Finally, a chain of events that was widely reported by the press and damaged the reputation and sales of the company forced the board to take the historically unprecedented and drastic action of voting him out. This case, in my view, shows how secure the president's position is in a large Japanese company, not only because such cases are so rare but also because, despite the fact that Okada's apparent mismanagement had been known within the company for many years, the board could not remove him until his bizarre wrongdoings, such as his instruction to procure from his mistress's company at high prices, became a widely known scandal and the Fair Trade Commission accused the company of violation of the Antimonopoly Law.

Two more interesting observations can be made from this case. First, Mitsukoshi's board had one outside non-executive director, a former chairman of Mitsui Bank. Mitsukoshi is a member of Mitsui's presidents' club (see Chapter 7) and was the very first business that the Mitsui family set up about three centuries ago. Currently, about 12 per cent of the shares are held by Mitsui's financial institutions. According to the news report, this director played an important role in ousting Okada. Second, despite the apparent failure of the internal control mechanism, it was an insider, once regarded as second in command but demoted by Okada to head a non-Tokyo (and hence, less prestigious) branch, who succeeded as the president. This clearly suggests the difficulty in a Japanese firm of bringing in a CEO from outside. Business expertise and human relations specific to the firm are indispensable in managing a Japanese company, as are the co-operative attitudes of employees that internal appointments are expected to create.

The Mitsukoshi episode raises the question of what mechanisms there are to remove inefficient management. In the USA or the UK, it is usually argued that such inefficiency causes the share price to fall and thereby invites take-overs which will eliminate such management. The disciplinary role of the take-over is weaker in Japan to the extent that take-overs are rarer.

What happens most usually in a Japanese firm is that, such a manager, having become aware of dissatisfaction among employees, particularly at managerial level, or among lending financial institutions, opts to resign voluntarily to 'save his face'. For instance, he may find it more and more difficult to persuade banks to extend loans to his company or, if the outstanding loans are in danger of default, it may be explicitly suggested to him that he resign. If, however, the company is not in a weak position *vis-à-vis* banks, the manager, despite its inefficiency, may opt to continue the *status quo* and succeed, as in the Mitsukoshi case. Of course, one ultimate mechanism of disciplining such a manager is bankruptcy. The more competitive the market is, the more effective this discipline must be. Particularly under the lifetime employment system prevalent in Japan, the hardship that bankruptcy imposes on employees is incomparably large, and any manager who has himself been promoted from inside must be very sympathetic to employees' concern about job security. Fear of company failure is a strong incentive for the management to strive for managerial efficiency and to work for the company's long-term prosperity. In others words, Japanese management regards itself as accountable not only to shareholders but also to a wide body of stakeholders, in particular its employees, and this makes the cost of bankruptcy disproportionately large. The threat of bankruptcy thus plays a strong disciplinary role. This view will be discussed again in the closing chapter.

2.5. THE BACKGROUND OF MANAGERS

I have argued that the management of a typical Japanese firm—from presidents to ordinary directors and further down the scale to middle management—consists of those people who have worked with the same firm for a long time and been promoted internally. In fact, this tendency can be observed in any country, to a varying degree. In the UK, for instance, Fidler (1981) found that 42 per cent among 130 CEOs of top UK companies worked for only one company in their career. The percentage is smaller, at 22 per cent, in the study conducted by Kohn/Ferry (1981) of 418 executives (not necessarily CEOs), but more than a third of them had been working with the firm for twenty-one years or longer and more than a half for sixteen years or longer. The average length of time in one company of all executive directors in 1981 was found by Cosh and Hughes (1987) to be twenty-two years in the UK and twenty-six years in the USA. For CEOs, these figures were twenty-three and twenty-nine years, respectively. Clearly, the popular picture of a successful executive moving from one company to another in pursuit of promotion and higher financial rewards does not match the behaviour of typical executives today.

Japan is therefore not the only country where executives are internally bred. The difference is that the tendency is found not only in many or the majority of cases but in almost all. It is the norm to elect a director and then a president from inside the firm. Any deviation from this norm will greatly disappoint employees and damage their morale, as well as adversely affecting the quality of job applicants to the company. A typical example of such deviation has been the recruitment of retired senior government officials called *amakudari*, translated literally as 'descent from heaven'. Unless such recruitment is expected to bring a significant benefit, or unless the incumbent manager is entirely dissatisfied with the quality of his subordinates, there will be no recruitment from outside. It is therefore no wonder that as the benefit from *amakudari* has become less and less important with the diminishing influence of the government (to be discussed in Chapter 11), there are fewer cases of *amakudari* to private companies.

There is another important difference between Japanese and American or British managers—their background. In Japan, the largest proportion of directors have come from production and technology departments, followed by marketing and export, which altogether have accounted for 50 to 70 per cent, a far larger figure than for those with financial and accounting backgrounds, which amount to merely 5–19 per cent (Kono 1984, 33). More recently, among the 126 presidents who assumed their posts during the first six months of 1987 in the firms listed in Tokyo Stock Exchange, 36 per cent had a background in marketing and 28 per cent in production and R&D. Those with financial backgrounds again accounted for a mere 11 per cent (*Nihon Keizai Shimbun*, 25 May 1987). The unimportance of any financial background forms a contrast to the USA or the UK where financial experience has been found most helpful in attaining managerial positions. In the UK, in both the Fidler and the Kohn/Ferry studies cited above, 'general management' was the answer most commonly given when executives were asked in which areas they spent the major part of their career, followed by finance/accounting. When, in the Kohn/Ferry study, they were asked in which areas business careers commenced, the largest proportion, 32 per cent, answered 'finance/accounting', followed by 24 per cent who answered 'professional/technical'. In the USA, according to Browne and Motamedi (1977), of 754 CEOs in top US firms in 1976, 25 per cent cited finance, 22 per cent administration, 15 per cent marketing, and 12 per cent legal, as the type of work they were engaged in prior to their appointment. In contrast, production and engineering/technology accounted for just 20 per cent. They found, furthermore, an increasing trend in the finance-based CEOs from 1970 to 1976.

How much reliance to place in this international comparison is hardly an easy question. The definition of areas or fields is not always easy. A person may move from one area to another during his career; for instance, a worker with an engineering diploma or with experience in production/research may work in the marketing department as a technical consultant, such cases being more likely in Japan where a wide-ranging rotation of workers is more common. Also, the results may be affected by sampling or by year. These deficiencies notwithstanding, the implication seems clear enough: finance, supposedly the quickest way to the top in the USA and the UK, is not a favoured field in Japan. More commonly, it is either production/technology/research or marketing/sales/export that are the favoured departments from which promotion to directorship takes place. This fact is consistent with the stronger influence of finance in American than in Japanese firms found by Kagono *et al.* (1985). They asked executives about the extent to which each of seven departments was likely to influence decision-making. For only one department—finance and control—did American executives give a higher score than Japanese executives, while in the other six—sales and marketing, research and development, production, personnel, corporate planning, and purchasing—Japanese managers gave higher scores.

This difference probably explains why business schools are not so popular in Japan as in the USA or the UK. Financial knowledge, which is more theoretical, more universal, and easier to teach in classrooms, counts less in Japanese management, and technological, manufacturing, or marketing knowledge, which is more firm-specific and more effectively learned on the job than through lectures, counts more. The importance of on-the-job training in Japanese firms, discussed in the next chapter, is closely related to their production/marketing orientation.

2.6. SUMMARY AND IMPLICATIONS FOR MANAGEMENT MOTIVATION

We have found in this chapter that there is an absence of classical corporate owners in Japanese companies. Also absent is the threat of take-overs, although these are praised by a number of American and British authors as an effective means of eliminating managers who fail to maximize shareholder interests whether because of inefficiency or by pursuing other goals. For these reasons, we infer that Japanese managers have more discretionary power than their American and British counterparts.

Share-ownership in Japan is characterized by larger participation on the part of banks and other financial institutions, and of industrial or commercial companies than in the USA or the UK. This tendency is a reflection of a closer bank–customer relationship and of the existence of business groups. The closer bank–lender relationship may have arisen from the low-interest policy adopted by the government until the 1960s to foster private investment, which resulted in an excess demand for funds from the industrial and commercial sector, making it advantageous for companies to maintain friendly relations with banks. Because companies were so dependent on loans, such relations were also necessary for banks so that they might be kept informed of the companies' activities and performance, so as to be able to evaluate their ability to repay the debt and the desirability of further loans. Shareholdings by these financial institutions were a natural consequence of this relationship.

These shareholdings, however, have not resulted in control by banks over industrial firms. Of course, when a firm is in financial trouble, a bank will have a strong incentive to interfere in management to secure its investment and the management has no choice but to follow the bank's advice in order to save the firm and the employees. Yet, when no risk of default can be foreseen, banks dare not interfere in management, and the management has tended to resist any such interference by, for instance, diversifying its financial transaction. With the current change in financial markets, in which firms are accumulating more and more internal funds, bank control of companies is increasingly less likely.

It is also worth noting that all the financial institutions in Japan are themselves management-controlled. No bank has a majority shareholder. Virtually all the top ten shareholders are other financial institutions and industrial companies, each holding less than 5 per cent of the shares. The senior manager of a financial institution, like his counterpart in the industrial sector, has invariably been promoted internally after long working experience with the institution. No doubt, therefore, he is sympathetic to the managers of borrowing companies who have spent their entire career with the one firm and who wish to make their own decisions in consultation with their own staff.

The same empathy is present among the managers of business groups (*kigyo shudan*). They therefore tend to avoid interfering with the decision of other managers unless it affects their companies, and to concentrate instead on planning those projects that will be beneficial, or at least not harmful, to other members. (Further discussion on *kigyo shudan* will follow in Chapter 7.)

These facts obviously imply that a typical Japanese manager has substantial freedom to pursue his own ideas and goals. What are these goals? We should remember that he has been internally promoted after long service with the firm. Typically, he was recruited directly from university, and has been working with the firm for more than thirty years, probably having gained experience in many of the firm's departments. The workers are familiar with him, some of them having worked together for many years. He understands what is important to them: he is keenly aware of it. The employees are very much closer to him than the shareholders he sees only a few times a year at most. They are the insiders, whose satisfaction he can share and for whose dissatisfaction he knows he is to blame. The Japanese manager, as a result, is more concerned with the welfare of the management staff and other employees. He lays more emphasis on the human aspect of the firm than the financial aspect. He believes that the accumulation of human resources and their full utilization are the keys to the success of the firm. The whole incentive system and the system of allocating the internal labour-force are geared to this end, and the manager intends to ensure that employees contribute to the company's success voluntarily and happily.

3

The Internal Labour System

3.1. LABOUR PRACTICES IN JAPANESE FIRMS: THE STEREOTYPE

Let us start by discussing the so-called 'three pillars' of the Japanese internal labour system. The first, *lifetime employment* (also called 'permanent employment' or 'lifetime commitment'), refers to the practice whereby a worker is hired immediately after school and is expected to stay with the same firm until retirement. The firm, in return, is expected to retain him until the age of mandatory retirement (typically 55 to 60) regardless of business conditions. According to Abegglen, who was among the first to propagate the concept to Western readers, 'At whatever level of organization in the Japanese factory, the worker commits himself on entrance to the company for the rest of his working career. The company will not discharge him even temporarily except in the most extreme circumstances. He will not quit the company for industrial employment elsewhere' (Abegglen 1958; reprinted 1973, 62).

The second is the *seniority system*, whereby wages and promotion are determined according to seniority. Seniority refers either to age or to the length of service within the firm, the difference being unimportant because, when everyone is recruited directly from school and stays with the same firm, seniority ranking among workers of the same educational background is unaffected by comparisons between age and length of service. Under the seniority system, an employee's wage is supposed to depend mostly on his seniority and education level, and less (if at all) on the job or his achievement. In addition, seniority is supposed to be the decisive factor in promotion. That is, an empty post is filled by the most senior among those subordinates and others who satisfy the required level of educational background.[1]

[1] Some authors use the term 'seniority system' to mean only the 'seniority wage system', and regard the 'seniority promotion system' as an indispensable part of the lifetime employment system (for instance, Koike 1988).

The third is *enterprise unionism*, which implies that all the employees of the firm, including both blue-collar and white-collar workers but excluding those in managerial positions above a certain rank, are represented by a single union. As a result, it is said, the basic attitude of the union to the management is not confrontational but co-operative. Indeed some people would go further and say that the unions consequently lack the power to promote workers' rights.

In addition to these three 'pillars', it is argued that the *bonus* system provides flexibility in the company's labour costs, because biannual bonuses are supposed to depend more on company profitability than monthly wages. In particular, when a company is in financial difficulty, workers accept a reduction in bonuses according to this argument, reducing the labour cost and making it easier for the company to survive.[2]

There is no denying that these practices are observed more often in Japan than in other countries, particularly the USA and the UK. And yet it is clearly an exaggeration to argue that they truly and wholly describe labour practices in Japan, or that they offer a clear distinction between Japanese firms and those in other countries. They are *not* entirely absent in the USA or the UK. Despite what we learn in neoclassical economic theory, even American and British workers do not always move from one firm to another when a better-paid job is offered. Neither are wages determined only by the nature of the job and workers' performance. A completely mobile labour market rarely exists, except possibly in a few rather minor sectors. The international differences are by no means absolute: rather, it is a question of degree. Abegglen's pioneering work recognized this fact: 'Reluctance on the part of the worker to quit and on the part of the firm to fire him are constant factors in the American [worker–company] relationship; the Japanese firm will discharge employees, and employees do occasionally quit' (ibid. 62). Nevertheless, many followers of Abegglen's book and subsequent observers from abroad have continued to be more impressed by the differences

[2] Weitzman (1984) even regards the bonus system as a form of profit-sharing between the owners and the employees. We will criticize this view in Chap. 9 because Japanese workers now expect bonuses more or less as part of regular pay. Pascale and Rohlen (1983), for instance, show that Mazda did not decrease bonuses even in the years when the company made losses.

than the similarities, ignoring his warning that the difference is not absolute.

However, there are studies, more reliable in my view, revealing, on the one hand, that the supposedly Japanese system is not strictly adopted among Japanese firms and, on the other, that similar systems are present in other countries. The aim of this chapter is to discuss how universal the supposedly Japanese system actually is, how much difference nevertheless remains between Japan and other countries, and what effects these differences may have in terms of worker motivation and corporate performance. We begin in Section 3.2 with a critical examination of the above stereotypes in general, and continue with three sections on specific topics. Section 3.3 focuses on labour adjustment; Section 3.4 on skill formation through training and job rotation; and Section 3.5 on the promotion tournament as a mechanism of internal competition. Section 3.6 presents a conclusion.

3.2. THE REALITY

The relevance of the three pillars varies across the Japanese economy. They are more relevant among big firms (and the government sector) than among small firms, and for male workers than female workers. It is difficult to estimate the proportion of the work-force covered by the lifetime employment and seniority system. Dore (1973, 305), for instance, assumed that the stereotype can be applied to government employment, firms with 500 employees or more, and smaller firms with a greater emphasis on non-manual labour, and estimated that about a half of the total number of employees and a third of all those gainfully occupied are involved in the system. Whether this estimate is accurate or not, the implication is clear: not all, and not even the majority, of Japanese workers are under the lifetime employment scheme. It is also true, however, that 'the importance of "the system" . . . is to be measured not only by its gradual absorption of a larger proportion of the Japanese labour force, but also by the influence it has as a normative model for the rest of society' (ibid.). In other words, lifetime employment is taken in Japan as a norm which the firm is expected to comply with, and regardless of the extent to which the firm pursues such a course, it is this that must be the crucial difference between Japanese and Anglo-American firms.[3]

Another fact to be noted is that the system of lifetime employment with internal promotion has not always been common in Japan. Most business historians believe that it became widespread around 1920 when the Japanese economy boomed following World War I (Hirschmeier and Yui 1975; Taira 1970). There was a great demand for labourers, particularly skilled workers. Many firms suffered labour shortages and offered a higher wage to entice skilled labourers from other firms. Many workers, as textbook economics would expect, moved from one firm to another seeking higher pay and a higher position. Realizing that this trend caused great harm to company stability, managers started to look instead to new graduates, training them internally, and offering permanent employment with seniority wages. This employment and wage system offered workers an incentive to stay with the firm, and the lifetime employment system gradually developed. The system, with some modifications, became more stable and more widespread when there was an even larger need for skilled workers during the post-World War II era of fast growth in the 1950s and 1960s.

The system, therefore, was by no means traditionally Japanese. It evolved as a response, perhaps one might say a 'rational' response, to market conditions. The popular argument which attributes it to Japanese culture is misleading, to say the least. Admittedly, the way firms responded to changing labour market conditions may have been influenced by Japanese culture and might have been different had they been American or British companies. Yet, such cultural factors played a role, if any, only in response to changing economic conditions. Furthermore, the fact that the labour market was quite mobile before that period, more like the market in the USA or the UK, suggests that the Japanese system may not be permanent.

To see if lifetime employment is really more common in Japan, an international comparison can be made of the separation rate, namely, the number of job-leavers as a proportion of the total labour force. Ono (1981) found that, though the rate was in general lower in Japan than in the USA or the UK, as expected, the difference between Japan and the UK is fairly small—25 per

[3] For a similar view, see also Clark (1979).

cent as opposed to 34 per cent. In particular, among smaller firms of 30 to 99 employees, the figure of 30 per cent in Japan was not much different from that in the UK, suggesting that the disparity between Japan and the UK is due to the lower separation rate in large Japanese firms. The ratio is much higher in the USA at 53 per cent, supporting the view that labour mobility is high in the USA.[4]

When separation rates were compared by age, Ono found that they decline with age or with the length of service (within the same company) in any of the three countries, and this tendency is strongest in the USA, and then in the UK. As a consequence, although the rate is clearly lowest in Japan among young workers or workers with service of under one year, it is rather similar in all three countries among older workers with long service.

A similar argument has been made by Koike (1988), who found that the proportion of male workers with more than ten years of service was, for blue-collar workers, 38 per cent in Japan, 37 per cent in West Germany, 32 per cent in France, and 35 per cent in the UK; and for white-collar workers, 52 per cent in Japan, 48 per cent in West Germany, 50 per cent in France, and 39 per cent in the UK. The percentages for large companies (with a thousand or more employees) are higher in Japan: 47 per cent for blue-collar workers and 62 per cent for white-collar workers. Yet the difference between Japan, even for workers in large companies, and European countries is hardly impressive, and it appears reasonable to conclude that 'if permanent employment is said to be characteristic of Japanese blue-collar male employees of large companies, then the same should be said about EC white-collar male employees' (Koike 1988, 61). Similarly, Main (1982) found that on average British workers stay with the same jobs for almost twenty years.

As regards the comparison between Japan and the USA, Koike found an interesting difference in trend. While in the USA the proportion of workers with ten years or more of service declined from 34 per cent in 1966 to 29 per cent in 1978, it increased in Japan from 35 per cent in 1969 to 50 per cent in 1979. This result indicates first, that the difference in terms of the length of service

[4] The data are not strictly comparable between the three countries: see Ono (1981, chap. 9) for details.

in Japan and the USA is a recent phenomenon and, second, that even in the USA the proportion of immobile workers is higher than is usually believed. A similar result has been reported by Hall (1982) in a study entitled 'The Importance of Lifetime Jobs in the US Economy', which estimates, for instance, that almost half of workers aged between 40 and 44 will remain with the same employer for ten years or more. Thus, though job tenure is on average longer in Japan than in the USA, the difference does not seem absolute.[5]

According to available labour statistics, therefore, worker–company attachment seems stable in virtually any country, with some international differences. It is perhaps strongest in Japan, followed by Germany and France and then the UK, and perhaps weakest in the USA. Another common finding is that young workers tend to move around seeking a good job match, but that once they find satisfactory jobs they tend to stay with the same employer.

Job separation takes place on the initiative either of the employee—through leaving and retirement—or of the employer—through lay-off, redundancy, and dismissal. For the workers, enforced redundancy is a particularly important question. They will be concerned to know how often employers resort to redundancy during depression, how many workers will be laid off, and which of them are likely to go, since all these things govern the extent of job security. Since none of these questions can be answered simply by looking at the statistics, a more careful examination of the mechanism of employment adjustment is needed. We shall return to this topic in Section 3.3.

Let us now look at the second 'pillar', the seniority system. A discussion of the importance (or unimportance) of seniority in promotion can be found in Section 3.5. At this point we confine ourselves to an examination of the seniority wage system. An easy way to do this is by comparing the age–wage profile across countries. Again, Koike (1988) found that an upward-sloping profile, that is, increasing wages according to age, is by no means unique to Japan. A clear difference was observed for male blue-collar workers between Japan and the EC countries: their wages remain more or less unchanged after the age of 25 in France,

[5] Also see Hashimoto and Raisian (1985).

Germany, Italy, and the UK, whereas in Japan they increase until the 50–4 age bracket in big companies and until 40–4 in small companies. For white-collar workers, however, an upward slope was found not only in Japan but also in Belgium, France, Germany, the Netherlands, and the UK. The difference between these countries is small, except that wages drop sharply in Japan after the age of 55, apparently due to the mandatory retirement system. Similarly, in the USA, an upward slope was found for white-collar workers. Thus in any of the developed countries, wages tend to increase with age for white-collar workers. As for blue-collar workers, Koike found a weak upward slope in the USA. It is clearly less steep than that for American white-collar workers or Japanese white-collar and blue-collar workers, but is nevertheless upward-sloping as opposed to the flat profile among European blue-collars.

These facts suggest that the extent of lifetime employment and seniority wages is probably more pronounced in Japan, but they are also present in European countries and the USA for white-collar workers. The difference is more conspicuous for blue-collar workers: Japanese blue-collar workers, like their white-collar colleagues, are employed on the basis of long-term employment and seniority wages, whereas this tendency is weaker or non-existent among American and European blue-collar workers. According to Koike, therefore, it is the 'white-collarization' of blue-collar workers that characterizes the Japanese internal labour system.

As for the third 'pillar', the enterprise union system, it is certainly common in Japan. This system is usually contrasted with that, prevalent in the UK, in which workers in a company belong to a variety of unions, each specialized to a particular occupation or a particular skill (Dore 1973). However, forms of organization which include all the non-managerial workers in a firm or an establishment do exist in other countries too. An example is local unions in the USA, which usually cover all the shop-floor workers in a plant regardless of occupation. Koike (1988) estimates that about 80 per cent of union members in manufacturing industries belong to such local unions, with probably a higher proportion in the heavy and chemical industries. Another example is the works councils in West Germany which are strictly-speaking distinct from unions and yet play similar roles as regards many matters. These works councils are legally required as a part of the country's co-determination policy, and are organized to include all the non-managerial workers in each establishment. Even in the UK, the recent movement toward single representation is unmistakable.[6]

Again, therefore, the difference is by no means absolute: unions or similar organizations of workers structured on the basis not of occupation but of company or establishment are found not only in Japan but also in many other countries, and appear to be increasing. What is characteristic of Japan, apart from such unions being regarded as a norm, is the amount of consultation between the management and the union; that is, the 'abundant flow of information [between unions and management in Japan] seems to be unmatched elsewhere' (Koike 1988, 257) and 'joint consultation channels are widespread throughout enterprises where there are labour unions' (ibid. 252). No wonder that the union leaders and the management tend to share mutual interests and motivation, rather than regarding each other as antagonists. Dore (1973, 200), after comparing industrial relations in a Japanese company (Hitachi) and a British company (English Electric), concluded that 'the major difference is that Hitachi union leaders share the managers' concern with the growth and prosperity of Hitachi as a corporation in competition with other corporations. Full-time British union officials may share with officials of the Employers Federation a concern with the future of "the industry" in the abstract but they have no special concern with the prosperity of particular concrete firms with it. (Shop stewards are in fact likely to have such a concern, but the union ethos as set by the full-time officials, operates to discourage it.)'[7]

To conclude, the 'three pillars' of the Japanese internal labour system are neither inflexible nor unique. They are found in many other countries to a varying extent. Yet, it is also true that they are more pronounced and more highly regarded in Japan, and this difference may have important consequences. To some of them we will now turn in more detail.

[6] This, apparently, has been influenced by the practice of many Japanese companies investing in the UK. We will return to this topic in Sec. 12.2.

[7] Despite the above discussion, the number of days lost in industrial disputes in Japan is not the lowest. It is lower than in the USA and the UK, but higher than in Germany. See Koike (1988, chap. 7).

3.3. EMPLOYMENT ADJUSTMENT

During a period of recession, in Japan as elsewhere, every firm will find the work-force to be in excess of what is really needed. Labour costs will have to be cut for the firm to survive against market competition. Thus, so long as business fluctuation remains a possibility, lifetime employment is not strictly sustainable anywhere. If the firm adheres too much to the ideal, bankruptcy is unavoidable, thereby causing job losses anyway. The important question, therefore, is how the burden of labour adjustment is to be shared among workers and, more generally, how the adverse effect of a contraction of demand is to be shared among company members from shareholders to workers (and possibly including customers and suppliers, as will be discussed in Chapter 6). An examination of the mechanism of employment adjustment, therefore, must take a central place in any discussion of the internal labour system.

There are several ways to adjust labour input without making 'permanent' (or 'regular') employees redundant. First, many Japanese firms employ part-time, seasonal, or temporary workers. They are usually unskilled and used primarily as a buffer to protect permanent employees from business fluctuation. That is, the firm will hire these workers during a boom to deal with a temporary labour shortage and, in recession, either lay them off or neglect to renew their work contracts. According to one set of statistics, 9 per cent of all the workers in 1986 were 'part-time' workers as defined by employers and, according to another, 13 per cent were 'part-time' or other 'non-regular' workers.[8] The percentage was higher in smaller firms and among female workers. Although I infer that these statistics only partly cover the non-permanent workers and underestimate their importance, they agree with the finding for Hitachi by Dore (1973, 33) that 'temporary' workers constituted about 9 per cent of the company's entire work-force. We also note that temporary workers in some firms are promoted to permanent status after having proved to be satisfactory: that is, firms may use the temporary contract as a probationary period. Usually this is the case only for mid-career recruits, as new graduates tend to be hired on a permanent basis.

[8] The first set of statistics is from the Ministry of Labour, *Koyo Doko Chosa*, and the second from the Management and Co-ordination Agency, *Rodoryoku Chosa Tokubetsu Chosa*.

Thus, although temporary workers are differentiated from permanent workers in many respects, such as compensation, recruitment, training, and job security, there are often links between the two categories.

The second method of employment adjustment is a reduction in new recruits from universities and high schools. Although this measure may appear the least damaging for the firm as well as for the workers, its long-term effect is more complicated. Suppose that the firm decides not to hire any new university graduates this year. This decision implies that the workers hired in the previous year will have no one to supervise and train, and, ten years hence, the firm will lack university-educated workers aged 32. This discontinuity can cause disruption to promotion and training schemes. To avoid this happening, the firm will wish to maintain a smooth age composition of the work-force, so that even if new recruits are not warranted from a short-run viewpoint, some may still be taken on, albeit a smaller number than in a normal year.

Thirdly, the firm will reduce working hours, by cutting overtime or encouraging workers to take holidays. In those work-places (usually for white-collar workers) where workers set their own working hours, the firm may determine the maximum number of hours for paid overtime.

Fourthly, the firm may meet changing demand by transferring workers from one department to another. Needless to say, if the best use is to be made of workers' skills, they will be moved to technically related areas. However, when the slump is severe and expected to last a long time, it may be necessary to transfer them further afield, for instance, from the production department to sales. Furthermore, the firm may even send some workers to other firms to be employed there temporarily. Affiliated firms, such as subcontractors and dealers, are natural candidates to act as short-term employers, but there have been cases of sending workers to basically unrelated firms in the local area, which, unlike the original company, need temporary workers to meet brisk demand. Wages will basically be paid by the temporary employer, but subsidized by the sending firm, which also provides fringe benefits such as insurance. The precise arrangement may vary but is almost always agreed by the union.[9]

[9] For case-studies, see Pascale and Rohlen (1983) who found that many workers at Mazda, an automobile assembler, were transferred from the plant to the dealers, and Muramatsu's (1983, chap. 3) study of a machinery manufacturer.

The two factors indispensable for any smooth temporary transfer are flexibility in work organization and a breadth of skills in each worker. As we will see in the next section, the use of rotation to enable workers to acquire a range of skills is a vital part of training schemes in Japan.

Following these measures it may be necessary to resort to lay-offs, which can be divided into two kinds. What is called a temporary lay-off (or a temporary rest from work, literally translated) in Japan means that the redundant worker retains the status of an employee, receives a reduced proportion, say, 80 per cent, of his basic wages, but does not come to work. Such a worker, therefore, is still bound by an employment contract, in contrast to the lay-off system in the USA where those workers who have been laid off and expect, without any guarantee, to be rehired in a short while are legally unemployed and treated as such in unemployment statistics. Under the US system these workers will receive unemployment benefits from the government. In the Japanese system, they receive wages, albeit less than usual, from the employer, though under certain conditions the employer can claim subsidies from the government to finance a part of their wages. The difference between Japan and the USA is in many ways superficial, therefore. Yet, the very fact that the temporary lay-off system is designed so as to maintain the employment relationship seems to testify to the strong feeling of workers and firms in favour of lifetime employment.

Finally, when the firm has no choice but to reduce the work-force on a permanent basis, it will start discharging workers. I will use the word 'discharge' in this chapter to mean (indefinite) job termination by employers (without implying disciplinary causes), that is, in the (British) sense of redundancy. In the USA, the word 'lay-off' is also used to indicate such job termination, but here it will be used only to indicate the kind of temporary separation outlined in the previous paragraph. The distinction is meaningful because, while in the USA many employer–union agreements stipulate that, when new recruits are again being sought, those workers previously discharged should take precedence, no such requirement or practice exists in Japan.

Discharges are naturally of the greatest concern to labour unions. During the 1950s, when discharges were more frequent, fierce industrial disputes were not unusual. Workers, in fear of being nominated for discharge, tended to participate actively in industrial action against employers. Such fierce and often long-lasting disputes damaged firms not only by stopping production but also by bringing about a deterioration in worker–company trust which lowered productivity. With this lesson behind them, many firms, when confronted with the recession and the rapid change in industrial structure following the oil crisis of the early 1970s, opted to use a softer approach by encouraging voluntary redundancies with an offer of favourable retirement benefits. Although consultation with the union was still generally needed to determine how many workers should be targeted in the voluntary redundancy scheme and how much premium should be paid in addition to the usual retirement benefits, negotiations became much less hostile because the final decision was left with each worker. The prevalence of this scheme explains why the number of labour disputes increased only modestly during the depression following the oil crisis.

However much this scheme may have contributed to maintaining good worker–company relations, the costs should not be overlooked. Those who volunteered to leave under the scheme tended to belong to one of two categories of worker. The first category included those workers confident of being able to obtain new jobs elsewhere. Apparently, these tended to be the workers with higher-than-average abilities or with special (but not firm-specific) skills, the kind of people the firm would prefer to retain. The second category consisted of older workers who decided to take advantage of the favourable retirement benefits. Although their leaving may be welcomed by the firm because of the higher wages paid to older workers under the seniority wage system,[10] a socially undesirable effect may result, because the additional premium is not usually enough to support early retirement. These workers, therefore, have usually sought other jobs, which turn out to be very difficult to find. Thus the scheme has tended to raise the unemployment ratio among older workers (Koike 1988, chap. 2). With the rapid 'ageing' of the Japanese population now in progress, such unemployment may create a grave social problem.[11]

[10] Indeed the management tended to encourage (or sometimes even actively page) these workers to leave under the scheme.

[11] The fact that older workers are usually the first to suffer from labour

Discharges, whether or not under the guise of the voluntary redundancy scheme, are by no means rare, despite the belief in a supposed lifetime employment system. A study of machine-tool manufacturers by Muramatsu (1985) and a study of cement producers by Koike (1988, chap. 4) both suggest that discharges usually take place after two to three years of loss-making in the company. Thus, 'lifetime' employment is clearly nowhere guaranteed.

Empirically, the sensitivity of employment to business fluctuation may be internationally compared by means of the output elasticity of employment, namely, the percentage of employment change in response to a 1 per cent change in output. Table 3.1 gives the elasticities estimated with the 1960–82 yearly data for each of five countries. Because the change in labour demand should depend on the change in target output less the change in labour productivity, the elasticity needs to be estimated as that of employment with respect to output per labour productivity. Two alternative assumptions were made: (1) labour productivity increases at a constant rate every year, and (2) the real wage rate increases at exactly the same rate at which productivity increases. The use of real GDP as the output measure is based on (1), because the constant rate of productivity change only affects the constant term in a regression of employment growth on output growth, whereas the use of GDP in wage units (GDP/W) is based on (2).[12]

Before looking at the results, a remark is in order. The use of macro-data in the estimation implies that the results reflect not only the behaviour of individual firms but also inter-firm employment shifts and a macro-equilibrium determination of aggregate demand. We will discuss the macro-equilibrium when individual firms hoard labour, namely, retain excess labour, in Chapter 9.

adjustment sharply differs from the practice prevalent in the US unionized sectors, where workers are laid off according to order of juniority and rehired according to order of seniority. See Abraham and Medoff (1984).

[12] The correlation coefficient between the labour productivity increase and the real wage increase was higher than 0.95 in every country. Note that the usual method of measuring labour productivity by output per employment cannot be used here because output divided by this productivity measure is nothing but employment itself. Alternatively to (1), a time trend may be added to the regression equations. The results were similar to those in Table 3.1 but with poorer Durbin–Watson statistics.

TABLE 3.1. Output elasticity of employment in five countries

Employment measure	Output measure	USA	Japan	FRG	France	UK
Man	Real GDP	0.401	0.090	0.377	0.294	0.272
(M)		(0.086)	(0.034)	(0.078)	(0.054)	(0.115)
	GDP/W	0.528	0.096	0.360	0.166	0.015
		(0.140)	(0.033)	(0.135)	(0.057)	(0.102)
Manhour	Real GDP	0.797	0.160	0.850	0.561	0.622
(M × H)		(0.087)	(0.110)	(0.131)	(0.110)	(0.133)
	GDP/W	1.059	0.205	1.065	0.339	0.275
		(0.171)	(0.106)	(0.208)	(0.110)	(0.139)

Note: The annual growth rates of output were regressed on the annual growth rates of employment using ordinary least squares with the 1961–82 yearly data. The estimated slope coefficients are shown with the standard errors in parentheses. None of the Durbin–Watson statistics was below the lower limit for the 5% significance level, suggesting a lack of autocorrelation. The variables, with data sources in parentheses, are as follows:

GDP Gross domestic product at current prices (OECD, *National Accounts*).
Real GDP Gross domestic product at the 1980 price levels (*National Accounts*).
W Wages in non-agricultural activities (ILO, *Year Book of Labour Statistics*).
M Civilian employment: all activities (OECD, *Labour Force Statistics*).
H Hours of work in non-agricultural sectors (*Year Book of Labour Statistics*).

Suffice it to say here that the international ranking in estimated elasticity would be unlikely to be affected were the data of individual firms used instead of the macro-data.

There are several important findings. First, all the elasticities except two are significantly less than one, suggesting that employment fluctuates only to a smaller extent than (productivity-adjusted) output. Second, as regards international comparison, the elasticities tend to be largest in the USA or Germany and smallest in Japan. Third, between the employment level in terms of the number of men (M) and that of manhours (MH), the elasticities are larger with MH in every country, suggesting a faster adjustment of hours over the number of men; yet, the international ranking stays the same, except for a slight reversal between the USA and Germany. And fourth, the choice of real GDP versus GDP/W matters little; nevertheless, in view of the rather peculiarly low elasticities estimated for the UK when GDP/W is used and of the untypically large elasticities estimated for the USA and Germany when GDP/W and MH are used, (1) appears to be a more acceptable assumption than (2).

That the elasticity is lowest in Japan and highest in the USA agrees with several other studies: see Abraham and Houseman (1989) and the literature cited therein. They showed not only that the elasticity is higher in the USA in terms of either employment or manhours, but also that, though the elasticity is higher for production workers than for non-production workers in both countries, Japanese production workers enjoy higher employment stability than their American counterparts. Here is further evidence of Koike's 'white-collarization of blue-collar workers' in Japan. Our international comparison also agrees with Ono (1981) and Shinotsuka (1989), who found that the elasticities in the European countries are not far from that in Japan but clearly smaller compared to that in the USA, and with Gordon (1982) who found a stable employment pattern in Japan and the UK in contrast to a volatile employment pattern in the USA. The frequent use of temporary lay-offs and resulting employment instability in the USA seems to be exceptional. See also the classic international comparison (excluding Japan) made by Brechling and O'Brien (1967), who regressed employment on lagged employment and time trend as well as on output in a log-linear equation. Inclusion of the lagged employment variable is expected to bring little change in the international ranking, in view of the finding by Miller (1971) that inter-industry ranking of the elasticity is essentially the same with or without the lagged variable (see also Greer and Rhoades 1977). The study of Brechling and O'Brien is for the period 1952–64 while ours is for 1960–82. Despite the many changes that took place during these years, the elasticity ranking among the four countries (excluding Japan) is basically the same in both the two studies.

Let us summarize this section. Japanese companies do adjust employment levels by several means, such as (1) making temporary workers redundant or not renewing contracts with them, (2) reducing the number of new recruits, (3) reducing overtime (4) transferring workers to other shops, other departments, or, temporarily, even to other companies, (5) temporarily laying off workers, and (6) discharges, which are usually attained by soliciting voluntary redundancies. The Labour Ministry's *Rodo Keizai Doko Chosa* (*Labour Market Survey*) shows the proportion of establishments taking these measures. In the last quarter of 1986, 40 per cent of the establishments in the sample, the highest figure for the period 1981–7, replied that they had taken one or more measures to adjust employment. The percentage of establishments adopting each of the measures listed above was as follows: (1) 6 per cent; (2) (confined to 'mid-career' recruitment) 12 per cent; (3) 26 per cent; (4) 20 per cent; (5) 3 per cent; and (6) 3 per cent, where the sum exceeds 40 owing to duplication. Apparently, reduction of overtime and transfers are the most popular means of adjustment, whereas discharges, even in the form of temporary lay-offs, are infrequent. In this regard, the notion of 'lifetime' employment appears to be justified.

The comparison of employment elasticity across countries also suggests that employment in Japan is least sensitive to business fluctuations. However, since the elasticity is rather small in European countries too, the difference between Japan and other countries is again not absolute, but one of degree.

It is possible to claim that the Japanese company is motivated to minimize lay-offs and discharges even when short-term profit maximization calls for them. Such 'lay-off minimization' behaviour is constrained, however, by the firm's need to survive; in particular, during periods of continuous loss the firm has no choice but to discharge workers. We will argue in Chapter 9 that this (constrained) lay-off minimization behaviour, that is, labour-hoarding, has a stabilizing effect on macroeconomic fluctuation.

Whether such behaviour is consistent with the maximization of long-term profits or the value of the firm is a delicate question, for, even though it works against profitability in the short run, this need not be so in the long run, for several reasons. First, frequent labour adjustment may impair dynamic efficiency through the loss of firm-specific skills possessed by the employees, the costs of discharging and rehiring workers, and the adverse effects on worker morale (Oi 1962; Okun 1981). Second, frequent discharges may impair the reputation of the firm as a good employer, causing the quality of job applicants to decline or requiring the firm to offer a higher starting salary. Third, given workers' risk aversion and in the absence of a full unemployment compensation scheme, it is possible to achieve a contract mutually beneficial to employer and employees, in which the employer promises to retain excess workers in periods of recession (Rosen 1985).

An equally attractive hypothesis is that the Japanese firm deliberately minimizes lay-offs and discharges even to an extent that is unjustifiable in terms of the shareholders' interests. Particularly under the weak capital market discipline described in the previous chapter, it appears very likely that the manager, feeling more sympathy for the employees than for the shareholders, will pursue such a course.

3.4. SKILL FORMATION: TRAINING AND ROTATION

Human resources, as we stressed in the introductory chapter, are the key to understanding the nature of a modern corporation, and the acquisition, enrichment, and maintenance of such resources is indispensable to corporate success. Human resources are not simply the collection of workers (including management staff) in a physical sense. More importantly, they have to embody the knowledge, skill, and experience needed to carry out the work and even to come up with ideas to improve the way the work is carried out. This knowledge, skill, and experience, to be simply called 'skills' in the following, are diverse. Some, like the mechanism of a machine, can be written on paper and learned in a classroom. Others, like the operation of a machine, can only be learned by actually handling the machine, although advice from someone already skilled in its operation is tremendously helpful. Yet others, such as acquaintance with someone who can help you or knowledge of how to deal with abnormal situations, can only be acquired through many years of experience, though, again, the help of somebody who already has such acquaintance and knowledge greatly shortens the time needed to acquire it.

Accordingly, the way a worker acquires skills or, to put it differently, the way the firm trains the workers, can be diverse. Apart from formal education at schools, which we will not discuss here,[13] there is an important distinction between off-the-job training (Off-JT) and on-the-job training (OJT). Off-JT is basically a series of lectures. As the Japanese word, *zagaku*, implies, it is to sit (*za*) and learn (*gaku*). This is an efficient way to teach the kind of skills given in the first example above, because one teacher can instruct a number of workers at the same time. On the other hand, it can never effectively teach the kind of skills cited in the other examples. These are acquired only while the worker is actually handling the machine or confronting an actual situation. For these skills OJT is a far more effective training method.

Hence, firms commonly use a combination of Off-JT and OJT. In offering a rich and varied programme of both forms of training, Japanese firms appear better equipped than most firms in other countries, though some foreign firms, such as IBM, are also known for their well-structured training programmes. It also appears that the Japanese internal labour market system has been conducive to OJT. To justify these arguments, we will first present a general account of the training system in large Japanese firms.

When a permanent (that is, a non-temporary) worker newly recruited from school starts working in April (the academic year ends in March) in a large firm, he is invariably given an induction training course. The purpose of this course is twofold. The first task is to familiarize him with the firm and give him a feeling of, say, belonging and identification. Thus he may learn the history of the firm from the president, the market situation from the sales manager, the organization and personnel policy from the personnel manager, the production system from the production manager, and so forth. The second task is more technological. Although technological training in the induction course is basically

[13] For English readers, Dore and Sako (1989) give a convenient account of the Japanese education system.

confined to general matters, such as the basic technology of the firm's products or an introduction to computers, the participants may be separated into groups on the basis of the jobs they are to be assigned, and given more specialized training, such as the use of a particular machine.

The length of this induction Off-JT course varies from one company to another. Also, the course tends to be shorter for middle or high school graduates than for university graduates. Thus, typically, for high school graduates, it will last from a couple of weeks to a couple of months, and for university graduates, from one to four months. Often, these classroom courses are followed by a series of, say, mini OJT, in which a participant is moved from one shop or department to another after short intervals. Again, the length of this training varies between companies. For instance, it may consist of one week in each of four shops in a particular plant. For university graduates, a more extensive and lengthier course may be provided, for instance, staying in several departments for several months each. Through this series of short assignments, the worker is expected to learn about the functions and activities of various departments within a company, as well as to acquire a certain number of skills related to each department. In view of the time generally required fully to acquire technical skills, it is perhaps reasonable to suppose that the main purpose is not to give technical knowledge *per se* but to give the new worker a familiarity with the entire activity of the firm, so that he gains a company-wide perspective.

Many firms also have a series of mid-career Off-JT. Again this varies a great deal from one company to another. In some cases, workers are given training of this kind at fixed intervals, say every three to five years. In others, those assigned to new positions and those who have been promoted attend courses related to their different jobs or to managerial skills. Each course may be just for a few days or last for some months. Sometimes, training may be given outside the firm, as is most common when a worker has to pass a qualification examination (administered by the government or by a private association) in order to get a licence for a particular job, for instance, boiler maintenance or a certain kind of welding. The worker may be then ordered to attend courses at training institutions to prepare for the examination.[14] In

[14] See Dore and Sako (1989) for the details concerning such qualifications.

other cases, a candidate for a managerial post may be assigned to attend a short executive course in a private school. Some large companies even send young but promising university-educated workers on two-year MBA courses in foreign or domestic business schools. Such training programmes do exist in a number of foreign companies, but the important difference seems to be that in Japan training is more organized and covers most of the (permanent) workers, blue-collar or white-collar, though, without doubt, it is usually biased in favour of white-collar workers.

The reason that blue-collar workers receive less Off-JT is presumably that most of the skills they need are better suited to OJT. While managerial skills may be learned through books, how to operate and maintain a machine and how to deal with any abnormality in the production process is better learned on the job. In fact, even for managerial skills, the emphasis on Off-JT, such as business-school education, has resulted in a bias towards the financial aspect of management, which is most easily defined and quantified and can therefore be taught in universal terms, at the expense of detailed information about manufacturing and technology which are more firm-specific. The strength of Japanese management, perhaps ironically, may be attributed to a neglect of off-the-job management education in favour of on-the-job accumulation of managerial experience.[15]

The importance of OJT, particularly for blue-collar workers, has become increasingly recognized not only in Japan but also in other countries. Doeringer and Piore's (1972) study for the USA is well known. More relevant to our purpose, Koike (1977), part of whose work is reproduced in Koike (1988), compared the practice of OJT in Japan and the USA based on detailed interviews and field observations. The following discussion heavily relies on this work. The same author also led a group of researchers in making a comparison between Japan, Thailand, and Malaysia (Koike and Inoki 1987), and concluded that OJT is the main means of skill formation not only in Japan but also in the south-east Asian countries. Further evidence on the prevalence of OJT in many countries has been provided by Shiba (1973) in his pioneering

[15] When Morita (1986, 154), the chairman of Sony, said 'management, despite the work of the Harvard Business School and others, and the increasing number of holders of advanced degrees in business administration, is an elusive thing that cannot always be judged by next quarter's bottom line', I presume he meant the same thing. See also Rosenbloom and Abernathy (1982).

study of electric power plants in eight countries. For European countries, the comparison between France and Germany by Maurice and Sellier (1979) and that between Britain and Germany by Sorge and Warner (1980) reveal interesting international differences.

These studies all suggest two important facts about the nature of skills; first, that most skills can be learned only by doing, and second, that at least some of them are specific to the firm or to the plant. In other words, the worker will lose some of the skills he has acquired if he moves to another firm, and the firm will not be able to replace him with a new recruit without some decrease in productivity. It is this that provides the basic incentive for both workers and firms to maintain lifetime employment and to use an internal mechanism, as opposed to external markets, to allocate human resources. (See Doeringer and Piore (1972) and Williamson *et al.* (1975). A theoretical analysis has been provided by Hashimoto (1981).) Lifetime employment, in turn, increases firm-specificity of skills, particularly in terms of administrative and social skills rather than technical skills, which makes OJT even more dominant.

How much skill can be acquired through OJT may be considered in two dimensions: depth and breadth. The word 'depth' is used to indicate how much skill is acquired on a certain job, or how easily and how firmly it is acquired, whereas the word 'breadth' indicates the number of jobs in which skills are acquired. For either dimension, I would suggest, the Japanese system has been more successful. Let us start with depth. What mainly determines depth must be the zeal with which a superior teaches his newly-assigned junior worker, because OJT can never be effective without adequate instruction and advice from an experienced superior. The Japanese internal labour system, in my view, increases workers' incentives to teach their junior members. Suppose that the skills of the junior have been improved by such teaching. While this obviously increases the productivity and profitability of the firm, how far is the worker likely to appreciate this effect? Under the prevalence of mobile labour markets, in which a worker's wage is essentially determined by the market, the enhanced profitability of the firm hardly affects the welfare of individual workers. If, on the contrary, lifetime employment is supposed to be the norm, the workers' welfare depends on the future prosperity of the firm; thus, any productivity increase must imply higher job security and faster growth, which in turn facilitates faster promotion. The latter scenario, needless to say, is more likely in Japan than in other countries, and gives senior workers an additional incentive to teach and guide junior members.

On a more micro-level, the improved skill of a junior worker may affect the evaluation of the senior worker. Again, there are two possibilities. On the one hand, if the junior's skill exceeds that of the senior, then management may decide to award a higher wage to the junior or to promote the junior first. If the senior regards this possibility as likely, he, naturally, has no incentive to help the junior. On the other hand, he may be highly valued for his contribution to training, and regarded as better suited for promotion. Again, the latter is more probable in Japan, where a detailed and long-term evaluation of the worker from various points of view is common, as will be discussed in more detail in the next section. Hence, the willingness of Japanese workers to teach and guide their juniors is a natural and perhaps rational response to the incentive scheme under the internal labour system.

Previous studies have tended to emphasize the psychological and sociological aspects, in particular the paternalistic vertical relationship (*oyabun-kobun*), to explain the willingness of senior workers to teach (Abegglen 1958; Rohlen 1974; also, for a more sceptical view, Cole 1971). Although there is an element of truth in such a view, it is quite doubtful that the same worker attitude would have been the result were it not for the economic incentives described here.

Let us now turn to the question of the breadth of skills acquired through OJT. What determines this breadth is how broad the worker's 'career' is, where career is defined as 'the way in which a worker progresses through a related series of jobs' (Koike 1988, 75). Koike's conclusion from a comparison of chemical, steel, and machinery plants in Japan and the USA is quite appropriate here: 'blue-collar workers in large Japanese companies have broader careers than their counterparts in US companies' (ibid. 177). In other words, he found mobility of workers within a workshop and, albeit less frequently, across workshops to be a common practice in Japan. Whereas in the USA job demarcation is clearer and the worker climbs a narrow promotion ladder according to a formula predetermined by union–employer agreement, such demarcation, if it exists at all, is ambiguous in Japan and there is no definite rule determining the career path a worker is expected to follow. 'Mobility in the Japanese machinery industry workshop does not depend on established rules about whom to move, to where and for what period of time' (ibid. 144). Usually, a lower-rank supervisor on the shop-floor, typically the foreman, has discretion on these matters, subject to custom and egalitarian considerations. It is worth noting that the decision is made not by high-ranking management at a distance from the shop-floor, but by the foreman, usually with the implicit or explicit consent of the workers. This fact suggests that the workers in a workshop possess a certain degree of autonomy, no doubt fostering the climate for worker participation at shop-floor level.

Koike is by no means alone in observing a broader mobility and rotation in Japan, and similar observations have been made not only for blue-collar but also for white-collar workers (Koike and Inoki 1987; Kono 1984). Although Koike's study is basically confined to comparing Japan with the USA, we note that the US plants he examines have local unions that cover the entire plant. If multiple representation by job-based unions is common, as in the UK, worker rotation must be even more limited.

As the worker experiences not one but several jobs by means of rotation, with a senior skilled worker helping him in each job, he is expected to gain familiarity and skill in all these jobs, and thus increase the breadth of his skills. This has several profound consequences, most important of which is that work organization becomes more flexible; that is, it becomes easier to rotate workers in response to changing patterns of labour demand. Not only are there more workers equipped with the skills required to carry out the new jobs, but they are psychologically better prepared to be transferred. Conversely, for lifetime employment to be maintained, flexibility of work organization to allow for workers' broad skills must be maintained as far as possible. Flexibility is also imperative in introducing new processes and new products to the shop-floor. For instance, the introduction of new machines may make all the workers in one job category redundant. In such a case, innovation and lifetime employment can both be maintained only by transferring these workers to other jobs. Adaptability of workers to new assignments is indispensable so that efficiency can remain unimpaired during the course of innovation.

There are two more consequences. First, the fact each worker possesses broader skills implies that there will be more candidates qualified for a certain post. The result is intensified competition among workers seeking promotion, as will be discussed in more detail in the next section. Second, broader rotation fosters the formation of a close communication network among workers, familiarity with the function of other sectors in the company, and a sharing of common goals. This tendency must be particularly strong among white-collar workers, who may move from one department to another or from one branch to another, that is, on a broader basis than most blue-collar workers. The consequences of these communicational or motivational aspects of broader skills will be discussed in several ways later in the book.

To conclude, Japanese firms have been generally more enthusiastic and effective in enriching human resources through off-the-job as well as on-the-job training.[16] The skills Japanese workers acquire appear to be deeper and broader, owing partly to the system of lifetime employment (as an ideal, if not necessarily as a reality), partly to the worker evaluation scheme, and partly to the frequency of broad rotation adopted by most Japanese firms. Consequently, flexibility is attained in work organization, innovation is more easily introduced, internal competition is maintained, a sense of participation is created among the workers (as witnessed by their willingness to participate in QC (quality control) and submit ideas for improving productivity), and worker interests tend to be identified with the company's. These human aspects will be repeatedly discussed in this book as the key to understanding the Japanese management system and its economic consequences.

3.5. INTERNAL COMPETITION FOR PROMOTION

According to popular myth, the diligence of Japanese workers can be ascribed to non-economic factors, in particular, the so-called paternalistic management–worker relationship. Abegglen (1958; reprinted 1973, 111), who popularized this notion, writes, 'the Western system emphasizes the impersonal exchange of job services

[16] Hashimoto and Raisian (1989) estimated the magnitudes of OJT in Japan and the USA and confirmed that it is in fact larger in Japan.

for cash reward. Responsibility for living and health standards is an individual problem for each worker. The Japanese employee is part of a very much more personal system, a system in which his total functioning as a person is seen as management's responsibility and in which his group membership transcends his individual privileges and responsibilities.' From this argument came the conclusion that 'motivation for work output rests in large part on loyalty and group identification' (ibid. 115). Such a view appears to have gained considerable popularity among Westerners.

The reality, however, is that Japanese workers are under constant pressure to achieve a better performance in the race against their colleagues to be selected for promotion.[17] Indeed, how else can a worker maintain motivation? How else can an organization maintain discipline?

In organizations everywhere, promotion plays the dual role of selecting the right person for each post and of rewarding the able and diligent worker. The latter role, apparently, provides an incentive for workers to acquire skills and to work hard. This scheme has been likened to a tournament by two studies, Lazear and Rosen (1981) and Rosenbaum (1984). Lazear and Rosen offer a theoretical model in which two players (workers) compete for promotion. Each player invests in skill acquisition to increase his productivity, which also depends on a random factor. The player with higher productivity is selected for promotion and earns a higher wage. The firm sets the winner's wage and the loser's wage in order to maximize profit, which, in equilibrium, is zero under the assumption of perfectly competitive (or contestable) output markets. They proved that, in equilibrium, the players (with identical utility functions) make exactly the same level of investment, which is as efficient as in the piece-rate scheme in which each worker earns his marginal product. The results thus imply that a tournament—competition by selection—is as efficient as the neoclassical competitive equilibrium in mobile labour markets.[18]

The importance of tournaments in the career of American

[17] Questionnaire studies on work satisfaction among employees do not suggest that Japanese workers are happier than their Western counterparts, in contradiction to the loyalty hypothesis. See Trevor (1983).

[18] For a criticism of the model, see Dye (1984). For extensions of the model, see Green and Stokey (1983) and Rosen (1986).

white-collar workers has been discussed by Rosenbaum, who argued that

> selections among the members of a cohort occur continually as their careers unfold, that employees' careers differ in their timetables for advancement and in their rates of advancement (trajectories), and that these timetables and trajectories will be related to employees' ultimate career attainment. Moreover, just as sports tournaments are used to identify the most able contestants, career tournaments may be used to create social signals of ability, which explain restrictions on opportunity and which legitimate investments in the winners of each stage (Rosenbaum 1984, 27).

It is indeed this aspect of the tournament that makes it a powerful incentive mechanism. With promotion, the worker gets not only a higher wage but also social recognition of his ability and efforts, and this social recognition gives him prestige and satisfaction. In fact, Japanese firms are known for internationally smaller wage differentials across ranks, while Japanese society is known for status-consciousness, perhaps owing to its racial homogeneity. Being in a well-known big company and being in a respectable position greatly enhance one's social standing, for instance, making it easier to find a spouse. Therefore, the non-pecuniary rewards of promotion are as important as, if not more than, pecuniary rewards, which provides a strong incentive for workers to strive for promotion.[19]

Many Japanese companies have developed elaborate criteria for promotion. Basically, they consist of seniority and merit, the latter being used here to include ability, achievement, qualification, effort, and so forth. The relative importance of these two factors varies from country to country, from company to company, and between white-collar and blue-collar workers. Apart from the public sector, those work-places in which seniority is most decisive in promotion appear to be some of the plants in the USA (Koike 1988). This observation contradicts the usual argument that the Japanese internal labour system is characterized by promotion according to seniority. It is true that seniority plays an important role in promotion in Japan, and may even be a necessary condition (no section head under 30, for example), but it is not the only factor, whereas the shop-floor in some US

[19] For a similar view, see Rohlen (1974) and Turcq (1985).

plants seniority is virtually the only criterion for promotion. Thus in the Japanese system, although it is hardly conceivable that a 30-year-old will be promoted before a 40-year-old, however clever he may be, it is common for one person to be promoted a few years earlier than the others in the same peer-group. Even just a few years' difference will greatly enhance the social standing of the promoted worker among his peers, for the reason stated above. Equally important in the Japanese system, is the fact that those not selected in the first round still have a chance to be selected in the second round; hence, one need not despair and give up making an effort.

In Japan or in the USA, the relative importance of seniority tends to be smaller for white-collar workers in comparison to blue-collar workers. Yet, for blue-collar workers alone, seniority is less important in Japan than in the USA, while for white-collar workers, it matters more in Japan. Here is further support for Koike's (1988) 'white-collarization of blue-collar workers' in Japan.

How much effort in terms of work and skill acquisition the promotion tournament is likely to encourage depends not only on the importance of merit relative to seniority, but also on how detailed, fair, and long-lasting the evaluation of merit may be. In this regard, the Japanese system, in our opinion, is more effective than that in other countries, because of the lifetime employment, internal promotion, and broader rotation mentioned in previous sections. In most companies, evaluation (called *satei*) of each worker is carried out by his supervisor on many counts. Note that workers' achievements can be a misleading measure of their abilities and effort if they are assigned to different tasks. Take, for example, sales workers. One worker may be assigned to a set of customers who have been more or less loyal to the company products, whereas another may be assigned to those customers who have previously bought rival products. Obviously, with other things being equal, the first will attain a higher sales volume, but evaluating him as capable on these grounds is clearly unfair and potentially discouraging to the second worker. Clearly the supervisor needs some knowledge of both markets so that he can evaluate achievement relative to the difficulty of the task assigned to each worker. The prevalence of internal promotion in Japanese firms means that supervisors do actually have sufficient knowledge and experience of the difficulty of the task assigned to all their subordinates. The fairness and accuracy of evaluation is expected to be reasonably high.

Achievement on the job is not the only thing to be judged. A worker will also be evaluated according to how much he has contributed to helping his subordinates and juniors in acquiring skills, how many ideas for improvement he has contributed and how good they were, how many skills and qualifications he has himself acquired through company-sponsored Off-JT or individual study, and how much potential he has in administrative posts. Very often, the supervisor asks for the opinion of the senior among his subordinates to make the evaluation as fair and accurate as possible. In some companies, internal examinations are held to measure the extent of skill level, or the suitability for certain posts. The results of these examinations, of course, form a part of the evaluation.

The prevalence of lifetime employment and broad internal rotation guarantees that the evaluation is made in the long term, and by numerous supervisors. A large organization with stable employment relations will be able to harness more information in this respect.[20] Even if a worker fails in his assignment in a particular year, he will be retained within the firm and will be given further chances to prove himself dedicated and able. In other words, return matches are available in this form of tournament.

Broad and frequent rotation implies that the worker is evaluated by several supervisors. Such diversification in evaluation must help to reduce the risk of a worker being given an extreme or unfair evaluation. It is more likely that his merits and demerits will be considered from diverse viewpoints, fostering fairness and reducing nepotism. It is also important to note that, by having a worker evaluated by several supervisors, the senior manager can compare the ability of supervisors to evaluate their subordinates. It is a tough world not only for subordinates but also for supervisors!

Fair and detailed evaluation over the long term makes the promotion tournament all the more competitive as the pool for

[20] 'Within a single organization, information about an employee's career history is more available, more interpretable, and more trustworthy than is such information when it is transferred across employing institutions' (Rosenbaum 1984, 28).

candidates is larger. When promotion can occur only within a narrow job hierarchy, candidates are few and, particularly if the abilities of the workers are apparently different, the less able will lose any hope of promotion and opt for the easy life without hard work. If, on the contrary, there is little job demarcation, workers have broad skills, and they are more or less homogeneous, then every worker will aspire to be promoted and internal competition will effectively lead to high worker motivation. In other words, as discussed in Chapter 1, competition with promotion prospects related to relative merits and over the long term can be expected to provide an effective incentive mechanism under such conditions and, I believe, is much more relevant in Japanese firms than elsewhere.

This discussion also suggests that the promotion tournament will be more likely to increase motivation when opportunities for promotion are constantly created and visible to the workers. This is one important reason why the firm might pursue expansion of organization, that is, corporate growth. Such bias towards growth is primarily the consequence of the human aspects of the firm. We will return to this topic in the next chapter.

To conclude, internal competition by means of the promotion tournament is intense in the Japanese firm. Seniority is one criterion for promotion but by no means the only one. Another equally important criterion, if not more so, is the evaluation of workers according to their abilities, achievements, and effort, and we have suggested that the Japanese internal labour system has been successful in achieving accurate and fair evaluation in the long term. This fact, together with the wide availability of candidates created through the rotation scheme, makes competition even more intense and contributes to maintaining high worker motivation. The diligence of Japanese workers is by no means cultural and psychological only. More importantly, there is a systematic economic mechanism.[21]

3.6. CONCLUSION

Human resources, more than financial and physical resources, are the key to understanding Japanese management—how Japanese

[21] The intensity of internal competition in Japanese firms has been recognized by only a few, including Turcq (1985) and Koike (1988).

firms behave, how they are organized, and their effect on the various industries and the economy. In this chapter we began our discussion with a critical view of the so-called 'three pillars' of the Japanese internal labour system, and went on to examine three major issues: employment adjustment, skill formation, and internal competition. As regards employment adjustment, we emphasized that lifetime employment exists as an idealized norm to which management is expected to aspire though not necessarily as a reality. In order to maintain employment under adverse demand conditions and changing inter-industrial patterns of demand it is essential that there be flexibility in human management. This flexibility is attained in Japanese companies by using temporary workers, by adjusting amounts of overtime, and, probably most important of all, by transferring workers to other jobs, other workshops, other departments, and even other companies. Such flexibility cannot be attained unless workers possess broad skills. In the area of skill formation, therefore, Japanese firms seek to ensure that their workers acquire both breadth and depth in their skills. The system of lifetime employment and internal promotion with a detailed and long-term evaluation scheme for workers, we argued, is conducive to efficient skill formation. Such evaluation as well as the broad skills possessed by workers contribute in turn to intense competition for promotion. There are clear economic incentives for workers to work hard, to make efforts to acquire skills, to help junior members acquire skills, and to feel a sense of participation in the affairs of the entire company.

The effects of this internal labour system on the motivation, behaviour, and organization of Japanese firms will be discussed in the following chapters. With regard to responses to business fluctuation, the above discussion suggests that the management will seek to minimize the number of lay-offs and discharges unless its survival is threatened. The impact of this behaviour on macroeconomic stability will be discussed in Chapter 9. With regard to its dynamic long-term consequences, we have emphasized that employees' concern for the long-term survival and growth of the firm is intensified under the system, because external job opportunities offering equal or better conditions are limited and growth creates opportunities for promotion. Managers, themselves having been promoted from within the firms, are sympathetic to this concern and pursue growth maximization (with constraints). The next chapter will discuss this behaviour more formally.

4

Dynamic Strategies

4.1. GROWTH PREFERENCE

We have suggested that the Japanese firm pursues faster growth than is warranted from the shareholders' standpoint. The senior manager of a typical Japanese firm has worked with the company for thirty to forty years, experienced several departments and jobs, climbed the promotion ladder, and has finally been chosen for the post by the out-going senior manager. Almost all the employees, particularly the senior staff, have been his colleagues for many years, and a close rapport has been established. His contact and communication with these employees happens on a daily basis, whereas contact with the shareholders occurs only a few times a year at most. He is therefore constantly reminded of what worries the employees and what they want. As he himself has been one of them for many years, how can he be distant from them? How can he not be sympathetic to their desires?

For a worker who expects to stay with the same firm until retirement, expected lifetime utility depends primarily on how the firm prospers and grows. His chief concern is that he should not be forced to terminate his employment relationship. To be unemployed, whether because of lay-off or bankruptcy, is a nightmare. It is disastrous not only financially but also psychologically, because in Japan finding a new job with similar pay is difficult in mid-career. Hence, the survival of the company, with a minimal chance of lay-off is the first priority for any employee.

Once survival is secured, the level of a worker's lifetime utility is a function of the probability (or speed) of promotion and the wage structure. The probability of promotion, in turn, is dependent on the rate of expansion of the firm and the span of control, namely, the number of subordinates supervised by any one manager. This relationship can be shown by a simple model. Suppose that there are two ranks only and that every worker works for two periods only. He is recruited at Rank 1 at the beginning of his first period, promoted to Rank 2 at the beginning of the second period with probability π, or otherwise remains at Rank 1, and retires at the end of his second period. His expected lifetime utility, U, is obviously

$$U = u + [\pi\beta u + (1 - \pi)u]/(1 + d), \quad (4.1)$$

where u is the utility level of a Rank 1 worker, βu is the utility level of a Rank 2 worker, and d is the rate of discount. The variables u and βu should depend not only on respective wage levels but also on the non-pecuniary satisfaction associated with each rank. To the extent that this latter factor is important, the utility ratio, β, is larger than the wage ratio.

Let N denote the number of recruits at the beginning of the current period and N_{-1}, the number of recruits in the previous period. Then the number of Rank 2 workers equals πN_{-1}, whereas the number of Rank 1 workers equals $(1 - \pi)N_{-1} + N$. The number of Rank 1 workers that every Rank 2 worker supervises is the span of control, denoted by c. It then follows that

$$(1 - \pi)N_{-1} + N = c\pi N_{-1}. \quad (4.2)$$

Rearranging and letting $N/N_{-1} = 1 + g$, we have

$$\pi = (2 + g)c/(1 + c). \quad (4.3)$$

Therefore, given the span of control for technological reasons, the probability of promotion, π, is a monotonically increasing function of g, the rate of increase in new recruitment.

Provided that the ratio of N_{-1} to N_{-2} (the number of recruits in two periods before now) was also $1 + g$, it is straightforward to show that the total labour-force increases at the rate g as well. It may be called the rate of growth of the firm.

Substituting (4.3) into (4.1), we have

$$U = [2 + d + (\beta - 1)(2 + g)c/(1 + c)]u/(1 + d). \quad (4.4)$$

This equation clearly demonstrates that the worker's lifetime utility depends primarily on the growth rate, g, the utility level at Rank 1, u, and the ratio of utility increase attained by being promoted, β, given c and d. Furthermore, the marginal effect of g on U is increasing with β; that is, the larger the utility increase through promotion, the larger should be the worker's incentive to seek faster expansion of the company.[1]

[1] Using this framework, Odagiri (1982) discussed bargaining between workers and shareholders on g, u, and β.

For the reasons mentioned earlier, management is sympathetic to the workers' desire to attain faster company growth. This is not peculiar to Japanese management. In fact, it was Marris (1964) of the UK and Galbraith (1967) of the USA (though of Canadian origin) who pioneered the growth maximization hypothesis as a behavioural principle of management, giving this promotion-enhancing effect of growth as an important cause. For instance, Marris (1964, 10) argued that 'when a man takes decisions leading to successful expansion, he not only creates new openings but also recommends himself and his colleagues as particularly suitable candidates to fill them.'

One way to compare the strength of growth preference is to compare β, because, as shown above, the marginal utility of growth depends on β. This parameter may be higher or lower in Japan than in the USA or the UK. It is a well-known fact that wages are more equal across ranks in Japan. For instance, a top executive's salary as compared to salaries at the bottom level is usually less than ten times as high in Japan but much more in the USA or the UK, though the presence of non-salary benefits associated with the position, such as company cars and meals, make the comparison difficult. On the other hand, the social satisfaction from being in a higher position seems higher in Japan. This is because, under the system of lifetime employment, promotion is virtually the only way a person can be rewarded for his talent and effort. This fact fosters the tendency of the society to evaluate somebody's worth according to how far and how fast he has been promoted.

To the extent that the non-pecuniary and social gains from promotion are more important than the pecuniary gains, β may be larger in Japan, thereby causing a stronger growth preference among employees. This preference, we have argued, is more likely to affect corporate decisions in Japan for two reasons: because top management is more sympathetic to the employees, and because capital markets have less power to control.

The manager's personal welfare is also enhanced by growth. Numerous empirical studies have shown that executive reward is a function of company size as much as, if not more than, profitability.[2] Furthermore, non-pecuniary gains are no less important:

[2] For American results, see Ciscel and Carroll (1980) and the literature cited therein. Iwasaki (1977) and Doi (1986) provide results for Japan.

leading a growing company or being the chief of a big organization gives satisfaction and social recognition. It is, for instance, pictures of the managers of growing companies that business journals usually use for their covers.

Psychological forces favouring growth have also been noted in Scitovsky's interesting study exploring the relation of psychology with economics. The key concept in understanding human satisfaction, according to him, is *arousal* or a level of brain activity, and 'feelings of comfort and discomfort have to do with the *level* of arousal and depend on whether arousal is or is not at its optimum level, whereas feelings of pleasure are created by *changes* in the arousal level' (Scitovsky 1976, 61, his emphasis). In the present context, managers may feel security and comfort in being with big and profitable companies, but it is more from changes—growth—that they derive pleasure. Very often, indeed, one enjoys climbing a mountain more than being at the summit.

There is another force which drives the firm to pursue growth beyond the value-maximizing level. To identify this force, we should note that decisions are actually made not by a single person, the president or whoever else, but by a group of managerial staff that may extend to the entire corporate organization. Admittedly the president makes the final decision. Yet his decision depends on information collected, selected, and edited by the staff. It is also common, particularly in Japanese firms, for top management to seek agreement, explicitly or implicitly, from the staff in charge of the project in question in order not to damage their morale. The decision is therefore in effect a team effort, however unequal the influence of its members. This fact was stressed by Galbraith, among others, who used the term 'technostructure' to describe this team. The technostructure, he says, 'extends from the most senior officials of the corporation to where it meets, at the outer perimeter, the white- and blue-collar workers whose function is to conform more or less mechanically to instruction or routine' (Galbraith 1967, 84).

Undoubtedly, a bias is present for the members of the technostructure to promote their own interests rather than the interests of shareholders they may never meet. This bias may come from conscious effort as they presume (correctly) that they will be more highly evaluated if they propose (and hopefully complete) more projects or sell more products. Though profitability is not disregarded, it is of secondary importance for average employees.

Another reason for conscious effort arises from the desire of team members to expand—a common tendency found in any organization (particularly among bureaucrats) known as the Parkinsonian Law of self-propagating organization.

There is also an unconscious force leading to the bias. Let us suppose that a certain project has been planned and proposed by a team representing a section or a plant, or by a temporary project team. Since the members of the team have spent a considerable time collecting information and planning the details of the project, they tend to identify themselves with the team and with the success of the project. They will be strongly motivated to favour adoption of the project and, consciously or not, their report to the top management will be biased in favour of it.

We would expect the extent of this bias and its effect on top-level decisions to be greater in Japan than in other countries, because the team members (employees) are more attached to the firm, the management is more concerned with attaining intra-organizational consensus, and shareholder control is weaker. Yet, Marsh *et al.* (1988) showed in a case-study of three strategic investment decisions that this bias is prevalent even in British firms. In particular, they found 'strong evidence of "selling" behaviour, born of a desire to put a strong case for the project' (ibid. 30) and that 'the managers involved had a strong emotional bias towards going ahead with the project' (26). In terms of motivation, they argued that 'the individual players identified strongly with their own business units' performance, and although there was in no case a direct formal link with their salaries, they seemed to view their own prosperity and promotion prospects as closely linked to the business unit' (60).

In other words, a bias towards adopting projects is present in any corporate organization and there are reasons to believe that this bias is stronger and more effective in Japan than in the USA or the UK. The growth maximization hypothesis, that is, the hypothesis that the company tends to pursue growth to a greater extent than the shareholders would prefer, is relevant as a behavioural principle of corporate management today in any country, but especially so in Japan.

The strong growth preference of Japanese companies has been also shown in a questionnaire study conducted on American and Japanese managers (Kagono *et al.* 1985). When the managers were asked to indicate the importance of selected goals on a scale of 0–3, American managers gave the highest points to two shareholder-related goals, 'return on investment' and 'capital gain for stockholders', which significantly outscored the points given to these goals by Japanese managers. By contrast, the two goals to which Japanese managers gave significantly higher points than their American counterparts were 'increase in market share' and 'new product ratio', both of which are clearly closely related to growth.[3]

Of course, the growth maximization hypothesis by no means implies that shareholders' interests are totally disregarded. Even in Japan, where shareholding is dispersed and take-overs are rare, the management will be under pressure if the market value of the firm becomes too low relative to its potential maximum or relative to the level of comparable firms. Such pressure may take the form of warnings from financial institutions, as discussed in Chapter 2, or an increased risk of bankruptcy, which will be of deep concern to the management not only to secure its position but also to secure the jobs of employees.

The growth hypothesis, therefore, should state that management pursues growth, subject to the constraint that a very low market value will endanger its security and independence. In Section 4.2, this hypothesis will be formally stated and analysed. In Section 4.3, the investment behaviour of Japanese firms is compared with that in other countries in order to discuss their growth bias. Section 4.4 turns to a discussion of the mode—direction and means—of growth, to show that the choice of mode is closely related to the internal management system. Section 4.5 examines investment in knowledge capital, that is, research and development, and discusses why Japanese firms have been more successful in making innovations. Finally, Section 4.6 offers some conclusions.

4.2. A MODEL OF CORPORATE GROWTH[4]

Shareholders' interests are summarized in the market value of the firm, denoted by V. This is the total value of the equity and debts of the firm as evaluated in capital markets. The well-known

[3] Neither the market value nor the growth rate is among the goals in the questionnaire.

[4] Details of the model can be found in Odagiri (1981), pt. I.

Modigliani–Miller theorem states that, given smooth capital markets, V is equated to the present value of current and future profits (or net cash flow) discounted at the prevailing shareholder rate of return. Also, under the same conditions, the total market value of shares, that is, V minus the value of debts, equals the present value of the dividend stream to be received by the current shareholders. Because the value of shareholders' wealth is maximized when the total market value of shares is maximized, it is maximized when V is maximized given the value of debts today, which is predetermined as a result of past debt issues. Thus, we take V as the variable representing shareholder interests.

Generally speaking, investment has two opposing effects on V. On the one hand, it enhances the growth of the firm, increases future profits, and increases V. On the other hand, investment incurs expenditure today, thereby decreasing V. Because a higher rate of growth tends to require more than a proportionally larger investment cost owing to increasing difficulties in marketing, research, capacity expansion, and management, the negative effect of growth becomes dominant as the firm pursues faster growth. Thus, even though V may increase with the growth rate for a range of low growth rates, eventually it begins to decrease; that is, a trade-off between V and the growth rate takes place, on which the management has to make a decision. This trade-off is called the value–growth frontier or, for short, the v–g frontier.

Let us derive this frontier formally. We denote by $P(t)$ the gross maximized profits of the firm at time t. They are 'gross' in the sense that investment cost has yet to be deducted, and are calculated as sales revenue less non-investment costs, such as material and labour costs. They are 'maximized' in the sense that all the static policy variables have been set at levels maximizing $P(t)$, where a policy variable is called static if its value at time t affects $P(t)$ but not $P(s)$ for all $s \neq t$. The levels of output, price, and employment are usually considered to be such static variables, though if today's price affects future demand by altering consumers' knowledge or habit, or if today's employment affects future productivity through the workers gaining experience, the variables are no longer static.

The net cash flow (NCF) to the firm at time t is $P(t)$ less the cost of investment at time t, $I(t)$. Because $V(0)$, the value today, equals the present value of NCF,

$$V(0) = \int [P(t) - I(t)] \exp(-it)\mathrm{d}t, \tag{4.5}$$

where i is the discount rate and the limits of integration are zero (today) and infinity (the infinite future). We make the analysis simpler by ignoring knowledge capital (and investment in this capital in the form of research and development) and assuming that physical capital is the only dynamic (non-static) policy variable.[5] Let $K(t)$ denote the book value (as opposed to market value) of this capital at time t. We furthermore assume the following: (A1) capital grows at a constant rate denoted by g; that is, $[\mathrm{d}K(t)/\mathrm{d}t]/K(t) = g$, for all t;[6] (A2) the profit rate on capital at time t, $P(t)/K(t)$, is constant over time at the level denoted by p; (A3) the ratio of investment cost to the value of capital, $I(t)/K(t)$, is independent of t, and denoted by ψ; and (A4) ψ is a function of g, $\psi(g)$, with $\psi(g) \geqslant 0$, $\psi'(g) > 0$, and $\psi''(g) > 0$ for all $g > 0$, $\psi(0) = 0$, and $\psi'(0) = 1$.

The first three assumptions together imply that the firm is aiming at *balanced* or *steady* growth. It is easy to prove that such a policy of steady growth is optimal for the firm provided that relative prices stay constant over time. For expository purposes, we omit this proof and concentrate on the firm's choice among steady growth rates.

(A4) implies that the cost of investment as a ratio to capital is an increasing and convex function of the growth rate of capital. Since the assumption implies that $\psi(g) > g$ for all $g > 0$, $I(t) > \mathrm{d}K(t)/\mathrm{d}t$ for all $I(t) > 0$. That is, the cost of increasing capital is greater than the increased value of capital. Such excess of cost over the attainable capital increment is due to the adjustment cost of capital. The particular formulation of the adjustment cost in (A4) follows Uzawa's (1969) 'Penrose curve'. Recall Penrose's view of the firm as a collection of productive resources (see Chapter 1). Recall, in particular, that in a choice between physical and human resources, she placed greater emphasis on human resources and argued that the managerial limit constrains the growth of the firm: 'the capacities of the *existing* managerial personnel of the firm necessarily set a limit to the expansion of the

[5] For an analysis with knowledge capital, see Odagiri (1981), chap. 3.

[6] We denote the growth rate of capital by g as we did for the growth rate of employment in the previous section, because along a steady growth path employment and capital grow at a common rate.

firm in any given period of time, for it is self-evident that such management cannot be hired in the market-place' (Penrose 1959, 45–6, her emphasis).

She clearly implies (as we did in Chapter 3) that skills, in particular the skills required of managerial staff, are firm-specific and can be accumulated only through experience and training, which takes time. For instance, when the firm builds two new plants instead of one, the firm can only appoint a less experienced and less able manager to head the second plant in comparison to the manager of the first plant, and for this and other reasons it requires greater costs to make the second plant as productive as the first. It is these that comprise the adjustment costs and (A4) is a simple but convenient way to formulate them.

Taking these assumptions, we have

$$P(t) - I(t) = [p - \psi(g)]K(t). \tag{4.6}$$

Since by (A1)

$$K(t) = K(0)\exp(gt), \tag{4.7}$$

substituting (4.6) into (4.5), we get

$$V(0) = \int [p - \psi(g)]K(0)\exp[-(i - g)t]\mathrm{d}t. \tag{4.8}$$

The ratio of $V(0)$ to $K(0)$, namely, the ratio of the market value of the firm to the book value or replacement cost of capital (assets) is called the valuation ratio (v) or Tobin's q.[7] Then, using the rule of integration, we have, given $i > g$,

$$v = [p - \psi(g)]/(i - g). \tag{4.9}$$

Given p and i, this equation gives a relation between v (Tobin's q) and g, which we call the v–g frontier. Given our assumptions, it is straightforward to prove that the frontier has the shape shown in Fig. 4.1; that is, v may (or may not) increase with g for a range of small g, but eventually reaches the maximum value (v^{**}) at $g = g^{**}$, and decreases with g for $g > g^{**}$. The relation is called a frontier because p is the maximized value, and hence inefficient management causes the firm to be inside the frontier.

Now the managerial decision can easily be analysed once the

[7] The term 'Tobin's q' comes from Tobin (1969), while the term 'valuation ratio' comes from Marris (1964), though in Marris' definition it represented the ratio of the market value of the shares to the book value of net assets (i.e., assets less debts).

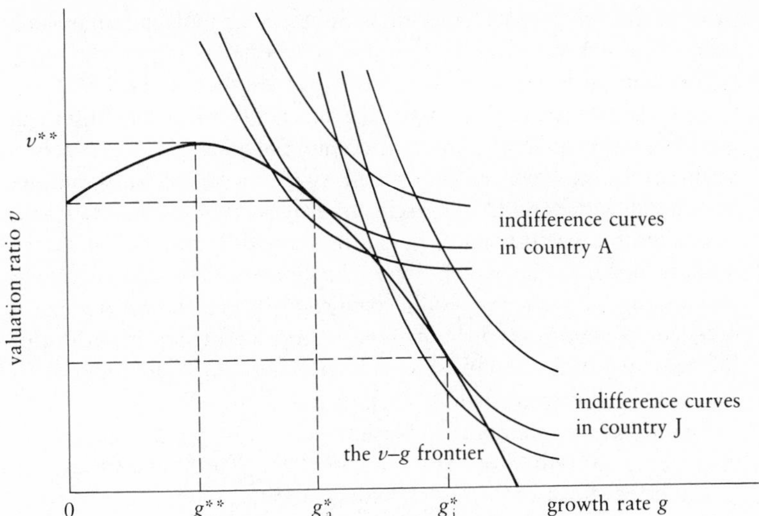

FIG. 4.1 Determination of corporate growth rate

managerial utility function is given. Let us write this utility function as $U(g, v)$. An extreme case occurs when the marginal utility of g is zero. This is the case of a value-maximizing management, and the indifference curves are horizontal: the optimal solution is obviously (g^{**}, v^{**}). If, on the other hand, the marginal utility is positive for both variables, the indifference curves are downward-sloping and the optimal growth rate is determined at the point where one of the indifference curves is tangential to the v–g frontier in the latter's downward-sloping section. Two sets of such indifference curves, one for the management in country A and the other for country J, and the resulting optimal growth rates, g_a^* and g_j^*, are shown in the diagram. Needless to say, the optimal growth rates in these cases, namely, under the (constrained) growth maximization hypothesis, are greater than g^{**}, namely, the solution under the value maximization hypothesis.

4.3. INVESTMENT BEHAVIOUR

The optimal growth rate is higher as the slope of the indifference curve, that is, the marginal rate of substitution, is higher, which, in turn, is higher as the marginal utility of growth is higher and that of value is smaller. Our previous arguments imply that such is the case with Japan relative to other countries, the USA and the UK in particular. In Japan, the marginal utility of growth is higher because of managers' and employees' strong concern about promotion and other social as well as psychological satisfactions associated with growth. The marginal disutility from lower value is smaller because threats of being discharged by unsatisfied shareholders or of being taken over are limited. We can therefore assume that Japan is more like country J in Fig. 4.1 with steeper indifference curves, and the firm will choose a higher growth rate, like g_j^* in Fig. 4.1, than in other countries, such as country A, which will choose g_a^*.

Two other arguments may be put forward to explain the choice of a lower growth rate in other countries. The first attributes it to imperfect information in the stock-market, which causes managerial myopia. Suppose that the real profitability is known only to the management, and investors in the stock-market observe only the reported profits. Then, the manager has an incentive to reduce investment today to claim a higher profit (at the expense of future profits, which investors cannot know) thereby raising the share price and discouraging take-over raiders. Stein (1988) showed that such 'managerial myopia' takes place even if the stock-market is aware of such opportunities for managerial manipulation. This result supports the popular view among American and British managers that the stock price is affected more by short-term profitability than by long-term consequences, deterring the management from adopting a long-term growth-oriented strategy. The effect of this myopia is equivalent to the effect of assuming that the stock-market applies a higher discount rate to evaluate the firm, because it places greater importance on today and less on some distant future. A comparative analysis can easily show that i affects both g^{**} and v^{**} negatively; that is, under myopia a value-maximizing management is led to choose a lower growth rate. Since a higher i implies a shift of the v–g frontier to the south-west, a growth-maximizing management is also forced to choose a lower growth rate and a lower valuation ratio.

The second argument suggests that American or British management is simply inefficient and has failed to maximize gross profits. This argument leads to the same consequence as the myopia theory, because the effects of a lower p on the frontier are qualitatively identical to those of a higher i. One reason for the relative efficiency of Japanese firms comes from the strength of internal competition discussed in Chapter 3, which leads the workers to work hard, resulting in static efficiency. The other reason comes from the long-term worker–company attachment, which encourages employees to think in terms of long-term consequences and come up with ideas to improve efficiency. Such a call for dynamic efficiency is often made under the Japanese term *kaizen*, meaning improvement, and is to be heard even in overseas plants of Japanese firms. For instance, the (British) personnel director of Nissan UK states that 'under the process known as *kaizen*—continuous improvement—Nissan seeks to create an environment in which *all* staff can contribute to improving quality, safety and productivity as a normal part of their job' (Wickens 1987, 46, his emphasis).

These arguments imply that the effective discount rate adopted in the stock-market is lower in Japan and/or that static and dynamic efficiency is higher under Japanese management. The 'perceived' frontier (which, if inefficient, must be inside the true frontier) is more toward the north-east in Japan than in other countries (say, country B) and this tendency reinforces its choice of a higher growth rate. These considerations suggest furthermore that the Japanese firm may be able to attain a higher valuation ratio despite its growth maximization. That is, though the management in country J with stronger growth motivation necessarily chooses a lower valuation ratio than the management in country A which has weaker growth motivation but the same v–g frontier, it may attain a higher v (as well as a higher g) than the management in country B with a lower 'perceived' frontier. Fig. 4.2 illustrates this possibility, where I_a, I_j, and I_b denote the indifference curves of the management in countries A, J, and B and g_a^*, g_j^*, and g_b^* denote the choice of g in countries A, J, and B.

This argument is consistent with the fact that the growth rate has been higher in Japan than in the USA or the UK but the difference in the valuation ratio (Tobin's q) has been less clear. According to Holland (1984), q has been, on average, 0.59 in Japan and 0.74 in the USA in 1965–81. A comparable figure is not available for the UK, but q based on a partial definition of assets (excluding land and monetary assets) was 1.03 in 1965–80.

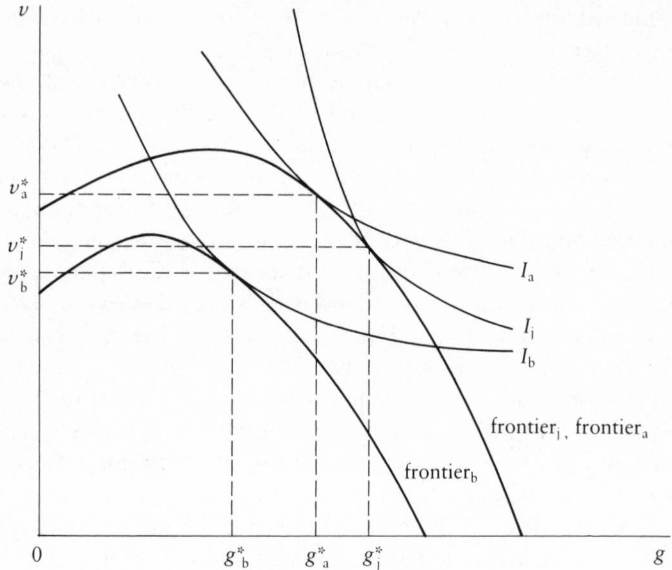

FIG. 4.2 Optimal growth rates under alternative v–g frontiers

The same q in the same period was 0.95 in the USA and 1.72 in Japan, apparently because of high land prices in Japan. Thus even if q has been smaller in Japan than in the USA or the UK, the difference is by no means great.[8] We also note that in all these countries q was smaller than unity (provided all the assets are taken into account). Since $q < 1$ means that the shareholders are better off liquidating the firm, selling all the assets, and sharing the proceeds among them, the fact that it has been persistent must support our argument that shareholder control is limited not only in Japan but everywhere.

Needless to say, a higher g is attained only with a higher ψ, that is, a higher investment/capital ratio. Since its international comparison is bound to be misleading because of the inaccuracy in estimating the value of capital,[9] let us take the investment/output

[8] We will return to this topic in Sec. 10.6. In particular, Table 10.2 will give a more detailed international comparison of Tobin's q.

[9] Estimates of real capital stock are available for Japan, the USA, and Germany: its average rate of annual increase during 1974–86 was 5.9% (Japan), 3.2% (USA), and 1.7% (Germany) in the manufacturing sector, and 8.2% (Japan), 3.6%

TABLE 4.1. Investment as % of GNP in five countries, 1970–1987

Period	Japan	USA	UK	FRG	France
	Gross private fixed capital formation as % of GNP[a]				
Total					
1970–4	26.0	15.3	14.7	20.3	21.5
1975–9	21.9	16.0	15.5	17.1	19.8
1980–4	20.8	15.6	14.8	18.2	18.1
1985–7	21.2	15.4	15.1	17.0	16.1
1970–87	22.6	15.6	15.0	18.3	19.2
Non-Residential Only					
1970–4	18.9	10.4	12.1	13.0	13.3
1975–9	14.9	10.9	12.9	11.2	12.2
1980–4	15.3	11.4	12.2	11.7	10.9
1985–7	16.2	10.4	12.2	11.7	10.9
1970–87	16.3	10.8	12.4	11.9	12.1
	Annual growth rate of real GNP[a]				
1970–4	4.8	3.1	3.0	3.0	4.4
1975–9	4.7	3.2	2.0	2.8	2.8
1980–4	3.9	1.9	0.7	1.1	1.5
1985–7	3.9	3.0	3.5	2.1	2.0
1970–87	4.3	2.8	2.1	2.2	2.6

[a] GDP in the UK and France.

Sources: National accounts.

ratio on the assumption that capital/output ratio is internationally similar. Table 4.1 compares Japan with four other industrialized economies, the USA, the UK, the FRG, and France, with respect to the proportion of GNP the private sector spent on gross fixed capital formation. Quite obviously, Japan has the highest proportion in any subperiod during the past two decades, and in total or for non-residential only. For instance, in terms of non-residential private investment, the proportion was on average 16 per cent in

(USA), and 4.1% (Germany) in the non-manufacturing sector: Economic Planning Agency (Japan), *Survey of Current Business* (USA), and *Statistisches Jahrbuch* (Germany), cited from Bank of Japan, *Comparative Economic and Financial Statistics*.

Japan but 10–12 per cent in the other four countries. Although one is tempted to argue that this high propensity to invest has been the main source of Japan's fast economic growth (see the rate of change in real GNP in the same table), one needs to be cautious because the intended growth rates of individual firms and the realized grorth rate of the national economy may not be the same, owing to the aggregation problem. That is, if external constraints, such as labour supply, set an upper limit to the speed at which the economy can grow, the growth preference of individual firms may merely change relative prices so that the realized growth rate is within the boundary of this limit. We shall discuss this aggregation problem in more detail in Chapter 10, but Japan's higher realized aggregate growth rate suggests that such external constraints were either absent or relaxed by the efforts of industries and/or government.

4.4. THE MODE OF GROWTH

When the firm intends to grow, it has to make strategic decisions, chiefly concerning where to grow and how to do so. The where-to question relates to the direction in which the firm should invest: should it strengthen the productive and marketing capacity in its current markets, expand into upstream or downstream businesses, or enter new fields unrelated to its current business? Following the usual classification for mergers, we can call these forms of growth horizontal, vertical, and diversifying, respectively. The how-to question relates to the means used to attain growth. A basic distinction has to be made between internal and external growth. External growth refers to merging with or acquiring the whole or part of existing outside businesses, whereas internal growth refers to growth without such mergers or acquisitions. Typically, internal growth is attained by investing within the firm, by such measures as building a new plant or increasing marketing and distribution capacity, but the establishment of subsidiaries should also be included.

Table 4.2 shows these two questions in a matrix form. 'Purely internal' growth refers to investment within the firm, while 'hive-off' denotes the establishment of subsidiaries. Three categories within external growth will be distinguished in the following chapter. Inter-firm activity is also included in the table as a means

TABLE 4.2. Modes of corporate growth

How to Grow	Where to Grow		
	Horizontal	Vertical	Diversifying
Internal Purely internal Hive-off			
External Mergers Acquisitions Capital participation			
Inter-firm Joint ventures Alliances Grouping			

of growth. Joint ventures are the typical example of such interfirm investment. Obviously, the question of which cell to choose from this matrix is no less important than the question of how much investment to make. It is also closely related to the question of which organizational form is best suited to the firm, which will be discussed extensively in Part II.

Although, theoretically, there can be any combination of direction and means, some combinations are more likely than others. In particular, internal and horizontal growth, and external and diversifying growth are more common than internal and diversifying growth. Recall again that the firm is essentially a collection of human and other managerial resources. Thus, diversification is costly, risky, and time-consuming without those human resources with skills and knowledge pertinent to the fields. Since these resources are unlikely to have been accumulated within the firm, and since the interfirm mobility of labour is limited, the scope for successful diversification is limited without recourse to acquisitions.

These considerations explain why internal and horizontal growth is most preferred in Japan whereas in the USA and the UK, by contrast, the most publicized form of growth is external and diversifying, as in the case of conglomerates.[10] Most importantly, only internal growth helps to utilize and enrich existing human resources, and to create opportunities for promotion. Since Japanese management purports to maintain employees even when they are redundant from the viewpoint of short-term profitability, the firm has a strong incentive to expand internally to utilize these employees during periods of contracting demand or following labour-saving innovations. The depth and breadth of skill-formation were emphasized in the previous chapter. The kind of knowledge ('undefinable knowledge') that cannot be conveyed through writing or speaking can be effectively acquired only on the job (with the help of supervisors or seniors) and, consequently, assigning workers to diverse jobs and diverse work-places (though not too distant from their current ones) is an indispensable part of OJT training. Internal expansion has the merit of creating related jobs to which workers can be assigned so that they acquire skills there.[11]

The importance of promotion for workers has been repeatedly emphasized. Only internal expansion can increase the number of posts relative to the number of incumbent employees, for while an acquisition also increases the number of posts, it increases the number of candidates as well. The management, keenly aware of the importance of promotion in every employee's career, is motivated to seek growth, and only internal growth will help in this respect.

Furthermore, Japanese management is less prepared to undertake acquisitions, partly because the employees of the acquired firm, identifying themselves with their firm, tend to view the acquisition as an intrusion and to resist it, and partly because integrating two separate human organizations with different cultures and conventions can cause many difficulties. More will be said on these issues in Chapter 5.

[10] According to Ravenscraft and Scherer (1987), of the lines of business added between 1950 and 1975 of 148 of the top 200 US companies surviving through the period (implying 74% survival rate), 41% were acquired and only 14% invested internally (with the remaining 45% unclassifiable).

[11] However, acquisitions, if successful, may be able to broaden the skills even further by creating opportunities for the workers of the acquiring firm (acquired firm) to learn from those of the acquired firm (acquiring firm). As we will see in the next chapter, Japanese firms do occasionally acquire other businesses for the purpose of diversification.

TABLE 4.3. Specialization versus diversification: Trend in Japan and international comparison

Country	Year	Sample size	% Single	Dominant	Related	Unrelated
Japan	1958	114	26.3	34.2	30.7	8.8
	1963	118	24.6	32.2	35.6	7.6
	1968	118	19.5	37.3	36.4	6.8
	1973	118	16.9	36.4	39.9	6.8
	1978	129	13.9	35.7	41.9	8.5
	1981	129	15.5	33.3	41.1	10.1
	1984	129	15.5	30.2	42.7	11.6
USA	1969	183	6.2	29.2	45.2	19.4
UK	1970	100	6.0	34.0	54.0	6.0
	1980	200	9.0	26.0	47.0	18.0
FRG	1970	100	22.0	22.0	38.0	18.0
France	1970	100	16.0	32.0	42.0	10.0
Italy	1970	100	10.0	33.0	52.0	5.0

Sources: Japan: 1958–73, Yoshihara *et al.* (1981), 1978–84, Suzuki (1987); USA: Rumelt (1974); UK 1980: Channon (1982). Others are taken from Yoshihara *et al.* (1981), but the original sources are: UK 1970: D. F. Channon, *The Strategy and Structure of British Enterprise*, MacMillan, 1973; FRG and France: G. P. Dyas and H. T. Thanheiser, *The Emerging European Enterprise*. MacMillan, 1976; Italy: R. J. Pavan, Strategy and Structure of Italian Enterprise. Unpublished dissertation, Harvard Business School, 1972.

The insistence on internal growth restrains the speed with which the firm can diversify its activity. This is why diversification is less extensive in Japan than in other developed countries, and why most diversification in Japan is into technologically or otherwise related fields in which the existing human resources of the firm can easily be utilized. Table 4.3 shows this international comparison. All the studies followed the same methodology of classifying each of 100 to 200 firms into one of four categories: 'single', which means that the proportion of one product in the firm's entire sales (called the specialization ratio) is larger than or equal to 95 per cent; 'dominant', which means that the specialization ratio is less than 95 per cent but larger than or equal to 70 per cent; 'related', which means that the specialization ratio is less than 70 per cent and the proportion of the largest group of related products (related in terms of technology or marketing) among the firm's entire sales (called the related ratio) is larger than or equal to 70 per cent; and 'unrelated', which means that both the specialization ratio and the related ratio are less than 70 per cent.[12]

Needless to say, the definition of a 'product' or 'related products' cannot be totally free from ambiguity, and the comparability of the studies is not beyond question. In addition, sample differences exist among them. Yet, two observations are evident from Table 4.3. The first is the increasing trend of diversification. The proportion of 'related' and 'unrelated' diversification increased in Japan from 40 per cent in 1958 to 54 per cent in 1984. A similar increase has been observed in other countries as well (Yoshihara *et al.* 1981). The second observation, more important for our purpose here, is the smaller proportion of diversified firms in Japan. For instance, the proportion of 'related' and 'unrelated' was less than 50 per cent in Japan until 1973 and was 54 per cent even in 1984, whereas in the USA and the UK the proportion was 60 per cent or more in 1969–70. In other words, diversification, particularly diversification to unrelated fields, is less common in Japan. This difference, we have already argued, relates to the Japanese preference for internal growth, which in turn relates to the internal management system.

To put it another way, Japanese firms have to adopt more external means of expansion if they really wish to diversify into unrelated fields. During a period of rapid industrial restructuring, and hard-pressed by declining demand and a bleak future for their main products, some firms have actually started using mergers and acquisitions to obtain the managerial resources needed to diversify into promising but unfamiliar fields, in the hope of combining them with existing resources. We will discuss this topic in the next chapter. None the less, the strategy used by American and British conglomerates of buying and selling totally unrelated businesses as if they are commodities will remain remote from Japanese management.[13]

[12] Suzuki's classification scheme is slightly different from others; however, this difference is unlikely to change the results substantially.

[13] Ravenscraft and Scherer (1987) estimates that about a third of businesses acquired in the 1960s and early 1970s were sold off by 1981.

4.5. RESEARCH AND DEVELOPMENT

The tendency of Japanese management to pursue growth implies a willingness to spend more on research and development (R & D) in order to attain a faster target growth rate. A similar view has been expressed recently by a few American authors, who have attributed the Japanese enthusiasm for innovation to their concern for long-term performance rather than short-term profitability: see Rosenbloom and Abernathy (1982) and Abegglen and Stalk (1985). That Japanese firms in many industries are now expending more of their resources on R & D than Anglo-American firms (excluding government-funded R & D; for more detail, see Section 11.4) is wholly consistent with the growth-maximization hypothesis.

There are several additional reasons why the Japanese firm is more concerned with R & D, and has been more effective in carrying out R & D and attaining product development and productivity increases. They include the managers' backgrounds, the link between R & D, production, and marketing, and the introduction of new technology into the work place.

One difference between Japanese managers and their American or British counterparts that we noted in Chapter 2 concerned their background: in Japan the largest proportion of directors came from production and technology departments, followed by marketing and export, whereas in the USA or the UK the majority came from administration, finance, and accounting. Japanese managers' better knowledge and wider experience in production and R & D provide them with a better understanding of the potential and limitations of R & D projects, an ability to make more accurate evaluations of the results from R & D, and more favourable attitudes towards R & D in general. Similarly, their knowledge and experience of sales and marketing provide them with a keen understanding of what kinds of products are in demand. The familiarity of Japanese managers with the seeds of technology and the needs of the market must be particularly valuable in technologically rapidly changing markets.

It was argued in Chapter 3 that the Japanese internal labour market system is characterized not only by long-term attachment but also by a carefully systematized training and rotation scheme. Commonly, the firm provides its workers with several months of well-programmed training at the time of entry, not only so that they acquire technical knowledge and skills but also so that they become familiar with the various activities of the firm, and then follows this with mid-career training every five years or so. In addition, rotation of workers from, say, R & D to production in the case of engineers, or from one shop to another in the case of production workers, occurs more frequently than in other countries. These practices help the workers to take a company-wide view and to acquire flexibility in changing work environments.

Furthermore, long-term employment naturally leads workers to form personal links across departments. If somebody has been working in R & D for many years, he will have had many opportunities to meet and talk with other people in the company, and also to visit other departments and other plants to discuss problems of mutual concern. Thus a close human relationship is created between the R & D department and other departments within the firm. Consequently, R & D staff will be more familiar with the technological needs arising from production and marketing, and non-R & D departments will be more familiar with what is going on in the laboratories. Company R & D therefore tends to be more pragmatic, that is, more production-based or market-oriented. The advantage of this is that the research undertaken will be more commercially relevant and a new product can reach the production and marketing stages more quickly. The disadvantage is that there may be less emphasis on truly original and basic research.

Two other features of Japanese firms make this link between R & D, production, and sales even more effective. One is the comparative lack in Japan of multi-divisional structures that permit substantial discretion within each division. Weaker divisional separation not only fosters easy rotation across divisions (which explains why the multi-divisional structure is unpopular in Japan; see Section 6.2), it also facilitates a company-wide use of technological knowledge. The other feature is a close link with suppliers and subcontractors. A stable buyer–supplier relationship with a constant flow of information is usually to be found in Japanese companies. As a result, they tend to share both the threat of market competition and the need for innovation. Improvements in the product or the production process by the supplier or subcontractor will be noted and rewarded by the parent company (possibly not in the short term but in the long term) and may also be utilized in other firms in the group. In many instances, co-operative R&D will be carried out by the parent and the supplier(s) working together. For example, when an automobile assembler develops a new model of car, it is essential that suitable components are developed at the same time. Such development will be carried out by the supplier(s) in close communication with the assembler's developing team, and often with technical advice from the assembling company. We will return to this topic in Section 6.4.[14]

In addition, we would suggest that the introduction of new processes or new products runs more smoothly in Japanese firms. We have already noted the existence of close communication between the R&D and production departments. Specifically, in the course of developing a product or process, production staff tend to participate from quite an early stage. This may not be efficient in terms of development itself but, since the views of the production department will be reflected in the development of the final product or process, the transfer from development to production will be more rapid and less prone to disruption and bottlenecks (Graves 1987).

Moreover, the engineers in the development team may be transferred to the production department and actively involve themselves in getting the new product or process into production (Sakakibara and Westney 1985). Such transfers are common in the careers of Japanese engineers because the ability for research tends to reach a peak during their late thirties (or even earlier) and, after this age, both management and the engineers themselves find it advantageous to use their ability and expertise in administrative and managerial positions in the production and R&D departments. A transfer, therefore, will not simply ease the introduction of a particular new product or process in which the engineer has been involved, but will also add to the sum of technological knowledge in the production department, while fostering an even tighter personal link between R&D and production.

Even if the production manager is familiar with the new product

[14] Also see Imai *et al.* (1985).

or process, its smooth introduction into the production stage requires skill and flexibility on the part of the workers. Here again the advantage of the Japanese internal labour system should be remembered. In Japan, given the expectation of lifetime employment, the management has ample incentives to provide training, both on and off the job, to its workers, whether white-collar or blue-collar. The breadth and flexibility of workers' skills make the adoption of new products and processes into shopfloor easier and faster.

In this adoption process, it is important that the management has a free hand in reorganizing the production organization. The prevalence of single and company-wide trade unions is crucial in this regard. For instance, when automobile producers introduced industrial robots, most of the welding jobs were eliminated and yet no Japanese firms discharged their welders for this reason. They were all retrained and transferred to other shops, such as metalwork and assembling; there was thus no reported incidence of grievance or industrial action. If, on the contrary, workers in different jobs are organized into different unions, as in many parts of British industry, no such transfers would have been possible and the introduction of new processes would have caused disputes. The relation between innovation and labour relations can indeed be quite important.

In this section, we have discussed four major aspects of Japanese management that help to promote efficient and large-scale R & D, and to introduce the results swiftly and easily into manufacturing and marketing. These are growth maximization; familiarity of management with research, production, and marketing; close links between R & D, production, and sales; and the smooth adoption of new processes and products in the workplace. Behind all these factors, we stressed the importance of the human aspect of management. The internal labour practices of Japanese management, particularly, long-term worker–company attachments with internal training and internal promotion, have been conducive to growth preference among managers and employees, to interdepartmental personal contact, and to easy adoption of production processes on the shop-floor. Innovation is predominantly a labour-intensive process, unlike, say, an automated production system. However big computers may be, it needs human brains to initiate ideas and to make a final evaluation of alternative projects.

However labour-saving the new process may be, it needs experienced workers to install and operate it. Creating the human resources and organizations that are most suitable for these needs is the key to innovative success, and we would suggest that, at this moment, the Japanese labour management system is more effective than the Anglo-American system in this regard.

Finally, we should note that these internal aspects must be accompanied by external factors. An organization, however capable of being efficient and flexible, need not be so unless presented with some external threat. Competition and rapid changes in industrial structure play a vital role in forming such a threat. Competition among rival firms has been very fierce in many industries in Japan, even where the concentration ratio is not particularly low. Entry into growing industries has been fast and frequent. And shifts in industrial structure have been drastic in past decades, with some of those industries which were once triumphant now fading into obscurity, for instance, ship-building, petrochemicals and aluminium-smelting. These realities have provided firms with a strong sense of crisis and a reason to be innovative. To maintain the smooth internal labour system, the firm has to seek growth and diversification internally and to acquire the necessary technology from within. Under the threat of competition and of rapidly changing technological and industrial structures, the very survival of the company is threatened unless it continues to innovate. More will be said on industrial competition in Chapter 8.

4.6. CONCLUSION

Based on the discussion in earlier chapters, this chapter has formulated the essence of the dynamic strategy of Japanese management, based on the growth maximization hypothesis, and presented a model by which to analyse the firm's choice of growth rate and the valuation ratio (Tobin's q). We have also looked at the implications on the investment behaviour of the firm, both investment in physical capital and investment in knowledge capital as typified by research and development, at the mode (direction and means) of growth, to be discussed further in Part II, and at the factors which contribute to the relative success of innovation in Japan.

In fact, research and development is not the only way to increase knowledge capital. This can also be brought about by training and by the accumulation of knowledge and experience that takes place as the cumulative output increases. This latter effect has been called learning-by-doing and is usually depicted by a learning curve or an experience curve—a downward-sloping curve between the unit cost of production (or the unit price) and the cumulative output. The most spectacular example of learning-by-doing has probably been the pocket calculator industry, in which the unit cost declined by 20 to 25 per cent with each doubling of cumulative output (Abegglen and Stalk 1985). Similarly, in the chemical processing industry in the USA, the unit price decreased by 20 to 30 per cent as cumulative output doubled (Lieberman 1984). The unit cost decrease through learning takes place partly because workers accumulate experience and partly because ideas for a better lay-out in production process are developed. Again the advantage of the Japanese internal labour system may be noted here. The long-term worker–company attachment, the broader experience of workers, and the encouragement of worker participation and worker proposals at the shop-floor level all point to more effective learning-by-doing.

The importance of learning-by-doing reinforces the hypothesis of growth maximization, because the cost reduction through increased cumulative output adds to the above-mentioned benefits of faster expansion. The effect is a shift of the v–g frontier to the right and upwards, and as a result the choice of a higher growth rate. Furthermore, the strategic importance of market share is strengthened because the firm with the largest market share can attain the largest cumulative output and consequently the largest cost reduction. The insistence of Japanese management on market share (see the finding of Kagono *et al.* cited in Section 4.1) must be partly a consequence of this effect.

PART II

HOW IT ORGANIZES

5
Mergers and Acquisitions

5.1. INTRODUCTION: WHY ARE THERE FEWER MERGERS AND ACQUISITIONS IN JAPAN?

Japanese management, as compared with American or British management, prefers internal growth (including the creation of subsidiaries) over external growth. A simple statistic illustrates this fact very clearly. Of the 899 manufacturing firms listed at the Tokyo Stock Exchange in 1964, only 67, or 7.5 per cent, had been acquired by 1984 twenty years later, which contrasts with the USA, where the percentage is five times larger at 38.4 per cent (384 out of the 1,000 largest manufacturing firms) during the twenty-two-year period 1950–72, and with the UK where the percentage was 42 per cent (1,265 out of 3,011 firms) during the twenty-seven-year period 1950–77 (Odagiri and Yamawaki 1990).

Many factors contribute to there being fewer mergers and acquisitions (M&As, hereafter) in Japan. One is the pattern of shareholding in Japan discussed in Chapter 2, particularly, large-scale ownership by financial institutions and inter-company shareholdings, including those within business groups. These 'stable' shareholders, it has been argued, will not sell their holdings even under rising stock prices unless they themselves are in financial difficulty and/or the current management agrees. The current management will expect them not to side with hostile take-over raiders. Of course, how far they really are stable is open to question. If, for instance, they are dissatisfied with the current management and offered a high premium on their shares, will they really decline the offer? It is difficult to answer this very interesting question, however, precisely because such cases have been rare.

In our view, the point is not so much that the Japanese company cannot use M&As as a means of corporate growth, but that it is unwilling to do so. We have already discussed the reasons why Japanese management prefers internal growth to M & As (see Section 4.4).

First, corporate growth is highly regarded and sought after primarily for its contribution to the use and enrichment of human resources and to the creation of promotion opportunities. For instance, firms in stagnating industries desperately seek opportunities to diversify, so as to enable their now redundant workers to support themselves in new fields. Obviously, only internal growth can help here, because acquiring a company also means acquiring its employees, which scarcely enhances the promotion prospects for employees of the acquiring firm.

Second, workers identify their interests with those of the company which, as a consequence, is regarded as a sort of community. Any offer to acquire the company is therefore likely to be taken as an intrusion. The management in this situation is unwilling to accept a tender offer, and a hostile take-over attempt is bound to meet furious resistance.

Third, because labour practices are in many ways firm-specific, unifying the practices of two different merging firms tends not only to be costly but also to create uneasiness and conflicts of interest in many areas, for example in the wage system, non-wage fringe benefits, the criteria for promotion and rotation, and even the quality of lunch the company provides. Thus, in order to secure the co-operation of employees, the merged firm usually has to adopt the higher of the wage structures of previously separate companies. There are also psychological or sociological costs. For instance, in mergers between firms under equal terms, such as Yawata Steel and Fuji Steel merging into Nippon Steel in 1970, great care has been taken to dispel the impression that either firm was 'acquired' by the other, since otherwise the morale of the employees of the supposedly 'acquired' firm would be damaged. Thus a lottery was held to decide which of the two presidents should be the first president of Nippon Steel, and for over twenty years since the merger the presidency has been taken alternately by ex-Fuji officials and ex-Yawata officials. Similarly great care was taken to ensure equal numbers of ex-Yawata men and ex-Fuji men at most hierarchical levels.

Fourth, as discussed in Chapter 2, the executives of Japanese firms are mostly internally promoted and are less constrained by the stock-market evaluation. As a consequence, they are not as anxious about short-term performance as American and British executives and can tolerate the initial losses that internal growth tends to create during the gestation period.

These considerations lead us to the following set of hypotheses on M & A activity in Japan relative to that in the USA or the UK.

Hypothesis 1: There will be fewer M & As. In particular, hostile M & As will be infrequent.
Hypothesis 2: Only those firms with financial or managerial difficulties will be willing to be acquired.
Hypothesis 3: The proportion of horizontal M & As will be smaller.
Hypothesis 4: A looser form of combination will be preferred to complete integration of the acquired firm's organization into the acquirer's.

All these hypotheses follow directly from the discussion above. Because employees and management identify themselves with the company, they are unwilling to be acquired. However, if the firm is under a serious threat of bankruptcy, or if they are aware that the lack of managerial resources is a serious impediment to the firm's growth, they may opt to be acquired.

The preference for internal growth should be particularly strong when the firm intends to grow horizontally, because the required resources, human or informational, are likely to be internally available or can be created without expending a great deal of time or capital. We thus expect a smaller proportion of horizontal M & As. In other words, only when the firm intends to expand into unfamiliar fields will the advantages of obtaining external resources outweigh the disadvantages already discussed.

Even when the firm opts to grow externally, a complete integration of two previously separate organizations is likely to be avoided. One reason for this is the cost of integration, discussed in the third point above. The other is to bolster the morale of employees who wish to view their company as an independent organization, however superficial the independence may be.

In this chapter, we shall be looking to see if these hypotheses are supported by observation of recent M & As in Japan. It has been reported that, notwithstanding the factors favouring internal growth, Japanese firms are now undertaking an increasing number of M & As. In particular, two types of M & A have recently become popular. One is the acquisition of foreign firms (or plants) in order to start overseas operations. Even Japanese firms find M & As more attractive for this purpose because they tend to lack the resources needed for efficient management and operation abroad, and because the target firms, being non-Japanese, can be more easily persuaded to agree to acquisitions. A discussion of acquisitions of this kind will be postponed until Chapter 12. The other type consists of acquisition as a means of diversification. In Japan, during the past twenty years, the industrial structure has changed at a speed hitherto unknown. This shift was caused partly by the oil shock in the early 1970s and the upsurge of the yen at a pace no one could have foreseen, and partly by rapid micro-electronization. The structural change forced many firms, such as those in the steel and ship-building industries, to contract their main operations and diversify into unfamiliar fields. When they found that retraining their own workers was too time-consuming and costly, many firms started to use M & As to acquire the necessary resources.

A natural question that arises is whether these M & As will become a dominant strategy, or whether the specifically Japanese factors mentioned above will prevent this tendency and managements will continue to prefer internal growth. Unfortunately, this question is extremely difficult to answer, partly because the supposed M & A wave is a recent phenomenon so that we only have a few years of observations to judge by, and partly because no comprehensive data exist on M & As. Furthermore, the lack of consolidated statements for most Japanese firms makes it difficult to assess the real impact of M & A. None the less, the characteristics and performance of recent M & As, to be discussed below, strongly suggest that human factors do play an important role in Japanese corporate M & A strategy.

This chapter is organized as follows. In Section 5.2, the trend in mergers is examined according to the data of the Japanese Fair Trade Commission (hereafter JFTC). In Section 5.3, we look at the characteristics of M & As—of Japanese firms by Japanese firms—in our sample. In Section 5.4, the average performance of M & As is examined by comparing profitability and growth rates before and after M & As, and Section 5.5 contains an inquiry into which M & As—which type, for what purpose, and how big—were most successful. In Section 5.6, the pre-merger performance of firms carrying out M & As is compared with that of non-merging firms to see if more profitable (or more rapidly growing) firms undertook more or less M & As, and to find out whether there is any difference in the characteristics of M & As according to their pre-merger performance. Section 5.7 offers a conclusion.

5.2. THE TREND OF MERGERS: THE JFTC DATA

The Antimonopoly Law in Japan requires any company to report to the JFTC its merger with another company or its acquisition of the whole or a substantial part of the business (or assets) of another company. The JFTC publishes the numbers of these mergers and acquisitions in its annual report, as well as the names of companies involved in large-scale mergers (JFTC 1988). The trend in these numbers is shown in Fig. 5.1. Roughly speaking, the number of mergers has remained constant around one thousand since 1963. There was a decreasing trend during the 1970s but there has been an increasing trend since 1980 with a record 1,223 mergers in the most recent year, 1987. Yet compared with the violent fluctuations in merger activity in the USA (see Scherer

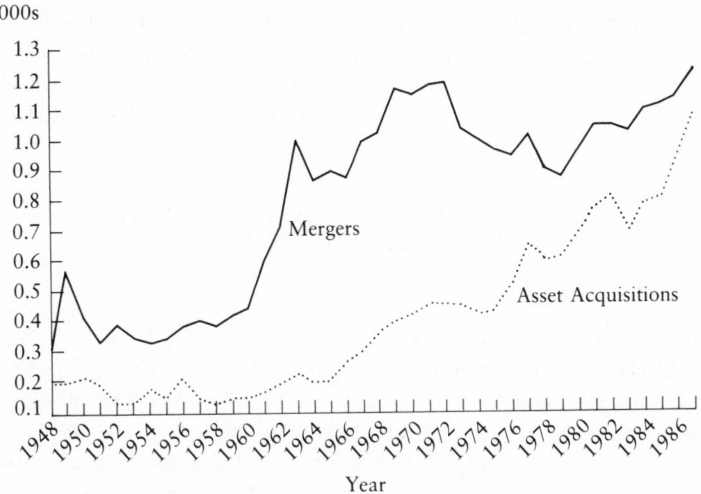

FIG. 5.1 Number of mergers and acquisitions in Japan: JFTC statistics

1980, chap. 4), the general impression in Japan is one of relative stability. The number of acquisitions as defined above, on the other hand, has been steadily increasing from around 200 in the 1950s to 1,086 in 1987.

Of these mergers, 26 per cent were horizontal; 15 per cent vertical; 15 per cent through geographical extension; 14 per cent through product extension; and 27 per cent others, which are regarded as pure conglomerates by the JFTC. These percentages are for 1987 but have been fairly stable over the years.

The proportion of horizontal mergers is slightly higher than that in the USA, where antitrust restrictions have been supposedly strongest (though weakened lately), but decidedly smaller than in most other countries, such as Australia, Canada, the FRG, Ireland, the UK, the Netherlands, and Sweden, where the proportion exceeded 50 per cent (OECD 1984). This fact supports our Hypothesis 3. Another reason for the existence of fewer horizontal mergers should be also noted which is that, as in the USA, the antitrust policy against horizontal mergers is stringent. Although mergers have seldom actually been stopped by the JFTC, this does not imply that the regulations on mergers have been weak or ineffective (see Section 11.2 for more detail). The JFTC has published guidelines which, for instance, state that any merger producing a post-merger market share of 25 per cent or more will be investigated, and this has probably worked as a deterrent to merger attempts. Also, there have been reports of several cases in which companies have asked for an informal prior assessment of the proposed mergers by the JFTC and then either abandoned or modified their original plans.

5.3. MERGERS AND ACQUISITIONS IN JAPAN, 1980–1987

5.3.1. Sample

The mergers and acquisitions reported by the JFTC do not represent the only means used by firms to expand externally, since they are restricted to those transactions in which two merging firms (or a firm and an acquired plant or other business unit) are unified to form a single corporation. They do not include cases in which company A acquires company B but keeps B as a subsidiary, that is, as another company under A's control, nor cases in which company A acquires only a portion of company B's shares, but effectively gains control of B. These omissions make the JFTC figures unreliable for our purposes, because it is these strategies that Japanese companies are said to be undertaking more frequently these days.

To make the terminology clear, let us define *merger* as a legal amalgamation of two or more companies to form a single company. *Acquisition* refers to the acquisition of control of another company without merging. It usually involves the acquisition of ownership, typically more than half of the shares, but there are cases in which company A acquires real control over company B without majority ownership of the shares. What we call *capital participation* refers to company B retaining its own control but falling under the influence of company A. The way A influences B may be, for instance, technological (A provides technology and know-how to B) or market-related (A utilizes B's market channels). We call these cases capital participation because, in nearly every case, A acquires some of the shares of B. Such share-ownership may be reciprocal, that is, B may acquire shares of A at the same time that A acquires shares of B. *M & A* here refers to all of these three methods of external corporate expansion. The firm undertaking an M & A is called an acquirer (or raider) regardless of whether the move is a merger, an acquisition, or capital participation. Similarly, the target firm of any M & A is called the acquired firm (or victim).

A problem when studying M & As in Japan is the lack of published data. In Odagiri and Hase (1989), we assembled data from *Nihon Keizai Shimbun* (The Japanese equivalent of the *Wall Street Journal* or *Financial Times*) during 1980–7. We are confident that this data set is reasonably comprehensive because all mergers for which the details were reported in the JFTC annual reports were also in our data. The data are also useful in that the declared objectives of the M & A by both the acquiring and the acquired firms are also reported, and they will be utilized in the following analyses. The sample thus collected consists of 243 M & As, undertaken by 183 firms.[1]

[1] Mergers between parents and their subsidiaries are excluded from the sample.

TABLE 5.1. Mergers and acquisitions in Japan, 1980–1987

Year	Mergers	Acquisitions	Capital participation	Total
1980	2	8	5	15
1981	11	10	8	29
1982	3	14	6	23
1983	7	14	2	23
1984	3	31	10	44
1985	6	25	13	44
1986	8	18	8	34
1987	3	15	13	31
TOTAL	43 (17.7%)	135 (55.6%)	65 (26.7%)	243 (100%)

5.3.2. *Trend and International Comparison*

Table 5.1 shows the number of mergers, acquisitions, and capital participations by year. From 1980 to 1984 the total number increased, but since 1985 it has been decreasing. Hence, it is difficult to conclude whether there has been any clear trend. We also observe that the number of acquisitions has been increasing (up to 1984) but the number of mergers has not.

It is difficult to make a precise international comparison of the number of M & As. In 1987, according to *Mergers & Acquisitions*, the number of M & As in the USA (US companies acquiring US companies) was 3,367, with an additional 363 US companies acquired by non-US companies and, according to *Acquisitions Monthly*, the number of M & As in UK companies was 1,937. In the same year, according to Yamaichi Securities, the number of M & As in major Japanese firms was 241 including those by foreign firms, and 219 excluding them.[2] This is seven times larger than the number of cases in our sample, suggesting that press reports have been selective, perhaps biasing our sample towards M & As involving larger firms. Thus, we find that American firms undertook fifteen times and British firms eight times more M & As than Japanese firms, if we base our comparison on the Yamaichi

[2] See Table 12.1 for more detail of the Yamaichi data.

data. However, if we use the JFTC data and include asset acquisitions as defined by the JFTC, then the Japanese number is roughly equal to the UK number and about two-thirds of the US number. If we adjust these numbers by the size of the economy, we find that it is about three times larger in the UK relative to Japan and is slightly smaller in the US, because as a ratio of Japanese GNP, the UK GNP stands at 0.3 and the US GNP at 1.9. However, the comparison very much depends on the coverage and definition of the data. The JFTC data cover all mergers and asset acquisitions (as defined by the JFTC) made by Japanese companies (public or private, stock company or not) and the majority of them relate to small companies. For instance, in 77 per cent of the 1,215 mergers in 1987, the acquired assets (in book value) were 1 billion yen or less and, in only 50 mergers (4 per cent), were the acquired assets 10 billion yen or more (JFTC 1988). The US data cover all M & As (and buy-outs) involving US companies valued at $1 million or more. Therefore, the coverage of companies is probably larger in the JFTC data. It is more difficult to compare the definition of M & As because acquisitions may mean different activities between the JFTC data and the US data. Among the 1,937 UK M & As, 197 involved acquisition of UK public companies. This appears more comparable to the Yamaichi data, but the majority of the M & As in the Yamaichi data must be those of Japanese listed companies acquiring smaller non-listed companies. Hence, my conjecture is that, though the total number of M & As may be similar in Japan and the UK, the figure becomes much smaller in Japan if we adjust the GNP difference. Furthermore, the number of cases of large companies acquired is definitely smaller in Japan. It is more difficult to compare the number of M & As in Japan and the USA. Again, however, it appears beyond doubt that M & As of large companies are much fewer in Japan. With these qualifications, there is evidence to support Hypothesis 1.

5.3.3. Methods

Let us return to our M & A sample and compare the frequency of the three methods in Table 5.1. Apparently acquisitions (A) are most popular, accounting for more than half of the cases, followed by capital participation (CP). Surprisingly, mergers (M) account for a mere 18 per cent. This preference for looser forms of combination must be, as we anticipated in Hypothesis 4, the result of the acquiring firm's desire to minimize the labour-related friction that is inevitable when two formerly separate organizations have to be integrated. Even though such a form of looser combination must suffer the disadvantages of weaker control and a slower or less reliable information flow, this drawback, it is suggested, is outweighed by the benefits of lessening labour friction in most cases. It may also suggest that the management prefers to maintain organizational flexibility to deal with unpredictable future changes in corporate environment that may force the firm to sell the business unit.

5.3.4. *Types*

We classified the M & As under examination into five categories following the definitions used by the US Federal Trade Commission: horizontal, vertical, product extension, market extension, and other (i.e., pure conglomerate). Some errors may remain in this system of classification because, first, the business composition of the acquired firm could not be fully known in some cases and, second, classification inevitably involved subjective judgement.[3]

Our results are shown in Table 5.2. The proportion of horizontal M & As, 28.8 per cent (70 out of 243), is about equal to the proportion of horizontal mergers, 26 per cent, reported in the JFTC data, again supporting our Hypothesis 3.

The proportion of vertical M & As is even smaller—a mere 7 per cent. This is less than the 15 per cent in the JFTC data, suggesting that the majority of vertical mergers have been by smaller firms (recall that our sample is likely to be biased towards those involving larger firms). The infrequent occurrence of vertical M & As suggests that the efficiency gains from vertical integration (Williamson 1971) were not important. The use of markets augmented by subcontracting networks and quasi-fixed groups of parts suppliers (see Chapter 6) is probably more advantageous to large Japanese firms.

The largest proportion of M & As took place for the purpose of

[3] For instance, should the acquisition by a food-manufacturing company of a pharmaceutical company be classified as product extension or pure conglomerate? To answer this question requires detailed information about the current activities of the acquiring and acquired firms and their proximity in both the technological and the marketing aspects. Such information was rarely available.

TABLE 5.2. Classification by type, method, and objective

Type	Acquirer's Objective ⟨1⟩	⟨2⟩	⟨3⟩	⟨4⟩	⟨5⟩	⟨6⟩	⟨7⟩	⟨8⟩	Subtotal	Total
Horizontal										
M	10		2	3	15				30	
	(1)		(1)	(2)	(10)				(14)	
A	20		1	2	3			5	31	70
	(16)		(1)	(2)	(2)			(5)	(26)	(43)
CP	1		5		1			2	9	
	(0)		(0)		(1)			(2)	(3)	
Vertical										
M		1							1	
		(0)							(0)	
A	7			2			1	1	11	17
	(4)			(0)			(0)	(1)	(5)	(6)
CP	2	1	1	1					5	
	(1)	(0)	(0)	(0)					(1)	
Product Extension										
M		7							7	
		(1)							(1)	
A	5	21	8	12	1		2		49	91
	(5)	(11)	(2)	(5)	(1)		(0)		(24)	(38)
CP	2	2	11	14			6		35	
	(1)	(1)	(6)	(4)			(1)		(13)	
Market Extension										
M	2		2					1	5	
	(1)		(0)					(1)	(2)	
A	6	1	8			11		1	27	41
	(2)	(1)	(4)			(6)		(1)	(14)	(21)
CP	1		2			6			9	
	(0)		(1)			(4)			(5)	

TABLE 5.2. (cont.)

Type	Acquirer's Objective								Subtotal	Total
	⟨1⟩	⟨2⟩	⟨3⟩	⟨4⟩	⟨5⟩	⟨6⟩	⟨7⟩	⟨8⟩		
Pure Conglomerate										
M									0 (0)	
A		12 (3)	3 (1)	1 (0)			1 (1)		17 (5)	24 (5)
CP		3 (0)	1 (0)	1 (0)			2 (0)		7 (0)	
Subtotal										
M	12 (2)	8 (1)	4 (1)	3 (2)	15 (10)	0 (0)	0 (0)	1 (1)	43 (17)	
A	38 (27)	34 (15)	20 (8)	17 (7)	4 (3)	11 (6)	4 (1)	7 (7)	135 (74)	
CP	6 (2)	6 (1)	20 (7)	16 (4)	1 (1)	6 (4)	8 (1)	2 (2)	65 (22)	
TOTAL	56 (31)	48 (17)	44 (16)	36 (13)	20 (14)	17 (10)	12 (2)	10 (10)		243 (113)

Notes: M = Merger, A = Acquisition, CP = Capital Participation.
For the numbering in the acquirer's objective, see the text.
Shown in parentheses are the number of cases in which the acquired firm raised management difficulty as the reason.

product extension. Market-extending M & As were also frequent. In contrast, pure conglomerate M & As account for only 9.9 per cent. Thus, in Japan, diversification by means of M & As is primarily directed at neighbouring fields, and diversification into unrelated industries, as often occurs among conglomerates in the USA and the UK, is still rare. In the USA the proportion of pure conglomerate mergers was 43.8 per cent in 1975 (JFTC 1981), forming a strong contrast with our result. This difference between Japan and the USA indicates an inclination on the part of Japanese management to make the newly acquired business complementary to its main business, thereby ensuring that it contributes to full utilization of existing human and other resources.[4]

5.3.5. *The Objectives of the Acquirers*

The press articles from which we obtained the data list the objectives claimed by the acquiring companies and the reasons for sale announced by the acquired companies in undertaking M & As. Although the truthfulness of these declarations may be open to question, in nearly all cases for which the details were available, the declared objectives appeared to fit the circumstances.

We classified the acquirers' objectives into eight categories. In order of frequency, they are as follows: ⟨1⟩ to increase productive capacity; ⟨2⟩ to diversify; ⟨3⟩ to strengthen marketing capacity; ⟨4⟩ to acquire technology; ⟨5⟩ to restructure the market; ⟨6⟩ to deal with government regulation; ⟨7⟩ to invest in a venture business; and ⟨8⟩ to save the acquired company from bankruptcy. ⟨1⟩ to ⟨4⟩ are self-explanatory. The business community in Japan often talks about the need for 'market restructuring' when, in its view, the production capacity of an industry is excessive and the number of producers must be reduced. Naturally, M & As intended to achieve market restructuring are mostly horizontal within stagnating or declining industries.

The sixth objective is to circumvent regulatory constraints. An example is the case of a trucking company in one geographical

[4] We also note that the percentage of pure conglomerates in the JFTC data was 27%, substantially higher than ours. This leads us to suspect that our criteria for product extension and market extension may have been wider than the criteria adopted by the JFTC. In terms of the Japan–USA ranking, however, the conclusion is unaffected.

area acquiring a trucking company in another area in order to obtain the licence needed to operate in the second area. The seventh, investment in a venture business, is probably a strategy for diversification or technology acquisition but is listed here as a separate objective. The eighth and final category, to save a failing company, is misleading because the true motivation may be something else. For instance, an M & A of this kind may not be undertaken unless the acquirer anticipates making a gain, by buying at an acquisition cost substantially lower than the asset resale value, or through low-interest loans promised by the bank(s) with outstanding loans to the failing company.

Table 5.2 shows that the first objective of expanding productive capacity was cited by the acquiring firms in about a quarter of cases. However, if we combine the three objectives immediately following that, they account for the majority of cases. These diversifying, marketing-oriented, and technology-oriented objectives are all intended to extend managerial resources into unfamiliar fields. We therefore conjecture that M & As are an important means of diversification even in Japan. In contrast, M & As of a defensive nature, as shown in objectives ⟨5⟩ and ⟨8⟩, appear less important.

5.3.6. The Reasons Given by Acquired Firms

The reasons for M & As cited by the acquired firms are less complete and totally unknown in 72 of the 243 cases. Those reasons that are known were classified into three categories. The first, mentioned in 113 cases, is the difficulty of continuing independent operation, for instance, due to suboptimal scale, financial difficulties, or simply bad management. The second (42 cases) is the desire to overcome growth constraints, which means that the firm was doing well but lacked the managerial (human or financial) resources needed to grow further, and thus opted to sell itself. The third (16 cases) is restructuring policy on the part of the former parent company. To save space, Table 5.2 gives only the number of acquired firms that cited the first reason, a defensive one. This reason was given in less than half (46.5 per cent) of the total number of 243 M & As, but in nearly two-thirds (66.1 per cent) of the 171 M & As for which reasons were given, consistent with Hypothesis 2 that Japanese firms are not willing to sell themselves unless their survival is threatened. Furthermore, even the second and third reasons imply that the acquired firms co-operated in the M & As. Hostile M & As have been virtually non-existent in Japan, as predicted in Hypothesis 1.

5.3.7. *Inter-Industry Merger Matrix*

Table 5.3 shows the number of M & As by the two-digit Standard Industrial Classification (SIC) to which the acquirer (raider) belongs and the SIC to which the acquired (victim) belongs. At the bottom is the total number of M & As conducted by the acquirers in each industry, and at the far right is the total number of victims from each industry. The classification was made according to the principal business of each firm.

An apparent concentration is found along the diagonal, suggesting that intra-industry M & As (146 cases or 60.1 per cent) are more popular than inter-industry M & As (97 cases or 39.9 per cent). Interestingly, this latter percentage is very close to what Goudie and Meeks (1982) found for mergers in the UK (38.9 per cent) during 1949–73. In the UK, however, they found an increasing trend of inter-industry mergers (or diversifying mergers, as they called them) with the percentage being 46.6 per cent in the most recent 1969–73 period. Thus, in recent years, preference for diversifying M & As may have been higher among British firms than among Japanese firms.[5]

Table 5.3 reveals that retail firms were most active in acquiring and second most active in being acquired. Most of their M & As were intra-industrial. This is in contrast to the electrical equipment industry. Firms in this industry were second in acquiring and first in being acquired, and yet 41 per cent of them acquired firms in other industries and 59 per cent were acquired by firms in other industries. In particular, M & As among four machinery-related industries—general machinery, electrical equipment, transportation equipment, and precision instruments—are prominent, suggesting technological proximity across these industries. Another industry active in making diversifying M & As is food-manufacturing. There are four M & As of chemical firms and four

[5] OECD (1984) reports that the proportion of inter-industrial mergers was 31.7% in Canada in 1976–7 and 58.2% in the FRG in 1980. Thus the percentage is much higher in Germany than in Japan, the UK, or Canada. However, because industrial classification is finer in the German study, its percentage is probably overstated.

TABLE 5.3. Inter-industry M & A matrix

Victim	Raider 06	09	12	14	16	18	19	20	21	23	25	26	27	28	29	30	31	32	34	40	43	44	45	49	53	61	69	72	Total
06																													0
09		5												1													1		7
12			8																					2					10
14				1															1									1	3
16																			1										1
18						8		1																					9
19			1												1				1										3
20		1	4					10			2													1					18
21									2		1																		3
23		1								1																			2
25		1						2							1														4
26												9																	9
27														1															1
28														4	1														5
29		3				1						4			4	4	2							1	1				20
30								2			5	3			6	14			2					1				1	34
31															1		2												3
32																4	1	4											9
34														2					1										3
40																				11									11
43																					1								1
44																						2							2
45			1																				1			2			4
49	1		1											1	1									9					13
53			1												1				1						27	1			31
61																										12		1	13
69																													0
72			1				1								1	1				3					2	1	4	10	24
Total	1	11	17	1	0	9	1	15	2	1	8	16	0	9	17	23	5	4	7	14	1	2	1	14	30	16	5	13	243

Notes: The industry classification is as follows: 06, mining; 09, construction; 12, food; 14, textile; 16, lumber; 18, paper and pulp; 19, publishing and printing; 20, chemicals; 21, petroleum; 23, rubber products; 25, glass, cement, and ceramics; 26, iron and steel; 27, non-ferrous metals; 28, metal products; 29, machinery; 30, electrical equipments; 31, transportation equipments; 32, precision instruments; 34, other manufacturing; 40, ground transportation; 43, water transportation; 44, flight transportation; 45, warehouse; 49, wholesale; 53, retail; 61, finance; 69, real estate; 72, miscellaneous services.

of firms in distribution, trade, and service. The former are all acquisitions or capital participations of pharmaceutical firms, suggesting that a technological link exists between food-processing (for instance, fermentation) and pharmacology. The latter are all related to marketing strategies.

These tendencies are also found in the UK (Goudie and Meeks 1982, table 1). Though the industrial distribution of raider or victim firms appears somewhat more widespread in the UK, a strict comparison is impossible because of different sample sizes (1,481 in Goudie and Meeks as opposed to 243 in ours).

We now compare Table 5.3 to Table 5.4, which shows the extent of internal diversification efforts in manufacturing industries. In the upper row for each industry is the percentage of sales revenue from each product field made by the industry's ten largest firms. In the lower row is the percentage of R & D expenditure made in each field by the firms in the relevant industry.[6] In both rows, the percentages add up to 100 horizontally. The figures are for 1979, while our M & A data are for 1980–7. Thus, the industrial distribution of sales or R & D in Table 5.4 precedes the M & As examined here.

Not surprisingly, the largest parts of both sales and R & D are directed towards own industries, in a similar way to the dominance of intra-industry M & As in Table 5.3. Comparison of the two tables also suggests that M & As are seldom undertaken into an industry in which no previous R & D effort has been made; that is, the direction in which an industry expands internally and the direction in which it undertakes M & As appear basically the same. Put differently, the choice of where to grow appears to be independent of whether growth is pursued internally or externally. Is this because the firm has to expend on R & D after the M & A to utilize fully the technological resources of the acquired business, or because the firm first attempts to grow internally and then, in the face of resource constraints, decides to acquire external

[6] For sales composition (upper rows in the table), the data are those of the 10 largest firms in the industry except four (SIC codes 16, 19, 23, and 25), for which the data of less than ten firms are used. For R & D composition (lower rows), the data source is *Report on the Survey of Research and Development* (Prime Minister's Office) in which the sample firms are more extensive and not restricted to the ten firms. This difference probably explains why the diversity of R & D across fields is more prominent than that of sales. Also, the definition of fields in the R & D data slightly differs from that of sales.

TABLE 5.4. The proportion of sales and R & D expenditures by field, 1979

Industry	Fields 12	14	16	18	19	20	21	23	25	26	27	28	29	30	31	32	34	Total
12	96.2					2.2											1.6	100
	67.3			*0.2*		*29.1*			*0.2*				*0.8*				*2.3*	*100*
14	0.9	66.3	0.9			26.9											4.9	100
	0.1	*45.2*		*0.4*		*40.4*			*1.9*				*3.4*	*2.5*	*2.3*		*3.8*	*100*
16			86.1														13.9	100
18			10.8	86.1		2.4											0.7	100
		0.1		*81.5*	*1.4*	*14.9*							*0.3*				*1.8*	*100*
19					100.0												0.04	100
	2.5	*0.7*		*0.8*	*74.0*	*4.5*			*0.4*	*0.7*		*0.8*	*6.9*	*2.2*	*1.5*		*5.1*	*100*
20	3.7					84.0			5.4				4.3			0.9	1.8	100
	1.3	*0.4*		*0.1*	*0.1*	*92.7*	*0.2*	*0.4*	*0.5*		*0.2*		*0.2*	*0.9*	*0.2*	*0.8*	*2.1*	*100*
21							99.2										0.8	100
						25.2	*54.3*		*3.3*	*0.1*	*11.0*	*0.1*			*0.1*		*5.9*	*100*
23						8.9		90.0							0.1		0.9	100
		0.1		*0.1*		*4.1*		*85.3*				*0.2*	*0.3*		*9.5*		*0.5*	*100*
25						10.2	4.7		74.7			1.2					9.2	100
	0.1	*0.1*				*24.5*		*0.1*	*57.6*		*0.4*	*0.7*	*5.7*	*3.5*	*0.2*	*0.1*	*7.1*	*100*
26										85.8	1.9	0.7	3.5		0.7		7.3	100
						0.6			*0.1*	*77.5*	*1.4*	*2.9*	*10.6*	*0.9*	*1.8*	*0.1*	*4.2*	*100*

27						1.7		0.3			88.9			0.6			8.6	100
	0.1			*0.7*	*0.2*	*2.7*		*0.9*	*1.2*	*11.1*	*57.8*	*5.1*	*0.5*	*13.6*	*2.0*		*4.3*	*100*
28		0.5				4.0						90.5	2.2			0.3	2.4	100
	0.2					*4.8*		*1.1*	*1.5*	*1.0*	*1.4*	*46.9*	*11.0*	*20.2*	*2.6*	*0.2*	*9.1*	*100*
29						0.9						10.6	82.5	1.4	1.8		2.8	100
	0.1			*0.1*		*1.7*	*0.1*	*0.1*	*0.6*	*1.2*		*2.2*	*75.6*	*9.3*	*5.4*	*2.0*	*0.8*	*100*
30												0.5	2.3	93.3	2.6		1.3	100
						0.8			*0.1*		*0.2*	*0.3*	*5.3*	*89.0*	*2.9*	*1.1*	*0.1*	*100*
31												1.4	18.0		79.4		1.1	100
		0.1				*0.3*			*0.1*	*0.3*		*0.1*	*11.4*	*0.7*	*86.6*	*0.2*	*0.2*	*100*
32												0.5	35.8	6.4		57.2	0.1	100
						1.9			*0.6*		*0.1*	*0.1*	*9.3*	*13.3*	*3.8*	*70.8*	*0.1*	*100*
34													0.6	3.3	2.0		72.3	100
	0.1	*0.3*		*0.4*		*26.8*	*1.3*	*1.2*	*1.1*		*0.4*	*1.2*	*1.7*	*6.0*	*5.1*	*0.9*	*53.4*	*100*
TOTAL	5.1	3.1	1.1	2.6	1.5	6.6	14.9	1.5	2.1	12.4	4.3	2.0	8.0	13.8	16.1	1.0	4.1	100
	2.1	*0.5*		*0.6*	*0.2*	*22.0*	*0.7*	*1.8*	*1.9*	*4.4*	*1.3*	*1.4*	*10.3*	*28.5*	*18.8*	*2.8*	*2.8*	*100*

Notes: Upper rows: composition of sales by field; Lower rows (in italics): composition of R & D expenditures by field.
See table 5.3 for the industrial classification code.
No R & D expenditure was reported in the lumber industry (SIC code 16).

Source: Niida *et al.* (1987), appendix tables 2.1 and 2.3.

resources? Although the time difference between the two data (the R & D data preceding the M & A data) appears favourable to the latter hypothesis, the evidence is hardly sufficient to give a convincing answer to this extremely interesting question.

5.4. ARE MERGERS AND ACQUISITIONS PROFITABLE OR CONTRIBUTING TO GROWTH?

5.4.1. Past Studies

The effects of mergers on performance have been studied by many economists, particularly for American firms. Basically these studies used either of two measures, stock-market evaluation or accounting data. The first methodology calculates the cumulative average residuals (or cumulative abnormal returns), CAR, that the stockholders of the bidding firm or the stockholders of the target firm will gain from the tender offer. Most of these studies suggest that the stockholders of target firms tend to gain from the bid, but those of bidding firms may or may not. For US results, see Jensen and Ruback (1983) and, for a critique, Magenheim and Mueller (1988); for UK results, see Franks and Harris (1989).

The second methodology compares the post-merger performance of acquiring firms with the pre-merger performance. The most frequently used measures of performance are profit rates and growth rates. To eliminate the effects of general business conditions and industrial differences, the changes in performance of acquiring firms are compared with those of matched non-acquiring firms. Some studies use this methodology to infer corporate objectives. For instance, if the merger is found to have increased the size or growth rate of the acquiring firm relative to that of the non-acquiring firm, but decreased the profit rate or the stock return, it is inferred that the merger was undertaken not to maximize stockholder wealth, but to maximize the size or growth rate as suggested by the growth maximization hypothesis: see Mueller (1980) for an international comparison (without Japan) along these lines.

A few studies of Japanese mergers have all used the second methodology. Hoshino (1981) found a significantly lower profit rate for acquiring firms in comparison to non-acquiring firms and an insignificant difference in the rate of sales growth. Ikeda and Doi (1983) found that just a half of the acquiring firms in their sample had improved either their profit rate or their growth rate three years after the merger, relative to matched non-acquiring firms. This proportion of improving acquirers tended to increase when firms were assessed five rather than three years after the merger. Taketoshi (1984) found that mergers improved the growth of the acquiring firms relative to non-acquiring firms, deteriorated the stock returns, and did not affect profitability. Muramatsu (1986), again comparing acquiring firms with matched non-acquiring firms, found that mergers relatively decreased the profit rate without affecting the growth rate.

These results suggest that mergers hardly improved the performance of acquiring companies in Japan. An exception is provided by the results of Ikeda and Doi, which weakly suggest that mergers may have contributed positively in the long run; however, using the same five-year period, neither Taketoshi nor Muramatsu found positive effects (except to the growth rate in Taketoshi's study). In a choice between the value-maximizing (or stockholder welfare-maximizing) hypothesis and the growth-maximizing (or managerial welfare-maximizing) hypothesis, these studies appear to be somewhat more favourable (or less unfavourable, to be more precise) to the latter.

Our complaint about these studies is that they concentrate on mergers, ignoring acquisitions or capital participations. Given the importance of these forms of external corporate growth, as shown above, this is certainly unsatisfactory.

5.4.2. Data and Variables

Let $x_M(t)$ be a performance measure in year t of a firm undertaking an M & A and $x_N(t)$, that of a firm not undertaking an M & A, matched on the basis of size and sales composition. Denote the ratio, $x_M(t)/x_N(t)$, by $X(t)$. Let $t = T$ indicate the year of M & A. If $X(T + a)$ is greater than $X(T - a)$, then we infer that the M & A contributed to an improvement in performance as measured by the x variable.

There is a trade-off in the choice of a. On the one hand, in view of the length of time required to realize the gains from M & A, we wish to take a large a. On the other hand, the larger a the fewer the observations we can obtain of $x_i(T + a)$, i = M or N, because T is quite recent, 1980–7. We decided to use either $a = 2$ or $a = 3$.

The two major variables we want to examine are the profit rate rate on assets and the rate of sales growth. The profit rate is defined as the ratio of profits gross of interest payments and corporate income tax to the book value of total assets. The growth rate (more accurately, the growth factor) is defined as the ratio of one year's sales revenue to that of the previous year. Although a few other variables have also been examined in our preliminary analyses, none of them appeared more suitable or yielded more interesting results. For instance, the profit–sales ratio is less useful, because it need not equalize across industries with different capital intensities; hence, its post-M & A level cannot be compared with the pre-M & A level in a diversifying merger. A similar argument can be made with regard to labour productivity. We therefore confine our analysis to the two variables as defined above.

The sample used in the following analysis consists of 46 pairs of M and N for $a = 2$, and 33 pairs for $a = 3$, after eliminating recent M & As for which $X(T + a)$ has not yet been observed, and the M & As by unlisted companies for which financial data are not available.[7] Because financial data are not consolidated, the contribution of a non-merger M & A can be assessed only through received dividends unless there exist indirect contributions, such as a reduction in material costs associated with an acquisition of a vertical nature. We have no way of knowing the extent of the bias caused by this use of unconsolidated data other than to conjecture that it is probably downward.

5.4.3. The Results

In Table 5.5, the effects of M & A are investigated in two ways. First, is $X(T + a)$ greater or less than $X(T - a)$ in terms of the average for the whole sample? Second, did more firms find that their performance had improved than that it had worsened?

To get the results, abnormal values, caused mostly by negative or near-zero profit rates, had to be eliminated. The table contains two sets of results. In part A, the abnormal values were eliminated only from calculating the mean of the relevant variable at the relevant time point. In part B, all firms with one or more ab-

[7] For firms undertaking two or more M & As during the sample period, we set T to be the year of the first M & A, because the later the M & A the less often are the data for $T + 3$ available.

TABLE 5.5. Relative performance of M & A-conducting firms before and after the M & As

	Profit rate	N	Growth rate	N
A: By separate sample				
(1) Mean of $X(T-3)$	1.145 (2.33)[b]	31	1.035 (1.59)	33
(2) Mean of $X(T-2)$	1.144 (2.71)[a]	43	1.003 (0.18)	46
(3) Mean of $X(T+2)$	1.067 (1.38)	41	1.005 (0.46)	46
(4) Mean of $X(T+3)$	1.102 (1.62)	29	0.998(−0.23)	33
(3) − (2)	−0.076(−1.06)		0.002 (0.11)	
(4) − (1)	−0.043(−0.49)		−0.037(−1.53)	
No. of cases: (3) > (2)	24 (53.3%)		21 (45.7%)	
(3) < (2)	21 (46.7%)		25 (54.3%)	
No. of cases: (4) > (1)	13 (40.6%)		12 (36.4%)	
(4) < (1)	19 (59.4%)		21 (63.6%)	
B: By common sample				
(1) Mean of $X(T-3)$	1.151 (2.44)[b]	26	1.019 (1.17)	26
(2) Mean of $X(T-2)$	1.128 (1.83)[c]	26	0.986(−0.63)	26
(3) Mean of $X(T+2)$	1.135 (2.01)[c]	26	1.006 (0.48)	26
(4) Mean of $X(T+3)$	1.110 (1.70)	26	1.001 (0.09)	26
(3) − (2)	0.007 (0.07)		0.020 (0.79)	
(4) − (1)	−0.041(−0.46)		−0.018(−0.88)	
No. of cases: (3) > (2)	16 (61.5%)		12 (46.2%)	
(3) < (2)	10 (38.5%)		14 (53.8%)	
No. of cases: (4) > (1)	10 (38.5%)		10 (38.5%)	
(4) < (1)	16 (61.5%)		16 (61.5%)	

Notes: In parentheses are the following: for (1), (2), (3), or (4); *t*-values to the hypothesis that the mean equals one; for (3) − (2) or (4) − (1); *t*-values to the hypothesis that the difference equals zero; for the number of cases; percentages to the whole sample.

[a], [b], and [c], respectively, indicate significance at 1, 5, and 10% levels two-tailed. *N* denotes the sample size.

normal value(s) were eliminated from calculating the mean of every variable in every time period, so that we can compare the means calculated from a common sample.

The results indicate a lack of any significant change caused by M & A. The profit rate decreased after M & A for either $a = 3$ or $a = 2$ (except the near zero value of $X(T+2) - X(T-2)$ in the common sample), but not significantly. The growth rate is also found to have insignificantly decreased over a longer period.

A comparison of the number of successful cases (those in which performance relatively improved after M & A) with the number of unsuccessful cases also fails to yield a clear tendency. At two years after M & A more firms found their relative profit rate to have increased compared to two years before the M & A, but that the relative growth rate had decreased. At three years after M & A, by contrast, more firms found their relative profit rate as well as the growth rate to have decreased compared to three years before M & A. This reversal of the result is due to the relatively good performance of acquiring firms at three years before M & A, as shown in the means of $X(T-3)$.

We can also compare $X(T+3)$ to $X(T+2)$ to inquire if the performance of firms undertaking M & As improves as the period of time since the M & A increases. Such an improvement is nowhere found except for the profit rate in the separate sample.

This absence of gains from M & A agrees with the previous Japanese findings discussed above. Only Ikeda and Doi found some positive results, particularly in relation to a five-year period after merger. Although the recent occurrence of M & As in our sample does not allow us to test their hypothesis of the lagged effects of mergers, the result of our comparing $X(T+3)$ to $X(T+2)$ appears rather unfavourable.

5.5. WHICH MERGERS AND ACQUISITIONS ARE MORE SUCCESSFUL?

To examine which M & As are doing better than the others, we regressed the change in profit rate or growth rate on a number of variables. The dependent variable is $[X(T+2)-X(T-2)]/X(T-2)$ where $X(T+a)$ is as defined in Section 5.4.2. No analysis is made for $a=3$ because the sample is smaller. Because the firms with abnormal values were eliminated, sample size differs across the regression equations. For explanatory variables, we started with several combinations of dummy variables in addition to the change in sales volume. This last variable, denoted by GSIZE, was included to capture the size effect. Since the dependent variable is the rate of change, GSIZE is the rate of change as well, namely, the rate of change in sales from $T-2$ to $T+2$.

One dummy variable, MANUF, was always included, which takes the value of one, if and only if the firm undertaking M & A belonged to one of the manufacturing industries. Additionally, we

TABLE 5.6. Determinants of M & A performance

Independent variables	Dependent variables			
	Profit rate change		Growth rate change	
	(1)	(2)	(3)	(4)
Constant	0.06	0.18	−0.03	−0.00
	(0.39)	(1.06)	(−0.33)	(−0.02)
GSIZE	−0.13	−0.09	−0.06	−0.05
	(−1.22)	(−0.75)	(−1.02)	(−0.88)
MANUF	−0.30[c]	−0.18	0.02	0.04
	(−1.99)	(−1.01)	(0.26)	(0.51)
PROEXT	0.32[a]		0.07	
	(3.27)		(1.33)	
HORIZ		−0.27[c]		−0.03
		(−1.76)		(−0.34)
MARKET	0.10	0.04	0.15[b]	0.15[c]
	(0.77)	(0.24)	(2.16)	(1.93)
$\bar{R}^2$	0.332	0.102	0.128	0.053
N	44	44	46	46

Notes: *t*-values in parentheses.

[a], [b], and [c], respectively, indicate significance at 1, 5, and 10% levels.
N denotes the sample size.

tried several dummies concerning the method, type, and acquirer's stated objective. None of the dummy variables for the method—merger, acquisition, or capital participation—produced a significant result, which may suggest that the contribution of acquisitions and capital participations is not seriously understated despite our use of unconsolidated data.

Consequently, we settled with the equations shown in Table 5.6. The variables, apart from GSIZE and MANUF, are defined as follows:

PROEXT = 1 if and only if the M & A is classified as product extension
HORIZ = 1 if and only if the M & A is classified as horizontal
MARKET = 1 if and only if the stated objective of the acquirer is to strengthen its marketing capacity

An interesting contrast is apparent from the table: M & As into different but related markets and M & As with the purpose of strengthening marketing capacity have performed better than other M & As in terms of both profitability and growth; yet, the former (PROEXT) significantly increased only profitability while the latter (MARKET) significantly increased only growth. This suggests that a lack of marketing resources has been the most serious impediment to growth, and the acquisition of such resources has tended effectively to overcome this impediment. On the other hand, if the firm wants to improve profitability through M & A, it should aim to extend its product line.

Horizontal M & As, on the contrary, were doing poorly, particularly in terms of profitability, that is, they tended to have worsened the profitability of firms undertaking M & As relative to that of firms not doing so. Since, as we will see in the next section, many of the horizontal M & As took place within declining industries, this casts doubts on the argument that horizontal M & As should be encouraged in declining industries to increase their efficiency.

M & As conducted by manufacturing firms are resulting in a poorer change in profitability than those undertaken by non-manufacturing firms. The effect of size on profit or growth is negative but insignificant.

5.6. WHAT FIRMS ARE UNDERTAKING MERGERS AND ACQUISITIONS?

5.6.1. Performance of Firms Undertaking Mergers and Acquisition.

The variables $X(T-3)$ and $X(T-2)$ for profit rate are, on average, significantly greater than one (see Table 5.5), implying that firms conducting M & As were usually more profitable before the M & As than matched firms not conducting M & As. Also, in twenty-four of the forty-five pairs, the firms conducting M & As were enjoying higher profit rates than the matched firms at two years before the M & As. By contrast, there was no indication that the two groups of firms differed in growth rates. Probably, therefore, it is not that firms performing poorly are seeking to get out of the crisis through M & A, but rather that profitable firms are seeking to obtain external resources to grow further. Industrial differences need to be discussed in this regard, however.

5.6.2. *Mergers and Acquisitions in Growing as Opposed to Declining Industries*

For each manufacturing industry defined on the basis of four-digit SIC, the rate of growth of shipments was calculated for the period 1981–5. This rate was compared with the rate for total manufacturing to determine whether the industry is in a state of relative growth or decline. We then assigned each of sixty-seven firms conducting M & As (listed firms only) into four-digit industries according to its major product. Eliminating three firms belonging to industries of average growth, we summarize the results in Table 5.7.

Thirty-one firms that undertook forty-eight M & As were in growing industries, and thirty-three that undertook forty-nine M & As were in declining industries. There are a few interesting differences between the two groups. First, acquisitions are the most popular method in both groups, with the proportion of mergers slightly higher in declining industries. Second, horizontal M & As account for about 10 per cent in growing industries, but 40 per cent in declining industries. Third, firms in declining industries cited market restructuring and prevention of bankruptcy in the acquired company as the objective of the M & As more often than firms in growing industries. Fourth, difficulty of survival was quoted as the reason for being acquired more often when the acquirer was in a declining industry. Finally, about 60 per cent of the M & As by declining industries were intra-industrial, whereas about the same proportion of M & As in growing industries were inter-industrial.

Roughly speaking, these results indicate that many M & As by firms in declining industries were of a defensive nature. They were intra-industrial and horizontal, and undertaken in order to reduce excess production capacity under declining demand or to save the acquired firm from going bankrupt. By contrast, many of the M & As by firms in growing industries are more positive and strategic, aiming to diversify into fields that are different from current main operations, but related in terms of production, technology, or market. We infer that on the whole M & As by

TABLE 5.7. M & A-conducting firms classified by growing or declining industries

	Growing industry	Declining industry
Total number of acquiring firms	31	33
Total cases of M & A	48 (100%)	49 (100%)
Method		
Mergers	5 (10.4%)	7 (14.3%)
Acquisitions	29 (60.4%)	31 (63.3%)
Capital participation	14 (29.2%)	11 (22.4%)
Type		
Horizontal	5 (10.4%)	19 (38.8%)
Vertical	5 (10.4%)	2 (4.1%)
Product extension	31 (64.6%)	20 (40.8%)
Market extension	0 (0.0%)	4 (8.2%)
Pure conglomerate	7 (14.6%)	4 (8.2%)
Acquirer's objective		
Increasing productive capacity	12 (25.0%)	12 (24.5%)
Diversification	17 (35.4%)	5 (10.2%)
Strengthening marketing capacity	5 (10.4%)	6 (12.2%)
Technology acquisition	10 (20.8%)	10 (20.4%)
Market restructuring	0 (0.0%)	5 (10.2%)
Dealing with regulation	0 (0.0%)	0 (0.0%)
Investing in venture business	3 (6.3%)	6 (12.2%)
Preventing victim's bankruptcy	1 (2.1%)	5 (10.2%)
Reasons cited by the acquired		
Difficulty in survival	21 (43.8%)	27 (55.1%)
Others or unknown	27 (56.2%)	22 (44.9%)
Two-digit SIC of the acquirer and the acquired		
Same	18 (37.5%)	29 (59.2%)
Different	30 (62.5%)	20 (40.8%)

firms in growing industries have resulted in entry into other (mostly related) markets, while those in declining industries fostered exits from the markets.

Another possibility is that M & As in declining industries are related to the adjustment policy of the Japanese government, because the policy may have created a co-operative atmosphere in the designated 'depressed' industries. We found that seventeen

M & As involved firms in these designated industries.[8] How many mergers were fostered by the policy is not known. The adjustment policy will be discussed again in Chapter 11.

5.7. CONCLUSION

Let us first briefly summarize the results of our inquiry into 243 cases of M & A—merger, acquisition, and capital participation—between Japanese firms from 1980 to 1987. (1) There is some tendency towards an increase in M & A, though the time period over which our analysis has been conducted is too short to make any confident prediction. (2) More than half of the M & As were classified as product or market extensions, and in more than half of cases the acquiring firms described their objectives as diversification, strengthening of marketing capacity, or technology acquisition, suggesting the use of M & As as a means of diversification in many cases. (3) By contrast, those M & As undertaken for defensive purposes were basically horizontal, made by firms in declining industries, and aimed at restructuring markets and/or saving the victims from management crisis. (4) The effects of M & As on the profitability or growth of the firm conducting them were ambiguous. (5) Horizontal M & As, many of which are defensive, did particularly poorly. (6) Product-extending M & As seem to have made a relative contribution to profitability, whereas market-oriented M & As have made a relative contribution to growth.

Are there peculiarities in the M & As in Japan as compared to those in other countries? We emphasized at the beginning of this chapter that human factors, such as labour practices and worker attitudes, must be taken into account, in order to understand M & A activity in Japanese companies. The results very much support this view.

First, as predicted by Hypothesis 4, the majority of cases are

[8] By industry, these 17 M & As were as follows: paper, liner-board, and corrugated paper, 8; electric furnace, 6; compound fertilizer, 1; aluminium smelting, 1; and ship-building, 1. In terms of method, 4 were mergers and 13 acquisitions. All were horizontal except two vertical M & As. Twelve firms undertook these 17 M & As, of which 7 firms (making 12 M & As) belonged to declining industries as defined above. Thus, of the 21 horizontal or vertical M & As by firms in declining industries (see Table 5.7) more than half might have been under the influence of the policy.

acquisitions and capital participation rather than mergers, suggesting a preference of Japanese management for looser forms of combination rather than complete integration. In other words, the costs and difficulty of integrating two previously separate corporate organizations after a merger must have outweighed the gains from internal reallocation of resources that can be attained only under a tighter form of integration.

Second, as predicted by Hypothesis 2, two-thirds of the target firms cited 'difficulty in survival' as the reason for being acquired. Apparently, only one-third would have accepted the M & A were it not for a management crisis, suggesting strong feelings among management and employees against being acquired. Again, this tendency can be fully appreciated only when the deep concern of Japanese management for employee satisfaction is understood.

Third, as predicted by Hypothesis 3, horizontal M & As are less frequent than in other countries (except the USA where the antitrust restriction on horizontal mergers was vigorous), presumably because a priority is placed on the use of internal resources when expanding horizontally. Furthermore, although more and more Japanese firms are now using M & As as a means of diversification, most of the diversifying M & As are directed towards fields with a close production, technology, or marketing link, and towards fields in which acquirers are also making internal efforts to expand, such as research and development. It is thus suggested that M & As are complementary to internal growth efforts or the M & As are made when internal growth efforts are hampered by internal resource constraints. This again supports our view that Japanese management is most concerned to achieve a full use of its resources, human resources in particular, to minimize the necessity of worker redundancy, and, with expansion, to increase the promotion prospects of employees. It appears quite unlikely that in the near future Japanese companies will start acting like American conglomerates, diversifying into numerous unrelated fields with little internal growth effort and with tender offers used as the main strategic weapon.

As regards managerial objectives, we have suggested in Part I that Japanese management is most concerned for the survival of the company in order to provide job security to its employees, and will pursue growth to provide promotion opportunities. The profitability or the value of the firm may constrain managerial decisions, but only as a minimum requirement. As predicted by this view, the study in this chapter gave no support to the hypothesis that M & As were made primarily to increase efficiency and enrich the stockholders. Although there is no precise support for the view that M & As have been made to foster the growth of the acquiring company (except for the specific increase in the company size immediately caused by the M & A), the indication that diversifying M & As are made in association with internal diversification efforts is consistent with the view that Japanese management is keen on diversification to attain growth. In some cases, particularly in declining industries, M & As are claimed to have been undertaken to save the acquired firms from bankruptcy and their employees from unemployment. In view of the motivation in Japanese companies, such considerations of employee welfare must have played an important role.

More and more Japanese firms will use M & As as a part of their growth strategy, particularly as changes in industrial structure are expected to accelerate in the future. Yet, distinctive differences will remain, both quantitative and qualitative, between the M & A strategy adopted by Japanese firms and that of American and British firms.

6

Divisional Form, Hive-off, and Manufacturer–Supplier Relations

6.1. INTRODUCTION

Firms organize their activities in a variety of ways. Probably the most popular distinction is between a functional structure and a divisional structure. Under a functional structure, an organization is partitioned according to business function, such as production, sales, finance, personnel, and research. Essentially, all the firm's products are produced in the production department and sold to any market by the sales department. This is also called the unitary form (U-form). Under a divisional structure, also called the multi-divisional form (M-form), an organization is partitioned primarily according to products and/or regional markets. Each division has its own production facilities, sales force, and research department and deals with its own accounting and personnel questions. It is quasi-autonomous and is solely responsible for its own operation unless that affects the other divisions. It is controlled by the top management in the general office who allocate financial resources and appoint divisional heads. Between these two totally different forms of organization there are intermediate ones, for instance, divisional separation for production with central control of personnel.

Choice of organizational form is inseparable from the question of how financial and human resources are organized within the firm, and how much the firm intends to decentralize decisions. In this regard, Williamson's (1970) argument concerning the implication of the M-form for the corporate behavioural rule is worth noting. He argued that control loss is reduced and internal efficiency is enhanced under the M-form, because of efficient and effective control by the general office. He likened this control to the capital market control of management, calling the M-form structure 'a miniature capital market', and argued that the general office is more efficient than the capital market for three reasons.

> First, it is an internal rather than external control mechanism with the constitutional authority, expertise and low-cost access to the requisite data which permit it to make detailed, contemporaneous evaluations of the performance of each of its operating parts. Second, it can make fine-tuning as well as discrete adjustments. Taken together, these permit the general office to intervene early in a selective, preventative way—a capability which is lacking in external control mechanisms in general and the capital market in particular . . . Finally, the costs of intervention by the general office are relatively low (Williamson 1970, 139–40).

The informational advantages and easier control within an M-form organization, he argued, lead to more internal efficiency than is observable in a U-form organization. Managerial discretional behaviour is more easily monitored and punished in an M-form organization, and this monitoring together with the more active take-over activities of M-form conglomerates results in the prevalence of neoclassical profit maximization.

We will see in this chapter that the M-form structure has its disadvantages, and that the relative dynamic efficiency of Japanese management may in fact be related to the fact that adoption of the M-form has been less widespread and less complete, quite contrary to Williamson's thesis.

Another organizational decision concerns the choice between putting all activities within a single legal 'company' or establishing subsidiaries for some or most activities. Although this may appear to be no more than a legal question without any substantial impact on the reality of corporate decisions, we will suggest that the distinction between parent companies and subsidiaries is an important one for Japanese management. Again, this importance is inseparable from the properties of the internal labour system in Japanese management.

The third organizational question pertains to the degree of vertical integration. Should the firm vertically integrate by producing materials and components internally? Should it rather purchase them from other firms? If it elects to purchase, should it purchase in spot markets or from more stable relations with suppliers? It is well known that Japanese firms, notably automobile assemblers, are less vertically integrated than their American rivals, and that the relations between Japanese assemblers and their suppliers are close and stable. Two questions immediately present themselves: what are the merits of such stable relations, and do they imply a lack of competition or the inefficiency of the competitive mechanism? These are also the questions we seek to approach in this chapter.

When the firm establishes subsidiaries, when it acquires other firms, and when it maintains a close relation with its suppliers and/or subcontractors, a group is created. Such a group, called a '*keiretsu*' in Japanese, is more or less part of a hierarchy, with the parent firm or the assembler maintaining a certain degree of control or influence over the entire group. In this regard it substantially differs from a loose grouping of independent firms, called a '*kigyo-shudan*', which is the topic of the next chapter.

The purpose of this chapter is to discuss such diverse internal or inter-firm relations as are frequently found in Japanese management. The question of functional versus divisional forms (U- versus M-forms) is discussed in Section 6.2. The question of hive-off, that is, the establishment of subsidiaries, is dealt with in Section 6.3, the question of supplier–assembler relations in Section 6.4, and the *keiretsu* in Section 6.5. Section 6.6 contains a summary of the points made.

6.2. THE FUNCTIONAL AS OPPOSED TO THE DIVISIONAL FORM

Table 6.1 presents an international comparison of the distribution of firms over four organizational categories. The definition for each category is as follows:[1] a 'functional' organization is one in which the major subunits are defined in terms of the business functions of stages in the manufacturing process, for instance, sales, manufacturing, research, and finance. A 'divisional' organization is one which is split into a number of quasi-autonomous divisions, each headed by a general manager and supplied with the resources necessary for it to operate as an independent economic entity. Each division may consist of a central office and a group of operating subdivisions, and is responsible for engineering,

[1] This definition is taken from Rumelt (1974). All the other studies follow this definition.

TABLE 6.1. Functional form as opposed to divisional form: Trend in Japan and international comparison

Country	Year	Sample size	%			
			Functional	Mixed	Divisional	Holding company
Japan	1963	118	55.9	15.3	28.8	0.0
	1968	118	45.8	20.3	33.9	0.0
	1973	118	40.7	17.8	41.5	0.0
	1967	102	53.0	7.0	40.0	0.0
	1976	102	45.0	11.0	43.0	0.0
	1980	102	42.0	13.0	44.0	0.0
USA	1969	183	11.2	9.4	77.0	2.4
UK	1970	96	8.3	0.0	70.8	20.8
Germany	1970	100	20.0	18.0	50.0	12.0
France	1970	100	14.0	20.0	54.0	12.0
Italy	1970	100	36.0	0.0	48.0	16.0

Source: Same as Table 4.3 except Japan 1967, 1976, 1980: Kono (1984).

producing, and marketing a product or set of products (possibly in a specific geographic area). A 'mixed' organization is a combination of these two. It is basically functional but has one or more separate product divisions which report to top management or, in some instances, to one of the functional managers. In a 'holding company' structure, a set of virtually independent firms are owned and controlled by a holding company.

The Antimonopoly Law stipulates that 'any company shall not operate as a holding company in Japan', where a holding company is defined as a company 'whose principal business is to control the business activities of a company or companies in Japan by means of holding stock'.[2] Therefore, although many Japanese companies own a number of subsidiaries, as will be observed later in this chapter, none of them is a holding company because the principal business is not to control the subsidiaries but is some form of real economic activity, such as manufacturing and retailing. This fact explains why in Table 6.1 no holding-company structure is observed in Japan.

There is a difference between the two Japanese studies of this subject. Yoshihara *et al.* (1981) seems to have classified more companies into the 'mixed' category than Kono (1984). Yet they agree in two observations. One is the increasing trend, albeit a slow one, in the divisional form in Japan, which has been observed in other countries too (see Rumelt 1974, for the American trend). The other is that a clearly smaller proportion of Japanese companies adopt the divisional form. Specifically, while this proportion (including holding companies) was 80 per cent in the USA and 90 per cent in the UK in 1969–70, it was only 44 per cent in Japan even in 1980. In contrast, the proportion of firms adopting the functional form is still more than 40 per cent in Japan but less than 20 per cent elsewhere, except Italy.

The findings that emerge from an international comparison are similar to those regarding diversification. As we found in Section 4.4, the proportion of firms diversifying into related or unrelated product fields is increasing in Japan but still smaller than in other countries. Here we find that the proportion of firms adopting the divisional form is increasing but still smaller in Japan. These two

[2] This prohibition has been enacted to prevent the resurrection of pre-war *zaibatsu*. See Chap. 7.

tendencies are related because, as the firm diversifies, the advantages of integrating, say, manufacturing of all the products into a single functional unit diminish, and instead the advantages of giving autonomy to each product division increase. In the jargon of economics, production economies of scale become less relevant and managerial diseconomies of scale start to prevail as the firm diversifies and expands.

We also note that the international difference in organizational form is more prominent than the difference in diversification. A comparison between Japan in 1973 and the USA in 1969, for instance, reveals that the proportion of firms adopting a divisional form (and holding companies) was 42 per cent in the former as against 79 per cent in the latter, while the proportion of (related and unrelated) diversification was 47 per cent as against 65 per cent. It therefore seems that the lower popularity of the divisional form in Japan cannot be entirely attributed to any difference in the extent of diversification.

Another explanation may be given in terms of the different means used to attain diversification. As shown in the previous chapter, mergers and acquisitions are less frequent in Japan than in the USA or the UK, and internal expansion is preferred. Thus, while keeping an acquired business in a separate division may be a natural solution, divisional separation between internally created businesses can be damaging, because the firm will fail to take advantage of the interaction and homogeneity between them. For instance, under internal expansion, the people in different production units all come from the same background, unlike those acquired through mergers and acquisitions, and encouraging interaction between them should help the firm's dynamic development, as suggested in Section 4.5.

Indeed, we believe that such management of human resources is essential to an understanding of Japanese reluctance to adopt a divisional form. A finding by Kagono *et al.* (1985) is quite suggestive in this regard. Table 6.2 shows the percentages of firms adopting a divisional form in general and for each function. For corporation-wide division, the percentage is 94 per cent in the US against 60 per cent in Japan, a difference corresponding to that in Table 6.1, though both percentages are higher in this study. As for the percentages by function, those directly related to production and marketing are more frequently divisionalized in both

TABLE 6.2. % of firms adopting divisional control system by function, 1980

	USA	Japan
Adoption of Divisional Form	94.4	59.8
Function		
Production	96.7	85.5
Sales	94.8	91.5
Marketing Planning	89.6	82.6
Personnel	84.4	35.5
Control	82.0	40.1
Finance	38.4	12.2
Basic Research	19.9	28.5
Applied Research and Development	62.1	75.6
Purchasing	77.3	52.4

Note: Sample size is 227 (USA), 291 (Japan).

Source: Kagono *et al.* (1985).

countries, whereas the functions spanning products and markets, such as finance and control, are infrequently divisionalized, and this tendency is stronger in Japan. The most obvious difference can be seen in regard to divisionalization of personnel management; 84 per cent of the US companies against 36 per cent of Japanese companies.

It appears therefore, that Japanese firms are not simply less willing to adopt a divisional form in general, they are also more concerned to maintain the allocation of personnel at company-wide management levels. In other words, cross-divisional mobility of workers is considered more important in Japanese firms than in American or British firms. To see why, we should recall the discussion on the internal labour system in Japan. Its salient features, as we found, are lifetime employment as a norm (and the mechanism of employment adjustment to support it), depth and breadth in skill formation, and internal competition. Take lifetime employment, for example. One of the reasons the firm diversifies is that the effect of business fluctuation can be spread among products. In other words, unless demand fluctuations are perfectly correlated among products, and particularly if they are negatively correlated, the loss of demand for one product is partly compensated for by the gain in demand for another. Hence, even if demand for labour decreases in one section, a diversified firm has a greater chance of avoiding lay-off by transferring the now redundant workers to other less adversely affected sections. Such transfers, needless to say, are easier when personnel management is centralized. This forms a contrast to the USA, where lay-offs are more readily implemented, because the contracting division will immediately lay off its workers while other divisions within the same firm may be hiring workers at the same time. This lack of inter-divisional labour mobility makes sense in the USA, where training is more job-specific than firm-specific, and therefore the firm does not provide training for anything not directly related to the job. By contrast, if, as in Japan, training is more firm-specific and provided within the firm, it is less costly to transfer a worker from a redundant job to a vacant job than to hire a new person to fill the vacant post and train him.[3] Thus, company-wide utilization of human resources is of the utmost importance to Japanese management and the adoption of a divisional form is likely to hamper such utilization. We have also emphasized the importance of the breadth of skill attained by means of transfer from job to job and division to division. Breadth of skill is valuable not only *per se* but also because it affects internal competition by enlarging the pool of candidates for promotion. This offers another explanation of why the divisional form, particularly the divisionalization of human management, is less appealing to Japanese management.

Put differently, the lack of divisional separation fosters human interaction across the entire corporate organization. An idea generated by a section or department can be more quickly diffused to others, and more easily combined with ideas from others. The favourable effect this has on innovation has been already noted (see Section 4.5). An argument can be made, admittedly an exaggerated one, that however much the divisional form may contribute to static efficiency, it may create unfavourable conditions for dynamic efficiency. Clearly, Williamson's thesis, mentioned earlier, lacks this viewpoint.

There is another reason why the divisional form can impair

[3] The difference between the USA and Japan here is exaggerated since, as we emphasized in Chap. 3, it is not absolute but one of degree.

dynamic efficiency: namely, an emphasis on short-term financial returns from each division. As Williamson argued, the performance of each division is monitored by the general office, and measures are taken to encourage improvements in divisional performance (as monitored by the general office) or to remove any manager whose performance the general office regards as unsatisfactory. Not surprisingly, therefore, as shown by Kagono *et al.* (1985), the relationship between divisional performance and financial remuneration of managers is significantly stronger in the USA than in Japan. And it is quite likely that evaluation is biased towards an assessment of financial performance, because of its quantitative nature. This bias may be less serious than that of the capital market because the general office has better access to information than the shareholders, as argued by Williamson; yet, taken together with the fact that more members of American and British top management come from financial backgrounds than their Japanese counterparts (see Section 2.5), it appears very likely that the management of an American or British divisionalized firm will emphasize short-term financial returns over long-term returns through innovation and real investment (as opposed to financial investment). That the 'success' of Japanese management (if it should be called a success) has been attained against a background of reluctance to adopt the divisional form and with a bias toward growth maximization (as opposed to 'profit maximization') is a clear antithesis to Williamson's hypothesis.

6.3. HIVE-OFF

An organizational strategy that has been gaining more popularity in Japan recently is '*bun-sha-ka*', literally translatable as to divide (bun*katsu*) companies (*kai*sha). As the firm expands, managerial diseconomies of scale become serious, owing to limitations in the capacity of top management to co-ordinate and supervise, a loss of control and information through layers of hierarchy, and loss of morale among staff as the organization becomes gigantic and bureaucratic attitudes prevail. If a divisional structure, a popular solution in the West, is not similarly popular in Japan, what can Japanese management do to avoid these diseconomies? One answer is to create subsidiaries and transfer some activities to them, or *bun-sha-ka*, which we shall call hive-off in the following.

There are several steps in hive-off. In the first step, the change may be merely legal and superficial, that is, from a section within a big company to a legally separate company, with the entire share held by the parent company and nearly all the staff maintained as before.[4] As the subsidiary expands, it starts hiring its own employees and often seeks to enlarge its financial basis by inviting other parties (other companies or the public) to invest in its shares. In some cases, this process continues up to the point at which the staff transferred from the parent company are in a minority or non-existent, the parent's share of ownership becomes less than half, and the management is chosen by internal promotion from among its own people. There are even cases where the subsidiary becomes totally independent of the parent firm due to the latter's restructuring policy, and other cases of the subsidiary expanding rapidly to dominate the former parent. Toyota Motor, hived off from Toyota Automatic Loom in 1937, is a typical example of the latter. Toyota Automatic Loom still owns a share of Toyota Motor, but only 4.3 per cent, and it is only the third largest shareholder. Conversely, Toyota Motor, whose sales are nearly twenty times larger, owns 25 per cent of shares in Toyota Automatic Loom, and is the largest and the dominant shareholder.

In Table 6.3 three indices were taken to measure the extent of hive-off: the number of consolidated subsidiaries; the ratio of sales in consolidated statements (that is, for the parent plus the subsidiaries) to those in unconsolidated statements (that is, for the parent company only); and a similar ratio for profit, as averages over 129 firms, the largest in the entire manufacturing and construction industries or in individual two-digit industries. Because of the incompleteness of consolidated statements in Japan, the figures are probably underestimated, making it difficult to say whether they are large or small. In terms of trend, however, all three figures increased over the years, indicating that more and more firms are adopting hive-off as an organizational strategy.

The table also indicates distribution across four categories defined in the same way as those used to investigate diversification

[4] Throughout this chapter, the word 'company' is always used to refer to a business unit (be it a stock company or not) that is legally recognized as a separate 'company'. Each subsidiary is a 'company', therefore. The word 'firm' may be used in this sense or loosely to indicate a business unit (a 'company' or more than two of them) under a single decision-making body.

TABLE 6.3. The trend and type of hive-off

	1978	1981	1984
Number of consolidated subsidiaries	13.12	14.74	17.64
Consolidated/unconsolidated ratio: sales	1.22	1.28	1.32
Consolidated/unconsolidated ratio: profit	1.26	1.28	1.54
Type (%)			
Single	25.6	24.8	21.7
Dominant	17.1	19.4	14.7
Related	32.6	33.3	38.0
Unrelated	24.8	22.5	25.6

Note: Number of sample is 129.

Source: Suzuki (1987).

(see Table 4.3). The main business of each subsidiary was classified according to one of three types: (1) same (in the same three-digit SIC), (2) related (in the same two-digit SIC but not in the same three-digit SIC), and (3) unrelated (not in the same two-digit SIC) to the main business of the parent company. Then the proportion of the parent company's investment in subsidiaries of the 'same' type was calculated as the specialization ratio (SR); the proportion in 'related' subsidiaries as the related ratio (RR); and the proportion in 'unrelated', as the unrelated ratio (NR). A consolidated group is classified as 'single' if $SR \geqslant 0.9$; 'dominant' if $0.9 > SR \geqslant 0.7$; 'related' if $SR < 0.7$ and $RR \geqslant NR$; and 'unrelated' if $SR < 0.7$ and $RR < NR$.

The percentages in Table 6.3 therefore indicate the degree of diversification outside the parent companies, while the percentages shown earlier in Table 4.3 indicate diversification within the parent companies. A comparison of the two tables suggests an interesting pattern: subsidiaries have higher proportions in the 'single' and the 'unrelated', namely, the two polar categories. In 1984, for instance, 22 per cent of firms were using their subsidiaries mainly for the same businesses as those being conducted by the parents, and 16 per cent had parents classified as a 'single' business. Also, 26 per cent used their subsidiaries mainly to diversify into 'unrelated' fields, while only 12 per cent of the parent companies themselves were classified as 'unrelated' diversification. Although the comparison is not strict because of the differences between the two measures,[5] one message appears clear: subsidiaries are more often used to expand within the same industry or into unrelated industries. This observation, which we shall examine shortly, is consistent with our view of why Japanese management prefers hive-off to the M-form.

Some subsidiaries are under control of the parent companies in almost every aspect of their business and may appear very little different in substance from sections within the parent company. So what are the advantages of organizing them as separate companies?

One obvious advantage is economic. The wage system in Japan is company-specific rather than job-specific; that is, a person's wage is more comparable to the wages of his fellow workers in the same company in a different job than to somebody doing the same job in a different company (particularly a company of a different size), given that age, years of service, education, and ability are similar. Together with the fact that wages are higher in larger firms,[6] this suggests that hiring a worker in a smaller subsidiary costs less than hiring the same person in a parent company. Of course, from the worker's viewpoint, a job in the subsidiary is less attractive not only because of the lower pay but also because of lower job security and lower social status. Thus first-class job-seekers will apply to larger companies and the subsidiary will be able to attract only second-rate workers. It is therefore sensible to transfer the job to a subsidiary only if it does not require a worker of higher quality. A plant requiring mostly simple jobs might more efficiently be hived off as a separate company on these grounds. Another argument for transferring the job to a separate company may occur when, even with the lower wages, the firm can attract job applicants for geographical reasons. Thus, a plant that can be built in a low-wage labour-surplus area is a natural candidate for hive-off.

A typical example of hive-off for these reasons is found in NEC. In addition to its own plants, mostly near Tokyo, NEC controls a

[5] In the classification concerning hive-off, each subsidiary is allotted to a single industry however diversified it is, and the three ratios (SR, RR, UR) are calculated on the basis of the parent's investment (not on sales as is the case of diversification classification).

[6] Wage differentials according to company size also exist in other countries and, according to Koike (1988), are similar in Japan and in European countries.

number of plants as wholly owned subsidiaries (Sakamoto and Shimotani 1987). Among the many divisions of NEC,[7] the electronic device division, whose main products are semiconductors, is typical. Because of the low transportation cost of semiconductors, NEC actively established its plants in areas at some distance from Tokyo, where there was a relatively ample supply of young workers, as wholly owned subsidiaries. Although most of the strategic decisions for these subsidiaries are made by the parent company, production management is generally the responsibility of each subsidiary. The company stresses that this delegation of control enhances the morale of production staff and gives them an opportunity to understand many of the managerial problems besetting NEC. While we by no means discount the importance of this motivation, it seems certain that the economic incentives mentioned above are what really lie behind the hive-off strategy.

We also note that the division has kept within the parent company two plants near Tokyo, where both the general office (including the main sales department) and the research laboratories are located. It is in these plants that both the more essential or sophisticated, and the more experimental or developmental parts of production are concentrated. We can make two conjectures. First, as discussed above, the parent company has a comparative advantage in the work requiring a trained work-force of high quality; hence, it is sensible to organize the division of labour between the parent company and its subsidiaries on the basis of required quality in production. Second, as discussed in Section 4.5, a close link between research and manufacturing as well as between sales and manufacturing is vital for the maintenance of flexibility to changing market needs and for the promotion of innovation. During the process of development, collaboration between the research laboratory and the plant is essential for trial manufacture and to establish the production method and evaluate the production cost. Product innovation and process innovation are often inseparable, and the development team may have to come up with a new production process to manufacture the new product it has invented. Similarly, the market demand for the product has to be assessed in order to examine its commercial

[7] NEC has a divisional structure for manufacturing, but most of its other functions, such as sales, personnel, finance, and basic research, are centralized, giving an example of the incompleteness of the divisional form in Japan.

feasibility. Geographical and organizational proximity between the main plant and both research laboratory and sales department is indispensable for this purpose, and must be particularly important in such high-technology products as semiconductors.[8]

Another reason for hive-off relates to the importance of promotion in a Japanese worker's career, since it may be used as a mechanism by which to increase the number of posts, such as directorial positions. '*Shukko*' is the Japanese word used to indicate the transfer (or secondment) of a worker from the parent company to a subsidiary (or to any other firm, for that matter). If somebody cannot be promoted within the parent company because there is no appropriate post or because his performance is below standard, he may be offered a post in a subsidiary instead. Usually his pay is guaranteed not to decrease as a result of the transfer: if the pay is lower at the subsidiary, the parent company covers the difference. Therefore, he suffers no disadvantage in financial terms and is still promoted, however superficial the promotion may be. The transfer may be temporary, with an explicit or implicit guarantee that he will be recalled to the parent company after a predetermined period of three years or so. Or it may be regarded as permanent, which is usually the case for older workers nearing retirement. Indeed, transfers may be carried out in order to provide jobs for those wishing to continue work after the age of mandatory retirement, in which case the lower wages paid at the subsidiary are likely to be applied. According to the statistics of the Ministry of Labour (1989), the proportion of companies who had one or more of their employees working in other companies as *shukko* was 14.2 per cent, but among the companies with more than 5,000 employees the figure reached 91.6 per cent. Of these large companies, 47 per cent specified the length of temporary transfer in labour contracts and so on, while 53 per cent did not.

These transferred workers work alongside the workers recruited by the subsidiary itself. The latter are paid according to the wage-scale of the subsidiary while, as mentioned above, the temporarily transferred workers are often paid (in effect) according to the higher wage-scale of the parent company. The firm therefore has

[8] A similar discussion applies to the distinction by Toshiba between a 'development factory' and other factories: see Fruin (1989).

an incentive to reduce the proportion of transferred workers in the subsidiaries. This incentive has to be balanced against the higher skills and experience such workers tend to have. Thus, for instance, when the subsidiary starts operations, because workers hired there still possess little skill, a fairly high proportion of transferred workers will be needed to maintain operations and help the new workers to acquire skills. As the subsidiary accumulates experience, in the form of both managerial and production skills, the need for transferred workers decreases. In other words, as a subsidiary acquires more experience and expands, the proportion of transferred workers invariably declines and in many cases becomes virtually nil, except for one or two directors who are retained in order to maintain links between parent and subsidiary, providing control and information flow. Another implication is that more of those jobs that require higher skill, longer experience, or greater ability will be done by transferred workers. The fact that the proportion of parent companies' employees currently in transfer is 7 per cent in general but 17 per cent among management staff (Ministry of Labour 1989) supports this view. Of course these staff may have been relocated to the subsidiaries for control purposes; however, the statistics also indicate that the proportion of the parent company's directors transferred to the subsidiaries is lower, at 12 per cent, than the proportion of management staff, which suggests that lack of managerial skills is a more important factor than control by the parent company.

Transfer to subsidiaries and other firms, as the statistics show, is a common practice among Japanese companies, and hive-off is a strategy that is inseparable from the internal labour system. It is an organizational device intended to foster flexibility and reduce costs in labour management, and to offer posts to middle-aged workers, mostly of a white-collar nature. Needless to say, psychological reasons, such as those mentioned by NEC, may be equally important, for instance, to encourage independence, to increase worker morale, and to help the workers acquire managerial views and responsibility; but these would not necessarily lead to the adoption of separate corporate entities rather than autonomous divisions within the company. As we argued in the previous section, the divisional structure is not particularly attractive for Japanese managements because they are more concerned with the company-wide use of human resources and interaction across business units. On the other hand, Japanese management will find it relatively advantageous to adopt a divisional form for, or to hive off, those business units which are basically unrelated to other businesses within the firm, and for which the required human resources are separable from those needed in other parts of the firm. This explains why more unrelated diversification has been undertaken by subsidiaries than by parent companies. We have also explained, using the case of NEC, why hive-off is used in order to carry out the same businesses as the parent companies. The observed difference between subsidiaries and parents as regards the emphasis on business fields in Table 6.3, that is, a wider use of hive-off for the same or unrelated fields, is therefore an expected consequence of the Japanese management system.

6.4. MANUFACTURER–SUPPLIER RELATIONSHIPS

The prevalence of continuous trading between a manufacturer and suppliers is known to be an aspect of Japanese management. When 94 large non-financial corporations (65 in manufacturing and 29 in non-manufacturing industries) in Japan took part in a questionnaire study conducted under the auspices of the Fair Trade Commission, 87 (92.6 per cent) of them replied that all or most of their non-investment purchases (materials, fuel, and so on) had been made on a continuous basis over the past five years (JFTC 1987). It is not that such continuous trading is totally absent in other countries. Marks and Spencer, a giant UK retailer, and Benetton, an Italian knitwear producer-retailer, are two well-known cases of companies that maintain continuous and almost familial relations with their suppliers (Tse 1985; Lorenzoni 1988). Nor is it that the trading relation in Japan has been literally continuous: in the same JFTC study, 51 per cent of the firms replied that they had changed suppliers within the past five years. Notwithstanding these reservations, one can reasonably say that the average trading relationship is more continuous and stable in Japan than in other countries.

Two myths seem to have been popularized among both foreign and a number of Japanese observers. The first states that the manufacturer–supplier relation is protected by paternalism and is not subject to market competition. It is typical of the advocates of this myth that they contrast a competitive relation in the West with a co-operative relationship in Japan (for instance, Oliver and Wilkinson 1988). The truth is that the relation changes over time even in Japan and, moreover, the lack of actual switching in suppliers does not by itself imply an absence of competitive threat. Indeed, how could Japanese industries maintain efficiency were it not for competitive pressure exerted on every aspect of economic activity?

The second myth, stressed by Marxists in Japan as well as by many foreign observers, alleges that the Japanese subcontracting system is a device by which large firms can exploit small and medium-sized firms and the workers in these smaller firms. The lower profit rates and lower wages in smaller firms have been cited as evidence supporting this view. The implication is also that large firms transfer the impact of business fluctuation to smaller firms, either by reducing the orders to suppliers by a larger proportion than the decrease in demand for the end product or by forcing the suppliers to accept less favourable terms in business down-turns, such as lower prices and delayed payment. Using the suppliers as a buffer is a common expression. This way, it is alleged, larger firms can reduce fluctuations in profitability and maintain employment.[9] Although there may be some truth in this argument, we believe that this is not the essence of the Japanese system. For instance, it is not exactly clear that suppliers and subcontractors are actually earning lower profit rates. The profit rate of small and medium-sized firms in the transportation, electric, and electronics equipment industries, those most known for the supplier and subcontracting system, is smaller than that of large firms, as suggested by the exploitation theory; yet, it is still higher than the average profit rate for the entire manufacturing industry (Yokokura 1988). Moreover, a difference in wage rate, profitability, or profit fluctuation across firm size is observed in many other countries.[10]

Before we discuss the reality, as opposed to these myths, we should identify several types of supplier–manufacturer relationship and clarify the terminology. We confine our discussion to the case of a manufacturer, such as an automobile assembler and an

[9] 'When business is bad the large principal firm cuts down on its orders to subcontractors and pays them lower prices' (Clark 1979, 68).

[10] See n. 6 above. For the size–profit relation in the USA, see Scherer (1980, 92).

electric or electronic equipment producer (hereafter to be called an assembler), buying the necessary components from outside suppliers. Apart from components, the assembler also orders other goods and services from outside, from catering at the factory canteen and cleaning the office floors to office equipment and company cars. In the former of these two sets of examples, the supplier provides labour only and uses the assembler's capital equipment, thereby corresponding more closely to the concept of subcontractor. The second set of examples may indicate no more than the normal seller–buyer relationship in markets. Most of the procurement of components rests somewhere between these two cases, and careful attention is required to understand the distinction between several types of supplier–assembler relation. Also, it is these component suppliers that play an important role in the '*kanban*' or 'Just-in-time' production system that originated in Toyota and became famous worldwide (see Monden 1983). The following discussion applies mostly to suppliers of this kind for these reasons.

The first distinction to be made is between marketed goods (or catalogued goods) and ordered goods, that is, between those goods that are standardized and ready-made and can be purchased in open markets, and those goods that are supplied according to the purchaser's specification. Of course, some suppliers supply both marketed and ordered goods; nevertheless, some firms tend to supply mostly marketed goods while others supply mostly ordered goods, and the distinction is useful. Ordered goods can be further divided into those with 'drawings supplied' (DS) and those with 'drawings approved' (DA) (Asanuma 1989). DS suppliers manufacture parts according to drawings supplied by the assembler, while DA suppliers manufacture parts according to drawings made by the suppliers themselves and approved by the assembler. Again, some suppliers manufacture some products on a DS basis and the rest on a DA basis.

Among the three categories—catalogued goods (CG), DA, and DS—some tendencies can be observed. First, a more standardized component is likely to be supplied as a CG and a more specific component as a DA or DS. Asanuma (1989) found that, in the electric machinery industry in comparison to the automobile industry, components are more standardized and consequently the proportion of CG is higher. By contrast, virtually all of the parts supplied to automobile assemblers are DA or DS. The fact that DS or DA suppliers produce according to each assembler's specification implies that asset specificity must be higher for these suppliers, who consequently become more dependent on the assembler. We will return to this topic later.

Second, a larger supplier and a supplier with higher technical expertise tend to supply more catalogued goods than ordered goods and, of the ordered goods, more DA than DS. This is partly because greater technological know-how and human resources enable the firms to produce high-quality drawings, and partly because they are in a better position to absorb the economies of scale that come from producing a large amount of standardized products. Consequently, some of the CG suppliers are large producers, such as Matsushita and Hitachi, who are also themselves assemblers of final products. These large firms also supply ordered goods on a DA basis but they rarely supply on a DS basis. Obviously, this is because they wish to utilize their technological resources and attain a higher profit margin from the supply contract. In other words, production on a DS basis can be achieved with technologically non-advanced manpower, and lower-wage small firms have a comparative advantage.

Third, larger assemblers tend to purchase more on a DS basis, while smaller assemblers tend to purchase more CG. Probably there are two reasons for this. The first is economies of scale. While a large quantity ordered by a large assembler may be sufficient to attain the minimum efficiency scale, the average order by a small assembler must be of a small amount, resulting in higher production costs unless the product can also be supplied to other assemblers. The second is the breadth of technological knowhow possessed by larger assemblers. Thus, whereas smaller assemblers may lack engineers with sufficient knowledge of many parts and therefore have to rely on the technological expertise of the suppliers, larger assemblers will be equipped with such knowledge.

From the suppliers' viewpoint, these facts offer an ample incentive to acquire sufficiently high technology to make their own drawings and be promoted from DS to DA, and hopefully to CG, so that they can reduce dependence on a single purchaser, differentiate from rival suppliers, and increase profit margins. They are therefore motivated to invest in technological acquisition and in nurturing engineers of high technological capability.

In the automobile industry, according to Asanuma (1984), one 'contract' period corresponds to the life of a car model, which is usually four years in the case of components to be changed only when the entire model is changed, and two years in the case of components to be changed when minor modifications are made to the model. It is convenient to divide this period into four stages. This division is conceptual rather than chronological, as some of the stages may be taking place simultaneously. Stage I is the pre-production period. The assembler starts development of a new model several years before the target introduction date. As development proceeds, the basic specification is written for the necessary parts. Unless parts are to be purchased on a CG basis, contact is made with DA/DS suppliers in order to assess which supplier is more suitable. The assembler may send the specification to DA suppliers and request a detailed design of a particular part or, if necessary, begin joint development with the supplier. If the part is to be provided on a DS basis, the in-house designer has to start preparing the drawing. Stage II takes place towards the end of this development stage, after the assembler has decided which CG part to buy and which DA/DS suppliers to order from, has approved DA suppliers' designs, and has sent completed designs to DS suppliers. A contract will be drawn up between each supplier and the assembler, specifying the price and quantity of the part to be supplied. The price will be based on the estimated unit cost plus a mark-up agreed upon by the supplier and the assembler. The quantity will be based on the target production level of the final product. The price and the quantity thus set are provisional, since fixing them in advance for a period of two to four years is too risky.

Stage III starts as the actual production of the model starts, and is a period of fine-tuning quantity and price. The level of car production has to be flexible to meet unpredictable changes in demand. As the level of production changes, the quantity of parts ordered through *kanban* changes as well, in order to keep the minimized stock of parts at a minimum under the just-in-time production system.[11] This adjustment, which takes place daily, is

[11] *Kanban* is literally translated as billboard. Although like a billboard, it is used to carry information, that commonly used in the *kanban* production system is a rather small board the size of a large card, say.

on a comparatively minor scale, whereas more important quantity adjustments are made on a monthly basis when a document is sent from the assembler to the supplier stipulating the quantity to be produced in the coming month. In fact, it is essential if the system is to be efficient that a detailed monthly production plan is made to level production based on a demand forecast which is as accurate as possible, and that suppliers are informed of this plan in advance. Otherwise the daily adjustment cannot be kept to the minimum, causing disruption in the suppliers' production (Monden 1983).

An adjustment of price may become necessary when the production cost changes. The most apparent cause is changes in the variable cost due to external reasons, for instance, increases in material prices and wages. Will the assembler accept a price increase on these grounds? The answer, Asanuma says, depends. Usually, it is accepted that an increase in material costs may be passed on to the price, whereas an increase in wage rates may not, because the assembler maintains that the supplier should absorb the cost increase with labour-saving devices. As regards energy prices, it is sometimes agreed that increases may be passed on to the price but sometimes not. A price increase was allowed on this basis, for instance, during the oil crisis, when the extent of the energy price increase was far more than expected and potentially damaging, but it is usually not allowed for a more modest and anticipated energy price increase. These practices suggest that the risk of external cost increases is shared between the assembler and the supplier, and particularly damaging cost increases are likely to be borne by the assembler. It is not a foregone conclusion that suppliers will be forced to accept all the risk, that is, to be exploited as a buffer.[12]

The second cause of cost changes is a change in production level, since this alters the fixed cost per unit. In producing the ordered component, the supplier has to invest in capital equipment that can be used only for this model. Dies, moulds, and tools are typical examples. To give a simple example, suppose that a die is expected to last over the contract period. In Stage II when the

[12] Kawasaki and McMillan (1987) estimate that, on average for all manufacturing industries, more than two-thirds of the risk is borne by the assembler, though many questions remain about the validity of their assumptions, for instance, the assumption that all firms with less than 300 employees are subcontractors.

assembler and the supplier draw up the basic contract, they divide the cost of the die by the expected total production level in order to calculate the per-unit cost, and use this as a basis for calculating the total unit cost and, with mark-ups, the price. Hence, if the actual level of production turns out to be smaller than the expected level, the actual unit cost becomes larger than the estimated cost used to determine the price, and the supplier would suffer from a decrease in profit margin. Similarly, if the actual level of production turns out to be larger than expected, the supplier would benefit by a windfall. In other words, if the price is not adjusted the supplier has to bear the risk, whereas if the price is adjusted for this reason the assembler has to bear the risk. The practice Asanuma (1984) found among Japanese car assemblers suggested that the assembler bears the risk: that is, if the actual production level is smaller than expected the assembler compensates the supplier for the increased unit fixed cost, while if the actual production level is larger the price is decreased by the amount of the unit fixed cost for production beyond the level agreed in the first contract. Again, therefore, we find evidence that contradicts the myth that suppliers are used as a buffer.

As a third possibility, the supplier may succeed in reducing the unit cost through an improvement in productivity. Who should benefit from this cost reduction? For the assembler, there is a trade-off to be considered. If it presses for a price reduction, it can increase its profits: yet, this will deprive the supplier of any incentive to seek a further productivity increase. A compromise has to be sought on the level of price reduction so as to satisfy both objectives reasonably. This price reduction will depend on several factors. Obviously, if a similar productivity increase is attained by rival suppliers (who may or may not be supplying to the current model), the supplier will have to accept the price reduction in order to remain competitive. Moreover, under the circumstances, the supplier will strive for a further productivity improvement whether or not he is rewarded for it. Hence, much of the cost reduction will be transferred to the assembler through a lowered price. The other important factor is the extent to which the assembler has been involved in the productivity improvement. It is not unusual for the assembler to forward information of various kinds to the suppliers, to send its engineers and management staff to the suppliers' plants to see if there is any room for improvements in efficiency, to accept the suppliers' workers in the assembler's training programmes, and to help them finance cost-saving machines, or purchase these machines and lease them to the suppliers. If cost-saving on the part of the supplier owes a great deal to such help, the supplier will be asked to reduce the price accordingly. If, on the contrary, the reduction is due mostly to the supplier's own initiative and effort, the assembler will agree that the supplier receives most of the increased profits.

Any innovatory effort by the supplier also plays an important role in Stage IV of the contract, which is evaluation after the contract period. The assembler makes a detailed evaluation of the supplier's performance over the period: how much effort the supplier has made to increase efficiency and to improve product quality; how reliable the product quality has been; how reliable delivery has been; how co-operative the supplier has been in general; how many proposals it has made for design improvement, and so forth. The result of this evaluation affects the next contract in several ways. If the supplier is to be congratulated on these accounts, particularly, as regards innovation and proposals, the assembler may allow the mark-up to increase in the next contract in order to encourage further efforts.[13] Furthermore, if the supplier is evaluated as more than satisfactory, it may be promoted to a higher 'rank' in the assembler's rating among suppliers, and thus secure more future orders either of similar products or of more technologically advanced products that promise higher profit margins; while if the supplier is evaluated as unsatisfactory, it will be demoted and may be punished by lower mark-ups, by interference on the part of the assembler in its production and management, or, at worst, by a refusal on the part of the assembler to place further orders (Asanuma 1989). The very mechanism of competition is clearly at work here.

The discussion above is, I believe, more than enough to dispel the two myths quoted at the beginning of this section: the lack of competition and the assembler's exploitation of the suppliers. Competition actually occurs in several ways. For CG (catalogued goods), it takes the form more or less of usual market competition. If the assembler is unsatisfied, it can and will switch supplier

[13] According to Asanuma (1984), an item called 'compensation for design suggestion' is incorporated in the pricing scheme for this purpose.

within a short period. To use Hirshman's term, competition is maintained through the use of the 'exit' mechanism. By contrast, for ordered goods, be they DA (drawings approved) or DS (drawings supplied), the 'voice' mechanism seems to be more at work. The voice is most clearly expressed during price negotiations, because if the cost estimate provided by the supplier is considered too high, the assembler expresses its dissatisfaction. What voice the assembler expresses must depend on whether the submitted cost estimate is high because the cost is really high or because the supplier is claiming a higher cost in order to seek larger profits. If the cost is genuinely high and the assembler knows this, it may give technical and managerial assistance in order to decrease the cost. If the supplier is falsely claiming a higher cost, the assembler is likely to find out this fact eventually and to suggest submission of a new estimate. What is essential here is that the assembler has sufficient information to evaluate whether the cost estimate is reasonable. Such information comes not only from the assembler's accumulated technological expertise and past experience with the suppliers, but also from the tenders of rival suppliers. In other words, there are three important factors here: that the assembler generally has superior managerial and technical staff, that the assembler has a long-term association with most of the suppliers, and that the assembler has at least two (existing or potential) suppliers for each and every kind of component it needs. This last policy is called the 'two-vendor policy' and implies that, if the assembler is dissatisfied with a supplier even after the exercise of the voice mechanism, it may not hesitate to switch supplier in favour of a rival. Clearly the exit mechanism is also at work here and, as Hirshman (1987, 219–20) stated, 'the availability and threat of exit on the part of an important customer or group of members may powerfully reinforce their voice'.

In actual fact, it is quite unlikely that a supplier will submit an estimate based on higher than true costs. There is more than a fair chance of the assembler discovering any dishonesty, and this is bound to damage the supplier's reputation severely. The negative consequence of damaged reputation can be far greater than any hazardous gains to be made from dishonesty, because the supplier is expecting a long-term relationship with the assembler, and because the number of potential buyers is small owing to the oligopolistic nature of the automobile industry and hence all buyers are likely to learn of the bad reputation. As we discussed in the introductory chapter, the reputation effect is very powerful in long-term competition, as the expected present value of the damage from a bad reputation easily outweighs the short-term gains one may expect from fraud.

We also suggested in the introductory chapter that long-term competition tends to be of an evolutionary nature. Competition among suppliers can be described as evolutionary in two respects. One is the constant improvement in productivity and quality that is strongly encouraged by the assembler, with provision of an appropriate incentive scheme and with the assembler offering assistance if necessary and if possible. The second is that, after the assembler's evaluation of the supplier in Stage IV, the assembler tends to avoid any such drastic measure as total elimination of unsatisfactory firms from its list of suppliers in favour of the more gradual measure of demoting them to a lower rank, leaving them a chance to work hard and improve their status. This offers an opportunity for a return match, as was the case for internal competition for promotion among employees discussed earlier in Chapter 3.

To sum up, competition is very much at work in supplier–assembler relations in Japan, and takes the form essentially of competition in the long term, and competition by voice reinforced by a threat of exit.

But why are such long-term supplier–assembler relationships maintained in many parts of Japanese industries? Many of the reasons have already been suggested. Rapid adjustability of quantity and delivery, which is the basis for the well-known just-in-time production system, is facilitated because compensation for the costs incurred is guaranteed on a long-term basis. Risk-sharing between the assembler and the supplier is attained as a result. Equally important, incentives for innovation—more incremental innovation than drastic—are better maintained under a long-term relationship. Rewards for quality and productivity improvements are guaranteed by means of higher profit margins or improved position in the ranking among suppliers. All of these, we stress, cannot be maintained without mutual trust established through long-term relations between the two parties, particularly, that trust established as a result of almost daily face-to-face contact between the procurement staff of the assembler and the managers of the suppliers. It is these people who support the long-term supplier–assembler relationship and, if they prove untrustworthy, the negative reputation effect is damaging. The reputation effect, as we discussed in the introductory chapter, is more effective in long-term than in short-term competition, and, insofar as this effect is at work, the competitive mechanism is also very much in operation, however stable the supplier–assembler relationship may appear and however seldom actual switching ('exit') of trading partners takes place.

We have seen that the pressure for innovative effort takes the form of a voice from the assembler as well as technical, managerial, or financial assistance. Collaboration in research and development between the assembler and a (usually DA) supplier is frequent, for instance, to develop new components associated with a new model. Such joint R&D enables them to utilize their complementary technological resources fully and to foster a close link between manufacturing and development in the group (see Section 4.5). The long-term relationship, therefore, is conducive not only to competition but also to innovation.[14]

6.5. *KEIRETSU*

An assembler and the firms supplying the assembler are usually regarded as forming a *keiretsu*, a group of firms with a dominant firm. Thus, the term Toyota *keiretsu* (Toyota group) is used to describe the group with Toyota Motor at its centre. Similarly, NEC and its subsidiaries are regarded as forming the NEC group. These *keiretsu* have to be clearly distinguished from *kigyo-shudan*, which are groups of independent firms (who may be the leaders of their own *keiretsu*) enjoying an equal standing, to be discussed in the next chapter. At the risk of oversimplification, a *keiretsu* may be called a hierarchical group whereas a *kigyo-shudan* is a horizontal group, where the word horizontal is used not in the same sense as horizontal mergers but in the sense of non-hierarchical co-ordination, though we will show in the next chapter that this co-ordination is actually very loose.

[14] Case-studies of suppliers' involvement in development are provided in Imai *et al.* (1985), and a statistical analysis applied to the automobile industry can be found in Clark *et al.* (1987).

The discussion up to the previous section suggests that a *keiretsu* may be formed between a firm and (1) acquired firms (as discussed in Chapter 5), (2) subsidiaries created through the hive-off policy (as discussed in Section 6.3), and (3) suppliers and subcontractors (as discussed in Section 6.4). Generally, the leader's control is stronger over acquired firms and subsidiaries because of share-ownership. Personal ties are also strong because executives and other management staff may be sent from the parent/acquirer. The NEC group discussed in Section 6.3, namely, NEC and its subsidiary production units (which actually form only a part of the entire NEC group), is a typical example of such a group. Needless to say, a close relationship also exists between NEC and its subsidiaries in terms of production flow, as these subsidiaries are suppliers to NEC.

In the case of an automobile assembler, say, Toyota, the vertical relationship is the main connection between Toyota and most of the group members. Share-ownership, if any, is on a minor scale, and sending directors from Toyota, though not unheard of, is infrequent. In this regard, control from the top is considered to be weaker than in a group with subsidiaries and acquired firms. Indeed, one may question whether there is any control at all, because the members join the group on their own initiative and the role of the leader firm may be no more than to co-ordinate.

Since Toyota purchases from thousands of suppliers, it is virtually impossible to draw a boundary for its *keiretsu*. A common definition utilizes Toyota's supplier association, *Kyohokai*, on the assumption that the members of this association are recognized by Toyota as its major suppliers. In 1985 there were 171 firms in the association, ranging from producers almost as big as Toyota, such as Matsushita and Toshiba, to those that are tiny relative to Toyota. Obviously neither Toyota nor Matsushita controls the other, and Matsushita supplies parts to other assemblers too. More delicate is the case of Nippondenso, the biggest electric and electronic car component producer in Japan and the second biggest in the world. This firm was hived off from Toyota in 1949, and a 30 per cent share is still owned by Toyota Motor and Toyota Automatic Loom. Yet it now supplies almost every Japanese automobile producer and has so high a technological capability that even Toyota is heavily dependent on its supply. Therefore, despite its history and the distribution of its shareholding, it hardly appears to be unilaterally controlled by Toyota, however closely the two companies are associated.

Including Nippondenso, thirty-six members of the association had 20 per cent or more of their shares owned by Toyota Motor in 1985. Put differently, only 21 per cent of the association members had significant numbers of the shares owned by Toyota, though admittedly the 20 per cent threshold is arbitrary. The relation between Toyota Motor and its suppliers therefore appears to be basically not one of shareholding but of division of labour in the production process.

Sakamoto and Shimotani (1987) conducted an investigation to see if any of these 'core' members of the Toyota supplier association also belong to the supplier associations of other automobile assemblers. They found that 16 (44 per cent) of them belonged to at least one other association. These tended to be larger firms, such as Nippondenso and Koyo Seiko (a bearing manufacturer), which are probably CG or DA suppliers. We find, therefore, not only that the assembler diversifies supplies, as discussed in the previous section, but also that quite a number of suppliers, particularly larger ones, diversify their customers. Competition exists not only between suppliers but also between assemblers (buyers). Another interesting finding from their study is that, though some suppliers joined up to six associations (apart from Toyota's), only three belonged to either of Nissan's two associations. It must be that Toyota is particularly nervous of information leaking to Nissan, its arch-rival, through the suppliers.

The contrast between the two examples above, the NEC group with strong control through shareholding and personal ties and the Toyota group with a looser association formed for supplying and technical purposes, is exaggerated. In addition, NEC has many suppliers with little or no shareholding, and subsidiaries for diversification purposes with varying degrees of shareholding. Toyota also owns many subsidiaries in many business fields and with varying degrees of shareholding. In addition, it owns more than 20 per cent of the share of each of some seventy car dealers. Furthermore both NEC and Toyota own numerous overseas subsidiaries for manufacturing, sales, and other purposes. Hence, it is misleading to discuss *keiretsu* in general without specifying which kind of *keiretsu* (and which part of a *keiretsu*) is being considered. Suffice it to say here that though a *keiretsu* is a group of firms with a dominant firm, the relation between this firm and other members is diverse and should not be generalized from one or two observations only.

6.6. CONCLUSION

In this chapter, we have discussed several aspects of intra- and inter-company organization in Japan. We first showed that the divisional form is less prevalent and less complete in Japan than in the USA and the UK, but that hive-off of some activities is common and increasing. We attributed the lower popularity of the divisional form to the human management system which aims at company-wide interaction and utilization of human resources, and the acquisition of broad as well as deep skills. As a motivation for hive-off we cited the firm's desire to employ lower-wage workers for jobs requiring less sophisticated skills or in local areas with a relatively abundant labour supply, while maintaining a company-specific wage system for every worker in the parent company. There are also cases of hive-off to promote diversification that requires little interaction with the main business of the parent firm, in order to enhance managers' morale and independence. Hive-off has also been used as a means of entry into those markets in which the target customers are less willing to trade with the parent firm. Suppose, for instance, that there is a steel company which wants to sell its construction, engineering, planning, or software services. Marketing must be easier if the service is provided by a separate company, when the target customers include those competing with the parent firm in the steel market.

In discussing the supplier–assembler relationship, we emphasized that the practice of continuous trading by no means implies lack of competition. In fact, fierce competition occurs in the long run rather than in the short run, and by use of the voice mechanism reinforced with the threat of exit. Thus there is a strong motivation to decrease cost, improve quality, and maintain delivery and service. Although there is no way of making an empirical comparison between the strength or effectiveness of such competition in the supplier–assembler relationship and the strength of the more neoclassical or textbook-type competition observed typically in spot markets, the relatively successful past performance of Japanese industries, the automobile industry in particular, seems more than indicative.

This long-term relationship, supported by continuous contact between the staffs in the two parties, has been indispensable to Japanese production systems, such as the now widely known just-in-time and *kanban* methods, by facilitating rapid quantity adjustments, punctual delivery, and quality control. A price adjustment scheme has been in effect in order to share risks, to guarantee returns on innovation, and to maintain the competitiveness of the final product, and this scheme has been respected by both parties because of the substantial and long-lasting penalties incurred by breaching it.[15]

Our discussion of the *keiretsu* implied a wide variety in the origin, form, and aims of such groups. Some are strongly controlled by the parent company, while in others the role of the leader firm is confined to co-ordination without control. Whichever is the case, the leader is identifiable in any *keiretsu*, and the group is unambiguously named after the leader firm, such as the Toyota group, the NEC group, and the Hitachi group. This marks a contrast to the Mitsubishi group or the Mitsui group, which have no clear leader and in which the members (each of which may have its own *keiretsu*) can be assumed to be of equal standing. We will discuss such groups in the next chapter.

Let us close this chapter by repeating our findings in a general fashion: the choice of intra- and inter-company organization cannot be separated from the question of how managerial resources, in particular, human resources, are accumulated and allocated, and must be the answer to the question of how competition and motivation are to be maintained. Given this, international differences are inevitable: yet, a universal logic must remain and, as long as this logic is respected, there should be little to deter one country or one firm from learning from others.

[15] For a view stressing the importance of trust in the Japanese supplier–assembler relationship, see Sako (1990). She also recognizes the importance of competition in this relationship.

7

Business Groups

7.1. INTRODUCTION

Inter-company combinations can take several forms: they may be loose or tight, with or without shareholding involved; they may be hierarchical or horizontal (in the sense of being equal partners); and they may be horizontal (in the sense of being in the same market), vertical, or diversifying. Accordingly, their functions and effects will greatly differ. It is this variety of forms in Japanese business combinations that appears to confuse many foreign observers. In particular, pre-war *zaibatsu* and present-day *kigyo-shudan* are completely different in terms of control and structure, and so is the *keiretsu* discussed in the last chapter. The competitive effects have to be clearly distinguished, therefore. This chapter discusses *zaibatsu* and *kigyo-shudan* in detail.

Let us begin by clarifying the terminology, though some distinctions have already been made (see Sections 2.3 and 6.5). A *zaibatsu* is a tightly knit group of companies that existed only before World War II. Mitsui Zaibatsu is a typical example. As will be explained in Section 7.3, it was dissolved after the war. A *kigyo-shudan*, literally a group of firms or a business group, is a loose combination of basically independent companies. The most distinctive features of a *kigyo-shudan* are its non-hierarchical structure and diversification as a group. Some, like the Mitsui group, are descendants of pre-war *zaibatsu*—hence the incorrect indentification of *kigyo-shudan* with *zaibatsu*. A *keiretsu*, such as the NEC group, Toyota group, or Nippon Steel group, consists of a parent company and its affiliates, of which some are subsidiaries owned by the parent company and some are more independent, their affiliation to the group confined to technological or trading aspects. The *keiretsu* relationship is usually associated with acquisition, hive-off, or subcontracting, as discussed in Chapter 6. A *keiretsu* need not have a non-manufacturing company at the top. For instance, general trading companies (*sogo shosha*) tend to have their own *keiretsu*, and so are retail giants. The Saison group is such an example, with the Seibu Department Store Co. at the top, and it includes a supermarket chain, a consumer credit company, insurance, and a hotel chain. There is also the Seibu Railway group, a brother group to Saison,[1] which has a railway business at its centre and comprises diverse leisure businesses.

The concept of *kinyu-keiretsu* needs to be distinguished from other *keiretsu*, because it usually refers to a group consisting of a bank (with its affiliated financial institutions of other kinds, such as an insurance company and a trust bank) and the companies for which it acts as the main bank (main supplier of funds). As a consequence, a *kinyu-keiretsu* substantially differs from a *keiretsu* in its wider variety of members and its weaker control (or lack of control). To the extent that a bank finances companies in whatever business, a *kinyu-keiretsu* extends to almost all the industries in the economy. And to the extent that the member companies, with their ample internal funds or with the availability of loans from other banks, become less dependent on the bank for financing, control by the bank becomes ineffective or non-existent. There are as many *kinyu-keiretsu* as there are major banks (called city banks) but how many of them have any real effect is questionable. Even if they were important during, say, the 1950s and 1960s when financial markets were tight and companies preferred to have close ties with the bank so as to secure loans, they retained little significance once financial markets became less tight and deregulated in the 1970s and 1980s. Furthermore, even in the earlier period, *kinyu-keiretsu* appeared to be little more than a collection of lender-borrower relations without much interaction among the borrowers. It is therefore questionable whether the relation should be regarded as a 'group'.

Those *kinyu-keiretsu* organized around the most influential six banks overlap with *kigyo-shudan*, because all the *kigyo-shudan* include banks as one of the core members. Thus, depending on which companies are to be numbered among the *kigyo-shudan*, a

[1] They are literally *brother* groups because their top managers are half-brothers, each having inherited a half of their father's business. The expansion of the two businesses into giant groups must be attributed to the two brothers, who are said to have turned hostile to each other. The two groups, therefore, are now only remotely affiliated.

kigyo-shudan may be regarded as identical to a *kinyu-keiretsu* or as a subset of it.

Section 7.2 gives a historical view of the origin and structure of the *zaibatsu*, which were forced to dissolve after World War II (hereafter the war) as will be explained in Section 7.3. The structure and activity of the present-day *kigyo-shudan* will be discussed in Section 7.4. The performance, in terms of profitability, stability and growth, of *kigyo-shudan* members is compared with that of non-members in Section 7.5. Finally in Section 7.6, we speculate on the future of the *kigyo-shudan*, and also discuss its implications on market competition.

7.2. THE *ZAIBATSU* BEFORE THE WAR

Let us start by looking at the history of the two largest and best-known *zaibatsu*, Mitsui and Mitsubishi.[2] They form a good contrast, in terms of the way they started. Mitsui began with a merchant named Takatoshi Mitsui, who opened a drapery in Edo (now Tokyo) in 1672 following some success in a provincial town. His success can be attributed to several innovative approaches to retailing, such as marking prices, no discount, cash only, and selling cloth in any dimensions desired by customers, none of which were normal commercial practices at the time. Another innovation was backward vertical integration by purchasing his own cloth at Kyoto, the main textile manufacturing centre. He then entered into financial business, investing the profits from the drapery as his starting capital. During the two centuries before the Meiji Restoration of 1868, the descendants of Takatoshi Mitsui successively assumed the position of the top management, maintaining the firm as one of the largest in the country. After the Restoration, it gradually diversified into trading, shipping, coal-mining, textiles, machinery, and so forth.

Mitsubishi, by contrast, was not started until after the Restoration, by Yataro Iwasaki, a former low-rank *samurai* (warrior), with a shipping company. The company expanded tremendously in the following ten years, as it collaborated with the government in transporting soldiers and supplies during the civil war. It then

[2] The description below is mostly due to Hirschmeier and Yui (1977), which is a revised Japanese edition of their English book (1975).

entered into related businesses, such as marine insurance, banking, coal-mining, warehouses, and shipbuilding.

Both Mitsui and Mitsubishi diversified and expanded to become the biggest business groups in Japan before the war. Together with Sumitomo (mainly a mining business) and Yasuda (mainly a finance business) these two are known as the Big Four Zaibatsu. Together, the four accounted for about a quarter of the paid-up capital in the Japanese economy at the end of the war. They were particularly dominant in the financial sector, in which their paid-in capital accounted for nearly a half.

Two important characteristics of the *zaibatsu* that clearly distinguish it from the post-war *kigyo-shudan* are the tight control

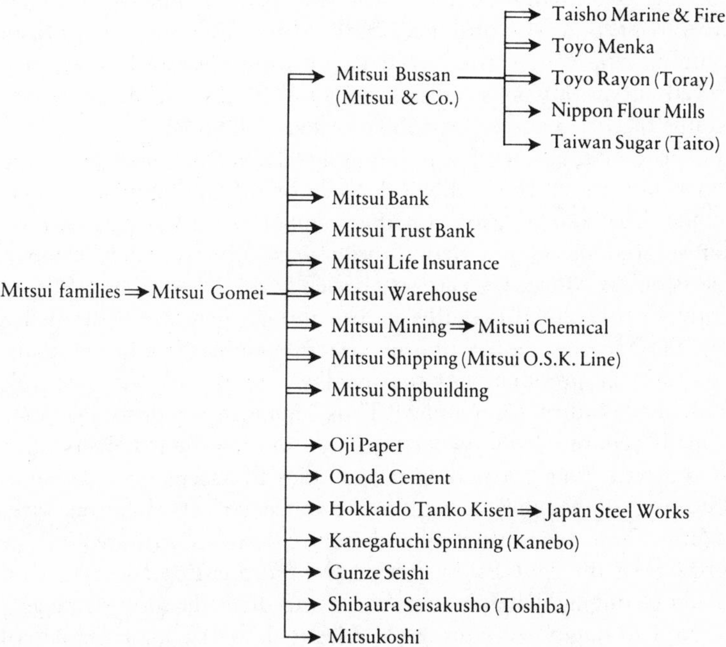

FIG. 7.1 The structure of the pre-war Mitsui Zaibatsu (abbreviated)
Notes:
⇒ indicates decisive control by means of majority shareholding, etc.
→ indicates weaker control.
In parentheses are the present company names.

maintained by the holding company which acted as the central decision-maker, and family ownership. Fig. 7.1 shows the structure of Mitsui Zaibatsu in a simplified form. Mitsui Gomei was a holding company owned by Mitsui families, and owned most of the main Mitsui companies. The structure changed from time to time and the figure ignores the details. For instance, the families often directly owned the shares of Mitsui companies, and shareholding among Mitsui companies was frequent. To give one example, a larger share of Mitsui Life Insurance was held by the families than by Mitsui Gomei. However, Mitsui Gomei was in charge of the control of the company.

Also simplified in the figure are the subsidiaries that were owned by many of the Mitsui companies. Mitsui Bussan (the present Mitsui & Co.), a trading giant, owned a particularly large number of subsidiaries. This ownership pattern changed considerably over time; for instance, both Mitsui Shipping and Mitsui Shipbuilding were started as divisions within Mitsui Bussan, then hived off as Bussan's subsidiaries, and finally promoted to the status of core members as shown in Fig. 7.1.

The combination of this hierarchical control with ownership does not mean that Mitsui Gomei or Mitsui families always made the major decisions for the member firms. On the contrary, substantial delegation of authority was common. For instance, decisions at Mitsui Gomei were basically delegated to non-Mitsui-family professional executives, even though it was wholly owned by the families. Some of the family members took the chairmanship or presidency of the member companies but their role remained rather ceremonial. Thus, managerial decisions were usually separate from ownership, even though the managers often had a hard time persuading the families to accept their decisions because the families tended to be more conservative and risk-averse. This separation may therefore have contributed to the growth of the *zaibatsu* by freeing the more entrepreneurial managers to pursue dynamic investment and diversification strategies.

Non-strategic decisions were relegated to the management of each member firm, and the role of Mitsui Gomei was essentially to co-ordinate such decisions among the members and to make strategic decisions for the group. In this regard, the structure was similar to the multi-divisional form adopted by US and UK conglomerates. Simply speaking, therefore, a *zaibatsu* was a multi-divisional firm highly diversified through internal investment (mainly) and owned by families.[3]

In Mitsubishi, the families took a more active part in management: the brother, son, and nephew of the founder successively assumed the presidency of the holding company, actually making top decisions. As in Mitsui, this holding company, Mitsubishi Goshi, owned other member firms, and control by Mitsubishi Goshi of member companies was tighter than in the case of Mitsui.

To repeat, there was a central decision-making unit in a *zaibatsu* before the war, with the control backed by share-ownership. Therefore, it may be regarded as a single firm, however huge and however diversified it may have been. In this sense it essentially differs from its post-war descendant, the *kigyoshudan*.

7.3. THE DISSOLUTION OF THE *ZAIBATSU*

When the army of occupation under General MacArthur took control of Japan after the war, one of the aims was to 'democratize' the economy. Most measures taken by the General Head Quarters (hereafter GHQ) of the Supreme Commander Allied Power's to achieve this end will be discussed in Chapter 11, but those related to the *zaibatsu* must be explained here.

It was GHQ's view, correct or not, that militarism in pre-war Japan had been enhanced by the presence of the *zaibatsu* and their connection with the military and politicians. The consequence of this view was GHQ's determination to break up the *zaibatsu*, which was reinforced by the view of its economic staff that Japan should have a competitive economy without anyone having a major influence on markets.[4]

The dissolution was achieved in four stages. First, in 1946, forty-two holding companies, including, of course, Mitsui Gomei and Mitsubishi Goshi, were forced to liquidate. The shares owned by these holding companies were all confiscated by a special committee organized under GHQ's instruction, which

[3] Acquisitions, however, were not rare. In fact, many of the weakly controlled members without 'Mitsui' in their names were first established by outsiders and then became affiliated to Mitsui Zaibatsu.

[4] The following description is mostly due to Hadley (1970), who was one of the economic staff at GHQ at the time.

then resold them gradually to the company employees and the public. The shares of the companies—holding, financial, trading, or industrial—held by designated *zaibatsu* families were also confiscated by the committee, with only nominal compensation paid. These families therefore lost most of their wealth literally overnight. Second, 1,575 top executives of more than four hundred companies, particularly those of *zaibatsu* companies, were purged, that is, prohibited to take managerial positions in companies. Interlocking directorships were also prohibited among a number of designated companies. Third, the two biggest trading companies, Mitsui Bussan and Mitsubishi Shoji (Mitsubishi Corporation), were ordered to liquidate and, furthermore, it was forbidden for two or more former directors (*buchos*) of these companies to join in order to form a new company. The result was that, as most of the employees soon restarted trading businesses, utilizing their knowhow and personal connections with customers and suppliers, more than two hundred companies were created out of each giant trading company. Fourth, GHQ announced that the use of the trademarks, Mitsui, Mitsubishi, Sumitomo, and Yasuda, would be prohibited, causing many ex-*zaibatsu* companies to adopt new names, although this prohibition never materialized because GHQ changed its policy in response to the Korean War.

It is beyond doubt that these drastic policies virtually wiped out the *zaibatsu*. Financial control supported by hierarchical shareholding was lost, leaving each ex-*zaibatsu* company without a major shareholder. The human connection through interlocking directorships that played an important role in the *zaibatsu* was also lost. The new executives who took over after the purge of their predecessors tended to be those who had worked with the firm (but little with other member firms of the *zaibatsu*) for many years, climbing up internal promotion ladders. As a consequence, member firms gained substantial independence in both financial and personal senses, being freed from the central decisions made by previous *zaibatsu* holding companies or *zaibatsu* families.

The dissolution remained effective even though many of the restrictions were relaxed after less than ten years. For instance, although the purged managers were allowed to resume managerial positions in 1950–1, hardly any returned (or were invited to return) to their original positions. The restriction on the formation of new companies by the former managers of the two trading companies was also relaxed, resulting in numerous mergers and finally in the reintegration of the present Mitsui & Co. (in 1959) and Mitsubishi Corporation (in 1952). These companies, however, lost the monopolistic position they had held within the *zaibatsu* because ex-*zaibatsu* industrial companies were now free to choose their own trading partners. That the use of the trademarks would not be banned became apparent by 1952, with many companies returning to the old names. An important exception is the Yasuda Bank, the centre of Yasuda Zaibatsu, which chose to retain its new name, Fuji Bank. This exception is interesting because, even though Yasuda was one of the Big Four, its activities were concentrated in finance, as is evident from the fact that it was the largest bank at the end of the war even though the entire Yasuda Zaibatsu was the smallest of the Big Four. Therefore, its decision to retain the new name suggests that the management opted for a strategy of widening the customer basis without setting it up as an ex-*zaibatsu* bank, rather than a strategy of exploiting the tie with ex-Yasuda companies. It also suggests a lack of cohesion in the post-war Yasuda/Fuji group and explains, at least partly, why it is distinguished from Mitsui, Mitsubishi, and Sumitomo in most discussions of the *kigyo-shudan*.

Although the restriction on shareholding among member firms was also relaxed, holding companies continued to be prohibited by the Antimonopoly Law enacted in 1947. The law also restricted shareholdings by financial institutions, as discussed in Chapter 2. The consequence was that, though shareholding among member firms gradually increased, these holdings remained far short of a majority, as will be shown in the next section.

The post-war *kigyo-shudan*, we conclude, is a group essentially different from the pre-war *zaibatsu*, even though the former, at least three of them, are descendants of the latter. There is neither a central decision-making unit nor tight financial control. The member firms are independent. Even if consultation within a group attempts to co-ordinate the conflicting interests of member firms, it can never force them to adopt policies they do not wish to.

What, then, are the functions of the current *kigyo-shudan*, and what are their merits? We will answer these questions in the following two sections, first by explaining their structure and activities, and then by empirically comparing the performance of group member firms with that of non-members.

7.4. BUSINESS GROUPS TODAY

We should first note that member firms are so loosely connected that it is not easy to identify *kigyo-shudan* (simply called groups in the remaining part of this chapter) nor to identify their members. All researchers agree that at least three should be identified as such groups. These are Mitsui, Mitsubishi, and Sumitomo, usually called ex-*zaibatsu* groups. Whether three other groups, Fuji (also called Fuyo after the name of its presidents' club), Sanwa, and Daiichi-Kangyo, should also be included is more questionable. These are essentially *kinyu-keiretsu* as defined in Section 7.1, with the respective banks, Fuji Bank, Sanwa Bank, and Daiichi-Kangyo Bank (DKB), at their centres. Although they are similar to ex-*zaibatsu* groups, in the sense, for example, that they have presidents' clubs (to be discussed below), the relation appears to be restricted rather to a collection of bank–client relations with little interaction among non-financial members. The reason for this view will become clear in the following discussion.

It is equally difficult to select companies to be included among the groups. Several alternative criteria have been proposed by different authors. These include membership of presidents' clubs, the strength of share-ownership by other group members, the proportion of loans from member financial institutions, and the use of trademarks. Depending on the criterion adopted, the number of members in the Mitsui group, for instance, can vary from 24 (according to presidents' club membership, as adopted in Ueno 1989) to 104 (according to share-ownership and loans, as quoted in Nakatani 1984).

In much of the following discussion, we refer to the results of an investigation by the Fair Trade Commission of Japan (JFTC 1984; Ueno 1989) into the six groups which are usually divided into three ex-*zaibatsu* groups—Mitsui, Mitsubishi, and Sumitomo (to be abbreviated as MMS in the following)—and three non-ex-*zaibatsu* groups—Fuyo, Sanwa, and DKB (abbreviated as FSD). The study uses participation in presidents' clubs as the criterion for group membership. This definition, as suggested above, is perhaps most conservative, restricting the members to the core of groups.

7.4.1. *Independent Decision-Making*

As the first and most important characteristic, let us repeat that each member firm is essentially an independent decision-maker unlike the firms in the pre-war *zaibatsu*. Hence, it is extremely unrealistic to assume that the group as a whole is pursuing, say, joint profit maximization.

7.4.2. *Diversification as a Group*

The group aims to be diversified as a whole and to include every industry within it. This tendency, called 'one-setism', can be verified by Table 7.1 which shows the number of members of each group according to industry.

We note first that every group has at least one bank (and a trust bank, except for DKB) and one general trading company (*sogo shosha*). These companies, often regarded as the financial and trading centres of each group, are usually the most enthusiastic supporters of group cohesion and attempt to play co-ordinating roles. Since the name of each group bank should be obvious, let me just list the names of the main trading companies: Mitsui & Co. for Mitsui, Mitsubishi Corporation for Mitsubishi, Sumitomo Corporation for Sumitomo, Marubeni for Fuyo, Nissho Iwai (and Nichimen) for Sanwa, and C. Itoh for DKB. However, Nissho Iwai also belongs to DKB, suggesting that, in the Sanwa and DKB groups at least, group activities are not mutually exclusive and in-group combinations are not tight. Such duplication of membership of both Sanwa and DKB actually occurs in three companies apart from Nissho Iwai, casting doubts on the substantiality of these groups. Another duplication is found in Hitachi, which belongs to all the three FSD groups. Duplication of this kind is one reason why we consider FSD to lack the same group cohesiveness as MMS.

This diversification as a group suggests that, as in the usual case for diversification, the group as a whole may be less prone to business fluctuation. This is the reason why Nakatani considers the main aim of the group to be mutual insurance. According to this view, a member firm in difficulty can expect support from the member financial institutions in the form of additional loans or a

TABLE 7.1. Presidents' club members

Industry	Mitsui	Mitsubishi	Sumitomo	Fuyo	Sanwa	DKB
Bank	1	1	1	1	1	1
Trust bank	1	1	1	1	1	
Life insurance	1	1	1	1	1	2
Marine and fire insurance	1	1	1	1		2
Securities						1
General trading	1	1	1	1	2*	3*
Other trading					1	1
Department store	1				1	1
Forestry			1			
Mining	2		1			
Construction	2	1	1	1	3	1
Beer		1		1		
Flour mills	1			1		
Other food				1	1	
Textile	1	1		2	2	1
Paper and pulp	1	1		1		1
Chemicals	2	5	2	3	4	3
Pharmaceuticals					2	1
Cosmetics and toiletries						2
Paints					1	
Petroleum refineries		1		1	1	1

Tire					1	1
Glass		1	1			
Cement	1	1	1	1	1	1
Iron and steel	1	1	1	1	4*	3*
Non-ferrous metals	1	2	3			2
Wires and cables			1		1	1
General machinery		1	1	1		3
Bearings				1	1	
Electrical equipment	1	1	1	3*	4*	5*
Automobile	1	1		1	1	1
Shipbuilding	1	1			1	2
Other transport equipment					1	
Optical equipment (camera)		1		1		1
Railroads				2	1	
Trucking					1*	1*
Shipping	1	1		1	1	1
Real estate	1	1	1	1		
Warehousing	1	1	1			1
Leasing					1	
Leisure						1
TOTAL	24	28	21	29	40	45

Note: The number shows the number of member firms in the industry. Membership is as of March 1982. * indicates duplicates; for example, in the electrical equipment industry, Hitachi belongs to Fuyo, Sanwa, and DKB groups.

cheaper interest rate, and from other member firms in the form of preferential trading terms. Thus, he argues that 'the setting up of a mutual insurance scheme among group members, and particularly between the banks and other group members, is an institutional response by the Japanese firm which aims at coping with apparent market failure in contingent claims markets of management risks' (Nakatani 1984, 229). We will examine this view empirically in the next section.

Another advantage of diversification as a group is the ease of entering into new markets by means of joint ventures, because combining managerial resources in different areas from different companies is easier when these companies have been continuously associated. More will be said about this advantage when we discuss joint ventures under a separate heading.

There is also a disadvantage to diversification—a high probability of creating conflicts with other members when a company diversifies. A well-known case is the plan formed by Sumitomo Light Metal, a subsidiary of Sumitomo Metal, to enter into aluminium-smelting, which was bound to create competition with Sumitomo Chemical which had already been involved in the business. The group, Sumitomo Bank in particular, tried to mediate between the two without success (which exemplifies the independence of decision-making stressed above).[5] Thus, group firms may feel more constrained in their diversification efforts.

Returning to Table 7.1, we find that there is more intra-industrial competition between the firms belonging to any one of FSD than those of MMS. Even though there are five chemical companies in Mitsubishi, they scarcely overlap with each other at more finely classified industrial levels. By contrast, in Sanwa there are two pharmaceutical companies and in DKB there are two integrated steel makers which must be directly competing with each other. This fact again illustrates the lack of co-ordinating capacity in FSD. To put it differently, an MMS firm is more

[5] A compromise between the two Sumitomo companies was finally made with the guidance of the Ministry of International Trade and Industry, and a new company, Sumikei Aluminium, was established with Sumitomo Light Metal holding a 40% share, Sumitomo Chemical 30%, and other Sumitomo companies 30%. It started production in 1977 but, ironically, the appreciation of the yen and the oil crisis that had disastrously hit the industry by this time forced the company to close down in just 5 years.

likely to find its diversification efforts constrained because of the membership.

7.4.3. *Reciprocal Shareholding*

A group shareholding ratio is defined as the ratio in a member company's total shares of those held by the other members, averaged over all the member firms in a group. In 1987, this ratio was 23 per cent on average over the six groups: that is, slightly less than a quarter of an average group member's shares are held by other members of the same group. Although this may appear substantial, we should note that these shares are held collectively by twenty or thirty firms, without any of them holding a major share. Typically, the largest shareholder is the member bank (or trust bank), whose shareholding is restricted to 5 per cent or less by the Antimonopoly Law.[6] Take Mitsubishi Heavy Industries as an example. This company is supposed to be one of the core members of the Mitsubishi group, together with the bank and the trading company, and Mitsubishi is said to be more tightly organized than Mitsui. The biggest shareholder in 1988 was, as expected, Mitsubishi Trust Bank (6.2 per cent) followed by Mitsubishi Bank (3.9 per cent). Meiji Life Insurance, a Mitsubishi member, owns 3.3 per cent and Tokio Marine & Fire Insurance, another member, owns 2.3 per cent. Also, Mitsubishi Corporation owns 1.7 per cent. Thus of the top ten shareholders, five are group members. The other five are non-members and, surprisingly, the fourth largest shareholder, at 3.3 per cent, is Sumitomo Trust Bank and the sixth and seventh largest are, respectively, Nippon Life Insurance and Toyo Trust Bank, both Sanwa group members. This illustrates that shareholding by an individual member is not large, usually up to 5 per cent by any member and far less by any non-financial member, and that shareholding by financial institutions of rival groups is not uncommon. Hence, even though the share collectively owned by the group may reach a quarter, no individual shareholding seems large enough to exert influence. This is a marked difference from the pre-war *zaibatsu* in which the holding company held a decisive share of any other group firm.

[6] This restriction does not apply to the shares not owned by a trust bank itself but merely entrusted to it. Needless to say, the trust bank cannot exercise voting rights on these shares. The restriction is relaxed to 10% for insurance companies.

Another difference compared with the *zaibatsu* is that shareholding is now reciprocal. In the case of Mitsubishi Heavy Industries, it owns 3.1 per cent of the share of Mitsubishi Bank, 3.0 per cent of Mitsubishi Trust Bank, 3.2 per cent of Mitsubishi Corporation, and so forth. Such reciprocity should lessen any incentive to exert influence through share-ownership.

The group shareholding ratio is significantly smaller in FSD (19 per cent) than in MMS (29 per cent), again showing weaker group cohesion in FSD. It is also noted that a shareholding relationship between member firms occurs less frequently in FSD. The frequency with which a member firm owns the share of any other member is 73 per cent in MMS but 34 per cent in FSD, and FSD's in-group shareholding is concentrated in that by financial institutions. We should also note that Fuji Bank of the Fuyo group and DKB are the two largest banks in Japan, and that Nippon Life Insurance, a Sanwa member, is the largest insurance company. Thus, the probability that these institutions hold shares in any company may be higher, regardless of group membership. These facts support the view that FSD should be regarded principally as a *kinyu-keiretsu* and not a *kigyo-shudan*.

7.4.4. *In-Group Loans*

An in-group loan ratio refers to the amount of loans provided by member financial institutions as a proportion of all the loans taken by the firms in a group. In 1987, this amounted to 17 per cent on average of the six groups, with MMS again showing a larger ratio, 22 per cent, than FSD, 15 per cent. Dependence on member banks in terms of loans appears not to be substantial.

Yet, in 68 per cent of group firms (in 1981) the largest proportion of loans came from financial institutions within the firms' own groups. This percentage was again higher in MMS (85 per cent) than FSD (52 per cent). In FSD, therefore, almost half of the member firms are using outside financial institutions as their main sources of loans. This is quite surprising because these are supposedly groups formed on the basis of a bank–borrower relationship (namely, *kinyu-keiretsu*). If the members' dependence on group financial institutions is not strong in such groups, what else remains?

An important question, of course, is to what extent in-group loans are preferential. There are two ways in which loans may be preferential. One is by charging a lower interest rate to borrowers. Thus one may hypothesize that group members are paying lower interest rates on loans from member banks. This hypothesis, however, is inconsistent with the empirical finding by Caves and Uekusa (1976), to be discussed in the next section, that the average rate of interest paid on debts was higher among group members in comparison to non-member independent firms.

The other more plausible hypothesis is that a bank applies looser criteria in evaluating the eligibility of member firms for loans. Even when other banks would refuse a firm's loan request on the ground of high risk or insufficient collateral, a member financial institution may comply with the request. If this is the case, the financial difficulty of a firm suffering declining demand must be greatly eased and its survival more assured. Thus Nakatani (1984, 241) argues that 'the "main" bank usually acts as an insurer of group-affiliated companies and when the latter are faced with financial and/or managerial difficulties, the former renders necessary assistance even beyond the level that normal business reciprocity requires'. The bank, therefore, plays a central role in his view of the *kigyo-shudan* as a scheme for mutual insurance.

But why does the bank make such a preferential offer? A number of hypotheses may be put forward. First, the bank may have better information about a member borrower through continuous information exchange within the group, and thus estimate the default risk to be smaller. Second, the bank, being also an important shareholder, may be able to participate in the management of the borrower, securing more efficient or less risky managerial practices and thereby reducing the default risk. Third, the bank may expect that other member firms will also help the firm by providing managerial assistance or offering preferential trading terms. Fourth, the bank may provide such preferential loans in return for the borrower's loyalty to the bank when the latter is prosperous. According to this last view, a higher interest rate paid by member firms (Caves and Uekusa's finding quoted above) and their higher debt–equity ratio (Nakatani's finding to be discussed in the next section) are the costs member firms pay in return for the insurance the bank provides against financial difficulty.

All these explanations suggest that preferential loans (if any) provided within groups are mutually beneficial to lenders and borrowers, resulting in Pareto superiority and suggesting an economic rationality behind grouping. One may also say, following the framework advocated by Williamson (1975) but criticized and revised by Imai and Itami (1984), that a group is an intermediate form between a market and a hierarchy, and is effective in remedying market failures due to information impactedness and the lack of contingency markets.[7]

However, we note that these explanations need not imply the superiority of grouping because at least some of the same results can be achieved through long-term bank–borrower relations, and we have already noted in Chapter 2 that such relations actually exist more commonly in Japan than in the USA or the UK, whether the borrower is a group member or not. Constant information gathering by the bank about the management of a borrower and the former's holding of the latter's share, as commonly occurs in Japan, should be able to produce basically the same effect even if the borrower does not belong to the group, and a mutual insurance scheme must be possible between any bank and its borrowers. Therefore, the economic role of groups has to be sought in any advantages that may come through the group as a whole and not through individual bank–borrower relations. A relevant question, for instance, is whether information exchange within a group is more effective than that between the bank and the borrowers individually, or whether non-bank member firms also provide help by offering managerial resources, preferential trading terms, opportunities for growth through joint ventures, and so forth. Some affirmative answers will be gained in the following.

7.4.5. *In-Group Trading*

A sales–dependence ratio is the proportion of sales to other members in the same group to total sales, and a purchase–dependence ratio is a similar proportion in terms of purchase. The average ratios for member manufacturing firms in 1981 were 20 per cent for sales and 12 per cent for purchase, with MMS again showing

[7] 'Information impactedness . . . exists in circumstances in which one of the parties to an exchange is much better informed than is the other regarding underlying conditions germane to the trade, and the second party cannot achieve information parity except at great cost—because he cannot rely on the first party to disclose the information in a fully candid manner' (Williamson 1975, 14).

significantly higher values than FSD. The percentages are not impressive, and it has often been found that a member firm buys from or sells to firms in other groups. Quantitatively, therefore, the extent of in-group trading appears small. The accuracy of these figures is questionable, unfortunately, because they are not free from the influence of vertical integration, and the definition of in-group sales or purchase may not be the same among the respondents to the JFTC questionnaire.

Casual observations suggest that in-group trading is preferential only in the sense that, if the price offers are similar, the firm will choose to trade with a group member, or that, if the firm is looking for a trading partner in a sequential fashion, it will first approach a group member and accept the offer, provided it is satisfactory. If, however, the offers are significantly different, or if the offer made by the member does not appear reasonable, the firm will not hesitate to trade with non-members, or to approach non-members (and even members of rival groups) to ask for their terms. Competition is by no means absent here. In particular, the use of voice must be effective in the group setting to attain a stable but efficient trading pattern. Whether Kirin Beer (made by a Mitsubishi member) would be served during business meals at Mitsubishi companies, even if prices of beers differ, is an interesting question.

There still remains a possibility that in-group trades, like in-group loans, play the role of mutual insurance by providing preferential trading terms to firms in difficulty. Even if the firm usually buys from the cheapest supplier regardless of its group affiliation, it may agree to buy from a member firm asking higher prices when the latter is in trouble. Needless to say, such a practice is only possible when the buyer firm is sufficiently profitable. If the buyer firm is not making a profit, for instance, if it is also in financial difficulty or in a perfectly competitive market, it cannot afford to pay a higher price without risking its own survival. However, if the profitability of a firm varies over time without being perfectly correlated across firms, a firm which is profitable at one time may support an ailing firm by paying a higher price, on the expectation that the latter will do the same when the situation is reversed. Diversification among member firms makes it likely that profitability is only imperfectly correlated among them, and group membership with constant information exchange may help to prevent free-riders who seek help at some time without helping others when they are in trouble.

If there is such mutual insurance through preferential trading, we should expect intertemporal profit variations to be smaller among firms belonging to groups as opposed to independent firms. Nakatani (1984) provides evidence to support this expectation; however, our own evidence, to be discussed in the next section, does not agree.

7.4.6. *Directorate Ties*

The proportion of firms in which at least one director had been sent from another member firm was 68 per cent in 1987, but the proportion of such directors among all directors was only 7 per cent.[8] The second proportion was higher in MMS but the first proportion was slightly higher in FSD (though higher in MMS in 1981). In other words, about two-thirds of group firms have within their boards at least one director from another group firm, creating directorate ties within the group, but the proportion of these directors is less than one-tenth.

The majority of these directors come from the member banks, and interlocking directorates among industrial members are less frequent. In view of the practice commonly adopted by firms, whether group members or not, to invite directors from the largest shareholder and/or the provider of the largest loan (see Table 2.2), directorate ties do not appear particularly strong within groups.

7.4.7. *Information Exchange*

The exchange of information among group members appears to occur frequently and at considerable depth. The most conspicuous forum of exchange is the monthly meeting of member company presidents. These members (shown earlier in Table 7.1) constitute what is called a presidents' club, though the word 'club' may be misleading because the only activity consists of monthly meetings and there are no facilities of the kind that exist in, say, golf clubs or social clubs. Although the subjects for discussion at these meetings can only be guessed at, some reports suggest that the topics most often raised include the evaluation and forecasting of general

[8] A director is regarded as having been 'sent' from another member firm when he is also a director in the latter, or when he assumed the directorship within 2 years of leaving the latter.

economic conditions, matters involving the entire group such as investment made jointly by most of the members and joint public-relations activities, and the use of group trademarks. Hence, they are confined to problems of interest to all the members: there are never discussions of management issues relevant to one particular member only, presumably to avoid internal conflict and antagonism.

There are also regular meetings of lower-rank managers in some groups, and meetings involving only the interested parties, for instance, those participating in joint ventures, occur frequently. Thus, the level of information-sharing among members is estimated to be high. This sharing is reinforced by human elements, including interlocking directorates, the experience of senior executives having worked in the same *zaibatsu*, and the interaction of people in common welfare facilities (to be discussed later). For these reasons I have regarded a group as essentially an information-sharing club (Odagiri 1975), while Imai has viewed it as an intermediate organization formed 'basically to cope with failures in both the market and in the organization' (Imai 1988, 25).

7.4.8. *Joint Ventures*

The group provides a favourable environment in which to organize joint ventures. When a firm plans to enter a new market, it often lacks the necessary resources, in particular informational and human resources, that is, the know-how and experience, frequently embodied in workers and managerial staff, that are needed to create production facilities, distribution networks, and consumer loyalty in new markets. One way to gain these resources, and a popular method in the USA and the UK, is by mergers and acquisitions. Given that, as discussed in Chapter 5, Japanese firms do not favour M & As, joint ventures with firms possessing related resources prove more attractive. The group, with its diversification and its constant information exchange, provides a perfect setting for joint ventures. The case of entry by a group into the atomic power plant market provides an illustration of this. Obviously, the creation of such a plant requires technology related to fields as diverse as construction, chemicals, machinery, electrics, and electronics. Since groups do contain firms with experience in these areas, by forming a joint venture among them they should be able to effect a faster and less risky entry.

The advantages of having member firms as partners are diverse. First, long acquaintance with the management of other companies will help the firm to assess their suitability as partners, and negotiation to form a joint venture will be easier. Second, even if negotiation fails, any information exchanged during negotiation will remain within the group, without risking leaks to outsiders. Third, information generated and exchanged in the course of joint ventures will similarly remain within the group, and the partners are unlikely to use it to the firm's disadvantage. Fourth, the constant flow of information within a group may make it easier for the managers participating in a joint venture to agree to any adjustment that has to be made to deal with a changing environment. And fifth, financing the joint venture will be easier because, again owing to information exchange, it should be easier to persuade not only the member bank to provide loans but also the other member firms to invest in the new venture.

The presence of financial institutions and a trading company in the group is essential here, for financial institutions can be expected to provide capital, and trading companies will possess international information and distribution channels to a higher degree than the other companies. It is no wonder that in virtually every group-wide joint venture—whether in petrochemicals, atomic power, space, or maritime activities—the member trading company has played a central role.

7.4.9. *Trademarks*

The use of the trademark, Mitsui, Mitsubishi, or Sumitomo, is said to be under strict control, and whether a company should be allowed to use the trademark is one of the important decisions made by the presidents' club. In general, therefore, companies adopting these names are regarded as legitimately recognized group members.

This does not mean that every member will wish to use the trademark. In fact, for such well-known companies as Toshiba and Toyota (Mitsui), Kirin and Nikon (Mitsubishi), and NEC (Sumitomo), advertising their group affiliation by using the group name is more likely to damage their marketability by alienating non-group customers. It has been reported that Mitsubishi Motor Company once considered eliminating 'Mitsubishi' from its company name in order to appeal to fashion-conscious young drivers, since the name 'Mitsubishi' is commonly regarded as being more closely related to heavy industries.

7.4.10. *Public Relations and Welfare Facilities*

Groups often undertake common public-relations activities, such as political donations, the setting up of research grants and fellowships, other contributions, advertising (of the group as a whole), and participation in international expositions. Economies of scale may be present in such areas, and the lack of market competition among members must make it easier for them to co-operate in these activities.

Welfare facilities for management and employees, such as hotels in resorts, are another common feature of groups (mostly MMS). Here again economies of scale should be present. Moreover, common public relations and welfare facilities seem to be undertaken in order to promote group-consciousness among the managements and employees of member firms.

7.4.11. *Conclusion*

The lengthy discussion in this section has explored the nature of existing business groups in Japan. They are essentially associations voluntarily formed by independently managed companies in pursuit of such benefits as information exchange and mutual insurance. These benefits are interdependent, since mutual insurance becomes feasible only because constant information exchange reduces the risk of supporting ailing member firms. Information exchange also makes in-group joint ventures more attractive, enhancing growth opportunities for members.

These considerations suggest that the value–growth frontier (see Section 4.2) of a member firm lies in a more north-easterly direction than that of a non-member, since larger growth opportunities and smaller risk should make the market value of the firm higher for any growth rate. In addition, the management of a member firm is likely to be less constrained by the capital market evaluation in its pursuit of growth, because reciprocal shareholding reduces the threat of hostile take-over. It is thus expected that a firm would be able to achieve a higher growth rate by joining a group, which explains the incentive for firms to form such a group. Whether this expected effect can in fact be observed is the subject of empirical analyses in the next section.

First, however, it is worth reiterating the weakness of group cohesion and group activities in FSD, non-ex-*zaibatsu* groups. The duplication of membership (across groups), the lack of a common trademark, the presence of market rivals within a group, the less frequent occurrence of group-wide joint ventures, in addition to smaller reciprocal shareholding, in-group loans, in-group trades, and less directorate ties, all point to the lack of any substantial effects as a result of grouping. It is therefore misleading to view these groups as business groups on the same terms as MMS. In our study in the next section, we include only MMS in our samples.

It is certain that this disparity between MMS and FSD mostly arises from the historical difference that all the member firms of MMS (except for newly emerged companies such as petrochemical firms and auto-makers) are ex-members of tightly organized *zaibatsu*, whereas this is not the case with FSD. Human elements, in particular the managers' mutual acquaintanceship as ex-colleagues in the *zaibatsu*, must have made a considerable contribution to the maintenance of bonds among the member firms. This fact, however, seems to suggest the possibility of weaker group cohesion in the future as those who have been recruited only since the war are now assuming an increasing number of top positions. We will return to this topic in the concluding section.

7.5. PERFORMANCE OF BUSINESS GROUPS

There have been some empirical studies of the performance of group member firms as compared to non-member independent firms. They are Caves and Uekusa (1976),[9] Nakatani (1984), and my own (Odagiri 1974, 1975). Before presenting the results of my own new study, let us quickly review the results of the past.

The first problem any researcher has to solve is which groups to include in the study and which firms to include as the members. Nobody questions the inclusion of Mitsui, Mitsubishi, and Sumitomo. Whether the other three, Fuyo, Sanwa, and DKB, should also be examined is more problematical. For the reasons stated in the previous section, I take the view that these three are

[9] The empirical results in this book are also shown in a more detailed study by Uekusa (1982).

not much more than a *kinyu-keiretsu*, namely, a group composed of a bank and its main borrowers. Intra-group interaction and cohesion are much weaker than in MMS, and joint venture activities less frequent. Hence, only MMS have been examined in my studies (both past and present). Caves and Uekusa, and Nakatani, on the other hand, include FSD as well as MMS in their studies, though they allow for the possibility that the effects of grouping differ from one group to another by using separate membership dummies.

As regards the extent of membership, I have confined my analyses to those members in the presidents' clubs, supposedly the core members, whereas Nakatani adopted a wider criterion of in-group shareholdings (larger than 20 per cent), in-group loans (more than 40 per cent of the company's debt), or historical connection. As one would expect, a larger number of firms are classified as group members according to Nakatani's criterion: more than a hundred firms for each of MMS, more than four times the size of each presidents' club. Consequently, in his empirical study using a sample of 317, only 69 are regarded as non-members.[10] As Hadley (1984) correctly pointed out in her comment on the Nakatani paper, this looser criterion leads to the serious error of including firms that are using group banks as their 'main' banks but do not have any other relation with the groups. Nobody, for example, would regard Sony as a Mitsui company, or Honda as a Mitsubishi company. Nevertheless, these firms have obtained loans mainly from, respectively, the Mitsui and Mitsubishi Banks for historical reasons, and are thus classified as group members in Nakatani's study.

Two methods have been employed to inquire into the performance of group firms as compared to that of non-group independents. The first method pairs group firms with comparable non-group firms, and compares the average performance between members and non-members. The second uses a sample of, for example, all the listed firms in manufacturing industries, and regresses the performance variable on a group dummy variable (taking the value of one for members and zero for non-members)

[10] In addition, 20 firms, regarded as subsidiaries to other (member or non-member) firms are excluded from group membership. Nakatani's criterion is actually more complicated than that given in the text: see Nakatani (1984, 233) for details.

and other explanatory variables. Both methods have their advantages and disadvantages. One drawback of the second method is that it is difficult fully to control differences between members and non-members in terms of size, market power, industrial distribution, diversification, and so on. This problem does not occur in the first methodology, provided the pairing is careful enough to eliminate these differences. However, it is often impossible to find a non-group firm that is exactly comparable with a member, and thus the pairs formed in such a study tend to be fewer than desirable.

In Odagiri (1975), I constructed thirty-six pairs, of which thirty-one are from manufacturing industries, and found that, in 1971, members had on average a lower profit rate on assets, a higher debt-asset ratio, and a higher or lower growth rate depending on the way in which growth is measured and over what period. Hardly any of the results were statistically significant. In a follow-up study (Odagiri 1974), using twenty-five pairs, twenty-two in manufacturing, I found mostly higher growth rates for the members when longer periods from 1956 or 1961 to 1971 were taken to measure these rates. Some of the results were significant and support the conjecture made at the end of the previous section, that member firms join the groups in order to pursue faster growth and not necessarily in order to enhance profitability.

Both Caves and Uekusa (1976) and Nakatani (1984) used the second methodology with samples of 243 firms and 317 firms, respectively, in manufacturing industries. By inquiring into the sign of the estimated coefficient of the group dummy variable, Caves and Uekusa found a negative and weakly significant effect of membership on the average profit rate over 1961–70, and a significantly positive effect on the average interest rate paid on loans. Nakatani similarly found a negative and weakly significant effect on the profit rate. His other findings are an insignificantly negative effect on growth rates, a weakly significant positive effect on the average wage paid to employees, a weakly significant negative effect on the ratio of net worth to assets (one minus debt-asset ratio), and negative effects on profit rate variability, some of which are significant.

A few interesting observations can be made on the basis of these results. First, none suggests that members are more profitable, and some actually suggest otherwise. Second, there was some indica-

TABLE 7.2. List of sample companies

No.	Industry	Group	Member company	Non-member company
1	Non-ferrous metal	S	Sumitomo Metal Mining	Furukawa
2	Flour	Mi	Nippon Flour Mills	Nisshin Flour Milling
3	Beer	Mb	Kirin Brewery	Sapporo Brewery
4	Textile	Mi	Toray	Teijin
5	Textile	Mb	Mitsubishi Rayon	Kuraray
6	Paper	Mi	Oji Paper	Daishowa Paper
7	Paper	Mb	Mitsubishi Paper	Kanzaki Paper
8	Chemical	Mb	Mitsubishi Chemical	Showa Denko
9	Chemical	S	Sumitomo Chemical	Sekisui Chemical
10	Iron and steel	S	Sumitomo Metal	Kawasaki Steel
11	Iron and steel	Mi	Japan Steel Works	Daido Steel
12	Iron and steel	Mb	Mitsubishi Steel	Aichi Steel Works
13	Electric cables	S	Sumitomo Electric	Furukawa Electric
14	Machinery	Mb	Mitsubishi Kakoki	Tsukishima Kikai
15	Electrical equipment	Mb	Mitsubishi Electric	Hitachi
16	Electronic and communication equipment	S	NEC	Fujitsu
17	Shipbuilding	Mi	Mitsui Engineering and Shipbuilding	Hitachi Zosen
18	Shipbuilding	Mb	Mitsubishi Heavy Industries	Ishikawajima-Harima Heavy Industries
19	Optical eqiupment	Mb	Nippon Kogaku	Olympus Optical

Note: Mi = Mitsui, Mb = Mitsubishi, S = Sumitomo.

tion of membership enhancing growth before 1971 but not after. Third, members tend to be more highly geared and to pay higher interest rates. One interpretation of this result has been already given: members are accepting these disadvantages in return for an implicit guarantee that the member banks should support them in case of financial difficulty: that is, they are paying a higher interest rate on disproportionally large debts, on the understanding that it includes an insurance premium. Such an argument appears consistent with another of Nakatani's findings, namely that members have been experiencing lower profit rate variability, which supports the argument that one of the main motivations for grouping is mutual insurance.

To pursue this conjecture further and examine whether the results still hold in more recent years, I have conducted another investigation using a sample of nineteen pairs from manufacturing industries (see Table 7.2). Although the pairing was carefully made in order to equate size and sales composition between the member and the non-member, some differences inevitably remain; nevertheless, systematic bias is unlikely because in some pairs the members are larger, while in others the non-members are larger. The results of my comparison are summarized in Table 7.3. The profit rate is the ratio of profits (inclusive of interest paid and taxes) to total assets. Sales growth and asset growth are measured by, respectively, sales and total assets divided by their value in the previous year; hence, it is one plus the growth rate. These are measured for each year and then averaged for the period 1964–85 for each firm. Profit rate variability is measured by the standard deviation of the profit rate over 1964–84. Furthermore, to investigate whether the effect of grouping differs for the period before the oil crisis of 1972–3 and the period after it, separate analyses were made for the subperiods of 1964–71 and 1974–84. Statistical tests were made against the hypotheses of the true difference being zero and of the true ratio being one.

As found in previous studies, members are on average less profitable than non-members, though the difference is insignificant. This tendency is common to both the two subperiods. An interesting inter-temporal change is observed as regards growth. Until 1971, members were on average growing faster than their non-member counterparts, whereas, since 1974, the ranking has been reversed and non-members have attained faster growth. It

TABLE 7.3. Comparison of performance: Group members and non-members

	1964–84	1964–71	1974–84
Profit rate			
Difference (M − N)	−0.536	−0.158	−0.665
	(−0.914)	(−0.258)	(−0.853)
Ratio (M/N)	0.956	0.987	0.973
	(−1.000)	(−0.370)	(−0.424)
%, M > N	42.1	42.1	42.1
Sales growth			
Difference (M − N)	0.296	1.992	−0.335
	(0.295)	(1.283)	(−0.274)
Ratio (M/N)	1.003	1.018[c]	0.997
	(0.544)	(1.771)	(−0.413)
%, M > N	52.7	73.7	47.4
Asset growth			
Difference (M − N)	−0.040	1.860	−1.114
	(−0.039)	(1.045)	(−0.886)
Ratio (M/N)	0.99998	1.018	0.990[c]
	(−0.005)	(1.559)	(−1.764)
%, M > N	47.4	63.2	47.4
Profit rate variability			
Difference (M − N)	−0.188	−0.034	0.002
	(−0.556)	(−0.106)	(0.008)
Ratio (M/N)	1.051	1.041	1.230
	(0.423)	(0.278)	(1.667)
%, M > N	47.4	47.4	52.7

Notes: M refers to the value of group members; N, to non-members. Differences and ratios are averages for 19 pairs. Percentages are the percentage of cases (among the total of 19) with M > N.

In parentheses are *t*-values. The null hypotheses are M − N = 0 (for differences) and M/N = 1 (for ratios). [c] indicates significance at 10% level.

appears that group firms have been less successful in adapting to the rapid industrial restructuring that followed the oil crisis. This result explains the difference between my earlier result and Nakatani's. No difference is observed in terms of profit rate variability between members and non-members, which does not support Nakatani's hypothesis of mutual insurance within groups. Though the variability was smaller for members before the oil crisis and larger after the crisis, neither difference is statistically significant.

The results are by no means encouraging. Hardly any benefit seems to accrue from grouping. Groups may have been helpful in creating growth opportunities until 1971, but this favourable effect seems to have evaporated after the oil crisis. In fact, we can see that the relative performance of members as opposed to non-members deteriorated according to all four measures; profitability, sales growth, asset growth, and profit variability. This finding casts a pessimistic view on the future of groups. Why have the groups been less successful in recent decades? Does anything substantial now remain of the organization and activity of groups?

7.6. CONCLUSIONS AND SPECULATIONS ON THE FUTURE OF GROUPS

We began this chapter by emphasizing the difference between business groups today (*kigyo-shudan*) and their predecessors before the war, *zaibatsu*. Unlike the *zaibatsu*, in which the group holding company controlled many firms through majority shareholdings and acted as the central decision-making unit, present-day groups are loose combinations of independent companies with equal power. Their main functions are presumably information exchange, the pursuit of growth through in-group joint ventures, and mutual insurance. The empirical results of past studies and our own new study have provided some, albeit weak, evidence to support this hypothesis. However, for the more recent period of 1974–84, the results have suggested slower growth of member firms as opposed to faster growth in earlier years. What has caused this change? Although no hard evidence is available, some conjectures seem appropriate.

Group firms, being the descendants of the *zaibatsu*, are generally older than independents. As a consequence, they have been biased towards more traditional industries. It is true that they entered newly developing industries after the war, but the more active (or successful) moves were made into the industries with large-scale plants, such as the petrochemical field, reflecting the group's enhanced ability to combine existing technologies and to finance new ventures. Their entry into technologically advanced fields or niche markets was either infrequent or unsuccessful compared to other firms. The result was that the industrial composition of the groups tended to be biased towards heavy industries, such as chemicals (but not pharmaceuticals or toiletries), iron and steel, machinery (for example, shipbuilding and heavy electric equipment rather than automobiles and electronic equipment), paper, glass, and cement. These were the industries most seriously hit by the oil crisis and the appreciation of the yen, which deprived Japan of her comparative advantage. Furthermore, the groups were less diversified into service industries (except for general trading and financing), which have recently been growing faster than manufacturing industries.

It has also been said that group firms were less capable of adjusting to new economic realities. The management may have overestimated their strength in the face of adversity because of their past reputation or the implicit mutual insurance scheme within the group. They may not have been used to severe market competition owing to the presence of in-group customers. Or their organizations may have become less flexible simply because of size or age. Simply speaking, therefore, group firms may have become less capable of being entrepreneurial in comparison to independent firms.

These arguments seem to explain their poorer performance after 1974, when industrial restructuring took place at a hitherto unknown speed, owing to higher oil prices, a higher yen, and microelectronization. The groups included firms in those industries most severely hit by these adversities and were probably slower to exit from these industries and/or diversify into more promising fields.

In addition, we can think of several factors that ought to work towards weakening group cohesion. The first is the weaker personal relationship among the top managers of member companies, because most of those recruited by the *zaibatsu* have retired and the few still remaining will retire in due course, to be replaced by those who were recruited by individual companies and have worked there (but in no other group firm) all the time. For these people, the sense of group unity must be much weaker than for those who created and maintained the group relationship during the decades immediately after the war.

The second is the change in financial markets, as described in Chapter 2. During the period of excess demand in financial markets, group membership often meant priority in the rationing of funds given by member financial institutions. However, since the 1970s, as the excess demand has disappeared and many firms have accumulated their own reserves, this benefit has been lost. Furthermore, Japanese financial markets have been deregulated to the extent that banks can now set their own terms on, for instance, the rate of interest to be paid on deposits, thereby causing price competition. This move obviously reduces an incentive for in-group loans and deposits. Insofar as terms are uniform among banks, in-group financial transactions are beneficial but never costly; however, if they are different, the cost of losing out on better terms may outweigh the benefit the firm can expect to receive in the long run by sticking to the group bank.

The third is the diminished need to depend on trading companies as industrial firms have acquired more expertise in international markets and more human resources familiar with business abroad. Most of them now have their own distribution channels overseas and can sell or buy without relying on trading companies.

The fourth is the increasing amount of in-group conflict as, under rapid industrial restructuring, the firms in declining industries desperately seek to diversify. Of course, the improved opportunities for joint ventures provided within groups may help diversification efforts. Yet, probably more often, the markets the firms wish to enter have already been served by other members, and entry is bound to create in-group market competition. The resulting conflicts will certainly lessen unity, harmony, and cohesion within groups.

It is unlikely that all the benefits of grouping will be lost. Information exchange may become even more valuable as competition becomes global and technology changes ever more quickly. The benefits of in-group shareholding increase as the threat of possible hostile take-overs by foreign raiders becomes more real. Public-relations activities by groups may remain effective. Groups, therefore, are likely to continue in existence in the long run and the presidents will maintain their monthly meetings. Yet, we infer that their substance will gradually diminish, with each member behaving more and more independently.

In terms of the consequences on market competition, we expect group affiliation to be less significant in the future. In the past, two opposing effects have been suggested. An anti-competitive effect has been expected from the practice of in-group trading and from the mere size of groups. According to the JFTC study (Ueno 1989), in 1987, the six groups accounted for 13 per cent of total assets and 15 per cent of sales (excluding the financial sector) of Japanese industries, with MMS accounting for 6 per cent of either assets or sales. These percentages for the six groups increase to 27 per cent of assets and 25 per cent of sales if subsidiaries and affiliates with more than 10 per cent share-ownership are included. As we have seen, however, the anti-competitive effect of in-group trading does not seem significant.

The other argument suggests a pro-competitive effect because groups may have fostered market entry through their one-setism and joint-venture activities. Thus, newly emerging industries such as atomic power, space and marine, have been subject to entry by Mitsui, Mitsubishi, and Sumitomo at a comparatively early stage; and the groups may have therefore made markets more contestable. If this effect was important in the past, will the loss of group cohesion as predicted above lessen contestability in the future? I do not regard this scenario as likely because entry efforts by individual firms are intensifying as mentioned above. An expected intensity of entry efforts by individual member firms was, after all, one of the main reasons why we expected business groups to play a weaker role in the future.

PART III

HOW IT AFFECTS

8

Industrial Organization

8.1. INTRODUCTION

Competition is a behavioural concept. When firms, existing or potential, strive to gain the advantage over others, competition results. It is, therefore, more intense in an economy where firms have a stronger motivation to strive to be ahead of others, and where there are more places and opportunities in which to confront one another. Our discussions in the preceding chapters have suggested the presence of several forces that make Japanese markets competitive. The most important of them is the growth-maximizing behaviour of Japanese management and its preference for internal growth over mergers and acquisitions, since only internal growth involves an expansion in production capacity. Whether the firm seeks growth in a horizontal direction, in which case production capacity will increase in the current industry, or by diversifying, in which case the threat of entry intensifies in the target industries, the result is increased competitive pressure. In this regard, the difference between internal growth and mergers and acquisitions is straightforward. Whether M & As are undertaken in order to expand horizontally or to diversify, they merely replace one manager with another without increasing productive capacity, unless they are accompanied by internal investment. In other words, even though merger and acquisition represents an investment for the purchasing company, it is a disinvestment for the seller of the ownership, with no net effect to the economy at large. In fact, if the M & A is horizontal, it results in a reduction in the number of producers, thereby intensifying concentration.

We have also suggested that the learning effect is more powerful in Japanese firms principally because of the internal labour system. To gain fully from the learning effect, firms have an incentive to increase the cumulative output level relative to that of their rivals. The consequence is the pursuit of market share. Even if responding to their rivals' lower prices or aggressive marketing efforts is too costly from the short-run viewpoint, the firm may have to counterattack in order to maintain its market share lest it suffer from a lagging productivity increase caused by a smaller accumulation of production experience. The same may be said of the race for innovation. In innovation the first mover attains a decisive advantage, as discussed in Chapter 1. Lest it lag behind the market leader who may capture a dominant position by being the first to invent and patent or the first to develop the product and gain market loyalty, the firm has a strong incentive to accelerate its research and development programmes. Innovation in the semiconductor industry offers a typical example. All the main Japanese electronics manufacturers—Hitachi, Toshiba, NEC, and Fujitsu among others—are making a huge effort, both in R & D and in physical investment, to be the first to develop a more powerful semiconductor (from 1 mega-byte memory to 4 mega-byte, and so on), to establish production capacity, and thus to gain the first-mover advantages that come from the learning effect and market dominance.[1]

The competition that results is very much of a long-term nature. And the importance of competition in the long run is enhanced by the rapid growth of the Japanese economy, which is in itself a consequence of the growth-maximizing behaviour of Japanese management, as we shall see in Chapter 10. Faster growth means of course that the long-run consequence is more important, and this encourages firms to adopt an aggressive strategy even if it damages short-term profitability. In this form of competition, relative ranking can be decisive, that is, whether you are the largest and the first can be more important than the absolute level of production and innovation, and this leads firms to behave more in a Bertrand manner than a Cournot manner. The resulting competition can be extremely intense.

We therefore hypothesize that Japanese markets are in general competitive and probably more so than in other countries. There are exceptions of course, where a few firms remain dominant, with little threat of entry and with a tendency to collude rather

[1] For the investment, R & D, and other strategies of the Japanese semiconductor industry, see Kimura (1988).

than compete. As expected from the discussion above, such exceptions are observed in more mature industries with smaller growth potential since the long-run gains from being ahead of rivals are less important. Examples might include the sheet glass industry and the beer industry, both of which are typical oligopolistic industries in Japan. Yet even here, the recent acceleration in innovation and internationalization, as well as changing consumer tastes, has started to disturb the established market order. For instance, the undisputed leader in beer brewing, Kirin, is now threatened by Asahi whose new 'Super Dry' beer has gained surprising popularity, more than doubling Asahi's market share. In addition, Kirin is threatened by imported beers which are gaining popularity among the internationally minded younger generation.

The difficulty lies in comparing the extent of competition internationally. Competition, as we have repeatedly argued, must be taken as a behavioural concept and may not be correlated with market structure. We have in fact suggested that an atomistic market structure can imply passive behaviour by the firm and thus a lack of competition in the behavioural sense. Therefore, the international comparison of market concentration made in the following Section 8.2 should not immediately be taken as a comparison of the extent of competition. However, the extent of competition may be inferred from the performance side, that is, from an international comparison of the level and variance of profit rates. Section 8.3 is devoted to this comparison. Although the indirect nature of this inference is subject to disturbances from other factors, it may be argued that it is still more reliable than the inference of behaviour from structure that has traditionally been made by many industrial economists. A criticism may be made that the profit rate variation across firms merely reflects temporary movement of profits. To examine this possibility, the extent of persistence of profits has to be investigated. This will be done in Section 8.4. Finally, in Section 8.5, there is a discussion of what we can learn from a rather traditional structure–performance correlation analysis. The results suggest that for Japan as well as for the USA collusion of oligopolistic firms may have been dominant in the 1960s, but has become rather irrelevant in recent years. Section 8.6 summarizes our arguments on competition.

8.2. MARKET STRUCTURE

The following comparisons of market structure will be confined to Japan and the USA, firstly because concentration ratios make more sense in these rather self-sustaining countries than in European countries (and Canada) where national borders are poor substitutes for economic borders, and secondly because US data are better organized than those in any other country. Let us first look at aggregate concentration.[2] In 1980, the largest 100 firms accounted for 21.4 per cent of the total assets of the Japanese non-financial sector. There has been a weak downward trend since 1967 when the percentage was 25.6. The percentage underestimates concentration because it is based on non-consolidated accounts. When the subsidiaries of these 100 firms (those with a shareholding of more than 50 per cent) are included, the percentage increases to 25.2 per cent in 1980. Roughly speaking, therefore, about one quarter of the assets in the Japanese non-financial sector is owned by the top 100 firms. Among these 100, a little more than a half, 54, were in the manufacturing industries, followed by 14 retail/wholesale companies and 11 electric power/gas companies. In manufacturing industries only, the concentration was higher, with the largest 100 firms (excluding subsidiaries) accounting for 33.8 per cent in 1980. Again a downward trend is observed since the percentage was 37.2 in 1967. Between 1967 and 1980, one quarter of the 100 companies, in either non-financial or manufacturing sectors, dropped out of the list.

In the USA, the equivalent percentages were 30.6 for the non-financial sector in 1975 and 49 for manufacturing in 1972. Clearly both percentages are larger than in Japan, even when subsidiaries are included in the Japanese data. Combined with the fact that the American economy was then almost three times larger (in terms of GNP) than the Japanese economy, this clearly suggests that large American firms must be gigantic compared to Japanese firms: compare, for instance, GM with Toyota, IBM with Fujitsu, and Exxon with Idemitsu. Although size alone cannot be any indication of market or political power, the contrast between Japan and the USA seems to accord with the hypothesized

[2] The following comparison is taken from Senoo (1983).

competitive nature of Japanese industries. One cause for higher aggregate concentration in the USA must be the frequency of mergers and acquisitions. Although the US antitrust authority is more stringent about horizontal mergers than the Japanese authority, many big US firms were created through mergers before the restriction tightened (for example, GM and US Steel) and others undertook diversifying acquisitions. This effect of M & As is also reflected in the difference concerning trend: while the aggregate concentration ratio has slightly decreased in the last twenty years for the non-manufacturing sector in the USA, similarly to the Japanese trend, it has increased in manufacturing in the USA, unlike in Japan. The intensified movement towards mergers and acquisitions in the USA in the last two decades must be at least partly responsible for this trend (Scherer 1980). The hypothesis that, unlike internal expansion, M & As are likely to foster concentration appears to be supported as far as aggregate concentration is concerned.

Comparison of market concentration ratios is more difficult and more ambiguous. The basic reason for the difficulty is the lack of comprehensive concentration data in Japan. The Fair Trade Commission in Japan (JFTC) has been publishing concentration ratio data since 1950. Unfortunately, however, these data do not cover all industries and the industrial classification used does not follow the standard classification scheme, because the main objective of the JFTC in compiling the data is to utilize them in its policy decisions. Consequently, the data cover 434 manufacturing industries in 1986 which, in terms of the value of shipment, account for less than half (46.5 per cent) of all manufacturing industries. They are biased towards concentrated industries because of JFTC's interest in these industries. In some of these industries, industrial classification is extremely detailed: for instance, the paper industry is further separated into eight categories (excluding cardboard) and the photographic film manufacturing is also separated into eight categories.

Theoretically the Ministry of International Trade and Industry (MITI) can calculate concentration ratios following standard industrial classification because it collects output data on this basis from each company for the Census of Manufacturers. It is believed that MITI has in fact calculated such ratios occasionally but limited the use of them strictly to internal purposes. One such data set, for 1963, has been used by Uekusa (1982) to make an international comparison. The average four-firm concentration ratio (weighted with the value of shipment) across the 512 four-digit industries was 35.4 per cent. This compares with 40.9 per cent for the equivalent average of 417 USA industries in the same year. Uekusa thus suggested that Japanese industries are on average somewhat less concentrated than in the USA.

A more recent comparison was made using the JFTC data by Unotoro (1988). Comparing the JFTC data with the US Census data, she found that for 209 industries (basically at the five-digit level) the Japanese and US data are comparable. Comparing the weighted average concentration ratio over these 209 industries, she found a result contrary to Uekusa's: 78.0 per cent in Japan in 1984 as opposed to 43.6 per cent in the USA in 1982 in terms of four-firm concentration ratio, and 1,333 in Japan as opposed to 857 in the USA in terms of the Herfindahl index. The reversal of the Japan–USA ranking is not because of different years, since the trend from 1963 to 1982 was basically constant in the USA and slightly downward in Japan. The main reason seems to be the bias of this sample towards concentrated industries. This bias is believed to be stronger for the Japanese data because the JFTC data is biased towards concentrated industries for the reasons mentioned earlier, whereas in the US Census, the concentration ratio is not published for highly concentrated industries to avoid the revelation of individual firms' market shares. Therefore, even though the 209 industries themselves are comparable in both countries, they represent those industries that are relatively concentrated in Japan irrespective of whether or not they are similarly concentrated in the USA.

Another reason may be that Unotoro used a more finely detailed industrial classification. That is, the results may suggest that Japanese markets are less concentrated at the four-digit industrial level but more concentrated at the five-digit level. This conjecture is consistent with the hypothesis that Japanese firms are more specialized at the five-digit level. Suppose that company X is specialized in a five-digit industry A, and Y is specialized in B, where A and B are different five-digit industries within the same four-digit industry. Then, the concentration ratio must be higher at the five-digit level but can be higher or lower at the four-digit level in comparison to the case where either company sells in both A and B. This explanation seems consistent with the discussion in Chapter 4 that Japanese firms are less diversified than American firms.

Thus the comparison of market concentration in Japan and the USA is inconclusive. Moreover, the concentration ratio is a measure with several limitations. For instance, it is measured at the production level without taking imports and exports into account; hence, it may not truly show the extent of competition in the markets. It does not take into account the threat of entry; hence, even if concentration is high, the market may be contestable. High concentration may actually be the result of competition rather than the deterrent to competition, as Demsetz (1973) has repeatedly argued. We will return to Demsetz's argument later.

8.3. COMPANY PROFIT RATES

Whenever the rate of profit is higher than in other industries, the industry attracts entry. As a consequence, when all the relevant markets (the product markets to which the firm sells its products, as well as the factor markets from which the firm buys its inputs) are perfectly competitive and mobile, in particular when there are no entry barriers (barriers a firm has to overcome to enter into a new market) or mobility barriers (barriers a firm has to overcome to move from one status or one strategy group in its market to another), the rate of profit must equalize across industries and across firms.

If the firms are value maximizers, their rate of profit (namely, the rate of return) should be equal not only to those in other industries but also to the cost of capital because entry should continue until and only until the rate of return goes down to equal the cost of capital. If they are growth maximizers they may enter into the market even if the rate of return is below the cost of capital, insofar as entry is expected to contribute to their long-run growth; hence, equalization of the rate of return to the cost of capital may not come about. None the less, equalization of the rate of return across industries should be approximately attained, as growth-seeking firms will enter the most profitable market.

This proposition suggests that, instead of measuring the extent of competition from structure, which we have argued is misleading, it may be measured by market performance, that is, by examining the extent to which profit rates are equalized across industries or firms.[3]

At the end of 1964, 458 manufacturing firms were listed in the First Section of the Tokyo Stock Exchange.[4] Tracing these firms over the following nineteen-year period of 1964–82, I found that 399 firms continued to be listed in one of the eight stock exchanges in Japan (not necessarily in Tokyo), 41 were acquired, 8 went bankrupt (including those that later succeeded in re-establishing themselves), and 10 became unlisted for other reasons. Thus the ratio of survival through the nineteen-year period is at least 87 per cent and probably higher, because some became unlisted or filed for bankruptcy and yet survived. That this ratio is surprisingly high compared to the USA or the UK has already been shown in Chapter 5.

Eliminating the 23 firms that undertook major mergers during 1964–82 which significantly changed the corporate identity, we obtained a sample of 376 firms. For each of these firms, the after-tax profit rate on assets—(operating profits plus receipt of interests and dividends minus corporate tax)/total assets—was calculated for each year. The profit rate on assets, not the rate on sales, is used because the return on investment is what is expected to equalize through the dynamic process of entry.

Fig. 8.1 shows this profit rate averaged over the sample firms. Similarly, the average profit rate of 413 American manufacturing firms for the period 1964–80, and the average profit rate of 243 British manufacturing firms for the period 1964–77 are shown.[5]

Clearly, the average profit rate has been highest in the UK,

[3] Another, more direct, possibility is to compare the entry behaviour internationally. Such a comparison, however, is difficult because of the lack of adequate entry data in Japan and many other countries. Yamawaki (1991) showed with cross-industry data that net entry (the change in the number of firms) responds positively to the growth of demand and the price–cost margin of the industry, but also that the result is sensitive to business fluctuation.

[4] The Tokyo Stock Exchange is separated into two sections, with the more prestigious First Section including nearly all the internationally known big companies. If the firms in the Second Section are included, the number of manufacturing firms listed in 1964 almost doubles to 900. The survival rate to be discussed presently is little affected by the inclusion of the Second Section firms (85% as opposed to 87%).

[5] The American data were collected by Odagiri and Yamawaki (1990) as an extension to the data collected by Mueller (1986). The British data were collected by Cubbin and Geroski (1990).

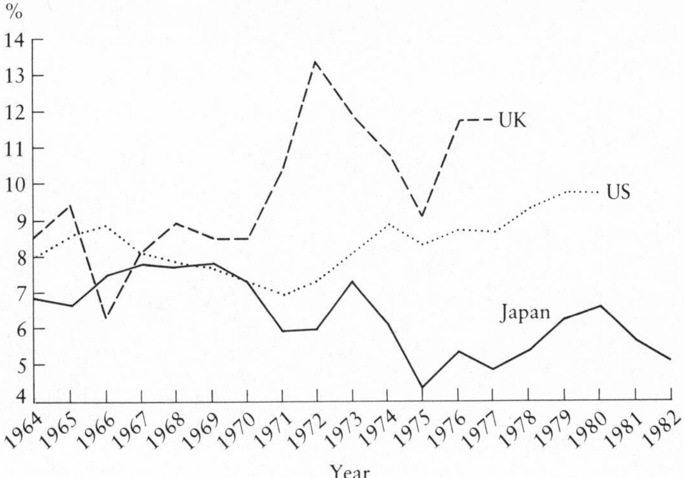

FIG. 8.1 Average reported profit rates in Japan, the USA, and the UK

followed by the USA, and lowest in Japan, except for 1966 (for the UK) and 1969 (for Japan). The average difference over the 1964–77 period is 3.3 per cent between the UK and Japan, and 1.6 per cent between the USA and Japan. Moreover, the difference became larger following the oil crisis of 1973–4, owing to an upward trend in the USA and, less smoothly, in the UK as opposed to a significant drop in Japan between 1973 and 1975.

Thus Japanese firms have been generally less profitable than American and British firms. However, a straightforward comparison of the level of accounting profit rate can be misleading owing to complications arising from international differences in accounting. One such complication comes from inflation. Since the book value of total assets is based on historical acquisition costs, it can be undervalued after inflation causing the profit rate on assets to be overvalued. An effort to estimate the current cost of assets and compare the *real* profit rate internationally has been made by a group organized by Holland (1984). Their estimates for the three countries are shown in Fig. 8.2. This profit rate is defined in a similar way to that above, except (1) total assets are re-evaluated at current cost, (2) profits are re-evaluated to take account of the change in value of inventory, and (3) profits are

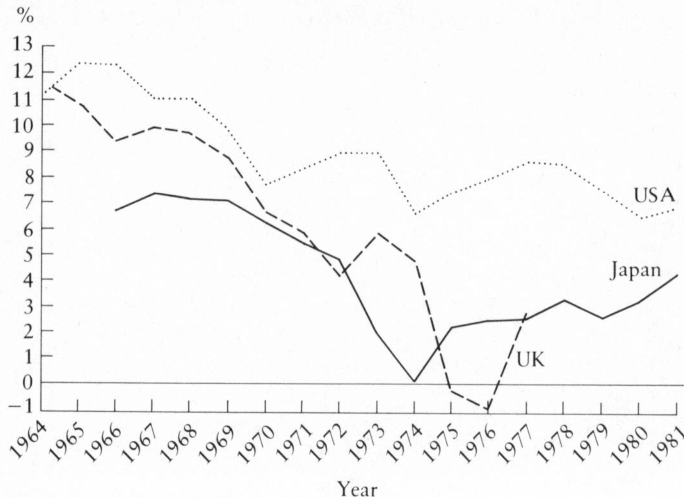

FIG. 8.2 Real profit rates in Japan, the USA, and the UK

computed before tax.[6] Their sample is larger than ours since it also includes non-financial non-manufacturing companies for Japan and the USA.

An obvious difference compared to Fig. 8.1 is the reversal of trend in the USA and the UK; that is, a downward rather than an upward trend can now be observed. Re-evaluation is particularly damaging to British profitability, making it trail behind American profitability and, in 1970–2 and 1975–7, even behind Japanese profitability. The Superior profitability of American over Japanese firms can still be observed; yet, the difference in the period after the oil crisis is now smaller. These results all imply that post-oil-crisis inflation caused the largest deviation of the accounting asset value from the economic value in the UK and then the USA.

Nevertheless, the profitability of Japanese firms remains the lowest (except for a few years in the 1970s when that of UK firms

[6] This is $ROC_w(BT)$ in their notation. Estimates are also provided of after-tax real profit rates for Japan and the USA. None of the following discussion is affected whether rates are computed after tax or before tax. Japanese real profit rates are the ratios of profits to assets at the end of the previous year, unlike our profit rates in the previous section and unlike real profit rates in the USA and the UK which are the ratios of profits to assets at the end of the same year. Because assets have been increasing in most firms, an upward bias in the real profit rate is likely to be present for Japan.

was even lower), implying that the lower profitability in Japan observed in Fig. 8.1 cannot be explained by the divergence between the accounting value and the economic value of assets. Indeed, there are reasons to believe that recalculation of profitability using current-cost assets should rather lower Japan's ranking in profitability. For one thing, the historic cost method of asset evaluation is strictly applied in Japan, whereas in the USA and the UK re-evaluation is sometimes made of assets acquired through mergers.[7] For another, when it comes to such durable assets as land, the price increase from the end of the war to the present day has been extraordinary in Japan, causing the assets of Japanese firms, particularly those with a long history, to be more undervalued than the assets of American and British firms. Hence, it is probably in Japan that assets are most undervalued and the profit rate on (nominal) assets most overvalued. Re-evaluation of assets is more likely to lower the relative profitability of Japanese firms than to raise it.

Another divergence between accounting profits and economic profits may arise from the omission of asset holding gains from accounting profits. Undervaluation due to this omission may be particularly acute in Japan where firms tend to hold a sizable amount of land and of shares in other companies, and the prices of land and shares have been rising at a pace far exceeding those in the USA or the UK.[8] Real profit rates taking these

[7] In the UK, re-evaluation of assets according to a current cost accounting (CCA) scheme became popular around 1980: see Nobes and Parker (1985). Our data are for 1964–77 and are unlikely to be subject to CCA.

[8] An interesting question is how much of these holding gains are recognized by management as profits. Of course, insofar as the firm is viewed as being owned and controlled by the shareholders, the question of whether the assets are owned by the firm or the shareholders themselves is superficial and all the gains have to be properly recognized by the management. However, if the firm is viewed as a more independent body serving the purposes not only of the shareholders but also of the employees and, possibly, of the suppliers and the customers, the assets will be viewed as indispensable and irreplaceable for its activity, and the holding gains may be regarded as gains which will never be realized. In such a firm, which must be a more accurate description of the Japanese firm, holding gains may never be properly recognized as a part of profits. Take Mitsubishi Estate for instance. This company owns a huge parcel of land in the Marunouchi area of Tokyo (equivalent to Wall Street in New York or the City in London), which is grossly undervalued in its books. From the viewpoint of the shareholders alone, there can be little doubt that they will be better off if the firm is liquidated, all land holdings are sold, and the gains are distributed among them. Yet the management would never think of taking such action. For liquidation means discharging workers!

holding gains into account have been estimated for Japanese companies by Wakasugi *et al.* (1984). The results suggest, as expected, that the inclusion of holding gains increases profit rates, though to what extent is ambiguous. In one estimate, the rate increases by an impressive 8.7 per cent for the 1966–81 period: in another, it increases only by 0.9 per cent.[9]

Apart from the effects of inflation, differences in accounting rules and business practices cannot be ignored in an international comparison. These differences are summarized in the appendix to this chapter. Some of them suggest an undervaluation of profit rate in Japanese firms, but some suggest otherwise, and the total effect is ambiguous. In other words, it is difficult to estimate how much of the difference in profitability between Japan and the USA or Japan and the UK observed in Figs. 8.1 and 8.2 is to be accounted for when all the adjustments are made.[10] In fact, it is not apparent how much adjustment should be made. Should we apply a completely identical criterion to countries with so many differences in institutions and business practices?

Therefore, although we can suggest for the moment that profit rates are likely to have been lower in Japan than in the USA or the UK until 1984, the results cannot be said to be conclusive. Since the cost of capital is unlikely to have been lower in Japan during this period, a suggestion is that the excess of the rate of profit over the cost of capital predicted by imperfect (or monopolistic) competition theory is least likely to be satisfied in Japan. We will confirm this suggestion in Section 10.6.

International comparison is less problematic when the inter-company variance rather than the level of profit rate is compared because inflation, accounting rules, and business practices are all country-specific and expected to affect the profit rates of all the companies in the country equally.

Fig. 8.3 shows the standard deviation of the profit rate calculated for each year across the sample firms used for Fig. 8.1. It gives a measure of the inter-firm dispersion of profit rate. A clear

[9] The result depends on whether or not the different timing between measuring profits and measuring assets is adjusted.

[10] Choi *et al.* (1983) and Ando and Auerbach (1988) give two such estimates, both implying that the Japan–USA ranking in profitability is unlikely to be reversed after the adjustments.

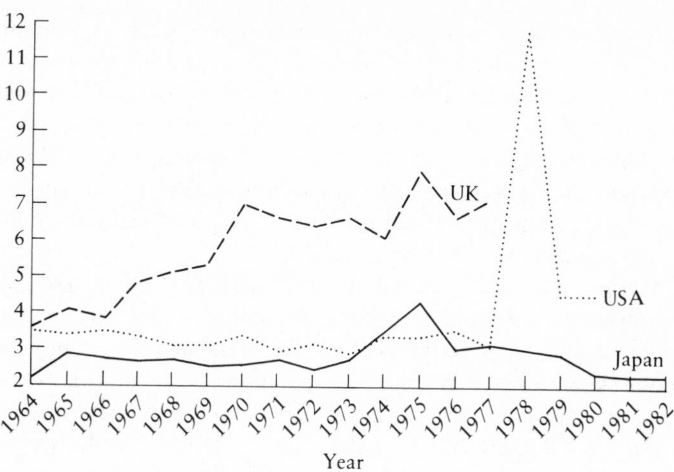

FIG. 8.3 Standard deviation of profit rates in Japan, the USA, and the UK

finding is that the UK has always had the largest dispersion, followed by the USA, except for the apparently abnormal peak in 1978 in the USA. The dispersion in Japan is even smaller than in the USA, a clear indication that Japanese companies are more homogeneous in terms of profitability than American or British companies. An exception to this tendency occurred in 1975 when Japan had a larger dispersion than the USA. That year also saw the lowest profitability (see Fig. 8.1), caused by severe depression after the oil crisis when some big-scale bankruptcies took place.

This fact suggests that, in Japan, the average level of profit rate and dispersion may have been negatively correlated over time, a conjecture confirmed with a correlation coefficient of −0.48. This negative correlation is contrary to the positive correlation in the other two countries; 0.46 in the USA (0.78 if the abnormal year of 1978 is excluded) and 0.10 in the UK. That is, the inter-firm dispersion has been smaller in more profitable years in Japan but larger in the USA and the UK.

A smaller standard deviation implies that there has been greater inter-firm equalization of the profit rate in Japan than in the USA or the UK. One interpretation of this, discussed earlier, is that Japanese markets are more competitive and entry and mobility barriers there are lower. Another interpretation, with contradictory implications is that Japanese firms have maintained uniform profitability by means of cartels, explicit or not. After all, the argument that the Japanese economy has been controlled by cartels and government–business collusion is popular among the authors of the 'conspiracy' theory of the Japanese economy (for instance, Prestowitz 1988). This interpretation, however, is inconsistent with the lack of evidence that profit rates are higher in Japan than in the USA and the UK.

A concept closely related to the inter-firm profit-rate dispersion is the so-called welfare triangle, that is, the loss of welfare (consumers' surplus plus producers' surplus) caused by monopolists' output restriction. Assuming that unit costs are constant and price elasticities of demand equal one in every industry, and approximating the cost of capital by the average rate of profit on assets, Harberger (1954) estimated the welfare loss as a sort of weighted profit-rate variance.[11] Therefore, our finding that the variance is smaller in Japan probably indicates that the welfare loss is also smaller.

Harberger estimated that in the US manufacturing sector in 1924–8, this loss was approximately 0.1 per cent of the GNP. More recently, Cowling and Mueller (1978) used US company data in 1963–6 to estimate the loss as 0.4 per cent of gross corporate products. They also estimated it to be 0.21 per cent in the UK in 1968–9. Shinjo and Doi (1989) also used company data to estimate the loss in Japan at 0.043 per cent in 1966–70 and 0.041 per cent in 1976–80. These results clearly indicate that the welfare loss has been lower in Japan in comparison to the USA and the UK, as we would expect.[12] Many criticisms have been made of Harberger's methodology, for example, his assumption that demand elasticities are one everywhere, and other formulas have been proposed. Yet, a comparison of the results of Shinjo and Doi and those of Cowling and Mueller clearly indicates that Japan has had a smaller welfare loss under any formula. We can therefore conclude that industries are more competitive in Japan than in the USA and the UK and, con-

[11] In his formula, the welfare loss equals the inter-industrial variance of profit rate weighted with sales times squared asset–sales ratio, multiplied by the number of industries divided by two.

[12] It is also lower than in France, since Jenny and Weber (1983) estimated that in France the same ratio was 0.13% in 1967–70 and 0.21% in 1971–4.

sequently, the loss of welfare caused by imperfect competition is smaller.

8.4. PERSISTENCE OF PROFITS

Competition, one may argue, will force the profit rate to equalize in the long run but not necessarily in the short run, and the larger inter-company variance of profitability in the USA and the UK may merely reflect the short-run disequilibrium. Even if the profit rates of individual firms have a propensity to converge in the long run, short-run disturbances may cause some firms to earn temporary supra- or sub-normal profits, thereby resulting in large inter-firm variance. The question is whether the larger variance comes from persistent profit-rate differences across firms or from inter-temporal fluctuation of individual profit rates. Brozen (1970, 292) argued that the concentration–profit correlation is a short-run disequilibrium phenomenon, by observing the 'lack of persistence of high rates of return in highly concentrated industries'.

Mueller (1977) criticized Brozen's view by estimating the long-run profit rate of each company by means of a regression equation fitted to the time series of its profit rate. His results suggested that the profit rates of firms with above-normal initial profit rates had a tendency to fall in the long run but not enough to achieve a convergence of profit rates across firms. The issue of whether profitability differences are persistent has been investigated by a number of studies since then (Mueller 1986; Connolly and Schwartz 1985; Mueller 1990). Here, let us discuss whether these studies throw any light on the extent of competition in Japan as compared internationally.

Let $P_i(t)$ denote the profit rate, as defined earlier, of firm i (= 1, . . . , n) in year t. To see if the firm is earning an above-average profit rate, we deduct from $P_i(t)$ the average profit rate of all the 376 manufacturing firms in the sample explained earlier (that is, n = 376), to get the normalized rate as follows:

$$\pi_i(t) = P_i(t) - \Sigma_i P_i(t)/n. \qquad (8.1)$$

Obviously an above-average profit rate implies a positive $\pi_i(t)$. We estimate the following autoregressive model for each firm using the 1964–82 time series of $\pi_i(t)$ (see Odagiri and Yamawaki 1986; Geroski 1990):

$$\pi_i(t) = \alpha_i + \lambda_i \pi_i(t - 1) + \varepsilon_i(t), \tag{8.2}$$

where α_i and λ_i are constants specific to firm i and $\varepsilon_i(t)$ is an error term assumed to be independently and identically distributed. The term λ_i indicates the extent that an above-average gain (or loss) in a certain year carries over to the following year; hence, it is interpreted as a measure of persistence of transitory (or short-run) excess rents. Its estimate will be denoted by LMD. Also, since (8.2) is a partial adjustment model, $(1 - \lambda_i)$ can be interpreted as the speed of adjustment.

The estimate of $\alpha_i/(1 - \lambda_i)$ gives the estimated long-run (or permanent) profit rate (denoted by PYLR). It is the profit rate towards which $\pi_i(t)$ converges provided $-1 < \lambda_i < 1$. If it is positive, the firm is estimated to earn above-average profits persistently.

In addition to PYLR and LMD, we define two profit variables for future use: PYIN, the initial profit rate, as defined by an average of $\pi_i(t)$ over the first two years (1964–5); and PYAV, its average over the entire period (1964–82). All are normalized to eliminate the effect of general business fluctuation.

It was found that the correlation coefficient (calculated from the sample of 376 firms) between PYLR and PYIN was significantly positive at 0.3: that is, a firm initially earning an above-average profit rate tends to earn an above-average profit rate into the indefinite future. In other words, the convergence of profit rates to the mean takes place only imperfectly even in the long run, showing that Mueller's (1977) finding in the USA of 'the persistence of profits' also applies to Japan.

A similar estimation of PYLR has been made for the USA and the UK, providing us with an opportunity to compare the extent of persistent interfirm profitability differences internationally.[13] In Table 8.1, the firms were grouped into six equally-sized subsamples in order of the initial profit rate (PYIN) and the means of PYLR, LMD, and PYIN were calculated for each subsample. By definition, therefore, PYIN is highest in subsample 1, the second highest in subsample 2 and so on. A clear finding is that in all countries PYLR has basically the same

[13] For details, see Odagiri and Yamawaki (1990) which also compares the results with those in Canada, the FRG, France, and Sweden. The UK result was taken from Cubbin and Geroski (1990).

Table 8.1. Persistence of profits

	Japan			UK			USA		
Period	1964–82			1951–77			1964–80		
Number of firms	376			243			413		
Variable	PYLR	LMD	PYIN	PYLR	LMD	PYIN	PYLR	LMD	PYIN
Subsamples									
1	0.74	0.63	3.41	1.91	0.57	9.08	1.49	0.58	5.62
2	0.28	0.46	1.16	0.89	0.45	3.83	0.79	0.49	1.41
3	0.15	0.46	0.42	0.14	0.45	1.56	−0.69	0.46	0.05
4	−0.19	0.39	−0.24	−0.58	0.46	−0.42	−0.23	0.42	−1.15
5	−0.63	0.44	−1.17	−1.05	0.47	−2.06	−1.27	0.47	−2.17
6	−0.76	0.41	−3.57	−0.67	0.55	−4.21	−2.23	0.41	−3.77
Correlation between									
PYLR and PYIN		0.305			0.339			0.275	
PYLR and PYAV		0.869			n.a.			0.398	

Source: Odagiri and Yamawaki (1990), table 10.4.

ranking across subsamples as PYIN, suggesting again that a firm with a high initial profit rate tends to earn a high profit rate even in the long run. The persistence of profits is observed in all of these countries.

Another finding is that the difference between the largest and the smallest PYLR is larger in the UK and the USA than in Japan. Our analysis in the previous section showed that the inter-company variance is smaller in Japan than in the UK and the USA in virtually every year, which agrees with the fact that the difference of PYIN between subsample 1 and subsample 6 is smallest in Japan of all three countries. This smaller profit-rate difference in Japan is further decreased in the long run: the most profitable group earns only 0.7 per cent points higher than the average while the least profitable group is behind the average by only 0.8 per cent points. By contrast, in the UK and the USA, the most profitable groups earn, respectively, 1.9 and 1.5 per cent points higher than the average. It is obvious, therefore, that the larger inter-company variance of profit rate observed earlier for the UK and the USA is not due to short-run disturbances but a persistently larger profit variance, that is, because profitable firms persistently earn larger profits.

The same conclusion can be reached by comparing the standard deviation of PYLR across firms, which was calculated only for Japan and the USA. This was 1.55 in Japan as opposed to 5.21 in the USA, a difference of more than three times—an even clearer indication that the profit-rate variance across firms in the USA is larger and more persistent than in Japan.

8.5. CHANGING BEHAVIOURAL MODES OF OLIGOPOLISTS

8.5.1. The Year 1964

Past studies in the USA indicate an interesting change that took place between the 1960s and the 1970s (Scherer *et al.* 1987). When the profit rate (of the firm or the line of business within a firm) was regressed on both the market share (of the firm or the LB) and the concentration ratio (of the industry), the coefficient to the concentration ratio was found by Shepherd (1972) to be positive, but by Ravenscraft (1983) and Martin (1983) to be negative. In addition, the positive effect of market share on profitability was found by Gale (1972) to be stronger in more concentrated industries, in contrast to the findings by Kwoka and Ravenscraft (1986) and by Mueller (1986) that the negative effect of rival firms' market share (namely, one minus the market share of the firm in question) was stronger in more concentrated industries.

Let us investigate whether the same change has occurred in Japan using two regression results, one for 1964 and the other for 1984.[14] They will show that the effect of market share has always been positive and significant, whereas the effect of concentration, with market share controlled, was positive in the 1960s but negative in 1984, similar to the change in the USA, suggesting that the change was caused by internationally common factors.

For the first study, which uses PYLR as well as PYIN and PYAV as the profit measure, the market structure variables are the four-firm concentration ratio (CR) and the market share (MS) for the main product of the firm.[15] Due to the lack of comprehensive data on concentration and market share (see Section 8.2), the CR data could be obtained only for 100 firms and the MS data for 88 firms (among these 100 firms) out of the original sample of 376 firms. Other independent variables are industry advertising intensity in 1965 (AD) and the rate of growth during 1964–82 of industrial shipment (IG). These are, again, for the main product of the firm.[16]

[14] Although a few studies have been conducted on the relationship between market share and profitability in Japan (Iwasaki 1974; Nakao 1979; Doi 1986), none analysed the concurrent effects of concentration and market share.

[15] It was impossible to obtain the CR or MS data as a sales-weighted average of each line of business of the firm because neither comprehensive CR or MS data nor the detailed sales composition of each firm was available. Thus we were forced to match each firm to the industry of its main product, eliminating diversified firms. On average the ratio of specialization to the matched industry was 73%. Basic data sources are the Fair Trade Commission (for CR) and *Toyo Keizai Tokei Geppo* (for MS). IG to be defined below was calculated using *Census of Manufactures* (Ministry of International Trade and Industry).

[16] A comparison was made between company advertising intensity (CAD)—the ratio of advertising expenditures to sales as reported in each company's income statement—and industry advertising intensity (AD)—the ratio of the amount of purchased advertising to the total domestic product as reported in the input–output table. Either variable has its advantages and disadvantages. The advantage of CAD is that it captures intra-firm differences in advertising intensity, whereas its drawbacks are that firms may be using a different accounting definition of advertising and that a number of firms did not report their advertis-

The ordinary least-squares estimation results are in Table 8.2, giving several valuable observations. First, with regard to the comparison between the four dependent variables, PYAV and PYIN performed better than PYLR, and the size of coefficient on CR or MS is largest with PYIN and then with PYAV. This finding is reasonable, because PYLR is an indirect measure estimated by means of least squares and may be vulnerable to estimation errors,[17] whereas PYAV and PYIN are not, and because the time lag between MS (measured for 1964) or CR (1964) and PYIN (1964–5) or PYAV (1964–82) is shorter than that between MS or CR and PYLR (indefinite future). Perhaps a more important fact is that the coefficients are significant even in the PYLR equation; that is, the market structure variables measured at a specific point in time are positively related to profit rates projected into the indefinite future. Clearly, the positive correlation between profitability and concentration or market share is not a short-run disequilibrium phenomenon, contrary to Brozen's contention quoted earlier.

Second, MS explains the profitability differences better than CR, suggesting that intra-industry differences are important and thus suggesting the crucial importance of using firm data.[18] By contrast, LMD is explained better by CR. The speed of erosion of excess short-run rents appears to be dependent not so much on firm characteristics as on industry characteristics, suggesting that

ing expenditures. The disadvantage of AD obviously is that firms in any one industry have to be assumed to have an identical level of advertising intensity. However, this drawback is not serious if the extent of product differentiation is due more to industry-specific factors, such as general product characteristics, than to firm-specific factors. Our preliminary estimation results suggested that AD has a stronger explanatory power than CAD; we therefore infer that industry-specific product differentiation is a more relevant factor of corporate profitability, and report only the results with AD. Another factor that affects profitability difference can be the R & D intensity, which again may be either at industry level or at firm level. However, the industrial R & D data can be obtained only at the two-digit level, whereas the company data suffer from definitional disturbances and the failure of more than a half of the firms to report R & D expenditures. Since preliminary regressions did not yield any significant effect of company R & D intensity, the results are not reported.

[17] Although these errors may be minimized by weighting the regressions with the inverted standard error of PYLR (Saxonhouse 1976), we found the estimation results to be insensitive to such weighting.

[18] It was confirmed that the difference in sample size (100 as opposed to 88) is not responsible for the difference in explanatory power between CR and MS.

TABLE 8.2. Effects of concentration and market share on profits, 1964

Dependent variable	Constant	CR	MS	AD	IG	$\bar{R}^2$
100 observations						
PYLR	−1.729[a]	0.018[b]		0.190[a]	0.015	0.126
	(−2.760)	(2.489)		(3.034)	(0.431)	
PYAV	−1.865[a]	0.025[a]		0.121[c]	0.004	0.127
	(−3.067)	(3.515)		(1.988)	(0.112)	
PYIN	−2.084[b]	0.035[a]		0.070	0.001	0.089
	(−2.400)	(3.408)		(0.805)	(0.028)	
LMD	0.358[a]	0.003[a]		0.021[a]	−0.009[b]	0.164
	(4.579)	(3.618)		(2.683)	(−2.012)	
88 observations						
PYLR	−1.730[a]		0.038[a]	0.115	0.042	0.167
	(−3.282)		(3.468)	(1.650)	(1.189)	
PYLR	−2.105[a]	0.010	0.029[b]	0.119[c]	0.033	0.168
	(−3.277)	(1.020)	(2.057)	(1.703)	(1.912)	
PYAV	−1.678[a]		0.049[a]	0.030	0.035	0.192
	(−3.250)		(4.500)	(0.435)	(0.994)	
PYAV	−2.241[a]	0.015	0.035[b]	0.036	0.021	0.206
	(−3.592)	(1.578)	(2.540)	(0.524)	(0.599)	
PYIN	−1.843[b]		0.073[a]	−0.049	0.033	0.183
	(−2.469)		(4.679)	(−0.499)	(0.665)	
PYIN	−2.594[a]	0.020	0.055[a]	−0.042	0.016	0.194
	(−2.869)	(1.452)	(2.752)	(−0.422)	(0.306)	
LMD	0.465[a]		0.004[b]	0.011	−0.006	0.079
	(6.644)		(2.391)	(1.208)	(−1.180)	
LMD	0.339[a]	0.003[a]	0.001	0.012	−0.009[c]	0.142
	(4.119)	(2.673)	(0.248)	(−1.396)	(−1.823)	

Notes: *t*-values in parentheses. Significance levels are: [a] 1%; [b] 5%; [c] 10%.

the speed of entry activity, presumably the major force of profit rate convergence, is influenced primarily by industrial characteristics. When both CR and MS are included as explanatory variables, CR tends to lose significance, though still positive, while MS remains significant with the exception of, again, the equation for LMD.[19]

As for the other explanatory variables, industrial advertising intensity, AD, exerts mostly positive effects on company profitability. These effects are more significant for PYLR and LMD than for PYAV and PYIN. The profit-enhancing effects of intensive industrial advertising appear to be lagged but long-lasting. Industrial growth, IG, has a positive but insignificant effect on PYLR, PYAV, or PYIN, and a significant negative effect on LMD. That LMD should be smaller in a growing industry is reasonable because growth will induce entry, thereby eroding the disequilibrium gains of incumbent firms more rapidly.

Finally, Table 8.3 shows the results when an interactive term between concentration, CR, and the market share of the rest of firms, 1 − MS, is introduced. The model is based on Kwoka and Ravenscraft (1986) and Mueller (1986). The use of advertising intensity multiplied by market share follows Mueller. We find contrasting results; that is, the coefficient of CR(1 − MS) is significantly negative in both of the US studies but positive here, which parallels the difference that the coefficient of CR, with MS controlled, is negative in recent US results such as Ravenscraft's (1983) but positive in our Table 8.2. These differences may have been caused by the difference between the USA and Japan or by the different time period. In fact, the similarity of our result to Shepherd's (1972) result for the US company data in the 1960s seems to suggest that intertemporal differences are

[19] The correlation coefficient (r) between CR and MS is a significantly high 0.619; no doubt, therefore, multicollinearity is present. To circumvent this problem, a proxy (or instrumental) variable for market share was sought. An inverted rank in terms of market share of the firm in the industry (RINV), namely, RINV = 1 for the top firm, RINV = $\frac{1}{2}$ for the second-ranking firm, etc., was found to be most suitable, because it is significantly correlated with MS (r = 0.573) and yet virtually uncorrelated with CR (r = 0.040): the results, not reported here, indicate that both CR and RINV become significant (with the exception of RINV in the LMD equation): that is, leading firms in concentrated industries are most profitable. Yet, in comparison with the equations using MS as the sole market structure variable (Table 8.2), the gain in explanatory power is unimpressive, suggesting that MS is sufficient as the market structure variable.

TABLE 8.3. Interactive effects of market share and concentration, 1964

Dependent variable	Constant	MS	CR(1 − MS)	AD × MS	IG	$\bar{R}^2$
PYLR	−2.180[a]	0.031[b]	0.016	0.362[b]	0.030	0.190
	(−2.977)	(2.485)	(1.358)	(2.264)	(0.833)	
PYAV	−2.518[a]	0.052[a]	0.018	0.0043	0.024	0.206
	(−3.495)	(4.318)	(1.613)	(0.027)	(0.683)	
PYIN	−3.026[a]	0.087[a]	0.021	−0.313	0.024	0.212
	(−2.931)	(4.998)	(1.265)	(−1.390)	(0.483)	
LMD	0.304[a]	0.0032[c]	0.0041[a]	0.034	−0.0084[c]	0.143
	(3.199)	(1.983)	(2.729)	(1.633)	(−1.812)	

Notes: Number of observations is 88. Significance levels are: [a] 1%; [b] 5%; [c] 10%.

more important. To inquire into this possibility further, let us now look at the study using more recent Japanese data.

8.5.2. The Year 1984

The JFTC possesses unpublished data on market share for a number of industries from which they calculate concentration ratios. Using this market share data the market share–profitability relationship was estimated for 1984.[20]

Table 8.4 lists the variables and data sources used in this study. There are two important differences from the study for the 1964 data. The first is the use of weighted averages of industrial data for several variables (those with asterisks in the table), as in the US studies. The second is the use of contemporaneous data (in 1984) for both the dependent variable, profit rate, and the independent variables. Unlike the study for 1964, therefore, one cannot here address the question of persistent profitability. In addition, the question of causality becomes more obscure. The sample consists of the 376 Japanese manufacturing firms listed in the First Section of the Tokyo Stock Exchange, for which all the data could be obtained.

The results, shown in Table 8.5, indicate a negative and significant coefficient for CR or for CR(1 − MS) when MS is controlled, in contrast to positive (though hardly significant) coefficients in Tables 8.2 and 8.3. That is, with MS fixed, the profit rate was higher in a more concentrated industry in the 1960s but lower in such an industry in 1984. Also, the negative effect of rivals' market shares was weaker in a more concentrated industry in the 1960s but stronger in 1984. These changes essentially agree with the changes observed in the USA. An inference can be made, therefore, that a change took place between the 1960s and the present day in a direction common to both the USA and Japan.

The effect of market share is again positive and quite strong. When MS is not controlled, CR does not have any significant effect on the profit rate, in contrast to the positive and significant effect obtained earlier. The effect of industrial growth, IG, is strongly positive, in contrast to the insignificant effect earlier.

[20] Because of the strict confidentiality of the market share data, this estimation was made by the JFTC staff under my supervision. I thank the staff, particularly T. Futagami, for the computation.

TABLE 8.4. List of variables for the JFTC study

Name	Definition	Source
PY	Profits (inclusive of interest payments) divided by total assets	Company reports
MS	Market share*	JFTC
CR	Four-firm concentration ratio*	JFTC
IG	1984/79 ratio of industry shipments*	*Census of Manufactures*
FS	Sales revenue in logarithm	Company reports
AD	Industry advertising/industry products*	*Input–Output Table*
RD	Firm R&D expenditures/sales	Company reports
TO	=1 if and only if the industry of the firm's main product has affluent technological opportunities	JFTC
IE	Industry exports/industry shipments*	*Monthly Report on Trade, Census of Manufactures*
IM	Industry imports/industry shipments*	*Monthly Report on Trade Census of Manufactures*

* The averages of the industrial values for the five (or fewer) main products of the firm, weighted with the sales proportions.

Industrial advertising intensity again has a positive effect. AD × MS performed slightly better than AD to explain PYLR in the previous study but not here. The R & D intensity has a positive effect, which is significant in equation (vi). Particularly interesting is the effect of trade. The result suggests that the profit rate is not affected by import competition but is lower in heavily exporting industries. An interpretation of the insignificant effect of imports is that competition among domestic suppliers was intense enough, whereas an interpretation of the negative effect of exports is that overseas markets were less profitable than domestic markets. Whether this is a permanent or temporary feature of Japanese exporting behaviour is unclear. For instance, because 1982–3 was a recession period with the capacity utilization index (100 in 1980) falling to 92.6, this lower capacity utilization may have prompted the firms to make an aggressive

TABLE 8.5. JFTC estimation results, 1984 (Dependent variable = PY)

Explanatory variables	(i)	(ii)	(iii)	(iv)	(v)	(vi)
Constant	5.13[a]	5.74[a]	6.20[a]	6.41[a]	7.74[a]	8.10[a]
	(10.11)	(7.86)	(8.73)	(8.30)	(3.91)	(4.05)
MS	0.076[a]		0.098[a]	0.077[a]	0.094[a]	0.074[c]
	(4.92)		(5.29)	(5.00)	(4.93)	(4.132)
CR		0.009	−0.024[b]		−0.014	
		(0.96)	(−2.14)		(−1.26)	
CR(1 − MS)				−0.027[b]		−0.015
				(−2.18)		(−1.221)
IG	1.42[a]	1.38[a]	1.45[a]	1.46[a]	1.30[a]	1.34[a]
	(5.07)	(4.77)	(5.21)	(5.21)	(4.34)	(4.48)
FS					−0.19	−0.21
					(−1.14)	(−1.20)
AD					0.32[c]	
					(1.77)	
AD × MS						0.57
						(1.04)
RD					0.12	0.196[b]
					(1.29)	(2.11)
TO					0.55	0.54
					(1.27)	(1.24)
IE					−0.024[a]	−0.025[a]
					(−2.64)	(−2.76)
IM					0.014	0.013
					(0.64)	(0.54)
$\bar{R}^2$	0.11	0.06	0.12	0.12	0.16	0.15

Notes: Number of observations is 376. *t*-values in parentheses. Significance levels are: [a] 1%; [b] 5%; [c] 10%.

export drive, its effect on profitability taking place in 1984. The evidence is not sufficient to confirm this interpretation, however.

8.5.3. *Interpretation*

Let us suppose that there are two firms, A and B, with the same market share in separate industries, and that A's industry is more concentrated than B's. Which firm should we expect to be more profitable? In one hypothesis, called the 'collusion hypothesis' or the 'shared-asset hypothesis', A will be more profitable than B, owing to the ease in collusion or the stronger influence enjoyed by the top firms. A higher price maintained by this collusion benefits every firm in the industry as a shared asset. Another hypothesis states that, if A and B have the same market share but A's industry is more concentrated, A's rival firms must be on average larger than B's. In terms of relative competitive strength, therefore, A's position is less favourable than B's. This will force A to employ more competitive strategies than B, cutting price margins, intensifying marketing efforts, speeding up inventive activities, and so forth. This 'rivalry hypothesis' predicts a lower profit rate for A.

Therefore, the two hypotheses form contrary predictions concerning the effect of concentration on the firm's profitability when the firm's market share is controlled. In addition, while an increase in the market share of all rivals combined (and a decrease in the firms' own share) is expected to decrease the profitability of the firm, this negative effect is expected to be smaller in a more concentrated industry under the collusion hypothesis, owing to the larger size of the average rival firm which is expected to foster effective collusion, but larger under the rivalry hypothesis, owing to intensified rivalry. Hence, the coefficient of the interactive term between CR and (1 − MS) is predicted to be positive under the collusion hypothesis but negative under the rivalry hypothesis.

The estimation results suggest that the collusion hypothesis was more relevant in the 1960s but that the rivalry hypothesis became more relevant in 1984. This shift in the relative explanatory power of the two hypotheses agrees with the US experience. It can therefore be inferred that oligopolists now behave less collusively but more competitively than twenty years ago in both the USA and Japan. Although no evidence is available for other countries, it does not appear far-fetched to assume that this change is consistent with the shifting economic conditions observed in every advanced nation during this period, such as rapid technological change including micro-electronization, faster and wider diffusion of information aided by this technological change, inter-industrial shifts of demand, and intensifying international competition.

A question that is more difficult to answer empirically is whether the high profit rate earned by a firm with a larger market share is the result of market power as traditionally argued, or of managerial as well as technological efficiency, as argued by Demsetz (1973). No previous study, in my view, has succeeded in separating these two hypotheses empirically, and whether it is at all possible to do so is questionable (Harris 1988). The findings above are consistent with either hypothesis. Indeed, insofar as collusion is rejected (as we have done with recent data), the separation of market power from efficiency may be irrelevant. Market power in a differentiated product market may originate from the exclusive use of certain inputs, better access to distribution, better product quality, or brand strength. Arguably, however, advantages in quality and brand are the consequence of efficient management and innovation. A better distribution channel is usually the result either of better management or of legal or other barriers in the way of other firms establishing a similar channel, and similar arguments can be made for the exclusive use of inputs. Therefore, the two supposedly opposing hypotheses are not as distinct as is usually believed.

8.6. CONCLUSION

The intensity of competition within markets and between markets can be influenced by a multitude of factors: the extent of market concentration as measured by, say, the four-firm concentration ratio, the distribution of market share among these top four firms, the height of legal, technological or strategic barriers to market entry and to intra-industry mobility, the speed of technological change, the importance of learning by doing, and the extent of internationalization are just some of those that are commonly discussed by industrial economists. In addition and perhaps more importantly, we have examined the behavioural aspects of competition. Does the firm place more emphasis on short-run profitability or long-run growth? Does it prefer acquisition to internal growth? Does it penetrate domestic and overseas markets by relying on local distributors or by making its own marketing efforts?[21] All these choices profoundly affect the intensity of competition in markets.

We have argued that Japanese management has a strong bias towards the latter strategy in any of these choices. All of these contribute to making competition more intense through entry activities and rivalry in pursuit of market share. This competitive aspect of Japanese management has seldom been noted by foreign observers. The 'cultural' theorists have tended to focus on the emphasis placed on harmonious human relations in Japan, while the 'conspiracy' theorists have tended to view the Japanese economy as a machine controlled by government guidance and cartels. Even such a knowledgeable Japanologist as Dore has written that 'the distinctively Japanese characteristics are that the "groupishness" of Japanese cultural traditions seems to make [cartels] form more easily' (Dore 1986, 75).[22]

The truth, however, is that Japan has always been a very competitive society. The education system is geared to competition (many people say excessively so) through a series of entrance examinations. Public examinations to gain qualifications are numerous and usually crowded with people aspiring to be accountants, welders, hairdressers, interior designers, and so on. Within companies, internal competition is intense, as described in Chapter 4. Perhaps, density—with more than two-thirds of the land being mountainous, Japan is the densest country in the world in terms of population and economic activity—and homogeneity—the Japanese basically belong to one ethnic group—have contributed to making the society competitive. Whatever the geographic and demographic reasons may be, the essential point is that competition in the Japanese economy is very intense, probably more so than in any other country. Competition, moreover, is the consequence as well as the cause of the entire Japanese management system.

[21] As for the willingness of the Japanese firm to bear a large marketing investment in entering foreign markets, see Chap. 12.

[22] In justice to Dore, I hasten to add that in the same book he also stated that 'in consumer markets competition is extremely keen' (83).

Some more recent authors, both foreign and Japanese, have begun to notice this fact. Abegglen and Stalk's book, *Kaisha*, a Japanese word for corporation, is probably the best example: 'Like heat in a chemical reaction, fast growth accelerates competitive interaction: relative cost position can change quickly, market share is liable to sudden change, investment requirements become massive, and immediate organizational adaptation is essential' (Abegglen and Stalk 1985, 19). To substantiate this argument, they give accounts of several cases, the most detailed of which is the dynamic competition between two motorcycle manufacturers, Honda and Yamaha. Among the Japanese authors writing in English, Kono noted that 'oligopoly, with similar-sized companies, is characteristic of the durable goods industry in Japan' (Kono 1984, 190), by showing that in six of the eight durable goods industries he examined, the ratio of market share between the largest firm and the second largest firm was only 1.4 or less. He then argued that 'it is a generally accepted theory that competition in an oligopoly of similar-size companies is the most intensive' (ibid. 191).

However persuasive they may be, discussions such as these that rely on a small number of cases remain open to doubt on grounds of lack of generality and statistical rigour. We have tried instead to approach the problem using a sufficiently large sample of companies, first by comparing the extent of concentration between Japan and the USA, second by comparing the mean, variance, and persistence of profit rates in Japan, the UK, and the USA, and thirdly by comparing the structure (market share and concentration)–profitability correlation. The distinctiveness of Japan does not become apparent so long as one's attention is confined to the structure, but can be observed more readily in the low profit rate and in its smaller inter-company variance, that is, by the performance measure of competition. This is perfectly consistent with our view that competition should be viewed primarily as a behavioural concept and not a structural concept. Irrespective of market concentration, competition is fully maintained if rivals compete fiercely with each other or if actual/potential entrants are actively seeking opportunities for entry. The consequence of this competition must be the long-run convergence of profit rates across firms.

Of course, in Japan as in any other country, some industries are notoriously monopolistic or collusive. The role of antitrust policy, therefore, should never be disregarded. In Japan the Fair Trade Commission has been watchful for any anti-competitive behaviour. The well-known fact that there have been fewer court cases under the antimonopoly law has often been attributed either to the weak stance of the JFTC or to the 'Japanese' custom of correcting wrongdoing by administrative guidance rather than prosecution. In this author's view, however, another explanation seems more pertinent: that the competitive nature of Japanese management and fewer mergers have actually kept the number of antitrust cases at a low level. We will return to this topic in Chapter 11.

Appendix: Accounting Rules and Profit Rates: International Differences

(1) *Depreciation.* The accelerated method, namely, the fixed-rate-on-declining-balance method, is common in Japan, whereas the straight-line method is common in the USA and the UK. Provided that Japanese firms are growing, this causes them to evaluate costs as higher, thereby depressing the reported profits. However, since the remaining value of assets should also be smaller, it is ambiguous whether the profit–asset ratio is higher or lower.

(2) *Retirement allowances.* A large lump-sum payment at the time of an employee's retirement is a well-established practice in Japanese companies, and allowances are made for this purpose during the employee's period of service. These allowances are regarded as deferred payment to the employee and included in the company's debts. They can be contrasted with the allowances for pensions, which are transferred to separate accounts without increasing the company's debts or assets. To the extent that the first is more important in Japan relative to the USA and the UK, the assets are expected to be larger and the profit–asset ratio smaller.

(3) *Loans to employees.* Most large Japanese firms provide housing or other loans to their employees on conditions more favourable than those commercially available, thereby providing, in effect, supplements to salaries and wages. Because these loans are treated as the firms' assets, the total assets of Japanese firms are likely to be inflated.

(4) *Receivables.* These are used more frequently in Japan to settle inter-firm trades. In consequence, there are more accounts payable remaining as debts and more accounts receivable as assets at the end of an accounting period, which again inflates the total assets in Japan.

(5) *Lease.* Leased assets are in principle included in assets in the USA and the UK but not in Japan. Hence, to the extent that Japanese firms use leases, their assets may be undervalued.

(6) *Consolidation.* The profit rates of Japanese firms are calculated from non-consolidated statements, whereas those of American and British firms come from consolidated statements. Until recently, few Japanese firms published consolidated statements. Now that many of

them publish both consolidated and non-consolidated statements, it is possible to make a comparison between the two statements, and this suggests that the profit rate is usually higher on a consolidated basis. Caution is needed here, however, because it may be only the firms with successful subsidiaries that are willing to publish consolidated statements, and only the successful subsidiaries that the parents are willing to consolidate.

Together with other differences in accounting rules between Japan and the USA or between Japan and the UK (see Choi *et al.* 1983; Nobes and Parker 1985; Wakasugi *et al.* 1984; Wakasugi *et al.* 1988; and Yamada 1989), these differences bias the international comparison of accounting profit rates. Unfortunately, the direction of this bias is ambiguous. Some of the differences discussed above suggest relative undervaluation of Japanese profit rates, but some suggest otherwise.

9

Macroeconomic Stability

9.1. INTRODUCTION

The performance of the Japanese macroeconomy has been impressive. Table 9.1 compares the economic growth rates of five leading nations since 1953. The most obvious fact to emerge is Japan's fast economic growth. In terms of real GDP, the Japanese economy grew at an average annual rate of almost 7 per cent during the thirty-five-year period from 1953 to 1987, in contrast to the US economy, which grew at the rate of 3 per cent and the UK economy which grew even more slowly. France and West Germany grew faster than these Anglo-American countries; yet, their growth rate of around 4 per cent is unimpressive compared to Japan's achievement. Japan's growth has slowed down since the oil crisis of 1973, but so has growth in other countries, which means that there has been no change in the international growth ranking.

In the lower half of the table, we have quoted from Dowrick and Nguyen (1989) the growth rates of per-capita GDP measured in terms of purchasing power parity. The result is similar to that in part A of the table. In fact, the difference between Japan on the one hand and the USA and the UK on the other is even larger here. Dowrick and Nguyen argued that a catch-up effect tends to boost the economic growth of initially poorer nations and slow down the growth of wealthier nations, owing to such factors as the public-goods nature of technological progress, changing preferences for quality of work and life rather than quantity of goods, and real and apparent differences in sectoral productivity growth. They estimated the rate of growth attributable to this effect and deducted this rate as well as the rate attributable to cyclical bias to calculate the 'adjusted' growth rate. This rate is shown in part C of Table 9.1. The difference, as expected, narrows after this adjustment; yet, there still remains an important difference between Japan (and Germany) on the

TABLE 9.1. Growth of real GDP in five countries, 1953–1987

Period	Japan	USA	UK	FRG	France
A: Annual growth rate of real GDP					
1953–63	8.28	2.80	2.78	6.22	5.02
	(2.19)	(2.77)	(1.54)	(2.59)	(1.35)
	[0.26]	[0.99]	[0.55]	[0.42]	[0.27]
1963–73	9.12	3.83	3.22	4.38	5.15
	(2.65)	(1.82)	(1.96)	(2.09)	(0.85)
	[0.29]	[0.48]	[0.61]	[0.48]	[0.17]
1973–87	3.67	2.48	1.63	1.79	2.12
	(1.71)	(2.69)	(2.08)	(1.83)	(1.20)
	[0.47]	[1.09]	[1.28]	[1.02]	[0.56]
1953–87	6.63	2.97	2.43	3.85	3.86
	(3.29)	(2.49)	(1.97)	(2.81)	(1.86)
	[0.50]	[0.84]	[0.81]	[0.73]	[0.48]
1953–87*	6.98	3.06	2.38	3.65	4.08
B: Annual growth rate of per-capita GDP in PPP					
1950–60	7.26	1.33	2.27	6.76	3.54
1960–73	8.45	2.80	2.53	3.59	4.63
1973–85	2.79	1.27	1.13	1.91	1.47
C: Adjusted annual growth rate of per-capita GDP in PPP					
1950–60	5.29	2.86	2.71	6.27	3.60
1960–73	7.29	3.97	2.78	4.05	5.03
1973–85	2.53	2.16	1.03	2.48	1.97

Notes: * indicates exponential growth rates estimated with regressions on trend terms; other rates in A are annual exponential growth rates averaged over the period. Figures in parentheses are the standard deviations of these annual rates and in square brackets are the coefficients of variation. PPP denotes purchasing power parity.

Sources: A: Calculated from OECD, National Accounts. B, C: Dowrick and Nguyen (1989).

one hand and the USA and the UK on the other. As an average for 1950–85 the adjusted rate is more than 5 per cent in Japan but 3 per cent in the USA and 2 per cent in the UK.[1]

Evidently therefore, the difference in growth performance between Japan and the USA and UK cannot be fully explained

[1] That Japan's growth rate for the period 1973–85 has decreased by adjustment is not due to the catch-up effect (which is in fact estimated to be negative) but to the cyclical bias supposedly caused by the high investment–GNP ratio. To this

by the 'convergence' of per-capita income that is expected to take place as lower-productivity countries catch up with high-productivity countries. There remains, so to speak, a missing link to explain the difference. In the next chapter, we will argue that the growth-maximizing behaviour of Japanese management provides such a link.

There is another important fact to be observed from Table 9.1. If we look at the fluctuation from year to year of the growth rate by the standard deviation (shown in parentheses), Japan's record is unimpressive. It actually appears to be the least stable country. However, if we look at the coefficient of variation (shown in square brackets), we find Japan (and France) to be most stable. This suggests that, even if its economy is hardly more stable than other economies in terms of the absolute level of business fluctuation, relative to the high growth rate fluctuation has been small.

Another well-known aspect of the Japanese macroeconomy is its low unemployment rate even during periods of recession. The rate has never exceeded 3 per cent in post-war Japan, whereas in many other developed economies, the worst rate has reached or exceeded 10 per cent.[2] This low unemployment rate may appear to be a direct consequence of the employment adjustment scheme in Japanese firms discussed in Chapter 3. However, even if each firm makes an effort to maintain lifetime employment, unemployment is bound to increase if firms go bankrupt following decreased demand and if surviving firms either cease new recruitment or dismiss existing temporary and part-time workers. Therefore, the lifetime employment scheme alone may not explain the relative stability of the Japanese economy.

With this end in view, the discussion in this chapter centres on how Japanese labour practice influences macroeconomic stability. A theoretical model is presented in Section 9.2, with an empirical application and interpretation in Section 9.3. In Section 9.4, we turn to the mark-up behaviour of Japanese firms during business

author it appears questionable whether this high ratio should be regarded as a cyclical phenomenon. If this 'cyclical' bias is not taken into consideration, the adjusted rate in the period is higher at 2.92.

[2] The international difference is partly due to internationally different definitions of unemployment; however, even when recalculated according to the American definition, the Japanese unemployment rate remains by far the lowest.

cycles and compare this with American findings. Section 9.5 offers some concluding remarks, with particular reference to Weitzman's view of Japan as a 'share economy'.

9.2. A MODEL OF LABOUR-HOARDING

Not only in Japan but probably in any economy, the level of employment is seldom reduced as much as might be implied by short-run profit maximization during periods of recession. This phenomenon, known as 'labour-hoarding' (Neild 1963; Solow 1968; Fay and Medoff 1985) or 'reserve labour' (Miller 1971), has been commonly observed across major developed economies. The effect of labour-hoarding on the aggregate supply as well as the aggregate demand of an economy has been discussed by Neild (1963, 29) who argued that 'the extent to which employers adjust their employment and hours governs the value of the short-run multiplier'. The assumption here is that labour-hoarding contributes to macroeconomic stability, though no formal analysis has been made to confirm this assumption or to derive the necessary conditions. It is by no means self-evident, because both aggregate demand and aggregate supply are affected by labour-hoarding. An equilibrium analysis is clearly needed to examine the consequences.

We will undertake such an equilibrium analysis using a Keynesian–Kaldorian framework. It is Keynesian in that the commodity-market balancing condition determines the level of national income, and the aggregate demand consists of consumption which is dependent on income level and other demands which are not. It is Kaldorian in that propensities to consume are assumed to be constant but different according to the two sources of income represented by wages and profits. The basic idea is simple: if labour is hoarded during a recession, the labour share of national income increases. Provided that the propensity to consume is larger with labour income than with corporate profits, the aggregate propensity to consume increases as the labour share increases. Since the Keynesian multiplier is the inverse of the aggregate propensity to save, the larger propensity to consume implies a larger multiplier, contributing to sustained aggregate demand under decreasing exogenous demand and stabilizing business fluctuation. A formal model now follows.

9.2.1. The Macroeconomy

Suppose that aggregate demand is composed of consumption expenditure C and autonomous (that is, exogenously given) non-consumption expenditure A. Suppose further that the propensity to consume is constant but may differ between the two income sources, aggregate labour compensation W and aggregate profits P. Let c_w and c_p denote the consumption propensities from W and P, respectively, and assume that $0 \leqslant c_p \leqslant c_w \leqslant 1$, $c_p < 1$, and $c_w > 0$. Then at a macro equilibrium, aggregate output Y is determined as follows:

$$Y = A + c_p P + c_w W. \tag{9.1}$$

Since the aggregate output is distributed between wages and profits, we have

$$Y = P + W. \tag{9.2}$$

(9.1) and (9.2) imply

$$A = (1 - c_p)Y - (c_w - c_p)W. \tag{9.3}$$

The equilibrium values of the endogenous variables, Y, W, and P, are affected by numerous factors, such as weather and technology. One such factor is the firm's decision rule determined by, among other things, the motivations of stockholders, managers, and employees, and their relative power. Let us consider two arbitrary decision rules, 1 and 2, and denote the equilibrium values under these rules by adding respective superscripts. Then, since A is independent of the rule, we have from (9.3)

$$(1 - c_p)(Y^1 - Y^2) = (c_w - c_p)(W^1 - W^2), \tag{9.4}$$

which immediately implies the following:

Proposition 1. Between any two decision rules, 1 and 2,
(i) if $c_p < c_w \leqslant 1$, $Y^1 > Y^2$ if and only if $W^1 > W^2$,
(ii) if $c_p = c_w < 1$, $Y^1 = Y^2$, and
(iii) if $c_w = 1$, $P^1 = P^2$.

Thus when the consumption propensity is constant irrespective of income source, the equilibrium national income cannot be affected by the decision rule. In fact, if $c_p = c_w$ $(= c)$, (9.3) reduces to

$$Y = A/(1 - c) \tag{9.5}$$

for any decision rule, which is nothing but the familiar Keynesian multiplier formula. (iii) follows from (9.2) and (9.4), indicating that if workers do not save, the equilibrium total profits are independent of the decision rule, and, if $W^1 > W^2$, then $Y^1 > Y^2$ and yet $P^1 = P^2$.

9.2.2. *The Firm*

Let x be an indicator of the size of demand for a monopolistic firm and let it distribute across firms according to a function $f(x)$: that is, $f(x)$ denotes the number of firms with a particular value of x. Suppose that firms are sufficiently many that $f(x)$ can be assumed to be a continuous function.[3] Every firm determines output q, price p, revenue y $(= pq)$, compensation to workers w, and profits p $(= y - w)$ as a function of x;[4] hence, we write these variables as $y(x)$ and so forth.

Since the aggregate output in value term is the sum of y for all firms,

$$Y = \int_0^\infty y(x)\, f(x)\, dx. \tag{9.6}$$

Integration does not extend to non-positive x because the firm with non-positive demand might as well cease operation. Hence, even though the number of potential firms is fixed, the number of operating firms may vary as the density function $f(x)$ shifts.

Notice that the density function is not free from the decision rule in a macro-equilibrium. To illustrate this fact, consider an extreme case where $c_p = c_w$. From Proposition 1 we know that $Y^1 = Y^2$ at equilibrium and therefore (suppressing the limits to integrals):

$$\int y^1(x) f^1(x) dx = \int y^2(x) f^2(x) dx. \tag{9.7}$$

Suppose that the two rules are such that $y^1(x) > y^2(x)$ for all x (say, rule 1 is revenue-maximization and rule 2 is profit-maximization). Then, apparently, (9.7) is satisfied only if the distribution given by $f^1(x)$ is mostly leftward of that given by $f^2(x)$. That is, the demand curve for an average firm must

[3] If the number of firms is small, x has to be regarded as a discrete variable with the function $f(x)$ non-continuous, and integrations in the following are replaced by summations. All the analyses remain the same.

[4] In this section, the variables for each firm are denoted by small letters and the aggregate variables by capital letters.

be leftward under rule 1 so that, despite the intended larger revenue, the same equilibrium revenue is realized on average to the effect that $Y^1 = Y^2$. This example shows that the distribution depends on the decision rule because of the constraint imposed by macro-equilibrium.

With the same aggregation applied to W and P, equation (9.3) is rewritten as

$$A = (1 - c_p) \int y(x)f(x)\mathrm{d}x - (c_w - c_p) \int w(x)f(x)\mathrm{d}x. \quad (9.8)$$

9.2.3. A Constant-Share Rule

Consider a decision rule, which we shall call a constant-share (CS) rule, in which the share of labour and thus the share of profits are constant irrespective of x. If we denote the values under this rule by superscript 0, $w^0(x) = \sigma y^0(x)$ for all x, with a constant σ $(0 < \sigma < 1)$. Now compare a macro-equilibrium under an arbitrary rule j with that under a CS rule, leaving other conditions, such as A, unchanged. First note that by (9.8)

$$\begin{aligned}(1 - c_p) &\int y^j(x)f^j(x)\mathrm{d}x - (c_w - c_p) \int w^j(x)f^j(x)\mathrm{d}x \\ &= (1 - c_p) \int y^0(x)f^0(x)\mathrm{d}x - (c_w - c_p) \int w^0(x)f^0(x)\mathrm{d}x \\ &= [1 - (1 - \sigma)c_p - \sigma c_w]\sigma^{-1} \int w^0(x)f^0(x)\mathrm{d}x, \qquad (9.9)\end{aligned}$$

where the second equality follows from the definition of the CS rule. Using (9.9), we can compare the aggregate labour compensation under the two rules as follows:

$$\begin{aligned}W^j - W^0 &= \int w^j(x)f^j(x)\mathrm{d}x - \int w^0(x)f^0(x)\mathrm{d}x \\ &= \int w^j(x)f^j(x)\mathrm{d}x - [1 - (1 - \sigma)c_p - \sigma c_w]^{-1}\sigma[(1 - c_p) \\ &\quad \int y^j(x)f^j(x)\mathrm{d}x - (c_w - c_p) \int w^j(x)f^j(x)\mathrm{d}x] \\ &= \{(1 - c_p)/[1 - (1 - \sigma)c_p - \sigma c_w]\} \\ &\quad \int [w^j(x) - \sigma y^j(x)]f^j(x)\mathrm{d}x. \qquad (9.10)\end{aligned}$$

Combining (9.10) with (9.2) and (9.4), we have

$$Y^j - Y^0 = \{(c_w - c_p)/[1 - (1 - \sigma)c_p - \sigma c_w]\} \int [w^j(x) - \sigma y^j(x)]f^j(x)\mathrm{d}x \quad (9.11)$$

$$P^j - P^0 = -\{(1 - c_w)/[1 - (1 - \sigma)c_p - \sigma c_w]\} \int [w^j(x) - \sigma y^j(x)]f^j(x)\mathrm{d}x \quad (9.12)$$

which yield the following proposition:

> *Proposition* 2. Suppose that the share of labour is larger than σ in at least one firm and equal to σ in all the others. Then, in comparison to the equilibrium in which every firm sets the share equal to σ,
> (i) if $c_p < c_w \leqslant 1$, the equilibrium aggregate labour compensation and the equilibrium national income are both larger;
> (ii) if $c_p = c_w < 1$, the equilibrium aggregate labour compensation is larger but the equilibrium national income is the same; and
> (iii) if $c_w = 1$, the equilibrium aggregate profits are the same.

Before discussing the implications of this proposition, let us consider the equilibrium under CS in more detail. By equations (9.2) and (9.8) and the definition of CS, it is straightforward to prove that

$$Y^0 = A/[1 - (1 - \sigma)c_p - \sigma c_w] \quad (9.13)$$

$$W^0 = sA/[1 - (1 - \sigma)c_p - \sigma c_w] \quad (9.14)$$

$$P^0 = (1 - \sigma)A/[1 - (1 - \sigma)c_p - \sigma c_w]. \quad (9.15)$$

Because $(1 - \sigma)c_p + \sigma c_w$ is the weighted average of consumption propensities and equals the aggregate consumption ratio, $(c_w W + c_p P)/Y$, (9.13) is a modified multiplier formula. These equations imply that, given the constancy of σ, c_p, and c_w, Y^0, W^0, and P^0 all change proportionally with A. If A is reduced by 10 per cent, Y^0, W^0, and P^0 also decrease by 10 per cent. Consequently, a unitary output elasticity of labour compensation must be observed in the CS economy.

9.2.4. An Example

An example of the constant-share rule is easy to find. Suppose that every firm is monopolistic with an iso-elastic demand function

$$q = xp^{-1/(1-\alpha)} \qquad 0 < \alpha < 1 \tag{9.16}$$

and a Cobb–Douglas production function:

$$q = ak^{1-\beta}w^{\beta} \qquad a > 0, 0 < \beta \leqslant 1, \tag{9.17}$$

where k denotes the amount of capital. Suppose also that the firm is a price-taker in the labour market; hence, without loss of generality, the wage rate is normalized to unity, which is why labour input is written as w in (9.17). Given a unit cost of capital by r, the profit is defined by

$$\pi = pq - rk - w. \tag{9.18}$$

Maximization of (9.18) subject to (9.16) and (9.17) is straightforward and yields the optimal values (denoted with asterisks) which depend on x, as follows:

$$w^*(x) = \alpha\beta p^*(x)q^*(x) = \alpha\beta y^*(x). \tag{9.19}$$

Obviously, the share of labour (σ) is constant at $\alpha\beta$: hence, profit maximization (PM) is a CS rule in this example.

9.2.5. *Labour-Hoarding and Macro-Equilibrium*

Suppose in this example that the level of demand to a certain firm, x, falls by 1 per cent. A simple calculation can show that the profit-maximizing levels of w and y both decrease by the proportion of $(1 - \alpha)/(1 - \alpha\beta)$; hence, the elasticity of employment with regard to output (in value term) is unity. By contrast, suppose that the firm opts to hoard labour, that is, to maintain the prior level of employment (which is now larger than the PM level) or to reduce it only by a proportion smaller than $(1 - \alpha)/(1 - \alpha\beta)$. If we write this labour-hoarding behaviour by LH and denote the values under LH by capped variables, we have $\hat{w}(x) > w^*(x)$. Consider an economy where at least one firm (and possibly all the firms) chooses LH whereas the rest of the firms choose PM. Since this economy satisfies the condition in Proposition 2, aggregate employment (W) and aggregate output (Y) decrease by a smaller proportion when A falls than in an economy in which all the firms follow PM. In this way, the firm's effort to retain extra labour in a period of recession contributes to smaller macro-unemployment and a smaller reduction in GDP.

Two remarks deserve attention. First, hoarding (that is, not laying off) one extra worker by a firm results in extra employment of strictly more than one worker in a macro-equilibrium. This is the multiplier effect. See equation (9.10). If $\hat{w}(x')$ is greater than $\sigma\hat{y}(x')$ by one (one more worker being retained) for x' such that $\hat{f}(x') = 1$ (one such firm) with $\hat{w}(x) = \sigma\hat{y}(x)$ for all $x \neq x'$, whereas $w^0(x) = \sigma y^0(x)$ for all x including x', $\hat{W}$ is greater than W^0 by $(1 - c_p)/[1 - (1 - \sigma)c_p - \sigma c_w] > 1$; for instance, if $c_p = 0.261$, $c_w = 0.903$, and $\sigma = 0.472$ (the estimates for Japan; see the next section), this multiplier equals 1.7. That is, hoarding one worker by any firm saves 0.7 additional worker from being discharged somewhere in the economy. By equation (9.11) the multiplier for GDP is $(c_w - c_p)/[1 - (1 - \sigma)c_p - \sigma c_w]$ which equals 1.5 in this example.

Second, equation (9.12) reveals that, not surprisingly, P^j, for any j, cannot be greater than P^0 but, interestingly, if $c_w = 1$, $P^j = P^0$. That is, when the workers spend all their income on consumption, the aggregate equilibrium profits are no smaller even if each firm sacrifices profits to retain is workers. Therefore, when $c_w = 1$, workers as a whole receive more and capitalists as a whole receive the same under LH in comparison to CS, such as PM in the example above, proving LH's superiority in Pareto's sense.

We have discussed labour-hoarding under contracting demand. When, on the contrary, demand is increasing, a plausible hypothesis is that a labour-hoarding firm will increase employment less that a profit-maximizing firm. One reason is that a firm that has hoarded labour during a previous slump can increase production (to a certain extent) without new recruitment. Another is that, even if the demand increase is large enough to warrant additional employment, the firm is unlikely to hire to the profit-maximizing level in anticipation of the cost of hoarding these workers in a future recession. Thus, in an expansionary period, $\hat{w}(x)$ is likely to be smaller than $w^0(x)$ for some or all x. The multiplier mechanism then works in a reverse direction, increasing aggregate employment and aggregate output by a smaller proportion. It is likely therefore that labour-hoarding contributes to a smaller fluctuation in business both in an upward and in a downward direction.

9.3. APPLICATION TO JAPAN'S EXPERIENCE

An international comparison of the extent of labour-hoarding can be made in two ways. The first is by comparing the output elasticities of employment, as in Section 3.3. The elasticities were significantly below one in most countries and particularly in Japan, a finding inconsistent with the constant-share rule but consistent with the labour-hoarding hypothesis.

The other method is by focusing on the parameters in the model, in particular, the share of labour (σ) and the consumption ratios (c_w and c_p). When labour is hoarded, σ is expected to be larger during a phase of contraction in the business cycle and smaller during a phase of expansion. A negative correlation is thus predicted between σ and the rate of change in real GDP. Table 9.2 supports this prediction with significantly negative coefficients of the rate of real GDP growth. In none of the five countries is the share of labour constant. In addition, the countercyclical movement of labour share is most prominent in Japan and the UK, followed by France. This international ranking agrees with the ranking in the output elasticity of employment (in reverse order) in Table 3.1, again suggesting that labour-hoarding is most prevalent in Japan (and perhaps the UK) and least prevalent in the USA and Germany.

The regression in Table 9.2 also indicates a significant increase in trend of labour share in every country except the UK. This trend is strongest in Japan implying that, despite the smallest labour share on average during 1960–82, the difference from the other countries is diminishing.

Table 9.3 shows the average aggregate consumption ratio ($\bar{c}$) in the first row and the estimated coefficient in a regression of this consumption ratio on the share of labour. Since

$$\bar{c} = (1 - \sigma)c_p + \sigma c_w = c_p + \sigma(c_w - c_p), \qquad (9.20)$$

the coefficient gives an estimate of $c_w - c_p$. Using this fact and (9.20), we can arrive at a solution for c_w and c_p as in the last two rows of Table 9.3. As expected, c_w is larger than c_p except in Germany. This difference between the two consumption ratios is largest in Japan where the statistical significance of the regression coefficient is also highest. In fact, of the five countries, Japan has the highest c_w and lowest c_p. Thus, when labour is hoarded, its positive impact on aggregate employment and aggregate income through the multiplier effect is expected to be largest in Japan and yet its adverse effect on aggregate profits is expected to be smallest: see (9.10), (9.11), and (9.12). That is, labour-hoarding is expected to contribute to the stability of employment and

TABLE 9.2. Labour share regressed on real GDP growth and trend for five countries

	US	Japan	FRG	France	UK
Mean labour share 1960–82	60.3	47.2	53.3	50.1	59.7
	(1.6)	(6.0)	(3.2)	(3.9)	(1.6)
Coefficient on real GDP growth	−0.145	−0.212	−0.135	−0.191	−0.224
	(0.042)	(0.063)	(0.061)	(0.072)	(0.090)
Coefficient on trend term	0.162	0.727	0.347	0.492	−0.080
	(0.054)	(0.114)	(0.082)	(0.055)	(0.100)
Durbin–Watson statistics	1.899	1.192	1.314	1.016	1.537
Adjusted R^2	0.988	0.894	0.966	0.979	0.955

Notes: In parentheses are the standard deviations (in the first row) and the standard errors (in the second and third rows). The Beach–Mckinnon iteration technique (AR1 procedure in TSP) was used in the estimation to minimize the bias due to serial correlation.

Data Source: OECD, National Accounts.

TABLE 9.3. Consumption ratios in five countries

	USA	Japan	FRG	France	UK
Mean aggregate consumption ratio 1960–82	0.629 (0.010)	0.563 (0.020)	0.561 (0.010)	0.618 (0.012)	0.623 (0.023)
Effect of labour share	0.425 (0.205)	0.642 (0.161)	−0.075 (0.194)	0.335 (0.147)	0.132 (0.135)
Estimated c_p	0.373	0.261	0.601	0.449	0.544
Estimated c_w	0.798	0.903	0.525	0.785	0.676

Notes: In parentheses are the standard deviations (in the first row) or the standard errors of the estimates (in the second row). The second row gives the estimated slope coefficient in a regression of the change in consumption ratio on the change in the share of labour (using changes rather than levels to avoid autocorrelation) without the constant term. The Durbin–Watson statistics were all greater than the lower limit for the 5% significance level.

Data Source: OECD, National Accounts.

GDP most strongly in Japan. This finding is quite consistent with Japan's relative economic stability discussed in Section 9.1.

9.4. PRICE MARK-UP AND BUSINESS FLUCTUATION

The question of how much labour to hoard is inseparable from the question of pricing or, in other words, the question of how much mark-up (gross of capital costs) to impose over labour and material costs. Suppose that the demand curve for an oligopolistic firm shifts to the left, thereby reducing the quantity demanded at the current price. At this quantity the marginal labour-related cost, namely, an additional labour cost to produce an extra unit of output, is zero if labour is hoarded, for instance, when the prior level of employment is maintained. Thus the firm has an incentive to reduce the price and increase the quantity demanded, and the required price-reduction is larger the smaller the price elasticity of demand. This fact can be easily established in our example in the previous section. In (9.16), suppose that x is decreased by 1 per cent. It is easy to establish that the price, p, must then be decreased by $1 - \alpha$ per cent to maintain the same level of demand, which is the inverse of the demand elasticity.

Since marginal cost is zero under the assumed labour-hoarding behaviour and the marginal revenue is always positive in this example, the firm has a strong incentive to reduce the price by this much.

It is possible to conjecture, therefore, that, if the firms with market power increase their prices more or reduce prices less in a period of recession than the firms in more competitive markets, they must be sacrificing employment stability. This conjecture, expected to hold if the demand elasticity is uniform across markets, is even more valid if, as usually supposed, the elasticity is smaller in monopolistic markets owing to, for instance, brand loyalty and control of the distribution network. Therefore, a study of how pricing behaviour is related to market concentration in the course of business fluctuation can give us a clue as to how firms under different market structures behave differently in terms of employment stability. In order to eliminate the effects of material costs, and also because of ease in obtaining comparable data, it is usual to use price–cost margins (PCM = (revenue − non-capital costs)/revenue) or mark-ups (MU = revenue/non-capital costs) in place of prices.[5] Thus the relation between PCM or MU and market concentration during recession has been an empirical issue of great concern to researchers as well as policy-makers.

Wachtel and Adelsheim (1977, 7) argued that 'firms operating in concentrated industries will increase their price mark-ups during recessions to the extent they can, in order to recapture revenues lost from declining sales', based on a finding from US industrial data (to be discussed in detail in the following). Similarly, Cowling (1983, 342) argued that 'the existence of excess capacity will tend to bolster collusion by making it clear to participants that rivals can react immediately—the existence of excess capacity makes the threat of retaliation more credible', and supported this argument using UK manufacturing time-series data. If these findings are correct, employment fluctuation over business cycles must be larger in more concentrated industries, which agrees with Feinberg's (1979) finding of a positive correlation between employment instability and concentration ratio from the US panel data of workers.

[5] Alternatively, price changes may be regressed on (weighted) material and labour cost changes as well as on concentration ratio: see Shinjo (1977).

Not all previous studies agree with these authors, however. Qualls (1979) found that the trend-free price–cost margin is positively correlated with concentration in 1966, the peak year of a business cycle, and negatively correlated in 1958 and 1970, the trough years. With this finding, he suggested that 'the same factors [such as high concentration] which allow for the maintenance of higher margins above cost also may allow for margins to be varied (in keeping with industry-wide profit maximizing considerations) in the face of fluctuating industry demand without interfirm coordination being destroyed' (Qualls 1979, 310, his parentheses). Domowitz *et al.* (1986) also found that the positive effect of concentration on the price–cost margin increases when the percentage change in industry output increases or economy-wide unemployment decreases. Both Qualls and Domowitz *et al.* used American industrial data. For Germany, Neumann *et al.* (1983) found that the effect of concentration on the price–cost margin is larger during periods of expansion than during recession.

Table 9.4 compares the mark-up behaviour of Japanese industries with the US results of Wachtel and Adelsheim. Each figure shows the average percentage change (from peak to trough) in MU, as defined above, for each period and for each of three groups separated on the basis of a four-firm concentration ratio (CR). Depending on whether CR is greater than or equal to

TABLE 9.4. Average % changes in mark-up by degree of concentration, Japan and the USA

Period	H	M	L
(*a*) *United States*			
1948–49 recession	10.78	−8.52	−8.16
1949–52 expansion	4.76	8.67	−4.54
1953–4 recession	14.15	−0.08	−0.32
1954–6 expansion	6.97	14.42	3.60
1957–8 recession	13.47	−4.91	−7.55
1958–60 expansion	−10.92	7.42	5.04
1960–1 recession	5.29	−1.86	1.34
1961–9 expansion	15.28	18.36	13.65
1969–70 recession	−1.05	0.82	2.54
Excluding the auto industry	1.75	—	—

TABLE 9.4. (cont.)

Period	H	M	L
(b) Japan			
1958–61 expansion	0.929	0.315	0.725
	(3.980)	(3.305)	(1.910)
1962 recession	1.040	1.845	1.199
	(8.226)	(6.132)	(4.786)
1963–4 expansion	0.909	−0.052	1.512
	(5.526)	(4.138)	(3.190)
1965 recession	−0.196	−0.327	0.036
	(9.129)	(5.550)	(7.751)
1966–70 expansion	0.402	0.447	0.408
	(2.143)	(1.626)	(1.359)
1971 recession	−0.149	3.149	−0.120
	(8.548)	(9.409)	(3.530)
1972–3 expansion	0.893	0.807	0.465
	(5.482)	(4.521)	(2.363)
1974 recession	−4.595	−2.817	−2.109
	(11.033)	(5.909)	(3.670)
1975–6 expansion	1.798	−0.551	−0.019
	(6.419)	(2.600)	(3.138)
1977 recession	−0.787	−1.051	0.285
	(7.167)	(4.548)	(3.866)
1978–9 expansion	1.467	1.877	0.870
	(4.804)	(3.468)	(1.641)
1980–2 recession	−0.412	−0.396	−0.600
	(2.393)	(1.868)	(1.723)

Notes: H refers to those industries with high concentration ($50 \leqslant$ CR); M, medium concentration ($25 \leqslant$ CR $\leqslant 50$); and L, low concentration ($25 <$ CR), where CR is the four-firm concentration ratio. In (*b*) the variances are given in parentheses. The number of sample industries for (*b*) is about 240 with a slight variation from period to period.

Sources: (*a*) Wachtel and Adelsheim (1977), table 2; (*b*) Odagiri and Yamashita (1987), table 1.

50 per cent, less than 50 but greater than or equal to 25 per cent, or less than 25 per cent, the industry is classified into a high (H), middle (M), or low (L) concentration industry, respectively. Part (*a*) of the table gives the American results of Wachtel and Adelsheim, who divided the twenty-two-year period into nine

subperiods according to business fluctuation. There is a clear finding: in every period of recession except 1969–70, the percentage change in MU is largest in the H industries. In fact, except for 1969–70 (and 1960–1 for L), MU increased during recession in the H industries but decreased in the M and L industries. In 1969–70, the H industries recorded a decrease in MU, but when the automobile industry (particularly hard hit by the competitive threat of imports during this period) is excluded, the change turns to positive. During expansion, by contrast, the change is largest in the M industries while it is either lowest or second lowest in the H industries.

Part (*b*) of Table 9.4 gives a comparable result for Japan.[6] Here the 1958–82 period is separated into twelve subperiods based on the business cycle as defined by the Economic Planning Agency. We notice that all recession periods except the most recent last no longer than one year, whereas all periods of expansion last two to five years, which of course means that Japan has been a growing country with only modest and short-lived downturns. The table shows a clear contrast with the USA: in none of the six recession periods is the change in MU largest in the H industries. It is lowest in three recession periods and second lowest in the other three. By contrast, it is highest in three of the six expansion periods. The thesis of Wachtel and Adelsheim and of Cowling clearly does not apply to Japan's experience.

The analysis is simplistic, and more detailed analyses, in particular multiple regression analyses taking account of the influences of other variables, are desirable. Such analyses were made in Odagiri and Yamashita (1987), which gave the following results. First, when the rate of change in MU was regressed on CR, capital requirement, advertising intensity, the growth rate of industrial shipment, and import penetration, the result was inconclusive concerning the effect of CR. Among the six recession periods, the effect was significantly positive once and significantly negative twice.[7] Among the six expansion periods, it

[6] CR is measured at 1971 and taken from the concentration ratio data of the Ministry of International Trade and Industry detailed in Sec. 8.2. MU is calculated from the Census of Manufactures (the Ministry of International Trade and Industry).

[7] Unless otherwise stated, the significance is always determined at the 5% level.

was significantly negative once and significantly positive twice. The result therefore appears to contradict the prediction of Wachtel and Adelsheim that the effect of CR on the change in MU is positive in recession and negative in expansion.

Second, when MU was regressed to the same list of variables (except for capacity utilization which replaces industrial growth), the effect of CR was significantly positive in every period until 1973 but only once among the five periods after 1974. Also the coefficient of CR has decreased over the periods. It is therefore suggested that the effect of concentration on MU has been declining in the past two or three decades and particularly after the oil crisis of 1973. This finding is consistent with the finding in Section 8.5 that the effect of CR on profit rate, when market share is not controlled, was significantly positive in 1964 but insignificant in 1984. When differentiating between recession and expansion, there is evidence of a weak tendency for the effect to be stronger in expansionary periods; however, this tendency also becomes obscure after the oil crisis. The observation for the pre-oil-crisis periods is consistent with Qualls but not with Wachtel and Adelsheim.

Third, intertemporal variation of MU was found to be higher in more concentrated industries, when capital requirement, advertising intensity, and import penetration are controlled. This finding is consistent with the above-mentioned larger effect of CR on MU in expansion because the average level of MU itself is higher in expansion. The finding is again at odds with the hypothesis of Wachtel and Adelsheim that firms in concentrated industries increase mark-up in recession to maintain profitability.

Fourth, when an interaction term of CR and industrial growth was introduced into the regression of the change in MU to take account of industry-specific business conditions, the coefficient was significantly negative in three of the twelve periods and significantly positive in one. This result is more favourable to the Wachtel–Adelsheim hypothesis than the results so far because the negative coefficient implies that the effect of concentration to increase MU is higher under a smaller increase (or larger decrease) in industrial demand. Nevertheless, the result is hardly clear-cut, with only seven of twelve being negative (significant or not) as hypothesized, and with only three significant.

To sum up, the results are hardly conclusive. There is more

evidence against the thesis of Wachtel and Adelsheim and of Cowling than there is to support it. For the reason stated at the beginning of this section, the result is consistent with the prevalence of labour-hoarding behaviour among big Japanese firms. Nevertheless, one should be cautious about making any inferences about the difference in employment adjustment in Japan and the USA from this rather weak evidence alone. First of all, as stressed in the last chapter, concentration is a far from perfect indicator of market power or of lack of competition; therefore, the lack of any significant or consistent effect of concentration may imply no more than the inadequacy of the measure. Second, the nature of business fluctuation was different between the two countries. In Japan during the period under study, recession lasted only for a year (except 1980–2) and tended to be modest, with a decrease in real GNP taking place merely once in 1974 as a consequence of the oil crisis. Hence, Japanese managers probably expected, correctly, that any recession would be short-lived and not serious. With this expectation they may have opted not to take any drastic action, such as laying off workers and changing mark-ups, thus obscuring the differences between expansion and recession. Moreover, we have to recall that not all studies agree with the Wachtel–Adelsheim thesis, even in the USA.

Notwithstanding these ambiguities, we believe that Japanese firms do make efforts to maintain employment as far as possible. That is, they tend to hoard labour more often than American firms, and as a result make aggressive pricing and marketing efforts during a recession. The results in this section are therefore consistent with the finding of low output elasticity of employment in Section 3.3. Abegglen (1973, 45) also noted this consequence of the Japanese employment system by saying that 'there is a clear incentive, when faced with reduced demand, or lower demand than anticipated, to operate facilities at capacity so long as a price can be obtained that is greater than variable costs. This can be a low price indeed. The Western tendency is more likely to be a cutback in output since a more considerable proportion of costs can be reduced.' The consequence can also be international because overseas markets can become the target of any aggressive marketing efforts. We will discuss this international aspect in Chapter 12.

9.5. CONCLUSION

It was not my intention in this chapter to discuss the whole of Japan's macroeconomic performance, but rather to focus on the employment adjustment behaviour of Japanese management and the effect of this on macroeconomic stability, and to argue that the labour-hoarding behaviour of Japanese management, namely, the lay-off minimization behaviour (with a certain profitability constraint), has contributed to macro-stability. Not only has it reduced unemployment by the amount of retained (excess) labour—the micro-effect, so to speak—but it has also reduced macro-unemployment through the multiplier effect—the macro-effect. In addition, this multiplier effect may have been more effective in Japan in view of the estimated larger difference between the propensity to consume from wage income and the propensity to consume from profits.

This argument marks a contrast to Gordon (1982), who emphasized the role of wage flexibility, and Weitzman (1984), who emphasized the role of profit-sharing to explain Japan's macroeconomic performance. According to Weitzman, profit-sharing contributes to employment stability because in the short run when, as he assumes, the level of employment is variable but the contract (that is, the percentage of gross profits to be shared by the workers as a whole) is fixed, the marginal cost of labour is smaller than the average cost to the extent that hiring an additional worker reduces the profit-related compensation not only of this worker but also of all the other incumbent workers, due to diminishing returns. Although Weitzman repeatedly cites the bonus system in Japan as the best example of profit-sharing, this is questionable on two accounts. First, the bargaining in a typical Japanese firm determines how many months' worth of salary is to be paid as a bonus to an average worker and not what percentage of profits is to be paid to the workers as a whole; therefore, employment of an additional worker cannot reduce the bonus payment to any other worker and consequently the marginal labour cost cannot differ from the average cost. Second, bargaining over bonuses is carried out at least once a year and very often twice a year because of the biannual bonus payment scheme; therefore, for the Weitzman thesis to make sense the firm must be able to change its employment level more than twice a year, which is extremely unlikely in an employment-conscious Japanese firm.[8]

In fact, according to the study by the Ministry of Labour (1989), 68 per cent of the firms investigated replied that they do not determine the amount of bonuses on the basis of 'performance-related' factors or 'profit-sharing', and this percentage is even larger, at 84 per cent, among firms with a thousand employees or more. Also, empirical results concerning the degree to which bonuses are profit-related are mixed. Freeman and Weitzman (1987) obtained a result indicating that bonuses are more profit-related than wages, but Brunello's (1989) finding indicates otherwise. These results do not imply that total worker compensation (bonuses plus regular wages) and profitability are not related. Many findings indicate they are; however, this may be not because of profit-sharing but rather because unions become more militant if profits are high. Furthermore, the relation of worker compensation to profit has been found in the USA too:[9] the difference between Japan and other countries is, again, not absolute but one of degree.

With this view we have emphasized in this chapter the macro-stabilizing effect of the constrained lay-off minimization behaviour of Japanese management more than that of wage flexibility. The other behavioural principle adopted by Japanese management is, of course, growth maximization. The role that this form of behaviour plays in the macroeconomy has to be a dynamic one, and it is to this subject that we turn in the next chapter.

[8] I should remind the readers that this stability applies to full-time employees only (and not to temporary or part-time workers); however, these are the very workers for whom bonuses constitute an important part of compensation.

[9] See Seidman (1979), for instance. Salinger (1984) and Karier (1985) both estimated that more than two-thirds of monopoly rents are distributed to workers as higher wages in unionized firms within the US concentrated industries.

10

Economic Growth

10.1. INTRODUCTION

We now turn our attention from short-run fluctuation and concentrate on the long-run growth path of a national economy. For this purpose, we assume steady economic growth with full employment, where steady growth (also called steady-state growth or balanced growth) refers to a growth path in which all the important economic variables—national product, national income, productivity, employment, profits, investment, and so forth—grow at constant rates, and prices, including interest rates and profit rates, and the division of income between wages and profits remain constant. By assuming continuous full employment, we ignore labour-hoarding: that is we assume that firms employ labour at the cost-minimizing level.

Whether the actual long-run growth path of the Japanese or any other economy may be approximated to steady growth is a difficult question. This approximation has been justified by numerous growth theorists by citing Kaldor's (1961) 'stylized facts'. Another known fact, however, is that economic growth as we usually envisage it began only after the Industrial Revolution at the earliest, and that, in Japan, the economic growth rate has been noticeably higher since World War II than it was before. Therefore, the period of constant growth may or may not be long enough to justify the use of the term 'steady' growth. Furthermore, as we have shown in Table 9.1, the growth rate fluctuates across periods and it is difficult to say if this fluctuation is a short-run disturbance around a steady growth path or a change in the growth path itself.

It is also known that the discrete nature of technological progress has a serious effect on the course of economic development. There are several examples of this—the invention of steam engines in the late eighteenth century, the construction of railroad networks in the late nineteenth century, the commercialization of automobiles in the early twentieth century, and more recently the development of electric and electronic devices including computers. These inventions have had the effect of creating new and growing industries and often of replacing obsolete industries, thereby providing an impetus for further economic growth or maintaining growth in an otherwise declining economy. As a result, the growth path may be a bumpy one. This process was described by Schumpeter as 'the process of creative destruction', and he claimed that 'capitalism is by nature a form or method of economic change and not only never is but never can be stationary' (Schumpeter 1942, 82).

These arguments do not necessarily deny the usefulness of the theory of steady growth. Even if inventions occur in a discrete manner causing bumps to the growth path, the long-run path may yet reasonably approximate to a steady one. Besides, by studying the properties of steady growth, we may arrive at propositions and predictions concerning the long-run effects of exogenous factors which are expected to occur even if the real path is not as smooth as the model predicts. Based on this belief, the majority of economic growth theories, whether neo-classical, Keynesian, or Marxist, have confined their attention to the study of steady growth. Needless to say, a big (and probably the biggest) motivation for this tendency is analytical ease. If, as Schumpeter claims, inventions occur in a discrete and stochastic manner with a decisive influence on economic growth, then growth theory cannot be a deterministic one. For instance, the 'evolutionary model' of Nelson and Winter (1982), that purported to capture the Schumpeterian spirit, had to rely on stochastic simulation to investigate the properties of the model. The price for this approach is obviously a lack of generality and the results may be seriously affected by the choice of parameters and particular equational forms used in the simulation. A model of steady growth, by contrast, not only eases the analytical manipulation but also provides deterministic conclusions.

With these caveats in mind, we present in this chapter a model of growth for what we call a 'corporate economy' and analyse the properties of the steady growth path.[1] We start in Section 10.2

[1] This model was fully and more rigorously discussed in Odagiri (1981), which also discusses the comparison with other popular growth models elaborated by Marx, Solow, Robinson, and Kaldor, and fiscal and monetary policies.

by describing what sort of economy we have in mind and inquire into the macroeconomic balancing condition there. The main discussion of the growth model will be concentrated in two sections: Section 10.3 for a model without R & D, and Section 10.4 for a model with R & D. The essential conclusion is that the speed of macroeconomic growth is affected by management growth preference if and only if firms undertake R & D to increase labour productivity. Together with our conclusion in Chapter 4 that growth maximization is the motivation of Japanese management, the applicability of the growth theory (with R & D) to Japan's growth performance is apparent. This argument is stated, together with an examination of the comparison of saving rates in Japan and the USA, in Section 10.5. In Section 10.6 we discuss the relation of the rate of return on stocks to the rate of company profit, in order to examine the extent to which and the reasons why they differ. The chapter concludes in Section 10.7 with a summary and remarks on alternative explanations of Japan's post-war economic growth, with a particular emphasis on Olson's theory of the rise and decline of nations.

10.2. AN EQUILIBRIUM MODEL OF A CORPORATE ECONOMY

Let us suppose that all production and research activities are carried out by corporations (that is joint-stock companies). The shares of these corporations are owned by households whose income therefore comprises returns from the shares (dividends and capital gains) and wages. These shares are the only means of possessing wealth available to the households; that is, neither money nor bonds exist (which is not an essential assumption) and households cannot own real capital (which is an essential assumption). This latter assumption implies that there is a substantial barrier against the non-corporate sector (households) entering the corporate sector (corporations). This barrier is most likely to be caused by the lack of managerial and technical skills and knowledge in the non-corporate sector, and implies that the rate of return on real capital (rate of profit) earned by the corporate sector may deviate from the rate of return (rate of interest) earned by the non-corporate sector from shareholding. The stock-market is perfect in the sense that any information is perfectly known, it is competitive both on the sellers' (corporations') side and the buyers' (households') side, and no participant differentiates return in the form of dividends from that of capital gains. The Modigliani–Miller theorem therefore holds, as discussed in Section 4.2, and the firms behave in the manner described there. An economy thus characterized is called a corporate economy. In addition, we assume it to be a closed economy (that is, with no foreign trade) without government for the sake of simplicity.

Let us first consider the balancing condition in the stock-market. The income of the non-corporate sector is the sum of wages, dividends, and capital gains. If the saving propensity is constant, then a constant fraction of this income goes towards saving. Since, under our assumption, saving is undertaken only by acquiring shares, the saving of the non-corporate sector must equal the incremental market value of total shares. This balancing condition in the stock-market, as we show in the appendix to this chapter, is satisfied if and only if the output market also balances, that is, if and only if the total output (of the corporate sector) equals the sum of consumption (in the non-corporate sector) and investment in physical capital (by the corporate sector). This equivalence of the two conditions arises from Walras' Law.[2]

The balancing condition determines the rate of interest, i, and the valuation ratio, v, where these two price measures are related as shown by (4.8) or, equivalently, by (10A.3) in the appendix.

Since the seminal work of Harrod (1939), the saving–investment balancing condition in steady growth has been known to be the equality of the growth rate of capital to saving ratio divided by capital–output ratio. This so-called Harrod-Domar condition becomes more complicated in our corporate economy because, first, the investment–capital ratio (our ψ) exceeds the growth rate owing to the Penrose effect (see Section 4.2), and, second, the valuation ratio need not equal one owing to the lack of arbitrage between corporate shares and physical capital. Nevertheless, the equilibrium condition in a corporate economy can be obtained in a similar fashion and includes the Harrod-Domar condition as a special case. This condition is shown in the appendix.

[2] Walras' Law in general states that if all markets except one are in equilibrium the remaining market has also to be in equilibrium: see any advanced microeconomics textbook, for instance, Varian (1984, chap. 5).

To obtain this condition, one has to assume that every individual applies the same saving ratio irrespective of income source. Alternatively, one may apply different saving ratios between wages and profits, as assumed in the previous chapter. In the previous chapter, however, saving included corporate saving whereas in the current model saving refers only to that made by the non-corporate sector. It is therefore more sensible to assume that there are two types or two classes of individuals in the non-corporate sector who, within a class, apply a common saving ratio to any income. Most reasonably, one may distinguish individuals according to whether they earn wages or not because, unless their saving ratio is zero, every individual owns shares from which he receives returns, whereas some individuals, the wealthy or the retired, may not be in a paying job. Assume therefore that there are two classes, workers who receive wages in addition, possibly, to dividends and capital gains from their shareholdings, and capitalists who receive dividends and capital gains from their shareholdings but no wages. Workers and capitalists may have different saving ratios and we assume that capitalists' saving ratio is larger than workers'.[3] Workers do not differentiate between the two sources of income and apply the same saving ratio to wage income and non-wage income.

A surprising fact is that, in any steady growth path of a two-class economy where the share of wealth between the two classes is constant over time, the equilibrium condition is independent of workers' saving ratio and is simply

$$g = s_c i, \tag{10.1}$$

where s_c is the constant saving ratio of capitalists and, as before, g is the steady growth rate of capital (and of income), and i is the interest rate or the rate of return to shareholding. The proof is given in the appendix. The equation is identical to the condition first proved by Pasinetti (1962), but (10.1) is a substantial generalization of Pasinetti's result because we have not assumed the equality of profit rate to interest rate.

In the following analysis, we use this equation as the equilibrium condition for the stock and goods markets. The major reason is its simplicity. One may instead use the condition for a

[3] If the saving ratio of capitalists is not larger than that of workers', the capitalists' share of wealth declines over time and eventually approaches zero; hence, a two-class economy cannot be sustained. See Samuelson and Modigliani (1966).

non-class economy (see the appendix), but the results are more ambiguous.

10.3. GROWTH WITHOUT INTERNALLY GENERATED PRODUCTIVITY INCREASE

Let us return to our discussion in Chapter 4 and examine the choice of growth rate by the firm. As shown in Figure 4.1, this choice is made at the tangency of the $v-g$ frontier and one of the indifference curves. The $v-g$ frontier is affected by two variables, profit rate (p) and interest rate (i). Profit rate is chiefly affected by wage rate (w) because a higher wage rate increases production costs and decreases profits (gross of capital costs). Therefore, either a higher w or a higher i shifts the $v-g$ frontier downward and decreases the optimal growth rate. Indifference curves are basically dependent on management's preference on growth. To capture this effect, let us introduce a parameter, z, and assume that the firm with a higher z chooses a higher growth rate given the $v-g$ frontier. In other words, z is a parameter in the management utility function, $U(g, v)$, indicating the marginal rate of substitution between g and v such that a higher z causes the indifference curves to be steeper, like those in country J in Figure 4.1. As a result, the firm with a higher z chooses a higher g.

Consequently, we write the management's choice of the growth rate as follows:

$$g = g\ (i, w, z), \tag{10.2}$$

with i and w having a negative effect and z a positive effect on g.

There remains an equilibrium condition of the labour market. Suppose that labour supply increases at an exogenous constant rate of n. Labour demand, on the other hand, increases at the rate of output increase (g) minus the rate of labour productivity increase which is denoted by a. Hence, in a steady growth equilibrium, we must have

$$g = n + a. \tag{10.3}$$

In other words, the right-hand side shows the rate of increase in labour supply in efficiency units and this must equal the rate of increase in output.

A critical question, of course, is how labour productivity growth is determined. Suppose first that the firms do not undertake any R & D activity. Then the only source of productivity increase must be exogenous, for instance, through an increase in general scientific knowledge: that is, a is a given constant. On this assumption, (10.1), (10.2), and (10.3) constitute a system of three equations that determine the values of three unknowns, g, i, and w, given s_c, z, n, and a.

Properties of the equilibrium in this model are easy to see. First, (10.3) determines g, given n and a. (10.1) then determines i at g/s_c, and these g and i, together with z, determine w by (10.2). Consequently, an increase in n or a increases g by the same amount, but neither s_c nor z affects g. Why is the macro-growth rate unaffected even though with a higher z all the firms attempt to choose a higher growth rate? Since neither g nor i is affected by z, it must be that w is higher if z is higher for (10.2) to hold. When the firms choose a higher growth rate, it increases the rate of growth of labour demand. Yet, because the rate of growth of labour supply is constrained exogenously, the wage rate has to go up, shifting the v–g frontier downward until the firm with a higher z ends up opting for the same growth rate as before. Here is another example of the so-called fallacy of aggregation, that is, the case of aggregation nullifying individuals' intentions.[4] Management's intention to achieve higher growth does not necessarily result in its realized growth rate and the macro-growth rate being higher. In order to explain Japan's faster economic growth by managerial growth preference, one has to analyse firms' efforts to raise labour productivity, because only through such efforts can firms increase the rate of growth of aggregate labour supply in efficiency units and thereby the rate of growth of output. Hence in the next section we consider the R & D activity undertaken by firms to increase labour productivity.

10.4. GROWTH WITH INTERNALLY GENERATED PRODUCTIVITY INCREASE

Suppose that by expending R on research and development the firm can increase its labour productivity by a. Needless to say, R

[4] Another example was given in the previous chapter that, given $c_w = 1$, despite firms' labour-hoarding at the expense of profits, the realized macro-profits stay the same as in the case of firms' maximizing profits.

is an increasing function of a. There is a trade-off in the firm's choice concerning a. On the one hand, the higher a is the smaller labour requirements and wage costs will be in the future. On the other hand, R has to be higher to attain a higher a, hence depressing profits today. The higher the wage rate today or the higher the expected rate of future wage increase (ξ), the greater must be the future cost reduction from any productivity increase and therefore the greater must be the incentive for R & D. A higher target growth rate also means a higher incentive for R & D because cost-saving from future productivity increases is proportional to the future output level. Since the choice concerning a is essentially intertemporal, with the cost incurred today and the benefit expected in the future, a lower discount rate increases the benefit relative to the cost, thereby encouraging R & D. It is therefore appropriate to write

$$a = a\,(w, i, g, \xi), \tag{10.4}$$

where the effect of i on a is negative and the effect of w, g, or ξ is positive.

The choice of growth rate now depends on ξ in addition to w, i, and z. Hence, (10.2) is rewritten as

$$g = g\,(i, w, \xi, z). \tag{10.5}$$

In the long run, the rate of wage increase ξ must equal the rate of productivity increase a, because if $\xi < a$ for instance, the marginal value product of labour will eventually exceed the marginal cost of labour, hence increasing labour demand and pushing ξ upward. Thus it must be that

$$\xi = a. \tag{10.6}$$

(10.1), (10.3), (10.4), (10.5), and (10.6) constitute a system of five equations to be solved for five unknowns: w, i, g, a, and ξ. The basic difference from the model without R & D is that now a and ξ are endogenously determined. As a result, the model is more complicated and analysis is not as easy as in the previous section. Therefore, we present the results without proof.[5] The exogenous parameters are, as before, s_c, n, and z. In equilibrium s_c unambiguously increases g and a (and hence ξ), but the effects on i

[5] Interested readers should see Odagiri (1981, chap. 5) for the proof.

and w are ambiguous. Although n increases g and i, it decreases a and w. And z increases everything, namely, g, a, i, and w.

The results are all plausible. A higher saving rate increases the fund for investment and hence promotes growth and productivity increases. A faster increase in labour supply makes economic growth easier but decreases the need for R & D to improve labour productivity. Management growth preference now affects macro-equilibrium growth positively, by increasing the rate of labour productivity increase at the same time. That is, if the firms have a preference for higher growth, they will expend more on R & D to make the faster target growth feasible without labour constraint. This growth preference should also increase the demand for funds, thereby raising the interest rate, and increase the demand for labour, which will raise the wage rate. Although the resulting higher i and w discourage growth by shifting the v–g frontier downward, the effect, unlike that in the previous section, is not strong enough to offset the higher growth preference. This explains why a high growth preference at the micro-level now results in high growth at the macro-level. The availability of R & D to increase labour productivity is the key to this result.

10.5. INTERPRETING JAPAN'S ECONOMIC GROWTH

Now the application of the theory to Japan's experience is straightforward. As we have argued repeatedly, Japanese management has a stronger growth preference; that is, z is higher in Japan. We also know that Japanese firms have been making considerable R & D efforts (see the next chapter) and there is evidence indicating that these R & D efforts contribute positively to productivity. Odagiri (1985), for instance, confirmed that labour productivity increase was positively affected by company R & D intensity measured as the ratio of R & D expenditure to sales during the two periods 1966–73 and 1973–7. Some studies have also estimated the rate of return from R & D by regressing the rate of total factor productivity increase on R & D expenditures as a fraction of value added. Although the rate varies across estimates—15 to 20 per cent according to Odagiri and Iwata (1986), 17 per cent according to Suzuki (1985), and 39 per cent according to Goto and Suzuki (1989)—all found significantly positive rates.[6] Obviously, therefore, productivity increase, at least in part, is internally generated through firms' conscious efforts to undertake R & D. According to our model, therefore, a higher z in Japan should result in a faster growth of labour productivity (that is, per-capita output) and national income, which is precisely what we observed in Table 9.1.

We also need to consider the effects of other parameters. There is no evidence that n, namely, the rate of increase in work-force or in population, has been particularly high in Japan. During 1970–86, the rate of increase in the work-force was actually higher in the USA (at 2.2 per cent) than in Japan (at 1.0 per cent), while in European countries it was approximately the same as or lower than in Japan—1.0 per cent in France, 0.3 per cent in the FRG, and 0.6 per cent in the UK. At any rate, these increases are small compared to their respective rates of economic growth (possibly with an exception of the USA), clearly indicating that an increase in labour productivity has been the major source of any increase in labour supply in efficiency units. Furthermore, as we have seen in Table 9.1, GDP per capita has grown faster in Japan than in any other country. Remembering that the rate of growth of per-capita GDP equals the rate of labour productivity increase (our a), given a constant labour participation ratio, and remembering that n exerts a negative influence on a in our model, we can easily conclude that the differential population growth rate does not explain Japan's higher economic growth rate.

The high saving rate in Japan has been widely known. The rate varies substantially according to the period and the definition of saving—whether it includes government and business saving, whether it includes purchases of consumer durables, whether it includes appreciation of assets, and so forth. Yet, a saving rate of more than or around 20 per cent has usually been quoted for Japan, in comparison to less than 10 per cent (or even less than 5 per cent) for the USA and the UK, and somewhere between these two rates for France and Germany; and there has been some discussion of the extent to which this high saving ratio has benefited Japan's economic growth. While we by no means disregard

[6] There is no evidence to suggest that these rates of return significantly differ from those in other countries. For the USA, for instance, Terleckyj (1980) estimated the rate to be 30% and Griliches (1986) 24%.

the contribution made by saving, some reservations have to be stated before any conclusion can be drawn.

Although it is the saving rate of capitalists that matters in our model, the distinction between capitalists' saving rate and the overall or average saving rate must not be emphasized on both theoretical and empirical grounds. Theoretically, as argued in Section 10.2, the assumption of two classes (within the non-corporate sector) is made more out of analytical convenience than out of empirical reality. The model can also be analysed for a one-class economy, assuming that every household in the non-corporate sector adopts a common saving rate. Though the conclusion is more ambiguous and the effect of saving rate or growth preference on equilibrium economic growth rate cannot be unambiguously determined, we may expect that, under normal circumstances, these parameters exert a positive contribution on growth. Empirically, estimating the capitalists' saving rate is very difficult. Note that these capitalists are individuals whose income consists solely of returns from financial assets. Corporate savings, namely, retained earnings, are not part of their savings and the saving ratio (one minus the consumption ratio) from profits, which was estimated in the previous chapter to be highest in Japan among five leading nations, may be totally different from s_c since the major part of that saving may be corporate retention. To my knowledge, no estimation has been made of s_c in the present sense, and thus whether it is higher in Japan or not is unknown. For both of these theoretical and empirical reasons, we confine ourself to a comparison of the overall saving rate.

Whether the international difference in saving rate is as high as is usually believed has been the concern of a number of recent researchers. According to Hayashi (1989), the difference between Japan and the USA has been exaggerated for two reasons. One is the different treatment of depreciation in the national accounts, because in Japan depreciation is estimated on the basis of the book or acquisition value of assets and not on the basis of replacement costs, as in the USA. The result is an underestimation of depreciation in Japan and consequently an overestimation of net saving. The other reason is the treatment of government capital formation. While this (together with government surplus) is taken to constitute government saving in Japan, government saving in the US national accounts only includes government surplus.

Hayashi argues that, in view of the difficulty in estimating depreciation of government capital, it is sensible to eliminate government saving from Japan's saving and make any comparisons between the two countries on the basis of private-sector saving.[7]

An adjustment on these two grounds makes a significant difference. The Japanese saving rate (non-government national saving as a percentage of net national product) is significantly reduced and the gap between it and the US rate significantly narrows. In fact, in 1979–81, the gap disappears altogether. In other years since 1958, Japan still has a higher rate but the difference between the two countries is not more than 5 per cent point except for the ten-year period of 1965–75. Indeed, another important finding of Hayashi's is Japan's exceptionally high saving rate during this period. The adjusted rate rarely exceeds 15 per cent in other years; yet, it exceeds 20 per cent in 1969–73 and reaches 26 per cent in the peak year of 1970. In the USA, by contrast, the rate remains stable over the same period at around 10 per cent; hence, the difference between Japan and the USA appears very large (though still smaller than the difference before adjusting the rates) if one looks only at this period. Hayashi regards Japan's high saving rate in this period as exceptional and attributes it to a temporary phenomenon associated with the process of catch-up, and to higher economic growth, which caused households to understate the permanent component of income and thus maintain a relatively low level of consumption.

It therefore appears that the well-publicized difference in saving propensity between Japan and the USA is somewhat exaggerated. None the less, the fact seems to remain that the Japanese are more savings-minded than the Americans. Several reasons have been suggested for this difference, in addition to those suggested by Hayashi, and they include the bonus system, the tax system, the inadequate social security scheme, a relatively underdeveloped system of consumer credit, and the high value attached to bequests.[8] Although many of these factors are gradually disappearing as the Japanese economy matures into one of the richest and the

[7] Boskin and Roberts (1988) also show that government saving makes a big difference in any comparison of saving rate in Japan and the USA.

[8] Horioka (1990), in an excellent survey article, enumerated more than 30 factors that have been suggested as possible causes of Japan's high household saving rate.

financial markets become freer, thereby suggesting that the international difference will narrow even further, Hayashi's calculation suggests that since 1984 (to 1987) the difference between Japan and the USA is on an increasing trend. Whether this trend is temporary or permanent has yet to be seen.

The higher saving rate in Japan, particularly during the 1960s to the mid-1970s, must have been one of the factors of economic growth, as suggested by its growth-enhancing effect in our model. This, together with the high management growth preference, explains both the demand for and the supply of high investment that have been the main characteristics of Japan's economic growth.

10.6. RATE OF RETURN AND RATE OF PROFIT

One of the mysteries of Japanese management has been the high rate of return enjoyed by shareholders despite management's relative disregard of profitability suggested by the growth maximization hypothesis, and despite the internationally low company profit rate, as discussed in Chapter 8. Table 10.1 compares the rates of return on stocks and bonds among five countries during

TABLE 10.1. Rates of return in five countries, 1971–1985

Country	Capital gain (1)	Dividend/interest (2)	Total return (1) + (2)	Risk
Stocks				
Japan	16.03	2.42	18.45	16.35
France	9.54	6.19	15.73	21.60
FRG	7.38	4.80	12.18	15.78
UK	11.33	6.01	17.34	24.95
USA	5.17	4.78	9.95	15.41
Bonds				
Japan	1.40	8.59	9.99	6.75
France	−0.21	12.09	11.88	6.69
FRG	0.40	8.37	8.77	6.91
UK	−0.47	12.27	11.80	11.38
USA	−0.92	9.68	8.76	9.20

Source: Solnik (1988), exhibit 2.5.

the period 1971–85. Two observations are immediately apparent. First, in terms of total return from stocks, Japan achieved the highest return, followed by the UK, while the lowest return is found in the USA. The difference between the UK and the USA may be explained by the higher risk (domestic risk only, without taking account of exchange risk) of UK stocks but the difference between Japan and the USA cannot be attributed to risk differences.[9] Second, Japanese investors have earned this higher return mostly in the form of capital gains: dividend rates, on the contrary, have been the lowest of those in all five countries.

How can these findings be reconciled with the growth maximization hypothesis? First of all, note that growth maximization predicts a lower stock price (relative to the assets in real value) but not necessarily a lower rate of return on stock. The latter is the rate an investor gains by holding a share from time t_1 to t_2; hence, with a low stock price at both t_1 and t_2, you buy a share cheaply and sell it cheaply, which is consistent with either a high or a low rate of return. In other words, the growth maximization hypothesis only suggests that by not maximizing the value today current shareholders are missing an opportunity to gain further.

Our model of growth for a corporate economy (where the rate of return and the rate of profit are determined independently) predicts that the equilibrium rate of return is higher but the equilibrium rate of profit is lower in an economy with a stronger management growth preference. To this extent the above findings for Japan are consistent with the theory. The reason for this result is easy to understand: management chooses a higher growth rate at the expense of profitability, but this increases the demand for funds, raising the rate of interest or the rate of return on financial assets. Does this imply that arbitrage between real capital and financial assets has been least active in Japan? Or, are the rate of return and the rate of profit actually so different as Table 10.1 implies? The answer to these questions turns out to be complicated because of international differences in financial structure and inflation. See Table 10.2. Here, the rate of return to investors at large is given as the weighted average of the rate of return on stocks and the rate of interest on debts. Also, both the

[9] See, however, Baldwin (1986), who argues that the risk has been considerably higher in Japan and that this difference mostly explains the difference in return.

TABLE 10.2. Real rate of return to investors, real profit rate, and Tobin's q: Non-financial corporations in four countries

Country	Rate of return and profit rate			Tobin's q			
	Period	Return	Profit	Period	$q(W)$	$q(F)$	$q(A)$
Japan	1965–81	3.6	3.5	1965–81	0.6	0.7	1.7
FRG	1963–79	1.7	2.6	1965–81	1.2	n.a.	n.a.
UK		n.a.	n.a.	1965–80	n.a.	n.a.	1.0
USA	1963–81	1.3	5.6	1965–81	0.7	n.a.	0.9

Note: Rate of return is the average of the rate of return on common stock and interest rate on debt with respective shares in finance as weights, deflated by consumer price index. Real profit rate is after-tax profits as a ratio to total assets in current value.

$q(W) = V/W$ where V is the market value and W is total assets in replacement value.
$q(F) = V/(W -$ Monetary Assets$)$.
$q(A) = V/(W -$ Monetary Assets $-$ Land$)$.

Source: Holland (1984), tables 1.9, 1.10, 9.2, and 9.8.

rate of return and the profit rate are calculated in real terms. The result is rather surprising: it is Japan that attained an equalization of the two rates. In both Germany and, more especially, the USA, the rate of return is lower than the profit rate. Thus the fact may be that there is most arbitrage between real capital and financial assets in Japan, whereas in the USA investors may have been deterred from investing in real capital despite its higher return.

But why is the rate of return in Table 10.2 so different from that in Table 10.1? Table 10.1 also gives (nominal) rates of interest on bonds, and this shows that the international difference is not as large as that of the rate of return on stocks. Therefore, apart from differences in inflation, the cause for the difference between the two tables must be the higher share of debt in the financing of Japanese firms. Indeed, the higher leverage ratio of Japanese firms has been well known, and this fact is also related to our second finding from Table 10.1 that Japanese stockholders' return comes overwhelmingly from capital gains. Why this difference in financing?[10]

If the stock-market is perfect in the sense of Modigliani and Miller, whether the returns are in the form of dividends or capital gains should not make any difference to the total rate of return to shareholders. If, however, interest payments on debts are deductible for the purpose of corporate taxes while dividends are not, or if income tax is levied more on dividends than on capital gains, then shareholders and management would prefer earnings to be retained rather than to be paid out as dividends, and would prefer to raise finance by debt rather than by issuing new shares. These conditions generally apply to both the USA and Japan, but Flath (1984) argues that a generally lower personal income tax rate makes debt financing relatively favourable in Japan, implying that the high leverage ratio of Japanese firms is a rational reaction to its tax system. Another consideration arises from information asymmetry and corporate control issues. If information is asymmetric between management and outside lenders, the latter are likely to estimate the risk of an investment project as higher than the management. They will therefore require a risk premium,

[10] However, Kuroda and Oritani (1980) showed that the apparent difference between Japan and the USA is significantly due to different accounting methods and business practices.

making the cost of borrowing higher than the cost of retained earnings, or they may demand some control mechanism to safeguard their loans, for instance, sending a director to the firm or requiring exceptional information about management affairs.[11] The management may thus evolve a pecking-order of preference concerning funds, with internal funds, if available, at the top of the order, then debts, and lastly new share issues. It has been argued that a 'pecking-order theory' of this kind can usefully be applied to explain the low dividend pay-out ratio and high leverage ratio of Japanese firms (Hoddar 1988).

Table 10.2 also compares Tobin's q or valuation ratio (see Chapter 4) among four countries. The large difference in Japan between $q(F)$ and $q(A)$ reflects the large replacement value of land held by the companies. When land is included, q is smaller than the ratio supposedly attained in the long run under free entry, which is unity. The same is observed in the USA but not in Germany. In the UK, excluding land, q is 1.025: inclusion of land is expected to decrease the value to below unity. A value of q smaller than one suggests that stockholders are better off if the firms are liquidated and the realized assets distributed to stockholders. The fact that a lower-than-one q is persistent without firms being liquidated thus suggests the prevalence of management discretion and, very plausibly in my view, management concern for other stakeholders, such as employees. Given that liquidation implies unemployment, how can Japanese management with a strong attachment to employees take such a measure? Even if q becomes lower than one, it will want to attain faster growth. This view is all that the growth maximization hypothesis claims and is what we have been suggesting throughout this book and particularly in Chapter 4. Such behaviour, as we have shown in this chapter, has been the essential driving force behind Japan's economic growth.

[11] Many Japanese firms are said to prefer borrowing from several banks to avoid demands for more control. However, this also has the effect that, if the firm gets into financial difficulties, the bank has less incentive to rescue it because of its smaller stake in the firm (recall the discussion in Chap. 2). Whether the firm should diversify banks in order to minimize the demand for control or concentrate on one bank in order that it may rescue in adversity will therefore depend on how vulnerable it is to business downturns.

10.7. CONCLUSION

In this chapter we have presented a macro-equilibrium model of steady growth to show that, provided corporate R&D efforts increase labour productivity, management growth preference results in rapid national economic growth. In our view, this preference, probably together with a higher saving rate, has been the main factor in Japan's rapid post-war economic growth. One should also note the role played by competition here. Both internal and inter-firm competition has been strong in Japan, as we have discussed in earlier chapters, and this has both forced and enabled firms to maintain efficiency. Only with such competition does the firm attain a point on the value–growth frontier and not inside it. If firms maximize growth without the threat of competition, the result must simply be lower profitability *and* lower growth. Therefore, measures which enhance management growth preference, say, limiting shareholder control, can be effective for the purpose of economic growth only if competition is maintained everywhere in the economy. In this sense, the result is hardly as paradoxical as Marris and Mueller (1980) have suggested.

The model has also indicated the importance of technical progress induced by firms' conscious R&D efforts. In this regard, we share Schumpeter's view to a large extent. Unlike Schumpeter, however, we have disregarded the discontinuity in growth path caused by innovations and, for analytical purposes at least, confined our attention to the continuous improvement in labour productivity. As discussed in Chapter 4, many aspects of the internal organization of Japanese firms suggest that they are efficient both in this respect and in taking full advantage of the learning effect, and there seems no question that this has been a contributory factor in the economic growth of the country.

Several other explanations have been given in the past for Japan's economic growth. One is the catch-up effect. The estimation results of Dowrick and Nguyen (1989) cited in Chapter 9 implied that until 1973, but not after 1974, this effect was a factor. However, a sizable proportion of the growth rate difference remained to be explained.

Another explanation has been offered by Olson (1982), in whose opinion Japan was able to attain fast growth because interest groups and distributional coalitions were mostly destroyed by her defeat in World War II. He says 'distributional coalitions slow down a society's capacity to adopt new technologies and to reallocate resources in response to changing conditions, and thereby reduce the rate of economic growth' (ibid. 65). Of such distributional coalitions, the most typical are trade unions, cartels, employer associations, and the military-business complex. And the best example of a coalition that was disbanded and banned following the war in Japan is probably the *zaibatsu*, which not only exercised a considerable controlling power in many markets, and particularly in financial markets, but also had connections with political parties and the military. As discussed in Chapter 7, the *zaibatsu* was dissolved by the occupation army as a part of its economic democratization policy and the present business groups are merely loose associations of independent firms without anti-competitive influences. As regards market competition, the post-war reform also forced the break-up of several monopolistic firms and established the Antimonopoly Law, as we will discuss in the next chapter. Trade unions, on the other hand, gained increased legal powers after the war and for some time caused a number of serious labour disputes.

Such reform, Olson argues, could be only attained under the traumatic conditions following defeat and 'the theory . . . predicts that with continued stability the Germans and Japanese will accumulate more distributional coalitions, which will have an adverse influence on their growth rates' (ibid. 76). I agree with Olson in stressing the growth-promoting consequence of competition that was made possible by the drastic measures taken after the war. However, whether his argument can explain Japan's continuous growth performance more than a generation after the end of the war is an interesting but very difficult question to answer.

Finally, some authors, whom we called 'the conspiracy theorists' in Chapter 1, have attributed Japan's economic growth to well-planned government guidance through a succession of industrial policies and to 'harmonious' business–government relations (see, for example, Johnson 1982). Postponing a more detailed discussion of industrial policies to the next chapter, we confine ourselves here to examining this view in relation to Olson's theory. As he puts it, 'the accumulation of distributional coalitions increases the complexity of regulation, the role of government, and the complexity of understandings, and changes the direction of social evolution' (Olson 1982, 73). 'At least in the first two decades after the war, the Japanese and West Germans had not developed the degree of regulatory complexity and scale of government that characterized more stable societies' (ibid. 76). It is the relative lack of coalitions and governmental control, and not the abundance of them, that has helped Japan's economic growth.

Appendix: Macro-Equilibrium in a Corporate Economy

Let us denote the aggregate income of the non-corporate sector by Y and aggregate production (in value terms) by Q. We first note that these are not necessarily the same because a rising stock price increases Y by increasing capital gains but not (at least not directly) Q. Denoting by W, P, D, and G the aggregate values of wages, profits, dividends, and capital gains, respectively, we have $Q = W + P$ and $Y = W + D + G$ by definition. The goods market is in equilibrium if and only if

$$Q = C + I, \tag{10A.1}$$

where C and I are aggregate consumption and investment, respectively.[1]

We now consider the budget constraints of the two sectors. For the non-corporate sector, it is obviously $Y = C + S$, where S refers to saving. In the corporate sector, firms can finance investment either through new share issues or retained earnings. The amount of money they can raise by new share issues is $q\dot{N}$ where q is the share price, N is the number of outstanding shares, and $\dot{N}$ is the number of new shares issued (dotted variables indicate the increments; e.g., $\dot{N} = dN/dt$). Retained earnings must equal $P - D$. Hence the budget constraint for the corporate sector is given by $I = q\dot{N} + P - D$. We also note that V, the total market value of shares, equals qN, and capital gains, G, equals $\dot{q}N$; therefore, $\dot{V} = \dot{q}N + q\dot{N} = G + q\dot{N}$. Putting all these together, (10A.1) can be rewritten as

$$S = \dot{V}. \tag{10A.2}$$

That is, total saving (new demand in value of shares) must equal the total increase in the value of shares (new supply in value of shares). It is therefore the equilibrium condition in the stock-market. In other words, the goods market is in equilibrium if and only if the stock-market is in equilibrium. This of course is Walras' Law. We therefore need to analyse only the equilibrium condition for either market (apart from the labour market) in order to analyse the general equilibrium of the economy.

We next investigate how the rate of interest, i, is determined. Since it is

[1] It should be helpful to compare this equation with the macro-equilibrium condition, (9.1), in the previous chapter. There we did not incorporate the stock market; hence, Q and Y were not separated. The autonomous expenditure, A, is most typically investment and government expenditures; hence, in the absence of government, it can be identified with investment. Except for these changes, the two equations are identical.

the rate of return to shareholding, we have $i = (D + G)/V$. Then, using the above facts, this equation can be rewritten as $i - \dot{V}/V = (P - I)/V$. Noting that $V = vK$, where v is the valuation ratio (or Tobin's q) and K is capital (total assets), we find that in steady growth,

$$v = (p - \psi)/(i - g), \qquad (10A.3)$$

because $p = P/K$ (profit rate on assets), $\psi = I/K$ (investment–capital ratio which may be greater than the growth rate because of the Penrose effect), and g is the growth rate of capital which is also the rate of growth of V in steady growth in which v is constant over time. This equation, of course, is identical to (4.8), the equation depicting the v–g frontier. We derived (4.8) by equating the value of the firm to the present value of net cash flow discounted at the market rate of interest, i. (10A.3) says that this relation can also be obtained from the equality of shareholder rate of return to i.

We now inquire into the equilibrium condition (10A.2) in more detail. Let us first assume that the saving rate is common to all households and equals s; that is, $S = sY$. Using the relations discussed earlier and noting that $V = vgK$ in a steady state, we can rewrite (10A.2) as follows:

$$(1 - s)vg = s(Q/K - \psi). \qquad (10A.4)$$

Given s, Q/K, g, and ψ, this equation determines v and, by (10A.3), determines i. This is a generalization of the well-known Harrod–Domar equilibrium condition. Suppose that $\psi = g$ (no Penrose effect) and $i = p$ (and hence $v = 1$). This latter condition is attained if arbitrage between real assets and shares is perfect. Then from (10A.3) and (10A.4) one obtains $g = sQ/K$, that is, the equality of growth rate to saving ratio divided by capital–output ratio, which is the condition for Harrod's (1939) warranted rate of growth. When the Penrose effect exists and the arbitrage is incomplete, the condition, as shown by (10A.3) and (10A.4), is more complicated but, like the Harrod–Domar condition, gives a relation that shows how saving, together with other variables, affects growth.

The condition can be substantially simplified in a two-class economy in which saving ratios differ between capitalists and workers (higher for capitalists), but are independent of income sources. In steady growth, the share of income between capitalists and workers has to be constant, which requires that the ratio of saving (increment in the value of shareholdings) between the two classes has to equal the ratio of wealth (value of shareholdings). Since returns to shares are proportional to the value of shares, the ratio of returns between the classes also has to equal the ratio of wealth. In consequence,

$$s_w(W + D_w + G_w)/s_c(D_c + G_c) = (D_w + G_w)/(D_c + G_c), \qquad (10A.5)$$

where subscripts w and c, respectively, refer to workers and capitalists, or

$$s_w(W + D_w + G_w) = s_c(D_w + G_w): \tag{10A.6}$$

that is, workers' saving exactly equals the amount capitalists would have saved were they to receive the workers' returns on shares. Consequently, we have the following expression for total saving:

$$\begin{aligned} S &= s_w(W + D_w + G_w) + s_c(D_c + G_c) \\ &= s_c(D_w + G_w) + s_c(D_c + G_c) \\ &= s_c(D + G) \\ &= s_c iV. \end{aligned} \tag{10A.7}$$

Together with the balancing condition (10A.2) and the condition that V grows at rate g, we have at a steady growth equilibrium,

$$g = s_c i: \tag{10A.8}$$

that is, growth rate equals the rate of interest multiplied by capitalists' saving rate.

Readers should note that differential saving rates apply not to different income sources as assumed in the last chapter but to different classes of households. Therefore, even though we have used a similar notation, c_w in the previous chapter referred to consumption ratio out of wages whoever received the wages, whereas s_w here refers to the saving ratio workers apply to whatever income they receive. Unless c_w is less than one, workers do save and acquire financial assets. From these assets they will receive returns and, provided they are 'rational' in the usual sense, they will not differentiate this income from wages in their consumption/saving decision. To this extent, the constancy of saving rates according to class seems a more plausible assumption than the constancy according to income source.[2] This is exactly the criticism of Pasinetti (1962) against Kaldor (1956), and (10A.8) is a generalized reformulation of Pasinetti's equilibrium condition. The difference is that the rate of profit, which was assumed to be identical to the rate of interest in Pasinetti, can now be determined independently of the equilibrium condition. Pasinetti's so-called 'paradox' that workers' saving behaviour has no effect at all on the equilibrium still stands here.

[2] This criticism by no means impairs the usefulness of the analysis in the last chapter, for as long as s_w in the present definition is smaller than s_c an increase in the share of wages in national income increases the aggregate demand in the short run.

11

Government Policies

11.1. INTRODUCTION

One of the myths commonly believed by Western observers, the press and politicians in particular but many academics as well, pertains to the role of government policies in Japan's economic achievements. For instance, 'the government-industry colossus known as Japan Inc.' was the expression used in a *Business Week* article entitled 'Does the US Need a High-Tech Industrial Policy to Battle Japan Inc.?'[1] No book on Japanese management and industry would be complete, therefore, without a discussion of this issue.

Let me first state my general view. It is not government policies but a management system favouring growth strategies and innovation, and its interaction with intra-firm and inter-firm competition that have been the central forces behind Japan's economic achievement. In high-tech industry, for instance, we shall see that, contrary to *Business Week's* view, actual government policies have been neither financially large nor particularly successful. A reasonable conclusion therefore is that it has been the will and effort of Japanese firms themselves that have given them a competitive edge. It is true that some policies have been helpful, notably in the years immediately following the end of World War II; yet, these policies would never have been effective unless the businesses were keen to grab the opportunities provided.

Our concern in this chapter is those policies that are directly related to firms and industries. Macroeconomic policies will not be discussed because, first, this book has been primarily concerned with the issues related to management and industries; second, if there are national differences they will be more apparent in micro-policies than macro-policies; and therefore, third, in my view, there have been more misunderstandings about micro-policies than about macro-policies. We shall therefore be examining what are

[1] *Business Week*, 5 Feb. 1990.

usually called industrial policies. However, the ambiguity of the term 'industrial policy' has first to be noted. The term is usually used, rather loosely, to refer to 'government policies such that, if they had not been adopted, there would have been a different allocation of resources among industries or a different level of some aspect of economic activity of the constituent firms of an industry' (Komiya 1975, 308). Apparently, industrial policy thus defined is hardly distinguishable from other policies. Even macroeconomic fiscal and monetary policies affect inter-industry allocation because an expansionary fiscal policy benefits the construction industry, among others, and an expansionary monetary policy benefits capital-intensive industries. Therefore, one can never determine a clear boundary between industrial policy and other policies. The difference is by no means absolute: it is one of emphasis, and may be more jurisdictional than economic. As one prominent Japanese economist once put it, 'industrial policies are the policies undertaken by the Ministry of International Trade and Industries (MITI)' (Kaizuka 1973).

Regulation is particularly difficult to distinguish from industrial policy. Though regulation typically refers to a set of policies aimed to deal with market failures such as economies of scale, externality, and public goods, price regulation and entry regulation directly affect inter- and intra-industry resource allocation and cannot be separated from industrial policy. We know that the political and bureaucratic costs of regulation are high owing to goal deflection, capture by clients, inflexibility and lags, and inefficiency in client organizations (Noll 1985). Some economists regard regulation as 'a powerful engine of redistribution' (Peltzman 1976). There is no reason to believe that these costs do not apply to industrial policy. Incentives abound for industries to persuade policy-makers to provide subsidies and protect markets from foreign competition, not for the sake of economic efficiency but for their own benefit. From this viewpoint, one may argue that what has helped Japan has not been industrial policy *per se* but the speed with which the Japanese government *reduced* its involvement in industries in order to make better use of the market mechanism. Ironically, then, Japanese success may have come not from an increase but from a decrease in governmental intervention and the MITI may be praised for restricting its activities in recognition of the superiority of the market mechanism.

In this chapter we examine three policies. First, in Section 11.2, there is a discussion of the drastic antitrust measures taken after the war and the antimonopoly policy in operation since then.[2] Second, in Section 11.3, there is a brief historical outline of industrial policy from the post-war period to the present day to show the enormous changes that the policy has undergone. And third, in Section 11.4, we discuss those aspects dealing with industrial innovation, an essential component of industrial policy, with an emphasis on the use of research associations as a policy tool. The computer industry is probably used most often as an example of a target industry for industrial and technology policies, and we give our account of this industry in Section 11.5. Section 11.6 offers some conclusions.

11.2. ANTIMONOPOLY POLICY

The history of antimonopoly policy in Japan began immediately after the war. The General Head Quarters (GHQ) of the Supreme Commander Allied Powers, the occupation army, was determined to create and maintain a competitive economy in Japan as the main plank of its economic democratization programme. The details of the antitrust reform undertaken by GHQ are well documented in Hadley (1970), who actually participated in the reform as a member of GHQ. The reform consisted basically of three policies; dissolution of the *zaibatsu*, dissolution of firms with excessive market power, and the enactment of the Antimonopoly Law.

On the subject of *zaibatsu* dissolution, it is necessary to add a few words to our discussion in Section 7.3. Although the measures taken for this purpose, such as the forced liquidation of holding companies and a purge of executives, were primarily aimed at the Big Four Zaibatsu and six so-called New Zaibatsu, their effects extended to many other firms as well. The number of holding companies forced to liquidate or to divest amounted to 83

[2] The term antitrust policy is probably more familiar to American readers. We use the term antimonopoly policy because it is basically the policy related to the implementation of the Antimonopoly Law (an abbreviation of the Act concerning Prohibition of Private Monopolization and the Maintenance of Fair Trade) in Japan.

and executives were purged from at least 391 firms. These measures significantly influenced the post-war formation of the Japanese management system by fostering the separation of management from control both in a financial sense—through dispersed share ownership—and in a human sense—by eliminating older shareholder-controlled executives and filling the vacant positions with internally promoted, younger, and more professional managers. They thus resulted in financial independence and in the prevalence of internal promotion, both of which form the backbone of Japanese management as discussed in Part I.

The Law for the Elimination of Excessive Concentrations of Economic Power (the Deconcentration Law) was passed in 1947, with the aim of reorganizing those companies with excessive market power. At first, 325 firms were designated under the law, but following strong resistance from designated firms and also from conservatives in the USA who became more concerned with the Soviets and their influence in Korea, the final plan implemented in 1949 designated only 11 firms for dissolution (apart from the Mitsubishi and Mitsui trading companies which had already been dissolved by that time) and 7 firms for divestiture (of plants or shares). The list of these 11 firms is in Table 11.1. Except for Mitsubishi Heavy Industries, which was the manufacturing centre of the Mitsubishi Zaibatsu, and three *zaibatsu*-owned mining companies, these firms were regarded as excessively monopolistic because their shares of their respective markets amounted to more than 70 per cent.

There is no doubt that this reorganization helped to make markets more competitive. Even though deconcentration took place in only nine industries, the effect extended to the whole economy partly because of the importance of these industries and partly because of the announcement effect: that is, it was now evident that the government had adopted an antimonopoly stance and moved away from its pre-war pro-monopoly, pro-cartel position. In addition, 61 firms reorganized and about 350 firms divested to comply with the Enterprise Reconstruction and Reorganization Law of 1946. The aim of this law was not to deconcentrate industries but to deal with the miscellaneous losses firms had necessarily suffered as a result of the war, and reorganization following this law was undertaken at the initiative of the firms themselves, or at least with their consent, which was not the case

TABLE 11.1. Reorganizations under the Law for the Elimination of Excessive Concentrations of Economic Power

Before reorganization	After reorganization	Capitalization (million yen)	Present name
Japan Iron and Steel	Yawata Iron and Steel	800	Nippon Steel (1969)
	Fuji Iron and Steel	400	
	Nittetsu Steamship	40	Shinwa Kaiun (1961)
	Harima Fire Brick	20	
Mitsubishi Heavy Industries	East Japan Heavy Ind.	700	
	Central Japan Heavy Ind.	1300	Mitsubishi Heavy Ind. (1964)
	West Japan Heavy Ind.	900	
Mitsui Mining	Mitsui Mining	1200	
	Kamioka Mining	600	Mitsui Mining and Smelting (1952)
Mitsubishi Mining	Mitsubishi Mining	900	
	Taihei Mining (metal)	700	Mitsubishi Metal (1952)
Seika (Sumitomo) Mining	Seika Mining	290	Sumitomo Coal Mining (1952)
	Besshi Mining	310	Sumitomo Metal Mining (1952)
	Besshi Construction	5	Sumitomo Construction (1962)
	Besshi Department Store	6	Niihama Daimaru (1975)

Oji Paper	Tomakomai Paper	400	Oji Paper (1952)
	Jujo Paper	280	
	Honshu Paper	250	
Teikoku Fiber	Imperial Hemp	180	Teikoku Sen-i (1959)
	Central Textile	240	
	Toho Rayon	120	
Daiken Industries	Kureha Cotton Spinning	700	Toyobo (1966)
	Marubeni	150	
	C. Itoh	150	
	Amagasaki Nail	10	Amatei (1969)
Toyo Can	Toyo Can		
	Hokkai Can	50	
Dainippon Beer	Japan Beer	100	Sapporo Breweries (1964)
	Asahi Breweries	100	
Hokkaiko Dairy Coop.	Hokkaido Butter	120	Snow Brand (1958)
	Snow Brand	360	

Note: In the far right column, the year that the company adopted a new name or the year that the merger took place is in parenthesis.
Source: Hadley (1970), table 9.1.

under the Deconcentration Law. In fact, there were many firms which had merged before or during the war under pressure from a government which regarded monopoly under government control as the most suitable production system to support the war effort, and these firms wished to de-merge to return to their original forms. Whatever the motivation, the competition-enhancing effects of these reorganizations were apparent in a number of industries.

Concentration in the designated nine industries decreased not only as a direct result of reorganization but also indirectly by lowering barriers to mobility and entry, so that smaller firms increased their share of the market and new firms entered it. A typical case can be found in the beer industry: even though in 1949 Kirin was the third largest company, behind the two descendants of Dainippon, Japan and Asahi, Kirin steadily increased its share to become the largest brewer within five years. In the steel industry, Nippon Kokan (now NKK), Kawasaki Steel, and Sumitomo Metal increased their shares to become viable competitors against Yawata and Fuji, which is why the Fair Trade Commission (JFTC) approved the Yawata–Fuji merger in 1969. The same can be said of the merger of three firms to re-establish Mitsubishi Heavy Industries. Both of these mergers, in particular the Yawata–Fuji merger, caused a controversy about the possible anti-competitive consequences. JFTC's decision was made even more delicate by MITI's support of the merger in order to pursue (supposedly large) scale economies. JFTC finally approved the merger but attached several conditions to it, such as the sale of rail production equipment to Nippon Kokan, so that Nippon Steel should not have a dominant position in any one product market. The heated public discussion of the Yawata–Fuji case also discouraged other firms from making similar large-scale mergers. For instance, Oji, Jujo, and Honshu, the descendants of pre-reorganization Oji Paper, had been planning to reunite but withdrew their plan. Although feelings about reunion were quite strong in the first decade or two, they have gradually abated as those recruited after reorganization have taken an increasing number of managerial positions. As a consequence, competition is now fierce among those firms created by reorganization.

To maintain those competitive markets which had been created by the temporary measures of dissolving the *zaibatsu* and enacting the Deconcentration Law, the Antimonopoly Law was passed in 1947. Since then it has been amended three times, twice, in 1949 and 1953, to relax restrictions and once, in 1977, to strengthen them. The law prohibits (1) private monopolization, that is, individual or collective action to exclude or control the business activities of others and thereby substantially to restrain, contrary to the public interest, competition in any particular field; (2) unreasonable restraint of trade, including cartels (with exemptions); and (3) unfair trade practices, such as price discrimination, dumping, false advertising, exclusive dealing, tie-ins, resale price maintenance (with exemptions), and unjust use of a dominant bargaining position. Two kinds of cartels are permitted with JFTC's consent: depression cartels and rationalization cartels. A depression cartel is allowed when excess supply is serious enough to threaten the survival of a sizeable proportion of producers, and a cartel is considered to be the only means to save them. A rationalization cartel is allowed when industry-wide technical improvement, quality improvement, or cost reduction cannot be achieved without a cartel. The number of these cartels reached 30 in 1966 but, with increasing reluctance on the part of JFTC to approve them, the number has fallen to 3 or less, and often to zero since 1980. In addition, exemptions apply to those cartels subject to other government regulation, those formed to protect small firms, and export or import cartels. The number of these cartels, which are of varying size and influence, was about 300 in 1988.

Another important aim of the law is to restrict the concentration of economic power. One of the measures designed for this purpose is the prohibition of holding companies, defined as those companies whose principal business is to control the business activities of other domestic companies by means of holdings of stock. This prohibition originated in the lesson of the pre-war *zaibatsu*. The law also restricts shareholding by a financial institution to a maximum of 5 per cent in any company (10 per cent by an insurance company). The consequence of this restriction on the pattern of shareholding was discussed in Chapter 2. Mergers, acquisitions of shares or assets, and interlocking directorates are prohibited where the effect may be substantially to restrain competition in any particular field of trade, or where unfair trade practices have been employed. Those firms intending to undertake mergers or acquisitions are required to report their intentions to JFTC thirty days in advance so that JFTC can stop them if necessary. The case of Yawata and Fuji has been mentioned above.

What strikes many American observers is the small number of court cases. The law stipulates three enforcement procedures. First, JFTC can warn the offender(s) and recommend whatever measure it thinks is appropriate. Second, JFTC can hold an official hearing and reach its own decision. This hearing may be held when the JFTC recommendation has been disputed by the offender or at the instigation of JFTC, without any prior recommendation. The offender may appeal to the High Court to quash the decision. Third, the law stipulates that when JFTC considers a crime to have been committed, it must bring an indictment before the court. In actual fact JFTC has rarely brought any indictments in a marked contrast with the USA where indictments are the normal rule. Even official hearings remain comparatively few: of the 130 to 200 annual instances of violation during 1985–9 hearings were held in less than 10 per cent of cases, and the rest were resolved by warnings or recommendations only. These statistics suggest that JFTC regards recommendations as a sufficiently effective means to eliminate monopolistic practices and that firms tend not to disagree with the recommendations. Whether the JFTC view is warranted remains an open question.

There is one notable exception to this tendency. In 1974 JFTC indicted twelve petroleum refineries and their executives in the Tokyo High Court for price-fixing and accused the Petroleum Federation of collusive output restriction. This case is noteworthy not only because it was an unprecedented move on the part of JFTC but also because of its relation with industrial policy, as the firms and the Federation offered the defence that they acted under MITI's administrative guidance. The central question therefore became whether the MITI's guidance had been in violation of the Antimonopoly Law and, if it had been, whether the firms following MITI's guidance should be prosecuted. The judgment of the court was thus destined to make a grave impact on MITI's industrial policy. In 1980, the High Court found the firms guilty, but not the Federation on the ground that JFTC had not warned MITI that its guidance to restrict output violated the Antimonopoly Law and, hence, the lack of recognition by the Federation of the violation could not be condemned. The judgment, however, clearly stated that MITI's policy violated the Antimonopoly Law, thereby forcing MITI to rethink its policy options and reminding JFTC to be watchful of the legality of the ministries' policies. The firms appealed to the Supreme Court, which in 1984 upheld the judgment of the High Court.

The importance of this case resided not only in its implications on industrial policy, which we will discuss in the next section, but also in convincing JFTC and the public of the need to strengthen the Antimonopoly Law. The result was the 1977 amendment which, among other things, gave JFTC the power to fine cartel-conducting firms (which JFTC has frequently done) and to break up firms in 'monopolistic situations' (which JFTC has never done).

The overall evaluation of antimonopoly policy in Japan as compared to, say the USA is extremely difficult. If one simply compares the number of cases brought to court, one is led to the conclusion that Japan's policy is ineffective. Alternatively, one may conclude that antimonopoly violation has actually occurred less often in Japan. Yet another interpretation, which JFTC seems to adopt, is a difference in attitude between JFTC and the American FTC or Department of Justice. JFTC appears to take a view that, if through warnings and recommendations the aim of maintaining competitive markets is fulfilled, then that is sufficient. The Americans, on the other hand, seem to believe that offenders should be legally prosecuted whether or not the prosecution is necessary for economic purposes, which appears not totally unrelated to the abundance of law suits in the USA and the high proportion of lawyers in the professional classes. One can never say which attitude is more fair or more efficient, though international misunderstanding appears to be increasing owing to this difference.

In view of the intensity of observed market competition, as discussed in Chapter 8, and of the achievement of Japanese industries, I am inclined to take the view that the antimonopoly policy in Japan has been sensibly carried out and/or sufficiently effective. In other words, I infer that the promotion of competition resulting from Japanese management has made antimonopoly policy less urgent than in the USA. Furthermore, thanks to the contestable market theory and the use of Demsetz's efficiency hypothesis to explain the concentration–profitability correlation, we now know that antimonopoly policies based on market concentration measurements alone may not be desirable. For instance, it may be better to approve a merger even if the combined market share exceeds, say, 30 per cent, provided that entry barriers are not substantial or effective rivals do exist. Whether intentionally or not, JFTC appears to have acted more in this spirit than the American authorities.

11.3. INDUSTRIAL POLICY

The history of industrial policy in Japan may be divided into four periods. The first period begins immediately after the war and ends before 1950. The key words for this period were *keisha seisan*, or priority production, with priority being given to the coal-mining and steel industries. The idea was to subsidize coal-mining, in order to produce low-cost coal which could be heavily allocated to steel production, and then in turn allocate the steel thus produced heavily into coal-mining. Subsidies, loans at a low interest rate, and the allocation of import quotas were the major policy instruments used to achieve this.

The second period is the 1950s, when the key words were *sangyo gorika* or industrial rationalization. It was considered necessary to rationalize industries by, for instance, introducing newer equipment and more efficient production systems, because much of the equipment had not been replaced since the beginning of the war. Special tax concessions and low-interest loans were awarded. This period also saw some support for *ikusei*, or nurturing of new industries, for the most part by means of protection against foreign competitors through quotas and tariffs.

The third period is the 1960s, when the key words were *shin sangyo taisei*, or the new industrial order. The country was in the process of rapidly liberalizing first trade and then foreign exchanges. The number of remaining import restrictions decreased from 466 in early 1962 to less than 100 by the end of 1970, and was further reduced to 27 by 1975. MITI, believing that in most industries the scale of production was too small and competition too excessive to enable them to compete with other industrial nations, encouraged mergers and investment co-ordination. One particular outcome of this policy, namely, the merger between Yawata and Fuji, was discussed in the previous section. The major policy instrument was *gyosei shido* or administrative guidance—

requests, suggestions, warnings, and so on—because the government was deprived of most of its explicit control devices including trade control and the allocation of foreign exchanges. To the extent that this guidance lacked legal power, its effect was limited.

The fourth and most recent period corresponds to the period after the oil crisis of 1973. Here two policies are relevant. One is the promotion of knowledge-intensive industries, such as the high-technology, fashion, and information-processing industries, though the government did little more than publicly announcing a 'vision'. The other is the adjustment policy for structurally depressed industries. The government used the Temporary Measures Law for the Stabilization of Designated Depressed Industries (abbreviated as *Tokuanho*) or its successor, *Sankoho*, to legalize the formation of cartels in order to co-ordinate scrapping production facilities in such industries as aluminium, synthetic fibres, and petrochemicals, and to create a fund to guarantee the firms against any debts incurred.[3]

It is not easy to evaluate these policies. We may differentiate between two issues: how much did the government really do and how far did its actions contribute to economic development. The first question may be examined relatively easily by looking at the evidence concerning subsidies, tax concessions, and so forth. The second question is more formidable because we know little about what would have happened had the policies not been pursued.

As regards the first question, the answer may be summarized as follows: (1) even in the early years the amount of government funding to industries, including subsidies, tax credits, and low-interest loans, was comparatively modest, though some industries, such as iron and steel, coal-mining, shipping, and electricity, benefited significantly. (2) There has been a clear tendency for such government funding to decrease overtime relative to the national economic level; in fact, over recent years it has come to appear minimal and by no means larger than in other industrialized countries. (3) In the early periods, protection against foreign competitors by means of tariffs and quotas may have been important

[3] A fifth period may be added, starting in the early 1980s and continuing up to the present day. During this period, MITI's main task has been to encourage imports and discourage exports, for instance, by persuading the industries to adopt voluntary export restraints.

in some industries, in particular, automobiles and electronics, but this has also been reduced over the years, so that Japan now has less trade restrictions (in manufactured goods) than any other country. In addition, (4) legalization of cartels and (5) collection and dissemination of information by means of published 'visions' or personal contacts between MITI staff and businesses have often been used as policy tools. Since the detailed quantitative evidence is available in Komiya *et al.* (1988), we will not discuss it here.

The second question of the evaluation of the effectiveness and contribution, positive or negative, of these policies is much more difficult. For instance, although we know that from 1946 to 1948, during which time the priority production policy was at its peak, coal production increased by 55 per cent, steel production more than tripled, and in the entire mining and manufacturing sectors overall production increased by 60 per cent, we cannot know the extent to which production would have increased without the policy. This was the period immediately after the war and the return of the labour-force from battlefields to production sites may have been an important factor in the production increase. One could also argue that the influences of wartime control that still remained were the reason for yet further control in the form of priority production. These influences included 'the continued impact of the economic control that were still in place, the problems of financially restructuring firms at the war's end, designations of facilities for reparation, inflation, the near-impossibility of obtaining private financing, and the generally poor working of the market in the confused social conditions of the time' (Kosai 1988, 33–4). The unfavourable effects of the policy were also apparent in the inflation over the following years and the delay in switching from coal to more economical imported petroleum as the major source of energy.

The nurturing policy in the 1950s was basically a direct application of the infant industry theory and appears to have helped the target industries to take off, most notably the automobile, electric and electronic equipment, and petrochemical industries.[4] Again,

[4] An industry satisfying the following three conditions is called *infant* (Negishi 1968): (1) entry entails substantial costs; these costs may come from the sunk entry costs, such as irreversible investment and R&D expenditures, or from the losses from higher costs during initial learning periods; (2) after these periods the entrant is expected to make positive profits; and (3) the present value of net profits to the

however, we do not know whether these industries would have failed to take off and been dominated by foreign producers had the policy not been adopted. Examples abound of firms that expanded without support, and even against government opposition, such as Kawasaki Steel and Honda.[5]

The loss of explicit policy tools in the 1960s forced the government to rely more on those means with little legal force. The most frequently used measure was administrative guidance, by which the MITI requested, suggested, or persuaded industries and firms. Sometimes it seems even to have threatened them with unfavourable consequences if they did not comply. This worked in many instances but not always. For instance, MITI's promotion of horizontal mergers or alliances to attain economies of scale and reduce what they thought was excessive competition succeeded in the case of Yawata and Fuji, perhaps because pre-war Japan Iron and Steel from which the two originated was partly government-owned and the president of Yawata at the time was an ex-MITI official. However, their attempt to integrate the automobile industry into two groups, Toyota and Nissan, and the computer industry into three groups, Fujitsu–Hitachi, NEC–Toshiba, and Oki–Mitsubishi Electric, did not succeed, and the enthusiasm for entry so outweighed MITI's pro-integration guidance that there were actually a larger number of firms and a lower concentration by the end of the period. A typical example is Honda's entry into the car industry. Although a top MITI official tried to persuade Mr Honda, Honda's founder and then president, to abandon its entry plan and strongly warned against the negative consequences, Mr Honda ignored this warning and went ahead with his own plan. Apparently, it was the firms' strong motivation for growth and not government policies that fostered investment in and entry

entrant is negative but the present value of increase in social welfare associated with entry is positive. The last condition guarantees that entry increases social welfare and yet will not be made under the market mechanism; hence, government support in order to promote entry is justified. Because social welfare is the sum of consumers' surplus and producers' surplus, and the increase in producers' surplus is negative by the first condition in (3), (3) requires that consumers' surplus increases with the entry, which in turn requires that the price decreases by the entry. See Odagiri (1986) for the detail.

[5] Kawasaki's plan in 1950 to build an integrated steel mill met with strong criticism from the government, though by 1951 the government had reluctantly agreed to provide a low-interest loan for part of the investment.

into Japanese industries. Had the firms been more obedient to the government, there would surely have been greater concentration in some industries now.

The petroleum cartel case discussed in the previous section further constrained MITI's discretion in the use of administrative guidance. It also forced MITI to be more conscious of the anti-competitive effect its policy might have. For instance, MITI is now less prepared to agree to cartels and, if cartels are considered really necessary, as in the adjustment policy, it consults with JFTC and explicitly legalizes exemption from the Antimonopoly Law. Furthermore, the case forced some MITI officials, particularly senior ones, who still maintained the non-*laissez-faire* view that co-ordination and guidance are needed for a smooth expansion of the market economy, to abandon their views in favour of respect for and reliance on market forces. The case also reminded the industries that complying with administrative guidance does not protect them from antimonopoly prosecution, and this, together with the decreasing need to seek approval or advice from MITI further weakened the personal connection between MITI and industry and reduced the effectiveness of administrative guidance.

As mentioned earlier, MITI has collected and disseminated information by various means—from councils that may include business executives, consumers, workers, and academics, to personal connections between MITI officials and businesses. Some authors, such as Komiya (1988) and Ozaki (1984), believe that information exchange of this kind has been the most important function of MITI and has helped to attain consensus among diverse interests. Yet two questions are appropriate. First, is the government better equipped to collect and disseminate information than businesses or the press who, needless to say, have a strong incentive as well as many channels through which to collect the information they need? Second, has this information exchange not created an anticompetitive climate among industries? For instance, businesses have often complained of excessive competition during recession and have argued that without a temporary cartel a damaging effect on the industry is inevitable. In this connection, one may actually argue that they engaged in such competition precisely because they could expect to form a cartel or to receive guidance from MITI during recession in order to avoid bankruptcy.

Another possibility is that the policy may have had the effect of signalling or announcing future intentions. For instance, publishing a 'vision' in which the government designates a particular industry as promising and essential for the economy's development may be taken by the private sector as a commitment to the industry. Expecting that the government will offer some help if the industry gets into trouble, the private sector may assume the risk to be lower, and there will thus be higher entry activity by industrialists and a greater willingness by financial institutions to make loans to the industry. Also the government's announcement may be taken by foreign firms as a credible commitment to deter their entry or to give domestic firms an advantageous bargaining position (Spencer and Brander 1983). According to these views, even if the government does not offer any financial or other assistance, the industry may be significantly helped by the mere announcement that the government has made. In other words, a sufficiently enthusiastic response to government signals from the private sector may have made further explicit government assistance redundant. It is hopelessly difficult to evaluate this hypothesis because available evidence, such as the amount of subsidies, may give no hint as to the extent and effectiveness of the policy in this sense.

As regards the adjustment policy in the 1970s and 1980s, the major policy tools were the legalization of capacity-scrapping cartels (with the approval of MITI and JFTC) and credit guarantees. Yet, according to both Sekiguchi and Horiuchi (1988) and Peck *et al.* (1988), the speed of capacity reduction was unrelated to the use of a cartel or a credit guarantee. Take, for instance, the aluminium industry which rapidly lost its competitiveness against imports during the 1970s owing to a sharp increase in electricity costs and the rising yen. The industry planned in 1977, with MITI's approval, to scrap 32 per cent of its facilities by 1981. Actually, 54 per cent had been scrapped by the time. Despite this more rapid progress of capacity reduction than had been planned, an interesting fact is that the industry neither formed a capacity-scrapping cartel nor utilized a credit guarantee. The implication appears very clear: it was a change in market conditions and not government policy that was the force behind rapid industrial restructuring. The proportion of imports in the total supply of aluminium increased from 33 per cent to 66 per cent during the period.

These examples cast doubt on the view that stresses the role of industrial policy in Japan's post-war economic growth. The policy probably has helped industries in several ways, from a fairly straightforward application of the infant industry theory to the automobile and computer industries in the early years, to the playing of more subtle roles as an information centre, co-ordinator, and signaller. Yet 'industrial policy is not the major reason for Japan's success' (Trezise 1983), and 'clearly, some part of the tendency to put the government in a central role is the search for a simple answer to a complex phenomenon' (Abegglen and Stalk 1985, 136). We have argued throughout this book that it is the Japanese management system that has promoted growth and competition in the industries. One may argue that this system made the industrial policy more effective (or less harmful) than in other countries, by encouraging management to respond to the opportunities provided by the policies, and by making use of personal connections. The management's own motivation to take advantage of the opportunities provided is therefore more important than the policies themselves. Industrial policy by itself would have never brought Japan the development it has attained in the post-war decades.

11.4. TECHNOLOGY POLICY

Science and technology are the areas in which the need for government assistance has been taken for granted because of their nature as public goods, which makes private benefit to the inventor smaller than overall social benefit: see Odagiri (1989) for a critical appraisal of theoretical and empirical arguments supporting this view.

Although many Westerners still tend to assume that the government is the main driving force behind Japan's technological 'success', an international comparison of R&D expenditure in Table 11.2 plainly indicates that quantitatively this assumption is wrong and that the part played by the government in both funding and carrying out R&D is smaller in Japan than in the USA, Germany, France, or the UK. One reason for this is that defence-related expenditure in Japan is small. Yet, even when defence-related R&D expenditure is excluded, the proportion of government funds in total R&D expenditures is smaller in Japan

TABLE 11.2. R & D expenditures and flows in five countries (%, except total R & D expenditures)

	Japan 1987	USA 1987	FRG 1987	France 1987	UK 1986
Total R & D expenditures (in billion dollars)	62.4	118.8	31.6	20.0	15.0
Total R & D expenditures as a ratio to GNP	2.57	2.59	2.81	2.28	2.29
Proportion of funds (expenditures) by					
Industry	74.4 (*72.0*)	47.6 (*72.5*)	62.3 (*73.1*)	42.0 (*56.8*)	49.5 (*69.2*)
Government	19.9 (*10.0*)	49.0 (*12.6*)	36.6 (*3.4*)	53.8 (*26.4*)	38.5 (*15.6*)
University	4.7 (*13.4*)	2.3 (*12.1*)	(*12.9*)	0.2 (*15.9*)	0.5 (*11.6*)
Private research institution	0.8 (*4.4*)	1.2 (*2.5*)	(*10.6*)	0.4 (*0.9*)	1.9 (*3.6*)
Foreign	0.1		1.1	3.6	9.6
Share of government funds in industry expenditures	1.7	35.5	15.3	22.4	25.7

Notes: Figures for USA, FRG, and France include social and humanistic sciences. Proportion of funds and expenditures and the share of government funds in France are for 1983. The proportion of funds by industry in FRG includes funds by private research institution which is probably less than 1%.

Source: Science and Technology Agency (1990), appendix tables 1 and 3.

TABLE 11.3. Government support to industrial R & D in Japan (in billion yen)

Year	(A) Total	(a) Subsidies and research contracts	(b) Preferential tax treatment	(c) Low interest rate loan	(B) R & D expenditure by industry	(A)/(B) (%)	(C) Payment for technology importation	(A)/(B + C) (%)
1960	9.8	0.7	9.1	—	124.4	7.88	34.2	6.18
1965	16.4	3.1	13.3	—	252.4	6.50	59.6	5.26
1970	31.0	11.0	19.1	0.9	823.3	3.77	155.1	3.17
1975	64.7	29.8	33.0	1.9	1684.8	3.84	211.3	3.41
1980	101.0	60.8	38.0	2.2	3142.3	3.21	326.2	2.91
1983	117.7	58.7	57.0	2.0	4560.1	2.58	493.8	2.33

Notes:
(a) is the amount of subsidies and research contracts.
(b) is the amount of tax forgone through the preferential tax treatments to promote R & D.
(c) is the interest payments savings due to the low interest rate loan to promote R & D.
(A) = (a) + (b) + (c).

Sources: (a) Somu-cho, 'Kagaku gijutsu kenkyu chosa hokoku' ('Report on the Survey of Research and Development'), each year; (b) Documents submitted to Tax System Council; (c) Estimated from Japan Development Bank documents.

Adapted from Goto and Wakasugi (1988), table 1.

than anywhere except the UK—19.3 per cent, as opposed to 26.8 per cent in the USA, 34.4 per cent in Germany, 40.5 per cent in France, and 17.2 per cent in the UK (Science and Technology Agency, 1990).[6]

Even more impressive is the comparison of government funds in industrial R & D expenditure. This amounts to less than 2 per cent in Japan, suggesting that industries are financing their proportionally larger R & D out of their own funds, which marks a contrast with the other four countries where 15 to 36 per cent of industrial R & D are supported by government funds. Although the gap narrows again if defence-related industries are excluded, the fact remains that the percentage is smallest in Japan.

These funds are usually transferred to the industries in the form of subsidies and research contracts. In addition, tax credits and low-interest loans on R & D investment have been granted, and one may be tempted to argue that the Japanese government has been effectively encouraging industrial R & D through these *de facto* subsidies. However, Table 11.3 shows that the tax revenue forgone due to preferential tax treatment has not been significantly different from subsidies and research contracts, and the amount of indirect subsidy in the form of reduced interest rates is quite small. In total, all these amounted to a little more than a hundred billion yen in 1983, or 2.6 per cent of industrial R & D expenditure. Of the sum of industrial R & D expenditure and payment for technology importation, which Goto and Wakasugi (1988) used as a better measure of industrial efforts to create or acquire technological knowledge, they constitute only 2.3 per cent.

We must inevitably conclude that industrial R & D in Japan is almost entirely funded by the industries themselves. Even if indirect subsidies in the form of tax credits and low-interest loans are included, the proportion of government finance in industrial R & D is far smaller than in other countries, where as much as a third of industrial R & D is financed by the government. An argument may be made, as in the previous section, that however small government funds may have been, their impact has been

[6] The smaller proportion in the UK than in Japan is only a recent phenomenon. In 1983, the proportion was 26.8% in the UK and 21.7% in Japan. During the 1970s the proportion in the UK always exceeded 30%.

significant because of the signalling effect they tended to create. There seems no way to measure this effect quantitatively.

Table 11.3 also reveals a clear downward trend in the importance of direct and indirect subsidies: the proportion of subsidies to industrial R & D was almost 8 per cent in 1960, still far lower than in other countries, but gradually declined to 2.6 per cent in 1983. In parallel with the generally diminishing importance of industrial policy, government support of industrial R & D has decreased rather dramatically in the past two to three decades.

Preferential tax treatment for R & D expenditure has been awarded by way of several measures. Since 1966, the most important has been credit (up to 10 per cent of the firm's total corporate tax payments) for 20 per cent of its R & D expenditure in excess of the previously highest expenditure. A similar measure has been taken in many other countries. For instance, in the USA since 1981, a 25 per cent tax credit for R & D expenditure in excess of the average of R & D expenditures in a base period (generally the previous three taxable years) is provided. Thus the tax credit in the USA has been more generous than in Japan in two senses: it has been based on 25 per cent of the excess rather than 20 per cent and on the excess over the past three years averaged rather than the excess over the past maximum. As a consequence, the revenue loss due to tax credits was estimated to be 0.6 to 1 billion dollars in the USA in 1981 (Mansfield 1985), while in Japan, the estimated revenue loss due to this credit and other less important R & D-related credits was 38 billion yen in 1980 or about 0.19 billion dollars (at the exchange rate then in operation) and 57 billion yen in 1983 or 0.25 billion dollars. Therefore, even taking into consideration the difference in national products or national R & D expenditures between the two countries, the evidence is against the view that industries in Japan enjoy more favourable tax treatment concerning R & D.[7]

Another policy tool used by the Japanese government has been

[7] Using the US data, Mansfield (1985) estimated that company-financed R & D would have decreased merely around 1% even without tax credits, indicating that unless private incentives are already there, tax credits cannot spur the firms to undertake R & D. He also estimated that the extra R & D stimulated by credits has been considerably smaller than the revenue loss to the government, suggesting the inefficiency of tax credits as a policy tool. These results seem to be true internationally, because he obtained similar results for Sweden and Canada.

the formation of research associations (RAs hereafter), partly financed by the government and partly by participating firms, based on the 1961 Act on the Mining and Manufacturing Industry Technology Research Association. During 1961–87 87 RAs were established of which 57 still existed (active or not) in 1987. Those among these 57 with a history of more than two years were approached by Fujishiro (1988) and 34 responded. All of them had received government subsidies at sometime during their history and in 1987, 27, or 80 per cent of the 34 RAs, received subsidies of 30.5 billion yen or about 80 per cent of their total R & D expenditure. Similarly, Wakasugi (1986) showed that 38 of the 44 RAs in 1983 received subsidies of 33 billion yen, or about a half of their total R & D expenditures. Since the total government R & D subsidies were about 59 billion yen in the same year (see Table 11.3), we infer that more than a half of them were supplied through RAs. A conjecture is that RAs have been used by MITI primarily as a means to distribute its subsidies, so as to avoid favouring a particular firm and to minimize the cost of supervising the use of subsidies. Given this view, it is not surprising that no joint research facility was established in any of the 87 associations except 2, while each member firm received its share of research funds and carried out the research in its own laboratory. The membership size of the RAs ranged from 3 to 45, with the median being about 10. Members are overwhelmingly private companies, though in some cases they included government research institutions.

The effectiveness of these technology associations is questionable despite the publicized success of the VLSI association (active from 1976 to 1979), which produced more than a thousand patents (Sakakibara 1981). According to Wakasugi's (1986) case-study of six RAs, the productivity as measured by the number of patents divided by the R & D expenditure was lower in every RA than that of the industrial average. Similarly, Fujishiro (1988) found that this productivity as an average for 20 RAs was 1.93 (per hundred million yen), less than a half of the average productivity, 5.06, of R & D expenditures by the 110 firms who participated in these 20 RAs. He also regressed in a log-linear equation the number of patents on R & D expenditures to estimate the marginal productivity as an elasticity. The result was 0.692 for RAs and 0.988 for the firms: that is, when R & D expenditures are increased by 1 per cent, the number of patents increases by about 1 per cent in private firms, suggesting constant returns to scale in their R & D activities, but by only 0.7 per cent in the RAs.

Admittedly, these results do not necessarily imply that RAs are inefficient. First, the RAs may have been engaged more heavily in basic research than private firms and therefore the research may have been more difficult and the results less patentable. Probably some of the research topics taken up by RAs, such as nuclear-powered steel-making, were too basic and too risky to be undertaken by individual firms. There were, however, research topics in RAs that were more application-oriented, as in the case of some of the computer-related RAs.

Second, when most of the actual and potential rivals are within the RA, there is little need for protective patents, that is, patents designed only to pre-empt rivals. In view of the high propensity of Japanese firms to apply for patents, of which some are believed to be for protective purposes only (which, incidentally, suggests the intensity of competition in Japanese industries), this factor may be an important explanation of the lower patent productivity in RAs.

Hence, it is impossible to estimate how much of the lower patent productivity of RAs as compared to that of private firms is attributable to the inefficiency of RAs (caused by free-riding, lack of control, lack of motivation, and so on) and how much to other factors, such as the orientation toward basic research. Suffice it here to say that it is misleading to make any inferences about the productivity of RAs by referring to the single successful case of the VLSI RA. The evidence above implies that the VLSI case was actually exceptional and RAs on average have produced fewer patents per expenditure than private R & D efforts.

Finally, as in the case of industrial policy, we need to note the role of the government, particularly MITI, in the collection and diffusion of information, for instance, the information on the availability of new technology. Before the trade and capital liberalization in the 1960s, firms had to make frequent contact with MITI to acquire approval or permission for many aspects of their activities.[8] Close human relations between MITI and the firms were created, which still remain to some degree. Con-

[8] An important consequence of foreign exchange control during this period was the better bargaining position of Japanese firms in technology importation because MITI tended to restrict the number of first importers to one. Consequently, competition among Japanese firms was minimized, making licensor–licensee

sequently MITI could easily play a useful role as a centre for the collection and dissemination of information. It could also obtain information on overseas markets through its Japan External Trade Organization (JETRO) and technological information through its Agency of Industry, Science and Technology, which has a number of laboratories. In the early years when firms tended to lack international or technological information, MITI's knowledge must have been appreciated by the companies. Many of these benefits have disappeared as the firms themselves have accumulated international experiences and technological knowledge.[9]

RAs may also have played an important role in disseminating information across member firms by offering opportunities for the scientists from different companies to get together. It is difficult to estimate how important this function of RAs has been. It has been reported that, in the VLSI RA, it took considerable talent and effort (and drinks!) on the part of the director to get the scientists from different companies to mingle (Sakakibara 1981). If we note that this RA was quite exceptional in having a common laboratory and a dedicated director from a third party (namely, a government research institution and not one of the companies), we can readily suppose that communication among scientists from different companies must have been infrequent in most other RAs. Thus, even though we dare not deny the RA's role in information exchange, we should not overemphasize it either.

11.5. A CASE-STUDY: THE COMPUTER INDUSTRY

Efforts to develop computers in Japan started in the 1950s. The leading companies, such as NEC, Fujitsu, and Hitachi, first developed computers of their own around 1960, but they were technologically far behind the larger foreign producers, in particular IBM. Naturally, this was one of the industries that MITI sought to nurture in the 1950s and 1960s. It protected domestic producers

bargaining bilaterally monopolistic and lowering the royalty payments. See Goto and Wakasugi (1988).

[9] An example is given by Lynn (1982) concerning a new steel-making technology invented in 1950 by Austrians called a basic oxygen furnace (BOF). MITI learned of the technology through the embassy in Austria in 1953. However, the information-gathering capacity of the private sector was surprisingly good even in this early period. Earlier than MITI, the engineers in Nippon Kokan (now NKK) found an article about BOF in a German specialist journal and started collecting more information.

TABLE 11.4. R & D expenditures by companies and major research associations in the Japanese computer industry (in million yen)

Year	Total R & D expenditure (A)	Joint R & Ds (B)	(a)	(b)	(c)	(d)	(e)	(f)	(g)	(B)/(A) %
1962	25 700	174	174							0.7
1963	33 740	240	240							0.7
1964	31 113	290	290							0.9
1965	31 205	30	30							0.1
1966	39 877	370		370						0.9
1967	55 467	1 190		1 190						2.1
1968	83 834	2 030		2 030						2.4
1969	93 366	2 780		2 780						3.0
1970	129 845	2 320		2 320						1.8
1971	131 656	1 330		1 330						1.0

1972	164 926	10 420			10 420					6.3
1973	194 587	35 480			35 480					18.2
1974	237 825	39 300			39 300					16.5
1975	233 839	29 150			29 150					12.5
1976	285 308	29 850			22 850	7 000				10.5
1977	272 147	17 280				17 280				6.3
1978	313 546	20 104				20 104				6.4
1979	382 688	13 863				13 812	51			3.6
1980	535 984	927					927			0.2
1981	664 307	2 464					2 419	30	15	0.4
1982	790 587	3 274					3 238	813	423	0.4
1983	958 643	7 619					3 332	1 567	2 720	0.8
1984	1 096 368	9 956					2 326	2 510	5 120	0.9
1985	1 321 973	10 484					3 438	2 270	4 776	0.8

Notes: (a) Computer Technology RA; (b) Super High Function Computer RA; (c) Super High Function Computer Development RA, New Computer Series Technology RA, and Super High Function Computer Technology RA; (d) Very-Large-Scale Integrated Circuits (VLSI) RA; (e) Opt-electronics Applied System RA; (f) High Speed Calculation Computer RA; (g) Fifth Generation Computer Development Project; (A) R & D expenditures in the electronics, communication, and computer industry; (B) = (a) + (b) + (c) + (d) + (e) + (f) + (g).

Source: Wakasugi (1988), table 4.

by restricting imports and direct investment by foreign producers. At the same time, subsidies were provided to encourage R & D to catch up with foreign rivals.

In 1961, IBM permitted seven Japanese firms to use its basic patents in exchange for Japanese government agreement to the company itself producing within Japan. In addition, many Japanese companies imported technology from other foreign computer makers. These arrangements gave Japanese firms opportunities to catch up with the advanced technology of foreign firms, but at the same time placed them under formidable competition from IBM. MITI, worried that domestic producers would be dominated by IBM and other foreign producers, postponed the liberalization of trade and direct investment until the early 1970s, and supported R & D in domestic firms by encouraging them to form research associations (RAs) under the 1961 Act on RA and by supporting them financially.

Table 11.4 shows the history of RAs in the computer industry since 1962, and the R & D expenditures made by these RAs as well as the total R & D expenditures by the industry as a whole. One can make several observations. First, quantitatively, the proportion of R & D expenditure by the RAs to that of the industry as a whole has been surprisingly small. It was relatively high during the exceptional years of 1973–6 when trade and investment liberalization was going on, but even then the proportion never exceeded one-fifth. It should be noted that the proportion of government funds was probably even smaller because, as explained earlier, RAs were also financed by the firms. Since 1980 in particular, the proportion has not reached even a mere 1 per cent, clearly showing that R & D expenditure in the industry is currently overwhelmingly funded by the companies.

Second, each RA was set up with a fixed time limit (with the possibility of extension), and never lasted more than a few years. Probably this has helped RAs to maintain flexibility and avoid organizational rigidity. Such flexibility must be crucial in an industry with a rapidly changing technological environment, because priorities among research projects may change rapidly. Also, the time limit helps to ensure easier personnel management. All researchers participating in these RAs came from the member firms, and no RA hired any researchers of its own, unlike similar associations in the USA, such as MCC (see Peck 1986) and

Sematec. Therefore, the researchers did not have to worry about their jobs when the RAs were disbanded. In fact most researchers wished to return to their own firms after several years, because under the Japanese system of lifetime employment and internal promotion, employees usually prefer to stay within the main body of the company in order to maintain contact with higher-rank managers and colleagues, and to impress supervisors with their achievements there.

Third, a sequence of RAs has been created in order to maintain continuity despite the short duration of each RA. Whenever an RA was disbanded, a new RA was started with a project selected to correspond to new scientific developments, new market needs, and the new technological level of participating firms. The subject for research may be proposed by the companies, the government-sponsored research institution, or MITI. MITI plays a role in fostering agreement among the prospective participants, and formalizing the RA under the Act. In these regards, the presence of MITI as a co-ordinator and as an information centre has been critical. It also explains why a close personal connection and frequent exchanges of information with MITI have been important to Japanese firms.

Fourth, partly as a consequence of MITI's role as a co-ordinator, the membership of various RAs in the computer industry has been stable and concentrated in the main six producers who were early entrants to the industry and have kept a close contact with MITI. These comprise three general electric and electronic equipment manufacturers—Hitachi, Toshiba, and Mitsubishi Electric—and three companies more specialized in communication and computation equipment—NEC, Fujitsu, and Oki. One exception was the VLSI RA, in which Oki did not participate. Other exceptions were the three RAs active during 1947–51 (shown in column (c) in Table 11.4), which each included two of the companies, without overlapping with the other two RAs. Hence all the six main companies participated in one of the RAs. This has been the only case of more than two RAs pursuing basically the same theme. The pairing for each RA was based on the MITI view, discussed in Section 11.3, that Japanese producers were too small and too many to compete against IBM and other big foreign companies, and that they therefore had to be integrated into three groups. Although this grouping did not last and they are now fiercely competing with each other, the strategic difference we still observe between, on the one hand, Hitachi and Fujitsu, who opted to pursue compatibility with IBM, and on the other, Toshiba and NEC, shows that some influences of MITI's policy still remain.

This stability of membership raises the possibility that the RAs may have discriminated against non-members who were mostly late entrants into the market. It is difficult to deny this possibility. Not all the firms wishing to join the RAs were allowed to do so, and not all the RA proposals were adopted. Therefore, whatever the beneficial aspects of RAs may have been, one has to balance them against the possible undesirable effects of concentration and entry barriers. If the observed growth of the industry and entry by a number of firms are any indicators that these negative effects have not in fact been serious, the reason is perhaps either the presence of a formidable outside competitor—IBM, of course—which kept the domestic market leaders from any monopolistic behaviour, or that RAs attained too little to give the participants any decisive advantage, or, indeed, both of these.

That RAs have been relatively inefficient in terms of patent production has already been noted. A possibility remains that, even though RAs themselves were unproductive, the member firms benefited from the spill-over of technological knowledge from the RAs. Such spill-over may take place when, for instance, the scientists sent from a member company to an RA return to the company. Fujishiro (1988) investigated this possibility in two ways. First, if the spill-over effect had been important, then the number of patents of the member firms would be expected to increase during or after the RA relative to those of non-members. Fig. 11.1 shows the share in patents of the RA member firms in those patent classifications relevant to the RAs. H01L, for instance, represents semiconductors. Since research by the VLSI RA, active during 1976–9, was concentrated in this field, if there was any spill-over, the share of the five members must have increased during or after this period. The figure, however, clearly suggests that their share has been steadily declining since 1976. Similarly, the share in any other field of the six firms that participated continuously in the RAs has been more or less declining. Evidence of RAs enhancing the relative patent position of the member firms is nowhere to be found.

The other, more sophisticated investigation by Fujishiro pre-

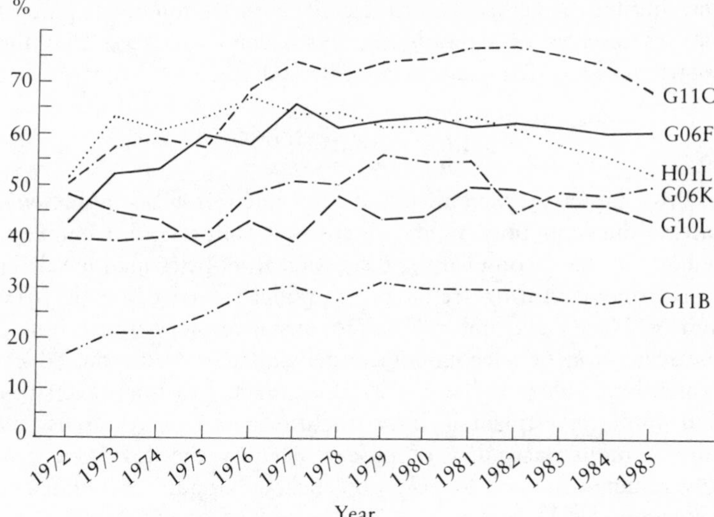

FIG. 11.1 Share in patents of the major six computer producers in Japan
Notes: The six firms are Fujitsu, Hitachi, Mitsubishi Electric, NEC, Oki, and Toshiba. For H01L only, Oki (not participating in the VLSI RA) is excluded.

The patent classifications are as follows: H01L, semiconductor; G06F, digital computer; G06K, data recognition and display; G10L, sound recognition; G11B, G11C, information storage.
Source: Fujishiro (1988).

dicted the numbér of patents of a firm in a certain year and patent classification based on the total number of patents of the firm in the year and the total number in the classification in the year. The residuals, according to the spill-over hypothesis, must be positive for member firms in the years (or several years after) they participated in the relevant RAs. The results did not support this hypothesis: some of the residuals were positive but some were negative, and only a few of them were significantly different from zero.

Both of these results therefore cast doubt on the importance of spill-overs from RAs, which is consistent with our discussion in the previous section that, except perhaps for the VLSI RA, the role of RAs in exchanging and disseminating information may have been limited. Together with the relatively small number of patents RAs themselves have produced, this seems to suggest that the contributions of RAs have been very modest.

11.6. CONCLUSION

In this chapter we have reviewed three micro-policies in post-war Japan: antimonopoly policy, industrial policy, and technology policy. We have confined the discussion to policies mainly related to the manufacturing sector and to policies carried out by JFTC and MITI. We did not discuss, for instance, agricultural policy, the regulation of telecommunications and transportation, education policy, policy on basic research conducted within universities, and public investment in infrastructure. Nor did we discuss the role in industrial policy of procurement by the government or government-affiliated organization such as Nippon Telephone and Telegram (NTT).

Apart from the short post-war period when GHQ took measures to further economic democratization and the government was comparatively directly involved in economic activities, the general picture that emerges is one of basic reliance on the market mechanism modified, if necessary, by the use of informal means of guidance and information dissemination. The use of direct control and financial means has been kept at a level probably lower than most other countries. Ironically, therefore, the success of government policy in Japan, if it can be called a success at all, may rest not in the exercising of power but rather in refraining from doing so. Such restraint, we should also note, was not entirely voluntary and very often the result of exogenous constraints, such as trade and exchange liberalization, the antimonopoly law, and budget constraint. Whether voluntary or not, the result was an effective use of the competitive market mechanism. Quite contrary to the general belief in the West, the Japanese economy may have been more in line with the spirit of *laissez faire* than elsewhere. Equally importantly this general policy attitude has had the effect of enabling managerial growth preference to contribute fully to economic growth and innovation.

Of course, an argument can be made that the presence of competent bureaucrats sympathetic to businesses and their stability have created an environment favourable to economic growth and that they must therefore be regarded as evidence of strong industry policy however small their interventions actually were. In this regard, the following assessment by Abegglen and Stalk (1985, 30) appears to agree with this argument:

> in such an atmosphere of growth, it helps if the government is competently staffed, and, in fact, the best of Japan's best educated university graduates enter government service by preference. It is helpful too if government staffing is kept small; proportionally, Japan has fewer of its labour force in government service than any other major country. It helps too if government is stable, avoiding abrupt swings in economic policy, and that economic policy making is in the hands of a competent bureaucracy which can take a long view of economic policy issues, relatively free from short-term political pressure groups.

What matters is the presence of a competitive and efficient market mechanism and a management system which has enhanced growth and competition. Without them no government, however competent and stable, would ever be able to achieve what Japan has achieved. Therefore, it is not at all surprising to find that many of the government policies in Japan that have been directed to those areas lacking these conditions, have proved totally unsuccessful and inefficient. Take, for example, the agricultural policy by which the government protects rice farmers from competition. The results are a persistence of inefficient producers, poor average quality, and a high price to the consumers. Take the transportation policy, in which politicians' pressure on the Transport Ministry to construct railways in their constituencies outweighs their concern for the national interest. The results are many railways with huge losses and higher fares for the consumer. Take the distribution and commercial policies, in which politicians are more concerned with attracting the votes of small-scale wholesalers and retailers. The results are restrictions on large-scale retailers and higher retail prices. Even within MITI, regulations against nine regionally monopolistic electricity companies are inefficient, with the result that innovation is discouraged and the companies are forced to employ large staffs to deal with the red tape. All the predicted vices of regulation can easily be found in many economic activities within the country and, if those vices have not been apparent in industrial and technology policies, I can think of only one reason: market competition.

12

Japanese Management in the World

12.1. GROWTH PREFERENCE, COMPETITION, AND ACCOUNTABILITY REVISITED BY WAY OF SUMMARY

I began this book by saying that the firm should be viewed primarily as a collection of human resources. By this I meant that the human aspect of the firm—what people want, what they can do and will do—constrains motivation, speed of expansion, its direction, and organizational structure. Of course this is hardly a new view. What surprises me is not that the importance of the human aspect is emphasized in Japan, but that it is often forgotten in the USA and the UK. Nowhere is this difference more evident than in the financial press. On 8 January 1990, not a particularly eventful day, the headlines of the company and industrial section of the *Financial Times* read:

> Campeau abandons attempt to sell Bloomingdale's
>
> Dixons launches counter attack on Kingfisher
>
> Apricot concentrate resources on computing services
>
> GrandMet considers Courage swap
>
> Balmoral back on the attack

On the next day, in *Nihon Keizai Shimbun*, the Japanese counterpart to the *Financial Times*, the headlines read:

> Japanese, European and Korean electronics companies to start selling DAT (digital audio tape) in the US from this summer
>
> Fujitsu develops a neuro-computer with a learning speed 400 times faster than the existing model
>
> JVC develops a video tape recorder with digital sound recording
>
> Toyota plans to produce a new wagon-type car in the US
>
> Suzuki Motor agreed to a joint venture in Hungary

Kowa's joint venture with a London company constructs buildings in the City

Nihon Yakuhin starts a clinical test of a new anti-cancer drug

The difference is all too clear. Except for the article about Apricot, all the news in the UK relates to the selling and buying of companies, or to fighting against proposed purchases. All the news in Japan, on the contrary, relates to product development and investment either internally or by joint ventures. Businesses, to the British, are something to be bought and sold like commodities. Businesses, to the Japanese, are something to be developed and expanded internally.

On 5 December 1989, IBM announced a restructuring plan. Here are two reports:

IBM said yesterday it would take a $2.3bn fourth-quarter charge for restructuring actions designed to improve the flagging performance of its US operations. The write-off will cover the cost of shedding 10,000 employees, or about 4.5 per cent of its US workforce, closing some plants, offices and development centres and changing the way it accounts for investments in other companies and new technologies. The actions, the latest in a series of cost-cutting measures by IBM since the mid-1980s, were immediately criticised by some Wall Street analysts. They argued that the company needed to cut between 40,000 and 60,000 from its worldwide workforce of 387,000 to make a big difference to its profits.

IBM's stock price edged up $1\frac{3}{4}$ to $101 after the announcement of the charge and the company's plan to buy back another $4bn of its stock. Coupled with previous repurchases, the world's largest computer maker will have reduced its equity by $10.5bn, or some 15 per cent, since mid-1986. From a 52-week high of $130, IBM's stock has sunk to a low of $96 as Wall Street began to appreciate the deterioration in IBM's performance during the second half of this year. Another round of restructuring was long anticipated. (*Financial Times*, 6 December 1989).

IBM announced yesterday a large-scale rationalization plan including redundancy for more than 10,000 employees and a concentration of manufacturing and sales activities. It plans to report a $2.3bn loss in the fourth quarter, and expects an annual cost reduction of $1bn. The growth in the US computer market is sluggish and many expect the slow growth to continue until the early nineties. IBM, in the face of this harsh environment, has decided to make a radical rationalization, and will prompt other computer makers to make similar rationalizations.

In addition to large-scale restructuring in manufacturing, development, sales, service and administration, the company will achieve employment

> reduction by cutting new recruitment and through an early retirement scheme. It aims to reduce its work-force in the USA by more than 10,000 to 206,000 by the end of 1990. According to the company, employment will then have been reduced by 37,000 since 1985 when they started a series of restructuring moves. (*Nihon Keizai Shimbun*, 6 December 1989)

Again, the implication is obvious. British readers are most interested in the reaction from Wall Street: Japanese readers are most interested in how many jobs are to be lost and how job reductions will be effected. Companies, for the British, are first of all objects of investment: for the Japanese, they are places in which people work together.

Of course, one should not exaggerate the differences. The *Financial Times* in fact reported later in the article that 'IBM, continuing its 40-year-old practice of no forced lay-offs, said the job losses would come from voluntary early retirement and natural attrition.' Japanese companies are also concerned with stock prices though, typically, the *Nihon Keizai Shimbun* article on IBM did not report the reaction from Wall Street. The difference is not overwhelming and may be simply one of emphasis. Yet the contrast is revealing.

It is against this background that we have emphasized the need for a full understanding of the Japanese internal labour system. The consequences of this system, as we have found, are a preference for corporate growth (which must be internal) and intense internal competition. Behind these two key concepts lie workers' long-term attachment to one company (as an ideal but not necessarily a reality), internal promotion based on detailed and long-run evaluation, and firm-specific skills, wage structure, and other work practices. Together with weaker financial control, the motivation of the firm can best be described by (constrained) maximization of growth in the long run and (constrained) minimization of lay-offs in the short run. The economic consequences of this behaviour, as we have shown, are industrial competition and economic stability and growth.

An understanding of the human side of the firm is also indispensable to a discussion of organizational issues. Why are hostile mergers and acquisitions so rare in Japan? Why are divisional forms of control less popular? Why do the Japanese prefer to hive off businesses—and, in particular, businesses requiring unrelated or lower skills? Why do they tend to maintain long-term relationships with suppliers and subcontractors? These questions are best answered, as we have done in Part II, by investigating the human said. Indeed, for management, the most appropriate issue is what organizational strategy to take in order fully to utilize and accumulate human resources, and to gain their full support. Acquiring a firm in the face of hostility from its management and employees may cause distrust among the employees of both the acquired and the acquiring firms and is unlikely to be as successful as internal investment in the long run.

In contrast to the vast majority of the literature in English, which depicts the Japanese economy as a harmonious society where the notion of competition is as alien as Confucianism is to the West,[1] we have argued that Japan is, on the contrary, a competitive society, possibly to a greater extent than in the West. This aspect of the Japanese economy may have been overlooked because the neoclassical concept of competition has been so dominant in these authors' thinking that they failed to realize the possibility of other forms of competition. Competition must be taken as a strategic concept, as it was for Adam Smith.[2] It is a concept far broader than the concept of perfect competition taught in economics courses. A market with a limited number of participants can be more competitive than an atomistic market. A market not perfectly competitive today may be still competitive in the long run, and such long-run competition may contribute more to long-run optimal resource allocation when specificity is high in human and other resources. An internal labour system and supplier–assembler relations are precisely the places where re-

[1] The best example of this view has been given by Morishima (1982), a Japanese who has been living in the UK for many years. Abegglen, an American who has been living in Japan for many years, offered a contrasting view of Japanese management in a book he wrote with Stalk (1985), which basically agrees with ours.

[2] For Smith's view on competition, see Stigler (1957) and McNulty (1967, 1968). Smith was by no means the first economist to discuss competition. Cantillon, for instance, explained the notion of competition by bargaining as follows: 'This proposition is come at by bargaining. The Butcher keeps up his Price [of Meat] according to the number of Buyers he sees; the Buyers, on their side, offer less according as they think the Butcher will have less sale: the Price set by some usually followed by others. Some are more clever in puffing up their wares, others in running them down' (Cantillon 1755; trans. Higgs 1964, 119).

source specificity is high, thus making long-run relations valuable and long-run competition effective. In such long-run relations, exit cannot be used as often as in a spot relation, but the use of the voice option (with a threat of exit) becomes more effective because ignoring the voice is expected to lead to the loss of a long-run opportunity.

In the financial market, the concept of the take-over as a disciplinary mechanism is based on the presumed effectiveness of the exit mechanism. If the shareholders are dissatisfied with the management, they will sell their shares, which will lower the share price and make take-over attractive. Is this mechanism really as efficient as usually believed? One answer to this question has been provided in Chapters 4 and 10. If the take-over mechanism is perfect and costless, then in the v–g frontier the management is forced to choose a rate of growth that maximizes the value of the firm. Compared to growth-maximizing management with incomplete shareholder control, the result is a lower growth rate for the firm which, as proved in Chapter 10, results in a lower economic growth rate, given that firms increase labour productivity through their R & D activity. Although the question of a socially optimal growth rate is beyond our concern in this book, a rather paradoxical result is that, if the economy prefers faster growth, the flawless working of take-overs as a disciplinary mechanism is undesirable.

Moreover, take-overs are costly. Premiums have to be paid over the market price, and legal fees and commissions can be huge. The latter item alone was estimated at £500 million in the UK in 1986 by Kay (1988), who suggests that it may outweigh any potential industrial inefficiencies which might be relieved. In one of the largest take-over attempts, Hoylake's failed bid against BAT industries, it has been reported that BAT spent at least £56 million on defence and Hoylake, £35 million on attack.[3] From the social viewpoint, these costs have no productive purpose: they only enrich lawyers and brokers whose talents could otherwise be used for productive purposes. Add to the cost the waste of time and energy that management has to spend in order to devise tactics to fend off and fight against take-over threats, and the result can be a

[3] *Financial Times*, 24 Apr. 1990.

huge underutilization of the productive capacity of the economy.[4]

The use of voice may be not only viable but also more efficient as a disciplinary mechanism. It is most likely that voice will be expressed by large shareholders or large debtholders, who usually are institutional investors and, particularly in Germany and Japan, banks. Their voice will be carefully listened to, because they not only have incentives to collect information on the firm's business conditions but will also be given access to the information normal investors cannot reach, and, furthermore, they have management know-how. The voice is therefore likely to be based on an accurate understanding of the real situation. The management has an incentive to listen to the voice because it may be accompanied by the threat of exit, that is, the threat to withdraw loans. Long-run human relations also play a role here, as the managers of the firm and the staff of the banks tend to form such relations.

Nevertheless, as discussed in Chapter 2, in Japan we consider this mechanism to be much weaker than is usually considered by Westerners. It is true that banks usually get involved when the firm is in difficulty; however, such involvement also occurs in the USA and the UK to a varying extent. At other times, the banks' interference in management appears quite small, which is exactly why we argue that management in Japan has substantial discretionary power—power strong enough for it to pursue growth (though not without limit). If the disciplinary role of banks is limited, as suggested here, how can management be disciplined and maintain efficiency in Japan? One answer to this question is simply that not all management in Japan is efficient. It is impossible to get quantitative evidence but one observes such inefficiency more in those markets which are shielded from competition—regulated industries such as agriculture and transportation, industries without international competition such as traditional crafts and food-processing, and industries with local market power such as (small-scale) retail. Therefore, we again come to the importance of competition.

When management is inefficient, the firm in a competitive market is expected to go bankrupt eventually. This fear of bank-

[4] Another possibility, that stock market evaluation based on asymmetric information causes managerial myopia, was discussed in Sec. 4.3.

ruptcy should prompt the management to be efficient. The effectiveness of bankruptcy fears as a disciplinary measure depends on two factors. The first relates to the question of how fast bankruptcy occurs as a result of inefficiency, which basically is a question of how competitive the product market is. The more competitive the market is the shorter time a high-cost firm will survive. Again, this competition should not be confined to the neoclassical concept of perfect competition. It may be Bertrand-type cut-throat competition among oligopolists, Schumpeterian dynamic competition with innovation, competitive threats from entrants (that is, contestability), or all of them. The growth maximizing behaviour of Japanese management strengthens competition in these senses because to attain growth the firm has to increase capacity in existing markets or enter into new markets. The two key concepts of growth maximization and competition thus become complementary.

Second, bankruptcy must be costly because otherwise fear of it will not prompt the management to make maximum efforts to maintain efficiency. This cost is small if the management's shareholding is small, an external market for executives is well developed, and labour can be easily dismissed. The last condition is satisfied if the demand in external labour markets is large so that dismissed workers can easily get new jobs (or unemployment insurance payment is generous), or if the management does not care about the worker's welfare. When these conditions are met, the managers of a bankrupt firm will simply dismiss all the workers and then find new jobs for themselves. It does not appear far-fetched to assume that these conditions are more likely to be met in the USA or the UK because an executive's quitting one company to become an executive in another is a common practice, and lay-off is a well-established custom. By contrast, neither of these conditions applies in Japan. The external market for managers is very limited. More importantly, the prevalence of long-term company–employee attachments with internal promotion on large companies makes it very difficult for the workers losing jobs in a bankrupt firm to find new jobs under acceptable conditions. And the managers in Japan do care about the welfare of these workers. Consequently, the costs, not necessarily pecuniary but also social and psychological, of bankruptcy are felt to be very large by Japanese management. To this extent, competition in the market works as an effective disciplinary device for the management.[5]

The issue can be restated in terms of accountability. The Anglo-American view is that the management must be accountable to the shareholders and, in the absence of controlling shareholders, take-overs are considered to be the devices to ensure this accountability. In Japan, the management considers itself to be accountable to all the stakeholders, from the shareholders to the employees, the suppliers, and the customers, and consequently the cost of bankruptcy is disproportionately large. Under the internal labour systems, accountability to the employees is felt especially strongly and this, together with competitive markets, provides an effective disciplinary mechanism.

These considerations do not imply that workers are happier in Japan. On the one hand, job security is probably better, though the intensity of product market competition may threaten them with possible bankruptcy. On the other hand, internal competition is intense and imposes a great deal of pressure on the workers. In addition, more restricted job opportunities outside not only increase their fear of bankruptcy but also deprive them of the option of quitting if they are dissatisfied with the current employer. It is therefore not surprising that many questionnaire studies have failed to reveal an internationally higher job satisfaction among Japanese workers.

12.2. JAPANESE MANAGEMENT ABROAD

The argument in this book implies that the so-called Japanese management system can be applied in a non-Japanese cultural setting. Indeed, very many excellent firms all over the world are known for management systems not so different from the Japanese management system described here. IBM in the USA and Marks and Spencer in the UK offer the best examples. IBM is known for its lifetime employment system and even in the restructuring plan reported in the articles quoted in the previous section, the company aimed to reduce employment in the same manner as

[5] Hart (1983) provides a theoretical analysis of the market mechanism as an incentive scheme. In his basically neoclassical model, however, the manager is not concerned with the employees' welfare.

Japanese firms would do, that is, by cutting down on new recruitment and encouraging early retirement, but without forced layoffs. Marks and Spencer is known for its emphasis on quality, its long-term relations with suppliers, and its efforts to maintain good human relations (Tse 1984). Again the similarity to Japanese management is evident. Similarly, the success of many Japanese firms abroad gives a clear indication that the system can be fruitfully applied in different cultures.

The increase of direct foreign investment by Japanese firms has been tremendous in the 1980s. By the end of the decade, the cumulative total direct foreign investment reached $250 billion, of which more than a half had been made since 1987. About 40 per cent of this investment has been made in North America. Although, because of historical connections and geographical proximity, Asia came second over the decades, with about 20 per cent, Europe came second in one year, 1989, with almost 22 per cent. The increasing importance of Europe is the result of basically two factors: first, the shift of marketing and/or production effort from the USA to Europe as many firms have now successfully localized in the USA, and second, the fear of increasing trade friction with Europe, particularly after 1992.

The majority of investment has been made in non-manufacturing sectors, such as finance, trade, and mining. Yet more and more investment is now made in manufacturing. According to the study by JETRO (1989), there were 411 Japanese manufacturing enterprises in Western Europe, where 'Japanese' meant minimum 10 per cent capital holding. The biggest proportion, 92 (22 per cent), were in the UK, followed by France (85) and the FRG (67). Electronics and electrical equipment, chemicals, general machinery, and transport machinery are the four largest industrial categories, together accounting for two-thirds. Slightly more than a half of them were established as wholly Japanese-owned while the rest were set up through joint ventures or acquisitions (including capital participation). Since joint ventures are more often found in Spain, where direct investment had been controlled until recently, we can infer that in general a 100 per cent investment in a greenfield site is preferred by Japanese firms, a preference which can be understood, as repeatedly discussed in this book, only when human side is considered. The following view of a Japanese colour TV producer in the UK is quite specific about this point (quoted in

Dunning 1986, 165): 'A new company can establish its operating philosophy from day one and select employees who are willing to accept the "ground rules". To engineer change is far more difficult as employee attitudes have been established by a history of ingrained habits'. In fact, performance has been on average higher for these firms than those established through joint ventures or acquisitions. There are a few successful cases of once failing companies that have been transformed by Japanese participation, such as Toshiba and Sumitomo Dunlop. In these cases, performance significantly improved after the Japanese side gained full control.[6]

A number of studies have been made of the management of Japanese companies abroad.[7] A brief look at these studies should suffice to convince the readers of the applicability of the Japanese management style in different cultures. The essence again lies in the human side of management. As in Japan, Japanese firms abroad prefer to recruit new people directly from schools, provide training, and minimize lay-off. They regard recruitment as vitally important, spending much time, effort, and cost in the selection process, and placing more emphasis on discipline and character (for instance, open-mindedness) than on particular skills. For they seek flexibility and want to avoid hiring workers whose attitudes have been influenced by their prior experience with other firms. In White and Trevor's observation, 'by recruiting younger workers, and by reinforcing values associated with work, the Japanese-owned company appears to have maintained the "work ethic" in a lively condition'. They even suggest that UK firms, on the contrary, tend to ruin the work ethic: 'the rate of decline of traditional values may be exaggerated; and it may also be that young people start work with values which are subsequently extinguished through adverse experiences' (White and Trevor 1983, 46).

[6] See Trevor (1988) for the case of Toshiba and Radford (1989) for Sumitomo Dunlop.

[7] My own reading of the literature is incomplete and biased towards the cases in the UK. These include Dunning (1986); Oliver and Wilkinson (1988); Takamiya and Thurley (1985), particularly the papers by Jenner and Trevor, Reitsperger, and M. Takamiya in this book; Trevor (1983); Trevor *et al.* (1986); and White and Trevor (1983), in addition to those cited in the previous footnote. Wickens' (1987) account of his experience as the personnel director of Nissan UK is also valuable.

There is also an emphasis on training. Though the budget for training is fairly modest, stress is laid on internal and on-the-job training which are often provided by Japanese expatriates, particularly in the early years after the start of operation. Equally often, British key workers are sent to the head office or plants in Japan to get first-hand experience of the work-place in Japan.

Third, the maintenance of work flexibility is considered vital. For this reason the management will seek to have no trade union or single union representation. Job demarcation is less; for instance, in Nissan UK, there are only two job titles, 'manufacturing staff' and 'technicians', in contrast to 516 job titles at Ford UK, which were subsequently reduced to 52 after learning from the Japanese experience (Wickens 1987, 44). Some firms regularly rotate workers across jobs and shops so that they acquire broad skills. Even without regular rotation, flexibility is emphasized so as to make transfers easier if there are changes in market demand or technology. Furthermore, participation and responsibility beyond a narrow job category are encouraged; for instance, workers in production lines may be encouraged to maintain the machines themselves or to co-operate with the maintenance men, or they may participate in production-planning or process improvement. Also, co-operation across shops or departments is fostered.

Fourth, management–worker communication is considered important and, based on this communication, workers' participation is encouraged. Morning meetings, newsletters, and notice boards are used in many firms to foster communication from the management to all workers. The extent and form of worker participation greatly varies across firms. Some companies have formal meetings of representatives from both management and labour to discuss management matters (called the Company Council in Nissan and the Company Advisory Board in Toshiba). Even in firms without such formal meetings, participation at lower levels is encouraged, as suggested in the previous paragraph. Two observations concerning these councils are particularly interesting. One is the fact that such councils are actually uncommon in Japan and Toshiba's Company Advisory Board, which allows for surprisingly large worker participation, was proposed and instituted by the British managing director and not by a Japanese manager, clearly suggesting the universality of the concept of worker participation. The other is that, owing to a rich and continuous flow of information between management and workers and to the presence of less formal but equally effective channels for participation or grievance, antagonism is virtually absent in these councils (which may explain why such formal councils are rare in Japan).

Fifth, egalitarianism is evident in many aspects, for instance, a common uniform worn by everyone in the firm including the management, a common restaurant, name-badges worn by everyone, and Christmas parties inviting every worker. Egalitarianism is also found in promotion procedures, which offer opportunities for advancement on the basis of ability and achievement.

Sixth, discipline, in terms of abiding by the rules, time-keeping, a ban on smoking and eating on the shop floor, cleanliness, and so forth, is strictly maintained. Of course, there is nothing unusual in this emphasis; yet, 'doing simple things but doing them very well and slowly improving them all the time'[8] may actually be surprisingly difficult.

All these practices (except for the councils) are identical to what we have described as the essence of the internal labour system in Japan. The method of recruitment, training, and employment adjustment is common and so is the emphasis on broad skills and flexibility. The use of promotion as an incentive scheme is also suggested in some studies. For instance, some companies regularly evaluate workers for promotion and establish a wide variety of ranks so as to offer more opportunities for advancement (White and Trevor 1983). These facts all point to one thing: the internal labour system in Japan is not particularly Japanese. It can be universally applied and mostly with good results.

The enthusiasm of Japanese firms abroad to establish a reliable group of suppliers is also observed by many. Firms make a careful evaluation before selecting their suppliers, but once they have made their choice they aim to maintain long-term relations and to give managerial and technical assistance to the suppliers. Some firms lend tools and machines to their suppliers in order to modernize the production process and educate the engineers. Some even send their suppliers to the Japanese parent companies or their suppliers in Japan so that they may acquire both managerial and technical knowledge at first hand. In return

[8] The impression Hayes (1981) got from visiting factories in Japan.

for this assistance, the firms tend to be much stricter than locally owned firms about quality, price and delivery. Voice, again, appears to be playing an important role in improving performance. These practices, needless to say, are quite similar to what we observed in Chapter 6.

The purpose of this discussion of Japanese management abroad is not to praise Japanese management. In fact, not all Japanese firms abroad have been successful. According to the JETRO (1989) report, more than a third of the 201 Japanese manufacturing firms in Europe that responded to the questionnaire reported losses on a cumulative basis.[9] Also it has been suggested that the human management system has been less successful with white-collar workers in Japanese financial institutions and trading companies abroad than with the blue-collar workers in factories discussed above.[10] Moreover, the management system adopted by Japanese firms abroad varies significantly. Hence, it is misleading to give a single picture. None the less, the following conclusion by Dunning (1986, 98) appears well warranted:

> the main reason for differences in Anglo-Japanese performances is not that the Japanese possess a secret formula for success, but UK industry has not applied well known and tried principles of management as it should have; and has paid insufficient attention to purchasing standards, inventory control, production management and employee motivation as keys to success. If the presence of Japanese affiliates in the UK has done anything, it has been to demonstrate that there is no Japanese technological, marketing or managerial miracle, or even a major cultural gap; and that much of the philosophy and strategic management of Japanese firms can be successfully transferred to a UK environment.

This is also the view advocated in the present book.

12.3. INVESTMENT IN OVERSEAS DISTRIBUTIONS

Japan's continuous trade surpluses since 1981, particularly a large imbalance in trade with the USA, have provoked a discussion of

[9] The percentage is lower for firms with 100% Japanese ownership (34%) than those with joint ventures and acquisitions (42%).

[10] The main reasons are lesser inhibition about changing jobs among educated workers in the UK and the USA, and higher dissatisfaction of staff about the lack of delegation of authority from Japanese headquarters and the tendency to appoint Japanese staff to high management positions.

Japan's structural impediments to trade. Blame was initially put on tariff and non-tariff barriers. As we have discussed in Chapter 11, Japanese markets for manufactured goods are equally, if not more, liberalized in comparison to other countries; hence, the target tended to be agricultural products and procurement by the government and quasi-government organizations, such as NTT. The fact that, even after the removal of these barriers, trade imbalance remained, prompted the Americans to blame Japan on the ground of more subtle 'structural impediments'. At the time of writing, the main issues are the government regulations governing large-scale retail stores and the Antimonopoly Law. As discussed in Chapter 11, the Japanese government restricts large-scale retail stores in order to protect small ones. The US government attacks this regulation because larger stores are expected to sell more imported goods than smaller ones. Although the expected relaxation of this regulation will be welcomed by Japanese consumers, its effect on imports must at best be modest. The US government also takes a view that JFTC should take more legal action against violations of the Antimonopoly Law and that penalties for violation should be strengthened, for instance, by increasing the fines to cartel-conducting firms. Again as discussed in Chapter 11, we take the view that Japanese markets are more or less competitive under the current law and are extremely unlikely to have worked as impediments to imports. Thus imports are unlikely to show a substantial increase even after these American demands are met.

The biggest question, of course, is whether any so-called structural impediments really exist in the Japanese economy. Will removing the impediments, assuming there are any, really solve the trade imbalance? Can our analysis in this book help us to suggest ways of solving this problem? The conclusion, unfortunately, turns out to be grim, for, regardless of structural impediments, there is an essential difference in corporate behaviour in Japan and the USA which is expected to cause a persistent imbalance for some decades.

One of the key concepts in understanding Japanese management, we have argued, is growth maximization or, equivalently, lower future discount and a longer time horizon. This implies that, even if creating distribution networks and marketing strength in overseas markets is costly and time-consuming, the Japanese firm is more likely to undertake such investment in order to attain an increase in sales through export. This is apparently what Japanese firms have done for many years. Many stories of successful Japanese firms clearly indicate the seemingly insuperable hurdles they had to overcome to get into American markets. Access to the US market for the Japanese, just as access to the Japanese market for the Americans, was neither open nor easy. As the chairman of Sony recalls, 'I think it is ironic that American businessmen now complain about our complex Japanese distribution system, because when I was first planning to export to the United States I was astonished and frustrated by the complexity of marketing in America.' None the less, he decided to keep struggling:

> I can understand the frustration of American and other foreign business men facing the Japanese distribution system and the complex Japanese language because it must seem as complex to them as the American system and language did to me several decades ago, but many of them have successfully figured out ways to work outside the traditional established system; that was what I felt I had to do in the United States. We needed a distribution route in which the message of our new technology and its benefits could be more easily and directly passed on to the consumer. It took us a long time to find the way. We also had to learn some hard lessons (Morita 1986, 86–7).

A similar story was told by Honda's Kawashima who was sent to the USA in 1958 with the task of selling motorcycles. In the eyes of the Americans, Honda at the time was a totally unknown and obscure manufacturer from a country known only for cheap and low-technology products. Kawashima says,

> my first reaction after travelling across the US was: How could we have been so stupid as to start a war with such a vast and wealthy country! My second reaction was discomfort. I spoke poor English. We dropped in on motorcycle dealers who treated us discourteously and in addition, gave the general impression of being motorcycle enthusiasts who, secondarily, were in business . . . My other impression was that everyone in the US drove an automobile—making it doubtful that motorcycles could ever do very well in the market.

Almost all the indications were discouraging and yet he formulated a plan to sell 6,000 motorcycles a year, or 10 per cent of total US imports, and reported this plan to the then vice-president, Fujisawa. According to Kawashima, '[Fujisawa] didn't probe that target quantitatively. We did not discuss profits or deadlines for breakeven. Fujisawa told me if anyone could succeed, I could and authorized $1 million for the venture' (Pascale 1984, 54).[11] Again, we find the strong entrepreneurship and strong growth motivation with which Japanese firms struggled to overcome the tremendous task of penetrating into unfamiliar markets against the impediments of different business practices, different cultures, and different languages.

This tendency of Japanese firms to engage heavily in investment in order to penetrate overseas markets can be confirmed by the statistics. The figures quoted in the previous section indicated that the Japanese have invested more in the non-manufacturing than in the manufacturing sector and that in the non-manufacturing sector trade (wholesale and retail) comes second to financial areas. In North America and Europe in particular, the amount of cumulative investment in trade is almost as large as total manufacturing. In terms of employment, the proportion of wholesale trade among non-banking Japanese-owned subsidiaries in the USA in 1986 was 46 per cent, which was far higher than the proportion for West German (16 per cent), French (15 per cent), and UK subsidiaries (7 per cent) (Yamawaki 1989). The result is that almost 40 per cent of the total stock of foreign-owned wholesale distribution assets in the USA in 1987 were owned by the Japanese, as compared to the 10 per cent each owned by British and West German firms (Williamson 1990).

There are a number of studies indicating that this heavy investment in distribution by Japanese firms contributed to their exports to the USA. Yamawaki (1989) measured the strength of Japanese distributional activities in the USA by the numbers employed in US distribution subsidiaries more than 50 per cent owned by Japanese manufacturing companies. Using a sample of forty-four industries, he found not only that this variable affects Japanese exports to the USA but also that the reverse causality (export affecting distributional activity) is weaker. Thus he concluded that 'Japanese manufacturing companies export their products

[11] Actually only $110,000 in cash could be taken to the USA after a long and uncertain struggle with the government, which controlled foreign currency, while the rest was taken to the USA in the form of parts and motorcycle inventory. This episode suggests, as did the previous chapter, that government control around this time (the 1950s and 1960s) often hindered private aspiration rather than promoting it.

successfully to the US markets because they have committed their resources to the local distributional activity and thereby created goodwill assets'. He also found that the extent of distributional activity is higher in industries where R & D by US firms is more intense. This result seems to suggest either that greater distributional activity is required in an industry with a higher entry barrier caused by R & D or that greater distributional activity is required to sell products with more complex and innovative attributes.[12] Japanese firms have undertaken such large-scale investment to overcome entry barriers; quite probably, therefore, they have entered industries which proved too daunting for firms in other countries to enter.

Williamson (1990) compared US imports from Japan, the FRG, and the UK using a sample of 462 products. For each of the three countries, he regressed the import share to several variables constructed from factor analyses. He found several international differences. First, MASS, a variable indicating the importance of mass marketing, affects the import share of the UK and the FRG negatively but not that of Japan. Second, GAPS, indicating a lack of well-developed networks of multi-layered distribution, affects import share negatively for the FRG but positively for Japan. Third, MSELL, indicating that manufacturers have a strong selling role, has a positive effect for the FRG and the UK, but an insignificant effect for Japan. Fourth, PUSH, indicating push marketing, in particular, higher selling expenses per sale, has a negative effect for the UK but a positive one for Japan. Fifth, LSNET, indicating the need for large networks of salesmen, has a negative effect for the USA and the FRG but not for Japan. These results suggest an important international difference. Whereas British and German firms tend to fail to penetrate an industry that requires mass and push marketing, with a large selling expenditure and a large selling force, Japanese firms have succeeded in capturing a larger market share. Conversely, British and German firms tend to succeed in, or be more attracted to, non-mass products where manufacturers are normally involved directly in the selling function. From these observations, Williamson concludes that 'an important contributor to Japanese success in export

[12] The effect of advertising intensity in US firms was also positive but insignificant.

strategy is the willingness to invest in local distribution where this is necessary to overcome this barrier to entry. British and West German exporters when faced with a distribution barrier, by contrast, tend not to invest and make little headway in the market' (ibid. 227).

Another finding of Williamson's is the lower price volatility (in terms of dollars) of Japanese imports to the USA in comparison to British and German imports. This price stability reflects the fact that a larger proportion of Japanese exports to the USA are priced in dollars. This is probably due to the historically weaker bargaining position of Japan, which has taught Japanese firms that to survive they have to adjust to US demand conditions and competition rather than to their own cost conditions. The long-run consequence of steady market penetration was more important to them than maintaining short-run profitability. This consideration was also the reason for lagging dollar-price increases to the rising yen. 'It appears that many Japanese exporters regard a rising yen as a signal that their cost must fall, rather than that foreign currency prices must rise. This reflects a strategy of long-term commitment to continuity of export sales' (ibid. 221).

The last study to be cited is Wong *et al.* (1988) which compared thirty Japanese firms selling in the UK with matched British and American firms in the UK. They found, for instance, that, when asked 'How well does "good short-term profits are the objective" describe your company?', 87 per cent of British firms and 80 per cent of American firms responded affirmatively but only 27 per cent of Japanese firms did, the difference being statistically significant. By contrast, 57 per cent of Japanese firms cited 'aggressive growth' as their strategy, while 13 per cent of British firms and 33 per cent of American firms did. Similarly, a significantly larger proportion of Japanese firms said yes to the question, 'How well does "winning share by beating competition" describe your strategic focus?', than the others. Accordingly, it is not surprising that only 7 per cent of Japanese firms gave profitability as an answer to the question, 'Which budget and performance criteria are most scrutinized by top management?' (multiple answers allowed), as compared to 60 per cent of British firms and 87 per cent of American firms. In contrast, a larger proportion of Japanese firms answered sales and market share to the same question, than Anglo-American firms. Thus, 'the Japanese approach reflects a managerial philosophy more oriented to long-term market position than short-term profit performance, and to exploiting new opportunities created by changing technologies and new market segments' (ibid. 127). In comparing American to Japanese firms, they say 'while the Japanese increased commitment to the UK market, and decisively exploited new "pockets" of growth, the Americans, with their excessive emphasis upon short-term financial gains, saw retrenchment, cost-cutting and rationalization as the best response to the competitive pressures in their market' (ibid. 128). This argument is quite consistent with our inference from Yamawaki's and Williamson's results.

They also found that a significantly larger proportion of Japanese firms depicted themselves as 'strong on efficient large scale manufacturing', agreeing with Williamson's finding of Japanese strength in markets where mass marketing is important. Another interesting finding of Wong *et al.* concerns the response to the question, 'Who is your major competitor in the UK market?' While a majority of British and American firms mentioned Western firms, more than three-quarters of Japanese firms cited other Japanese firms. The intensity of competition between Japanese rivals is apparent in these answers.

These results all indicate that Japanese firms succeeded in overcoming entry barriers and penetrating foreign markets only because they invested heavily in order to establish distribution channels regardless of short-run profitability. Trade barriers and structural impediments were not the main causes for the Japanese trade surplus. Clear support for this view is found in the presence of several foreign firms which have patiently made distributional and marketing investments and succeeded in becoming major competitors in Japanese markets. The case of the German company Braun, which started selling electric shavers in Japan in 1961, is typical. Its success came only after constant efforts in advertising and improving product quality. Braun realized that the differences between Japan and Germany are not confined to electrical voltage and safety regulations. Japanese hair is thick and round whereas German hair is thin and flat, and the original German model was too big in a Japanese hand. To comply with these different requirements, the product was remodelled and improved to the satisfaction of Japanese consumers. This continuous effort has been rewarded with a 40 per cent market share (in value terms), surpassing such formidable rivals as Matsushita. Other examples are easy to find, from IBM and Proctor and Gamble, to Lego toys and Tabasco sauce.

In the car market, the difference in attitudes to export in Japan and the USA can best be illustrated by the fact that until several years ago, all the US cars sold in Japan had steering-wheels on the left even though people drive on the left in Japan, whereas all the Japanese cars exported to the USA were altered for American drivers. It was only in 1981 that the first foreign car manufacturer, BMW, established its own distribution channel in Japan, which was then followed by other German producers, Mercedes and Volkswagen. After a few years of struggle, sales of these cars dramatically increased. US-made cars, by contrast, still rely on Japanese agents and their sales lag far behind their German rivals'.

These examples all point to a simple fact: a long-run commitment to distribution, marketing, and innovation is the key to success in international trade. Japan's relative success comes not from trade barriers but from a larger proportion of management who have not hesitated to make this investment even if it means a sacrifice of short-run profitability. Such behaviour is consistent only with the growth maximization hypothesis repeatedly discussed in this book. As long as the majority of Japanese management continues to adopt such a strategy while firms in other countries pursue (or are forced to pursue) value maximization, trade imbalance is unlikely to disappear.

Finally, one more consequence of Japanese management has to be discussed, namely, the export drive to maintain employment under conditions of slack domestic demand. This drive may be particularly strong among Japanese firms because of the extremely small marginal cost incurred by the labour hording behaviour described in Chapter 8. To this author, however, the more important question seems to be their strategy after domestic demand recovers: do they reduce exports to meet increased domestic demand, or do they try to maintain (or even increase) their export market share by meeting domestic demand with an expansion of capacity? Williamson (1990, 216) suggests that the first is true with British firms, referring to their tendency 'to relegate exports to a "capacity filling" role'. In contrast, I believe that the strategy of Japanese firms are better described by the second scenario. The essential difference between the two countries seems to be not the extent to which exports are used for capacity filling, but the extent to which persistent efforts are directed towards export during and after recessions in order to attain export market penetration. Again, the emphasis on long-run consequences must be the distinctive characteristic of Japanese export behaviour.

12.4. ACQUISITIONS OF FOREIGN FIRMS, ACQUISITIONS BY FOREIGN FIRMS

In Chapter 5, we discussed mergers and acquisitions (M & As) between Japanese firms, but not M & As by Japanese firms of foreign firms or by foreign firms of Japanese firms. In fact, acquisitions of foreign firms by Japanese firms have been increasing with great speed, as shown in Table 12.1.[13] Since the number of mergers between Japanese firms in 1988 was 1,336 according to the JFTC statistics, the numbers in Table 12.1 are clearly underestimated and confined to M & As involving large firms. The table clearly indicates that the number of acquisitions of foreign firms by Japanese firms increased by four times in the five years since 1985 and, in recent years, has outweighed the number of M & As between Japanese firms. By contrast, acquisitions of Japanese

TABLE 12.1. Major mergers and acquisitions involving Japanese firms, 1985–1989

Nationality of		Number of Mergers and Acquisitions in				
Acquirer	Acquired	1985	1986	1987	1988	1989
Japan	Japan	163	226	219	223	240
Japan	Foreign	100	204	228	315	405
Japan	USA	56	126	120	167	190
Foreign	Japan	26	21	22	17	15
USA	Japan	21	15	13	11	n.a.

Source: Yamaichi Securities.

[13] Since most of these M & As between Japanese and foreign firms are acquisitions (including minority shareholdings or capital participations) as defined in Chap. 5, we will simply call them acquisitions in this section.

firms by foreign firms have been much fewer and show no signs of increasing. As in trade, this imbalance has caused Americans and other Westerners to accuse Japan of unfairness. American irritation has been aggravated by Japanese acquisitions of increasingly large and symbolic US firms, such as Sony's acquisition of Columbia Pictures and Matsushita's acquisition of MCA.

However, one should note that, despite such complaints by American politicians and others, many of these acquisitions were originally proposed by incumbent American managers or shareholders, and none of them has been hostile. It has been reported, furthermore, that, in most cases, the employees of the acquired firms felt happier after acquisition. Take the example of the acquisition in 1990 of Southland, the 7-Eleven chain-store group, by its Japanese licensee, 7-Eleven Japan, and its parent, Ito-Yokado. Acquisition was undertaken at the request of the management, which was labouring under a heavy interest burden against the junk bonds it had issued in 1987 in a management buy-out to defend against a hostile take-over attempt. This example is worth considering not only for the hazardous consequences of take-over battles, which we discussed in Section 12.1, but also for the fact that the management chose its Japanese licensee as the acquirer. Clearly, the management recognized the managerial and technical capability of 7-Eleven Japan, which has been quite profitable, and also expected that Japanese management would be friendly to their American counterparts.

The reasons why Japanese firms do not feel themselves inhibited from acquiring foreign firms and why they are not eager to be acquired can be found in our discussion in Chapter 5, where we raised the importance of the human side of the firm. First, corporate growth is sought to utilize and enrich human resources and to create promotion opportunities. The firm will thus use M&As only when the resources needed for expansion are not available internally or when the acquired resources are complementary to existing internal resources. Japanese firms tend to lack the human resources required for international operation and these resources, if acquired through M&A, are expected to complement the internal resources and increase the overseas experiences of the Japanese staff.

Second, we argued that workers' identification of their interests with those of the firm makes hostile take-overs difficult. Thus

M & As take place most usually with failing firms, in which the workers would rather have the firm acquired than see it going bankrupt. The findings for M & As between Japanese firms confirmed this hypothesis (see Table 5.2). This argument also applies to acquisitions by foreign firms; that is, hostile take-over attempts will be met by strong resistance from the incumbent Japanese management and the employees, but friendly take-overs of companies in financial difficulty will take place even if the acquirers are foreigners. Koito and Sansui offer contrasting cases. Koito, a car-part manufacturer, has been the target of a take-over attempt by Boone Pickens, a well-known corporate raider from the USA, who owns about 30 per cent of Koito's share. Pickens demanded seats on the Koito board and increased dividends. Koito's management refused these demands and with the help of Toyota, the second largest shareholder after Pickens and the largest customer, have successfully defended the company against Pickens' threat. In contrast, Sansui, an audio equipment producer that had been in financial difficulty for several years, was peacefully acquired by Polly Peck of the UK.[14]

Third, unifying the different labour practices of the two firms to be merged is likely to cause pecuniary and non-pecuniary costs. We thus found that the majority of M & As in Japan were not mergers but looser combinations of acquisitions and capital participations. Japanese acquisitions of foreign firms all take these looser forms of combination. They need not integrate labour practices between the Japanese parent company and the foreign subsidiaries; hence, such costs do not arise in acquisitions of foreign firms.

Therefore, even though acquiring other Japanese companies may be neither advantageous nor easy for Japanese firms, this is not the case when acquiring foreign firms. In fact, many foreign firms are happy to be acquired (unlike in Japan), and gaining their resources may be the best way to penetrate unfamiliar foreign markets and to use this experience to enrich the knowledge of

[14] Polly Peck's collapse within two years of the acquisition was due to reasons unrelated to Sansui. According to press reports, Sansui had been planning to use Polly Peck's international marketing channel and is bewildered by the collapse, again suggesting the different length in planning time horizon between a Japanese firm and a British firm.

Japanese staff as well. For this reason, acquisitions are often used as the easiest way to enter foreign markets. A likely scenario is that, once the firm is established in foreign markets, it will prefer to expand internally for the first reason mentioned above. Yet to the extent that the second and third reasons are not important outside Japan, we should expect firms to use acquisitions more often than in Japan as a means of growth strategy. These acquisitions have been, and are expected to remain, mostly friendly because Japanese firms wish to retain the current managers (unless, of course, they are unbearably bad) in order to utilize their capacity and learn from their experience. Another difference between Japanese and Anglo-American acquisitions is that the Japanese aim is to maintain the acquired firm for good or, at least, for a longer period than UK or US acquirers. This difference clearly accords with the Japanese emphasis on long-term relations and long-run growth. Purchasing a firm for the purpose of reselling part or all of it, a practice frequently observed in the UK and the USA, is highly unlikely to be undertaken by Japanese firms.

Acquiring Japanese firms, on the other hand, is likely to remain difficult for the second reason above. Although it has been said that younger generations feel increasingly less attached to firms and less resistant to being acquired, and although financial deregulation will make foreign acquisitions easier, we do not foresee hostile take-overs occurring on the same scale as observed in the UK and the USA. Needless to say, the large shareholding by friendly financial institutions and other firms prevalent in Japan, discussed in Chapter 2, also makes hostile take-overs by foreign firms difficult.

12.5 WHAT CAN WE EXPECT IN THE FUTURE?

Will the Japanese management system change following changes in technology, life-style, and international relations? Yes, of course it will. After all, what we have described as the Japanese management system in this book is not an old phenomenon. The internal labour system started to take shape only around 1920 (see Chapter 3) and was not firmly established until after the Second World War. Similarly, the present financial system, including close bank–company relations and inter-company shareholding, as well as the separation of management from ownership, is the product of post-war circumstances. Needless to say, the system is founded on a long history of Japanese development—not only on the modern industrial development since the Meiji Restoration of 1868, but also on the accumulated education and commercial experience of the several centuries preceding it. No management system can be free from historical development and the Japanese system is no exception. Yet, the economic, social and cultural changes of the past century have been faster than in other countries, and so has the change in the management system.

Therefore the question is not whether the present system will survive as it is now—it will not. A more relevant question is whether the two key characteristics of the system, growth maximization and competition, will survive whatever superficial changes the system undergoes. If they do, we would expect the system to continue contributing to efficiency and growth.

Take for instance the argument that, owing to weaker discipline and impatience among the younger generations for whom affluence is a fact of life, identification of workers' interests with those of the firms and the feeling of the firm as a community are getting less and less common. Will this weaken the merit of the Japanese management system? To answer this question, we have to ask how much these factors are likely to lessen growth maximization and competition. To succeed in competition, whether internal or external, brings not only an economic reward but also a non-pecuniary satisfaction, say, a feeling of achievement. Indeed, as argued by Maslow (1954), social recognition and self-fulfilment can be more important than physiological needs; even if the latter needs are satisfied, therefore, people will strive to gain the first. Scitovsky's (1976, 61) finding from the psychology literature that 'feelings of comfort and discomfort have to do with the level of arousal . . . whereas feelings of pleasure are created by changes in the arousal level' also indicates that people, however rich they may become, will keep striving to gain pleasure. Insofar as they do, growth motivation and competition must remain strong.

Second, the lifetime employment system is under serious threat. As a consequence of rapid changes in industrial structure, many firms find that they can only survive by contracting current businesses and entering new markets. The skills acquired through many years of experience may become useless and the accumulation of human resources experienced in target markets may take too long without recourse to external resources. Rapid changes in technology, such as the shift to informational technology, accelerate this tendency by making the accumulated skills obsolete. As a consequence, firms find it more and more difficult to maintain lifetime employment and more and more attractive to recruit skilled mid-career workers.

An ageing population further adds to the problem. The system works most efficiently when young workers—who are more flexible to new assignments, easier to train, and paid less—outnumber older workers, who are gradually promoted to supervisory or managerial positions that require more experience. This division of work becomes more difficult as the proportion of older workers increases, and people's hopes of promotion at a reasonable age are not satisfied. The results are increasing wage costs, an increasing difficulty in maintaining flexibility in workers (though the emphasis on breadth of skill in Japan eases this difficulty), and an increasing difficulty in supplying promotion opportunities large enough to maintain worker incentives.

We should therefore assume that lifetime employment, which in fact has never been perfect, as discussed earlier, will become even less perfect. In terms of its effect on growth maximization and competition, one can imagine two scenarios. On the one hand, the labour system may become more external, as it is in other countries, so that any discussion of growth and efficiency being enhanced by an internal system becomes less relevant. On the other hand, in order to create opportunities for promotion and for utilizing existing internal human resources, management may make even greater efforts to grow. Both of these tendencies are currently observable, and it is premature to predict which of these two scenarios is likely to dominate.

The declining importance of manufacturing in the economy may also have a profound effect. Our discussion has been based for the most part on manufacturing industries. Yet, these industries currently account for only about a third of GDP and about a quarter of employment. Furthermore, an increasing part of manufacturing has been moved offshore, leaving less and less production and proportionally more and more control and other white-collar work in Japan. A worrying aspect of this trend is a loss of production skills or first-hand experience at production work-shops, which may undermine both flexibility and innovation capability through weaker research–production or management–shopfloor links. To avoid this, some production facilities should be retained inside Japan even if the major part is transferred to overseas subsidiaries. Such precautions seem particularly valuable because the loss of skills can be rapid but accumulating them takes time.

The applicability of our discussion to non-manufacturing industries depends on whether the merit of internal labour system is also evident in such industries. To answer this question, we must return to the nature of skills. Take car-driving for example. The required skills consist not only of knowledge of how to handle a car and how to change the oil, that is, the kinds of skill you learn at driving schools. Equally importantly, you have to know how to deal with erratic driving by other people, to recognize engine trouble from vibrations or from the exhaust, and you have to know whom to contact when your engine is in trouble or when you have an accident. Moreover, if you are a taxi driver, you should also know how to deal with passengers' complaints and how to keep smiling! These skills and knowledge you can acquire only through experience, and their relative importance may matter even more in non-manufacturing industries and jobs outside production because they involve human relations. They are, for the same reason, more firm-specific than job-specific. It therefore seems unlikely that the importance of the internal labour system will decline as the importance of non-manufacturing work-places increases. To this extent, I would expect the main discussion in this book to apply to the non-manufacturing sector as well.

Finally, the influences of internationalization or globalization have to be considered. Internationalization is taking place in many areas. Overseas production, trade, and acquisitions have been discussed already. Internationalization is also evident in the influx of foreign people and foreign businesses into Japan. Racial homogeneity, probably one of the two most important demographic characteristics of Japan, is bound to be lost. Together with the density of population, the other important characteristic, homogeneity is said to have contributed to the consensus-seeking management style and to the capacity to solve problems without recourse to legal means. If this argument is correct, internationalization may appear to undermine the efficiency of Japanese management by damaging homogeneity. The culture theorists will certainly take this view. Internationalization also forces the government to abandon consensus-seeking and guidance-led policies approach in favour of deregulation and, if necessary, explicit rules. The conspiracy theorists will say that such changes are bound to undermine Japan's strength. We disagree with both of them. We see no reason why these changes should conflict with growth maximization and competition. In fact, we take the view, quite contrary to the conspiracy theorists but consistent with mainstream economic thought, that any policy change in the direction of deregulation can be expected to contribute to competition and efficiency in industry. The only irony is that this change may not be brought about internally by the voting power of consumers but by external pressure.

BIBLIOGRAPHY

Abegglen, J. C. (1958). *The Japanese Factory: Aspects of Its Social Organization*. Glencoe, Ill.: Free Press. Repr. in Abegglen (1973), pt. 2.

—— (1973). *Management and Worker: The Japanese Solution*. Tokyo: Sophia University (with Kodansha International).

—— and Stalk, G., Jr. (1985). *Kaisha, The Japanese Corporation*. New York: Basic Books.

Abraham, K. G., and Houseman, S. N. (1989). 'Job Security and Work Force Adjustment: How Different Are US and Japanese Practices?', *Journal of the Japanese and International Economies*, 3:4 (Dec.), 500–21.

—— and Medoff, J. L. (1984). 'Length of Service and Layoffs in Union and Nonunion Work Groups', *Industrial and Labor Relations Review*, 38:1 (Oct.), 87–97.

Ando, A., and Auerbach, A. (1988). 'The Corporate Cost of Capital in Japan and the United States: A Comparison', in J. B. Shoven (ed.), *Government Policy towards Industry in the United States and Japan*. Cambridge: Cambridge University Press, 21–49.

Asanuma, B. (1984). 'Jidosha Sangyo ni Okeru Buhin Torihiki no Kozo', *Kikan Gendai Keizai* (Summer), 38–48; translated as 'The Organization of Parts Purchases in the Japanese Automotive Industry', *Japanese Economic Studies* (Summer 1985), 32–53.

—— (1989). 'Manufacturer–Supplier Relationships in Japan and the Concept of Relation-Specific Skills', *Journal of the Japanese and International Economies*, 3:1 (Mar.), 1–30.

Baldwin, C. Y. (1986). 'The Capital Factor: Competing for Capital in a Global Environment', in M. E. Porter (ed.), *Competition in Global Industries*. Boston: Harvard Business School Press, 185–223.

Baumol, W. J., Panzar, J., and Willig, R. (1982). *Contestable Markets and the Theory of Industry Structure*. New York: Harcourt Brace Jovanovich.

Berle, A. J., and Means, G. C. (1932). *The Modern Corporation and Private Property*. New York: Harcourt Brace and World.

Boskin, M. J., and Roberts, J. M. (1988). 'A Closer Look at Saving Rates in the United States and Japan', in J. B. Shoven (ed.), *Government Policy towards Industry in the United States and Japan*. Cambridge: Cambridge University Press, 121–43.

Brechling, F., and O'Brien, P. (1967). 'Short-Run Employment Functions in Manufacturing Industries: An International Comparison', *Review of Economics and Statistics*, 49:3 (Aug.), 277–87.

Browne, W. G., and Motamedi, K. K. (1977). 'Transition at the Top',

California Management Review, 20:2 (Winter), 67–73.

Brozen, Y. (1970). 'The Antitrust Task Force Deconcentration Recommendation', *Journal of Law and Economics*, 13:2 (Oct.), 279–92.

Brunello, G. (1989). 'Bonuses, Wages and Performance in Japan: Evidence from Micro Data', Discussion Paper No. 359, Centre for Labour Economics, London School of Economics.

Cable, J. (1985). 'Capital Market Information and Industrial Performance: The Role of West German Banks', *Economic Journal*, 95 (Mar.), 118–32.

Cantillon, R. (1755). *Essai sur la nature du commerce en général.* Ed. with an English translation by Henry Higgs (1964), New York: Augustus M. Kelly.

Caves, R. E., and Uekusa, M. (1976). *Industrial Organization in Japan.* Washington, DC: The Brookings Institution.

Channon, D. (1982). 'Industrial Structure', *Long Range Planning*, 15:5 (Oct.), 78–93.

Choi, F. D. S., Hino, H., Min, S. K., Nam, S. O., Ujiie, J., and Stonehill, A. I. (1983). 'Analyzing Foreign Financial Statements: The Use and Misuse of International Ratio Analysis', *Journal of International Business Studies*, 14:1 (Spring/Summer), 113–32.

Ciscel, D. H., and Carroll, T. M. (1980). 'The Determinants of Executive Salaries: An Econometric Survey', *Review of Economics and Statistics*, 62:1 (Feb.), 7–13.

Clark, K. B., Chew, W. B., and Fujimoto, T. (1987). 'Product Development in the World Auto Industry', *Brookings Papers on Economic Activity*, 3, 729–81.

Clark, R. (1979). *The Japanese Company.* New Haven, Conn.: Yale University Press.

Cole, R. E. (1971). *Japanese Blue Collar.* Berkeley, Calif.: University of California Press.

Connolly, R. A., and Schwartz, S. (1985). 'The Intertemporal Behavior of Economic Profits', *International Journal of Industrial Organization*, 3:4 (Dec.), 379–400.

Cosh, A. D., and Hughes, A. (1987). 'The Anatomy of Corporate Control: Directors, Shareholders and Executive Remuneration in Giant US and UK Corporations', *Cambridge Journal of Economics*, 11, 285–313.

Cowling, K. (1983). 'Excess Capacity and the Degree of Collusion: Oligopoly Behaviour in the Slump', *Manchester School of Economics and Social Studies*, 51:4 (Dec.), 341–59.

—— and Mueller, D. C. (1978). 'The Social Costs of Monopoly Power', *Economic Journal*, 88 (Dec.), 727–48.

—— and Waterson, M. (1976). 'Price–Cost Margins and Market Structure', *Economica*, 43 (Aug.), 267–74.

Cubbin, J., and Geroski, P. (1990). 'The Persistence of Profits in the United Kingdom', in Mueller (1990), 147–67.

Dansby, R. E., and Willig, R. D. (1979). 'Industry Performance Gradient Indexes', *American Economic Review*, 69:3 (June), 249–60.

Demsetz, H. (1973). 'Industry Structure, Market Rivalry, and Public Policy', *Journal of Law and Economics*, 16:1 (Apr.), 1–9.

—— and Lehn, K. (1985). 'The Structure of Corporate Ownership: Causes and Consequences', *Journal of Political Economy*, 93:6 (Dec.), 1155–77.

Doeringer, P. B., and Piore, M. (1972). *Internal Labor Markets and Manpower Analysis*. Berkeley and Los Angeles: University of California Press.

Doi, N. (1986). *Kasen to Kokyo Seisaku* (*Oligopoly and Public Policy*). Tokyo: Yuhikaku.

Domowitz, I., Hubbard, R. G., and Petersen, B. C. (1986). 'Business Cycles and the Relationship between Concentration and Price–Cost Margins', *Rand Journal of Economics*, 17:1 (Spring), 1–17.

Dore, R. (1973). *British Factory, Japanese Factory*. London: George Allen and Unwin.

—— (1986). *Flexible Rigidities*. London: The Athlone Press.

—— and Sako, M. (1989). *How the Japanese Learn to Work*. London: Routledge.

Dowrick, S., and Nguyen, Duc-Tho (1989). 'OECD Comparative Economic Growth 1950–85: Catch-Up and Convergence', *American Economic Review*, 79:5 (Dec.), 1010–30.

Dunning, J. H. (1986). *Japanese Participation in British Industry*. London: Croom Helm.

Dye, R. A. (1984). 'The Trouble with Tournaments', *Economic Inquiry*, 22:1 (Jan.), 147–9.

Fair Trade Commission (JFTC) (1984). *Keizai no Henka to Dokusen Kinshi Seisaku* (*Economic Changes and Antimonopoly Policy*). Tokyo: Printing Bureau of the Ministry of Finance.

—— (1987). 'Waga Kuni Kigyo no Keizoku-teki Torihiki no Jittai ni Tsuite' ('On the Continuous Trading of Japanese Firms') Unpublished report of the Research Group on Trade Friction and Market Structure.

—— (1988). *Kosei Torihiki Iinkai Nenji Hokoku* (*Annual Report of the Fair Trade Commission*). Tokyo: Printing Bureau of the Ministry of Finance.

Fay, J. A., and Medoff, J. L. (1985). 'Labor and Output over the Business Cycle: Some Direct Evidence', *American Economic Review*, 75:4 (Sept.), 638–55.

Feinberg, R. M. (1979). 'Market Structure and Employment Stability', *Review of Economics and Statistics*, 61:4 (Nov.), 497–505.

Fidler, J. (1981). *The British Business Elite: Its Attitudes to Class, Status and Power*. London: Routledge and Kegan Paul.

Flath, D. (1984). 'Debt and Taxes: Japan Compared with the US', *International Journal of Industrial Organization*, 2:4 (Dec.), 311–26.

Franks, J. R., and Harris, R. S. (1989). 'Shareholder Wealth Effects of Corporate Takeovers: The UK Experience 1955–1985', *Journal of Financial Economics*, 23:2 (Aug.), 225–49.

Freeman, R. B., and Medoff, J. L. (1984). *What Do Unions Do?*. New York: Basic Books.

—— and Weitzman, M. L. (1987). 'Bonuses and Employment in Japan', *Journal of the Japanese and International Economies*, 1:2 (June), 168–94.

Fruin, M. (1989). 'History, Strategy and the Development Factory in Japan: Production for Competitive Advantage', Unpublished, INSEAD.

Fujishiro, N. (1988). 'Computer Sangyo ni Okeru Kyodo-Kenkyu no Yakuwari' ('The Role of Joint R&D in the Computer Industry'). Unpublished master's thesis, University of Tsukuba.

Galbraith, J. K. (1967). *The New Industrial State*. Boston: Houghton Mifflin.

Gale, B. T. (1972). 'Market Share and Rate of Return', *Review of Economics and Statistics*, 54:4 (Nov.), 412–23.

Geroski, P. A. (1990). 'Modelling Persistent Profitability', in Mueller (1990), 15–34.

Gordon, R. J. (1982). 'Why US Wage and Employment Behaviour Differs from That in Britain and Japan', *Economic Journal*, 92 (Mar.), 13–44.

Goto, A., and Suzuki, K. (1989). 'R&D Capital, Rate of Return on R&D Investment and Spillover of R&D in Japanese Manufacturing Industries', *Review of Economics and Statistics*, 71:4 (Nov.), 555–64.

—— and Wakasugi, R. (1988). 'Technology Policy', in Komiya *et al.* (1988), 183–204.

Goudie, A. W., and Meeks, G. (1982). 'Diversification by Merger', *Economica*, 49, 447–59.

Graves, A. (1987). 'Comparative Trends in Automotive Research and Development', DRC Discussion Paper No. 54, Science Policy Research Unit, University of Sussex.

Green, J. R., and Stokey, N. L. (1983). 'A Comparison of Tournaments and Contracts', *Journal of Political Economy*, 91:3 (June), 349–64.

Greer, D. F., and Rhoades, S. A. (1977). 'A Test of the Reserve Labour Hypothesis', *Economic Journal*, 87 (June), 290–9.

Griliches, Z. (1986). 'Productivity, R&D, and Basic Research at the Firm Level in the 1970s', *American Economic Review*, 76:1 (Mar.), 141–54.

Hadley, E. M. (1970). *Anti-trust in Japan*. Princeton, NJ: Princeton University Press.

—— (1984). 'Counterpoint on Business Groupings and Government-Industry Relations in Automobiles', in M. Aoki (ed.), *The Economic Analysis of the Japanese Firm*. Amsterdam: Elsevier, 319–27.

Hall, R. E. (1982). 'The Importance of Lifetime Jobs in the US Economy', *American Economic Review*, 72:4 (Sept.), 716–24.

Harberger, A. C. (1954). 'Monopoly and Resource Allocation', *American Economic Review*, 44:2 (May), 77–87.

Harris, F. (1988). 'Testable Competing Hypotheses from Structure–Performance Theory: Efficient Structure versus Market Power', *Journal of Industrial Economics*, 36:3 (Mar.), 267–80.

Harrod, R. F. (1939). 'An Essay in Dynamic Theory', *Economic Journal*, 49 (Mar.) 14–33.

Hart, O. D. (1983). 'The Market Mechanism as an Incentive Scheme', *Bell Journal of Economics*, 14:2 (Autumn), 366–82.

Hashimoto, M. (1981). 'Firm-Specific Human Capital as a Shared Investment', *American Economic Review*, 71:3 (June), 475–82.

—— and Raisian, J. (1985). 'Employment Tenure and Earnings Profiles in Japan and the United States', *American Economic Review*, 75:4 (Sept.), 721–35.

—— —— (1989). 'Investments in Employer–Employee Attachments by Japanese and U.S. Workers in Firms of Varying Size', *Journal of the Japanese and International Economies*, 3:1 (Mar.), 31–48.

Hayashi, F. (1989). 'Japan's Saving Rate: New Data and Reflections', Working Paper No. 3205, National Bureau of Economic Research.

Hayes, R. H. (1981). 'Why Japanese Factories Work', *Harvard Business Review* (July–Aug.), 57–66.

Hirschman, A. O. (1970). *Exit, Voice, and Loyalty*. Cambridge, Mass.: Harvard University Press.

—— (1987) 'Exit and Voice', in J. Eatwell, M. Milgate, and P. Newman (eds.), *The New Palgrave: A Dictionary of Economics*, ii. London: Macmillan, 219–24.

Hirschmeier, J., and Yui, T. (1975). *The Development of Japanese Business, 1600–1973*. London: George Allen and Unwin.

—— —— (1977). *Nihon no Keiei Hatten: Kindai-ka to Kigyo Keiei* (*The Development of Japanese Business: Modernization and Management*). Tokyo: Toyo Keizai Shinpo Sha.

Hoddar, J. E. (1988). 'Corporate Capital Structure in the United States and Japan: Financial Intermediation and Implications of Financial Deregulation', in J. B. Shoven (ed.), *Government Policy towards Industry in the United States and Japan*. Cambridge: Cambridge University Press, 241–63.

Holland, D. M. (ed.) (1984). *Measuring Profitability and Capital Costs*. Lexington, Mass.: Lexington Books.

Horioka, C. Y. (1990). 'Why Is Japan's Household Saving Rate So High?: A Literature Survey', *Journal of the Japanese and International Economies*, 4:1 (Mar.), 49–92.

Hoshino, Y. (1981). *Kigyo Gappei no Keiryo Bunseki* (*An Econometric Analysis of Corporate Mergers*). Tokyo: Hakuto Shobo.

Ikeda, K., and Doi, N. (1983). 'The Performances of Merging Firms in Japanese Manufacturing Industry: 1964–75', *Journal of Industrial Economics*, 31:3 (Mar.), 257–66.

Imai, K. (1988). 'Japan's Corporate Networks'. Paper presented at the Mini-JPERC Conference in Stanford.

—— and Itami, H. (1984). 'Interpenetration of Organization and Market: Japan's Firm and Market in Comparison with the US', *International Journal of Industrial Organization*, 2:4 (Dec.), 285–310.

—— Nonaka, I., and Takeuchi, H. (1985). 'Managing the New Product Development Process: How Japanese Companies Learn and Unlearn', in K. B. Clark, R. H. Hayes, and C. Lorenz (eds.), *The Uneasy Alliance*. Boston: Harvard Business School Press, 337–75.

Iwasaki, A. (1974). 'Kigyo Rijun-Ritsu no Kettei Yoin: 1966–70' ('Determinants of Firm Profit Rates: 1966–70'), *Konan Keizaigaku Ronsyu*, 15:1 (June), 92–105.

—— (1977). 'Kigyo no Kibo, Rijunritsu to Juyaku Hosyu' ('Corporate Size, Profitability and Executive Compensation'), *Konan Keizaigaku Ronsyu*, 17:4 (Mar.), 494–512.

Jenny, F., and Weber, A.-P. (1983). 'Aggregate Welfare Loss Due to Monopoly Power in the French Economy: Some Tentative Estimates', *Journal of Industrial Economics*, 32:2 (Dec.), 113–30.

Jensen, M. C. (1988). 'Takeovers: Their Causes and Consequences', *Journal of Economic Perspectives*, 2:1 (Winter), 21–48.

—— and Ruback, R. S. (1983). 'The Market for Corporate Control: The Scientific Evidence', *Journal of Financial Economics*, 11:1 (Apr.), 5–50.

JETRO (Japan External Trade Organization) (1989). 'Current Management Situation of Japanese Manufacturing Enterprises in Europe: The 5th Survey Report'. Unpublished report.

JFTC. See Fair Trade Commission.

Johnson, C. (1982). *MITI and the Japanese Miracle*. Stanford, Calif.: Stanford University Press.

Kagono, T., Nonaka, I., Sakakibara, K., and Okumura, A. (1985). *Strategic vs. Evolutionary Management: A US–Japan Comparison of Strategy and Organization*. Amsterdam: North-Holland.

Kaizuka, K. (1973). *Keizai Seisaku no Kadai* (Tasks of Economic Policy). Tokyo: University of Tokyo Press.

Kaldor, N. (1956). 'Alternative Theories of Distribution', *Review of Economic Studies*, 23:2, 83–100.

—— (1961). 'Capital Accumulation and Economic Growth', in F. A. Lutz and D. C. Hague (eds.), *The Theory of Capital*. London: Macmillan, 177–222.

Kamien, M. I., and Schwartz, N. L. (1982). *Market Structure and Innovation*. Cambridge: Cambridge University Press.

Karier, T. (1985). 'Unions and Monopoly Profits', *Review of Economics and Statistics*, 67:1 (Feb.), 34–42.

Kawasaki, S., and McMillan, J. (1987). 'The Design of Contracts: Evidence from Japanese Subcontracting', *Journal of the Japanese and International Economies*, 1:3 (Sept.), 327–49.

Kay, J. (1988). 'The Economic Role of Mergers', *London Business School Journal*, 12:1 (Summer), 21–6.

Kimura, Y. (1988). *The Japanese Semiconductor Industry: Structure, Competitive Strategies, and Performance*. Greenwich, Conn.: JAI Press.

Kohn/Ferry International in Conjunction with the London Business School (1981). *British Corporate Leaders—A Profile*. London: Kohn/Ferry International.

Koike, K. (1977). *Shokuba no Rodo Kumiai to Sanka—Roshi Kankei no Nichibei Hikaku* (*A Comparative Study of Industrial Relations on the Shopfloor in the United States and Japan*). Tokyo: Toyo Keizai Shinpo Sha.

—— (1988). *Understanding Industrial Relations in Modern Japan*. London: Macmillan.

—— and Inoki, T. (eds.) (1987). *Jinzai Keisei no Kokusai Hikaku—Tonan Asia to Nippon* (*An International Comparison of Skill Formation: Southeast Asia and Japan*). Tokyo: Toyo Keizai Shinpo Sha.

Komiya, R. (1975). *Gendai Nihon Keizai Kenkyu* (*A Study of Contemporary Japanese Economy*). Tokyo: University of Tokyo Press.

—— (1988). 'Introduction', in Komiya *et al.* (1988), 1–22.

—— Okuno, M., and Suzumura, K. (eds.) (1988). *Industrial Policy of Japan*. San Diego: Academic Press.

Kono, T. (1984). *Strategy and Structure of Japanese Enterprises*. London: Macmillan.

Kosai, Y. (1988). 'The Reconstruction Period', in Komiya *et al.* (1988), 25–48.

Kuroda, I., and Oritani, Y. (1980). 'A Re-Examination of the Unique Features of Japan's Corporate Financial Structure: A Comparison of

Corporate Balance Sheets in Japan and the United States', *Japanese Economic Studies*, 8:4 (Summer), 82–117.

Kwoka, J. E., Jr., and Ravenscraft, D. J. (1986). 'Cooperation v. Rivalry: Price–Cost Margins by Line of Business', *Economica*, 53 (Aug.), 351–63.

Lazear, E. P., and Rosen, S. (1981). 'Rank-Order Tournaments as Optimum Labor Contracts', *Journal of Political Economy*, 89:5 (Oct.), 841–64.

Lieberman, M. B. (1984). 'The Learning Curve and Pricing in the Chemical Processing Industries', *Rand Journal of Economics*, 15:2 (Summer), 213–28.

—— and Montgomery, D. B. (1988). 'First-Mover Advantages', *Strategic Management Journal*, 9:1 (Jan.–Feb.), 41–58.

Lorenzoni, G. (1988). 'Benetton', Case Series No. 4, London Business School.

Lynn, L. H. (1982). *How Japan Innovates*. Boulder, Colo.: Westview Press.

McNulty, P. J. (1967). 'A Note on the History of Perfect Competition', *Journal of Political Economy*, 75:4 (Aug.), 395–9.

—— (1968). 'Economic Theory and the Meaning of Competition', *Quarterly Journal of Economics*, 82:4 (Nov.), 639–56.

Magenheim, E. B., and Mueller, D. C. (1988). 'On Measuring the Effects of Acquisitions on Acquiring Firm Shareholders or Are Acquiring Firm Shareholders Better off after an Acquisition than They Were Before?', in J. C. Coffee, Jr., L. Lowenstein, and S. Rose-Ackerman (eds.), *Knights, Raiders and Targets: The Impact of the Hostile Takeover*. Oxford: Oxford University Press, 171–93.

Main, B. G. M. (1982). 'The Length of a Job in Great Britain', *Economica*, 49 (Aug.), 325–33.

Manne, H. G. (1965). 'Mergers and the Market for Corporate Control', *Journal of Political Economy*, 73:2 (Apr.), 110–20.

Mansfield, E. (1985). 'Public Policy toward Industrial Innovation: An International Study of Direct Tax Incentives for Research and Development', in K. B. Clark, R. H. Hayes, and C. Lorenz (eds.), *The Uneasy Alliance*. Boston: Harvard Business School Press, 383–407.

Marris, R. L. (1964). *The Economic Theory of 'Managerial' Capitalism*. London: Macmillan.

—— and Mueller, D. C. (1980). 'The Corporation, Competition, and the Invisible Hand', *Journal of Economic Literature*, 18:1 (Mar.) 32–63.

Marsh, P., Barwise, P., Thomas, K., and Wensley, R. (1988). *Managing Strategic Investment Decisions in Large Diversified Companies*. Centre for Business Strategy, London Business School.

Martin, S. (1983). *Market, Firm, and Economic Performance*. The Monograph Series in Finance and Economics, 1983–1. New York: New York University Graduate School of Business Administration.

Maslow, A. H. (1954). *Motivation and Personality*. New York: Harper and Row.

Maurice, M., and Sellier, F. (1979). 'Societal Analysis of Industrial Relations: A Comparison between France and West Germany', *British Journal of Industrial Relations*, 17:3 (Nov.), 322–36.

Miller, R. Le Roy (1971). 'The Reserve Labour Hypothesis: Some Tests of Its Implications', *Economic Journal*, 81 (Mar.), 17–35.

Ministry of Labour (1989). *Sangyo Rodo Report* (*Industry and Labour Report*). Tokyo: Printing Bureau of the Ministry of Finance.

Mintz, B., and Schwartz, M. (1985). *The Power Structure of American Business*. Chicago: The University of Chicago Press.

Monden, Y. (1983). *Toyota Production System*. Atlanta: Industrial Engineering and Management Press.

Morishima, M. (1982). *Why Has Japan 'Succeeded'?: Western Technology and the Japanese Ethos*. Cambridge: Cambridge University Press.

Morita, A. (1986). *Made in Japan*. New York: E. P. Dutton.

Mueller, D. C. (1977). 'The Persistence of Profits above the Norm', *Economica*, 44 (Nov.), 369–80.

—— (ed.) (1980). *The Determinants and Effects of Mergers: An International Comparison*. Cambridge, Mass.: Oelgeschlager, Gunn, and Hain.

—— (1986). *Profits in the Long Run*. Cambridge: Cambridge University Press.

—— (ed.) (1990). *The Dynamics of Company Profits: An International Comparison*. Cambridge: Cambridge University Press.

Muramatsu, K. (1983). *Nihon no Rodo Shijo Bunseki* (*Analyses of Labour Markets in Japan*). Tokyo: Hakuto Shobo.

—— (1985). 'Kaiko wa Itsu Okoruka' ('When Do Discharges Occur?'), *Aichi no Rodo Keizai*, 41, 29 June.

Muramatsu, S. (1986). 'Zaimu Deta ni Yoru Gappei Koka no Bunseki' ('An Analysis of the Effects of Mergers with Financial Data'), *Kigyo Kaikei*, 38:5 (May), 668–77.

Nakane, C. (1970). *Japanese Society*. London: Weidenfeld and Nicolson.

Nakao, T. (1979). 'Profit Rates and Market Shares of Leading Industrial Firms in Japan', *Journal of Industrial Economics*, 27:4 (June), 371–83.

Nakatani, I. (1984). 'The Economic Role of Financial Corporate Grouping', in M. Aoki (ed.), *The Economic Analysis of the Japanese Firm*. Amsterdam: Elsevier, 227–327.

Negishi, T. (1968). 'Protection of the Infant Industry and Dynamic Internal Economies', *Economic Record*, 44:1 (Mar.), 56–67.

Neild, R. R. (1963). *Pricing and Employment in the Trade Cycle.* Cambridge: Cambridge University Press.

Nelson, R. R., and Winter, S. G. (1982). *An Evolutionary Theory of Economic Change*. Cambridge, Mass.: Belknap Press.

Neumann, M., Böbel, I., and Haid, A. (1983) 'Business Cycle and Industrial Market Power: An Empirical Investigation for West German Industries, 1965–77', *Journal of Industrial Economics*, 32:2 (Dec.), 187–96.

Niida, H., Goto, A., and Nambu, T. (eds.) (1987). *Nihon Keizai no Kozo Henka to Sangyo Soshiki* (*Structural Change and Industrial Organization in the Japanese Economy*). Tokyo: Toyo Keizai Shinpo Sha.

Nishiyama, T. (1975). *Gendai Kigyo no Shihai Kozo* (The Structure of Control in Modern Corporations). Tokyo: Yuhikaku.

—— (1982). 'The Structure of Managerial Control: Who Owns and Controls Japanese Businesses', *Japanese Economic Studies*, 11:1 (Autumn), 37–77.

Nobes, C., and Parker, R. (eds.) (1985). *Comparative International Accounting*, 2nd edn. Oxford: Philip Allan.

Noll, R. G. (1985). 'Government Regulatory Behavior: A Multidisciplinary Survey and Synthesis', in R. G. Noll (ed.), *Regulatory Policy and the Social Sciences*. Berkeley, Calif.: University of California Press, 9–63.

Odagiri, H. (1974). 'Kigyo no Choki Seichoritsu ni Ataeru Shudanka no Koka ni Tsuite' ('The Grouping of Firms: Its Effect on Their Long-run Growth Rates'), *Osaka Economic Papers*, 24:1–2 (Sept.), 89–96.

—— (1975). 'Kigyo Shudan no Riron' ('A Theory of the Grouping of Firms'), *Economic Studies Quarterly*, 26:2 (Aug.), 144–54.

—— (1981). *The Theory of Growth in a Corporate Economy: Management Preference, Research and Development, and Economic Growth*. Cambridge: Cambridge University Press.

—— (1982). 'Internal Promotion, Intrafirm Wage Structure, and Corporate Growth', *Economic Studies Quarterly*, 33:3 (Dec.), 193–210.

—— (1985). 'Research Activity, Output Growth, and Productivity Increase in Japanese Manufacturing Industries', *Research Policy*, 14:3 (June), 117–30.

—— (1986). 'Industrial Policy in Theory and Reality', in H. De Jong and W. G. Shepherd (eds.), *Mainstreams in Industrial Organization*. Dordrecht: Martinus Nijhoff, 387–412.

—— (1989). 'Government Policies toward Industrial R&D: Theory,

Empirical Findings, and Japan's Experience', in M. Neumann (ed.), *Public Finance and Performance of Enterprises*. Detroit: Wayne State University Press, 211–26.

—— and Hase, T. (1989). 'Are Mergers and Acquisitions Going to Be Popular in Japan Too?: An Empirical Study', *International Journal of Industrial Organization*, 7:1 (Mar.), 49–72.

—— and Iwata, H. (1986). 'The Impact of R&D on Productivity Increase in Japanese Manufacturing Companies', *Research Policy*, 15:1 (Feb.), 13–19.

—— and Yamashita, T. (1987). 'Price Mark-ups, Market Structure, and Business Fluctuation in Japanese Manufacturing Industries', *Journal of Industrial Economics*, 35:3 (Mar.) 317–31.

—— and Yamawaki, H. (1986). 'A Study of Company Profit-Rate Time Series: Japan and the United States', *International Journal of Industrial Organization*, 4:1 (Mar.) 1–23.

—— —— (1990). 'The Persistence of Profits: International Comparison', in Mueller (1990), 169–85.

Oi, W. Y. (1962). 'Labor as a Quasi-Fixed Factor', *Journal of Political Economy*, 70:6 (Dec.), 538–55.

Okun, A. M. (1981). *Prices and Quantities*. Washington, DC: The Brookings Institution.

Oliver, N., and Wilkinson, B. (1988). *The Japanization of British Industry*. Oxford: Basil Blackwell.

Olson, M. (1982). *The Rise and Decline of Nations*. New Haven, Conn.: Yale University Press.

Ono, A. (1981). *Nippon no Rodo Shijo* (*Labour Markets in Japan*). Tokyo: Toyo Keizai Shinpo Sha.

Organization for Economic Co-operation and Development (OECD) (1984). *Merger Policies and Recent Trends in Mergers*. Paris: Organization for Economic Co-operation and Development.

Ozaki, R. S. (1985). 'How Japanese Industrial Policy Works', in C. Johnson (ed.), *The New Industrial Policy Debate*. San Francisco: ICS Press, 47–70.

Pascale, R. T. (1984). 'Perspectives on Strategy: The Real Story behind Honda's Success', *California Management Review*, 26:3 (Spring), 47–72.

—— and Rohlen, T. P. (1983). 'The Mazda Turnaround', *Journal of Japanese Studies*, 9:2 (Summer), 219–63.

Pasinetti, L. L. (1962). 'Rate of Profit and Income Distribution in Relation to the Rate of Economic Growth', *Review of Economic Studies*, 29:4 (Oct.), 184–96.

Peck, M. J. (1986). 'Joint R&D: The Case of Microelectronics and Computer Technology Corporation', *Research Policy*, 15:5 (Oct.), 219–31.

—— Levin, R. C., and Goto, A. (1988). 'Picking Losers: Public Policy toward Declining Industries in Japan', in J. B. Shoven (ed.), *Government Policy towards Industry in the United States and Japan*. Cambridge: Cambridge University Press, 195–239.

Peltzman, S. (1976). 'Toward a More General Theory of Regulation,' *Journal of Law and Economics*, 19:2 (Aug.), 211–40.

Penrose, E. T. (1955). 'Limits to the Growth and Size of Firms', *American Economic Review*, 45:2 (May), 531–43.

—— (1959). *The Theory of the Growth of the Firm*. Oxford: Basil Blackwell.

Pitelis, C. N., and Sugden, R. (1986). 'The Separation of Ownership and Control in the Theory of the Firm: A Reappraisal', *International Journal of Industrial Organization*, 4:1 (Mar.), 69–86.

Prestowitz, C. (1988). 'Japanese vs. Western Economics: Why Each Side Is a Mystery to the Other,' *Technology Review*, 91:4 (May/June), 27–36.

Qualls, P. D. (1979). 'Market Structure and the Cyclical Flexibility of Price–Cost Margins', *Journal of Business*, 52:3 (Apr.), 305–25.

Radford, G. D. (1989). 'How Sumitomo Transformed Dunlop Tyres', *Long Range Planning*, 22:3 (June), 28–33.

Ravenscraft, D. J. (1983). 'Structure-Profit Relationships at the Line of Business and Industry Levels', *Review of Economics and Statistics*, 65:1 (Feb.), 22–31.

—— and Scherer, F. M. (1987). *Mergers, Sell-Offs, and Economic Efficiency*. Washington, DC: The Brookings Institution.

Rohlen, T. P. (1974). *For Harmony and Strength: Japanese White-Collar Organization in Anthropological Perspective*. Berkeley, Calif.: University of California Press.

Rosen, S. (1985). 'Implicit Contracts: A Survey', *Journal of Economic Literature*, 23:3 (Sept.), 1144–75.

—— (1986). 'Prizes and Incentives in Elimination Tournaments', *American Economic Review*, 76:4 (Sept.), 701–15.

Rosenbaum, J. E. (1984). *Career Mobility in a Corporate Hierarchy*. Orlando, Fla.: Academic Press.

Rosenbloom, R. S., and Abernathy, W. J. (1982). 'The Climate for Innovation in Industry: The Role of Management Attitudes and Practices in Consumer Electronics', *Research Policy*, 11:4 (Aug.), 209–25.

Rumelt, R. P. (1974). *Strategy, Structure and Economic Performance*. Boston: Harvard Business School.

Sakakibara, K. (1981). 'Soshiki to Innovation: Jirei Kenkyu, Cho-LSI Gijutsu Kenkyu Kumiai' ('Organization and Innovation: A Case Study of VLSI Technology Association'), *Hitotsubashi Review*, 86:2 (Aug.), 160–75.

—— and Westney, D. E. (1985). 'Comparative Study of the Training, Careers, and Organization of Engineers in the Computer Industry in the United States and Japan', *Hitotsubashi Journal of Commerce and Management*, 20:1 (Dec.), 1–20.

Sakamoto, K., and Shimotani, M. (1987). *Gendai Nihon no Kigyo Group* (*Business Groups in Modern Japan*). Tokyo: Toyo Keizai Shinpo Sha.

Sako, M. (1990). 'Buyer–Supplier Relationships and Economic Performance: Evidence from Britain and Japan'. Unpublished Ph.D. thesis, University of London.

Salinger, M. A. (1984). 'Tobin's *q*, Unionization, and the Concentration–Profits Relationship', *Rand Journal of Economics*, 15:2 (Summer), 159–70.

Samuelson, P. A., and Modigliani, F. (1966). 'The Pasinetti Paradox in Neoclassical and More General Models', *Review of Economic Studies*, 33:4, 269–301.

Saxonhouse, G. R. (1976). 'Estimated Parameters as Dependent Variables', *American Economic Review*, 66:1 (Mar.), 178–83.

Scherer, F. M. (1980). *Industrial Market Structure and Economic Performance*, 2nd edn. Boston: Houghton Mifflin.

—— Long, W. F., Martin, S., Mueller, D. C., Pascoe, G., Ravenscraft, D. J., Scott, J. T., and Weiss, L. W. (1987). 'The Validity of Studies with Line of Business Data: Comment', *American Economic Review*, 77:1 (Mar.), 205–17.

Schmalensee, R. (1982). 'Product Differentiation Advantages of Pioneering Brands', *American Economic Review*, 72:3 (June), 349–65.

Schumpeter, J. (1942). *Capitalism, Socialism, and Democracy*. New York: Harper and Row.

Science and Technology Agency (1990). *Kagaku Gijutsu Hakusho* (*White Paper on Science and Technology*). Tokyo: Printing Bureau of the Ministry of Finance.

Scitovsky, T. (1976). *The Joyless Economy: An Inquiry into Human Satisfaction and Consumer Dissatisfaction*. Oxford: Oxford University Press.

Scott, J. (1986). *Capitalist Property and Financial Power: A Comparative Study of Britain, the United States and Japan*. Brighton: Wheatsheaf Books.

Seidman, L. S. (1979). 'The Return of the Profit Rate to the Wage Equation', *Review of Economics and Statistics*, 61:1 (Feb.), 139–42.

Sekiguchi, S., and Horiuchi, T. (1988). 'Trade and Adjustment Assistance', in Komiya *et al.* (1988), 369–93.

Senoo, A. (1983). *Gendai Nihon no Sangyo Shuchu, 1971–1980*

(*Industrial Concentration in Contemporary Japan, 1971–1980*). Tokyo: Nihon Keizai Shimbun Sha.

Sheard, P. (1989). 'The Main Bank System and Corporate Monitoring and Control in Japan', *Journal of Economic Behavior and Organization*, 11:3 (May), 399–422.

Shepherd, W. G. (1972). 'The Elements of Market Structure', *Review of Economics and Statistics*, 54:1 (Feb.), 25–37.

Shiba, S. (1973). *Rodo no Kokusai Hikaku* (*International Comparison of Labour*). Tokyo: Toyo Keizai Shinpo Sha.

Shinjo, K. (1977). 'Business Pricing Policies and Inflation: The Japanese Case', *Review of Economics and Statistics*, 59:4 (Nov.), 447–55.

—— and Doi, N. (1989). 'Welfare Loss Calculation for Japanese Industries', *International Journal of Industrial Organization*, 7:2 (June), 243–56.

Shinotsuka, E. (1989). *Nihon no Koyo Chosei* (*Employment Adjustment of Japan*). Tokyo: Toyo Keizai Shinpo Sha.

Smith, A. (1776). *The Wealth of Nations*. Repr. Oxford: Oxford University Press, 1976.

Solnik, B. (1988). *International Investment*. Reading, Mass.: Addison Wesley.

Solow, R. M. (1968). 'Short-Run Adjustment of Employment to Output', in J. N. Wolfe (ed.), *Value, Capital, and Growth*. Edinburgh: Edinburgh University Press, 481–4.

Sorge, A., and Warner, M. (1980). 'Manpower Training, Manufacturing Organization and Workplace Relations in Great Britain and West Germany', *British Journal of Industrial Relations*, 18:3 (Nov.), 318–33.

Spencer, B. J., and Brander, J. A. (1983). 'International R & D Rivalry and Industrial Strategy', *Review of Economic Studies*, 43:2 (June), 217–35.

Stein, J. C. (1988). 'Takeover Threats and Managerial Myopia', *Journal of Political Economy*, 96:1 (Feb.), 61–80.

Stigler, G. J. (1957). 'Perfect Competition, Historically Contemplated', *Journal of Political Economy*, 65:1 (Feb.), 1–17.

Suzuki, Kazuyuki (1985). 'Knowledge Capital and the Private Rate of Return to R & D in Japanese Manufacturing Industries', *International Journal of Industrial Organization*, 3:3 (Sept.), 293–305.

Suzuki, Kyoichi (1987). 'Kigyo no Takakuka Kodo no Bunseki' ('The Analysis of Corporate Diversification Behaviour'). Unpublished Master's thesis, University of Tsukuba.

Taira, K. (1970). *Economic Development and the Labor Market in Japan*. New York: Columbia University Press.

Takamiya, S., and Thurley, K. (eds.), (1985). *Japan's Emerging*

Multinationals. Tokyo: University of Tokyo Press.

Taketoshi, R. (1984). 'Waga Kuni Seizogyo no Gappei ni Kansuru Kenkyu' ('A Study on Mergers in Japanese Manufacturing Industries'). Unpublished Master's thesis, University of Tsukuba.

Terleckyj, N. E. (1980). 'Direct and Indirect Effects of Industrial Research and Development on the Productivity Growth of Industries', in J. W. Kendrick and B. N. Vaccara (eds.), *New Developments in Productivity Measurement and Analysis*. Chicago: University of Chicago Press, 359–77.

Tobin, J. (1969). 'A General Equilibrium Approach to Monetary Theory', *Journal of Money, Credit and Banking*, 1:1 (Feb.), 15–29.

Trevor, M. (1983). *Japan's Reluctant Multinationals*. London: Frances Pinter.

—— (1988). *Toshiba's New British Company*. London: Policy Studies Institute.

—— Schendel, J., and Wilpert, B. (1986). *The Japanese Management Development System*. London: Frances Pinter.

Trezise, P. H. (1983). 'Industrial Policy is Not the Major Reason for Japan's Success', *Brookings Review* (Spring), 13–18.

Tse, K. K. (1985). *Marks & Spencer: Anatomy of Britain's Most Efficiently Managed Company*. Oxford: Pergamon Press.

Turcq, D. (1985). *L'Animal stratégique: l'ambiguité du pouvoir chez les cadres japonais*. Paris: Éditions de l'École des Hautes Études en Sciences Sociales.

Uekusa, M. (1982). *Sangyo Soshiki Ron* (*Industrial Organization*). Tokyo: Chikuma Shobo.

Ueno, T. (1989). 'Rokudai Kigyo-Shudan no Jittai ni Tsuite' ('On the Current Situation of the Six Business Groups'), *Kosei Torihiki*, 464 (June), 46–56.

Unotoro, K. (1988). 'Shuchu-do no Nichi-Bei Hikaku ni Tsuite' ('On the Japan–US Comparison of Concentration Ratio'), *Kosei Torihiki*, 448 (Feb.), 75–9.

Uzawa, H. (1969). 'Time Preference and the Penrose Effect in a Two-Class Model of Economic Growth', *Journal of Political Economy*, 77:4 (July), pt. 2, 628–52.

Varian, H. R. (1984). *Microeconomic Analysis*, 2nd edn. New York: W. W. Norton.

Wachtel, H. M., and Adelsheim, P. D. (1977). 'How Recession Feeds Inflation: Price Markups in a Concentrated Economy', *Challenge*, 20:4 (Sept.–Oct.), 6–13.

Wakasugi, R. (1986). *Gijutsu Kakushin to Kenkyu Kaihatsu no Keizai Bunseki* (*Economic Analysis of Technological Innovation and R & D*). Tokyo: Toyo Keizai Shinpo Sha.

—— (1988). 'A Consideration of Innovative Organization: Joint R&D of Japanese Firms', Staff Paper Series 88-05, Faculty of Economics, Shinshu University.

Wakasugi, T., Nishina, K., Kon-ya, F., and Tsuchiya, M. (1984). 'Measuring the Profitability of the Nonfinancial Sector in Japan', in Holland (1984).

—— *et al.* (1988). *Nihon no Kabuka Suijun Kenkyu Group, Houkokusho* (*Report of the Research Group on Share Price Level in Japan*). Tokyo: Nihon Shoken Keizai Kenkyu Sho.

Weber, M. (1904). *Die Protestantische Ethik und der Geist des Kapitalismus*. English trans. Talcott Parsons, *The Protestant Ethic and the Spirit of Capitalism*. London: Allen Unwin, 1974.

Weitzman, M. L. (1984). *The Share Economy*. Cambridge, Mass.: Harvard University Press.

White, M., and Trevor, M. (1983). *Under Japanese Management*. London: Heinemann.

Wickens, P. (1987). *The Road to Nissan: Flexibility, Quality, Teamwork*. London: Macmillan.

Williamson, O. E. (1970). *Corporate Control and Business Behavior*. Englewood Cliffs, NJ: Prentice Hall.

—— (1971). 'The Vertical Integration of Production: Market Failure Considerations', *American Economic Review*, 61:2 (May), 112–23.

—— (1975). *Markets and Hierarchy*. New York: Free Press.

—— Wachter, M. L., and Harris, J. E. (1975). 'Understanding the Employment Relation: The Analysis of Idiosyncratic Exchange', *Bell Journal of Economics*, 6:1 (Spring), 250–78.

Williamson, P. J. (1990). 'Winning the Export War: British, Japanese and West German Exporters' Strategy Compared', *British Journal of Management*, 1, 215–30.

Wong, V., Saunders, J., and Doyle, P. (1988). 'The Quality of British Marketing: A Comparison with US and Japanese Multinationals in the UK Market', *Journal of Marketing Management*, 4:2 (Winter), 107–30.

Yamada, A. (1989). *America Zaimu Shohyo Nyumon* (*Introduction to American Financial Statements*). Tokyo: Chuo Keizai Sha.

Yamawaki, H. (1989). 'Exports and Foreign Distributional Activities: Evidence on Japanese Firms in the United States', unpublished paper, Wissenschaftszentrum Berlin. Forthcoming in *Review of Economics and Statistics*.

—— (1991). 'The Effects of Business Conditions on Net Entry: Evidence from Japan', in P. A. Geroski and J. Schwalbach (eds.), *Entry and Market Contestability: An International Comparison*. Oxford: Basil Blackwell.

Yokokura, H. (1988). 'Medium and Small Firms', in Komiya *et al.* (1988), 513–39.

Yoshihara, H., Sakuma, A., Itami, H., and Kagono, T. (1981). *Nihon Kigyo no Takakuka Senryaku* (*Diversification Strategies of Japanese Firms*). Tokyo: Nihon Keizai Shimbun Sha.

SUBJECT AND COMPANY INDEX

(Company names in Fig. 7.1 and Tables 7.2 and 11.1 are not indexed.)

AUTHOR INDEX